New Religions Perspective

D1145751

New Religions in Global Perspective is a fresh in-depth account of new religious movements, and of new forms of spirituality from a global vantage point. Ranging from North America and Europe to Japan, Latin America, South Asia, Africa and the Caribbean, this book provides students with a complete introduction to NRMs such as Falun Gong, Aum Shinrikyo, the Brahma Kumaris movement, the Ikhwan or Muslim Brotherhood, Sufism, the Engaged Buddhist and Neo-Hindu movements, Messianic Judaism, and African diaspora movements including Rastafarianism.

Peter Clarke explores the innovative character of new religious movements, charting their cultural significance and global impact, and how various religious traditions are shaping, rather than displacing, each other's understanding of notions such as transcendence and faith, good and evil, of the meaning, purpose and function of religion, and of religious belonging. In addition to exploring the responses of governments, churches, the media and general public to new religious movements, Clarke examines the reactions to older, increasingly influential religions, such as Buddhism and Islam, in new geographical and cultural contexts. Taking into account the degree of continuity between old and new religions, each chapter contains not only an account of the rise of the NRMs and new forms of spirituality in a particular region, but also an overview of change in the regions' mainstream religions.

Peter Clarke is Professor Emeritus of the History and Sociology of Religion at King's College, University of London, and a professorial member of the Faculty of Theology, University of Oxford. Among his publications are (with Peter Byrne) *Religion Defined and Explained* (1993) and *Japanese New Religions: In Global Perspective* (ed.) (2000). He is the founding editor and present co-editor of the *Journal of Contemporary Religion*.

New Religions in Global Perspective

A study of religious change in the modern world

Peter B. Clarke

 Routledge
Taylor & Francis Group

LONDON AND NEW YORK

First published 2006
by Routledge
2 Park Square, Milton Park, Abingdon, Oxon OX14 4RN

Simultaneously published in the USA and Canada
by Routledge
270 Madison Ave, New York, NY 10016

Routledge is an imprint of the Taylor & Francis Group

© 2006 Peter B. Clarke

Typeset in Sabon by Book Now Ltd
Printed and bound in Great Britain by
Antony Rowe Ltd, Chippenham, Wiltshire

British Library Cataloguing in Publication Data
A catalogue record for this book is available from the British
Library

Library of Congress Cataloging in Publication Data
A catalog record for this book has been requested

ISBN10: 0–415–25747–6 (hbk)
ISBN10: 0–415–25748–4 (pbk)

ISBN13: 9–78–0–415–25747–3 (hbk)
ISBN13: 9–78–0–415–25748–0 (pbk)

Contents

Acknowledgements

I am most grateful to my family and friends who have been, as always, helpful and patient, and to all those colleagues in the sociology and other branches of the study of religion whose research and writings on this and related topics I have greatly benefited from reading.

My own research has taken me to Africa, mainland Europe, North and South America (Brazil), Japan and other parts of Asia. Many, many people have been most generous with their time and to all of them I am extremely grateful.

I am also very greateful to Kofuku no Kagaku (Institute of Research in Human Happiness) for generously funding a three-year research project (1994–97) on Japanese New Religions Abroad, which I co-ordinated from the Centre for New Religions at King's College London and which created for me many opportunities to extend my fieldwork on New Religions in Asia, Europe and North and South America.

Finally, but by no means last, I want to sincerely thank all my research students – a global cohort themselves – from whose research findings and insights I have benefited greatly in the course of supervising their dissertations. A selection of these is given in Chapter 3 without, of course, intending to suggest that these are necessarily of a higher quality than those not mentioned.

Whatever misunderstandings of interpretation or fact there may be are mine alone.

Peter Clarke
Oxford, April 2005

Introduction

The significance for the future of religion generally and the social impact of New Religious Movements (NRMs) and New Spirituality Movements (NSMs) (Shimazono, 2004) appear strikingly different when seen from a global rather than a country by country or regional standpoint. This is not to suggest that the latter are not important vantage points but simply that the impact of the phenomenon, to be fully appreciated, needs also to be seen for what it is, a religious reformation on a worldwide scale, and as such can only be fully understood in the context of global society. Without this perspective it will continue to be dismissed as marginal and superficial and its relevance to our understanding of the religious history of the modern world largely ignored.

The numbers of those involved in new religions and new types of spirituality movements are difficult to assess, not simply because of lack of good quality statistical data, but also because the meaning of the terms 'membership' and 'belonging' are not always clearly defined. However, reasonable estimates suggest that considerable numbers of NRMs, to confine the discussion to them, are now global religions in their own right, with a following that has to be counted in millions and one that outnumbers that of many branches of the so-called mainstream religions.

Looked at globally, modern NRMs (since NRMs are the main but not the exclusive concern of this volume, I will mostly use this label except when explicitly referring to an NSM) reflect the variety of modernities of which modernity itself is composed. They provide in each case new foundations for being religious, introducing new beliefs and practices, often by reshaping and transforming the purposes of old ones, and act as catalysts for change within the older religions. This includes not only change in beliefs and practice but also change at the epistemological level. For example, by influencing the way faith based on divine sources of revelation, as traditionally understood in the monotheistic traditions, comes to be replaced by knowledge derived from experience and experimentation, and notions of sin by that of ignorance, and ideas on paradise as a future state of bliss by the concept of self-realization in the here and now. Also evident is change in the function and purpose of religion. Such core notions as liberation (moksha) and enlightenment (nirvana) are increasingly being interpreted as a means to an end, the end being the profound transformation of society rather than as individual goals.

NRMs and NSMs challenge us to question not only the meaning of such concepts as faith and the purpose of religion but also most of what we traditionally take for granted about religion, including our understanding of the concept itself. They ask important questions about the future of standard, congregational religion, questions to which others (Shimazono, 2004; Heelas and Woodhead, 2005; Stark *et al.*, 2005) have already tried to respond, and to which I attempt a reply at the end of this volume.

It is made clear throughout this volume, beginning with the opening chapter, that religious change is constituted differently in different religious and cultural contexts. In certain Asian cultures a development such as that of Engaged Buddhism or Engaged Hinduism can represent as profound an innovation for adherents of those religions as any major doctrinal 'deviation' in, for example, Christianity.

Religious innovations serve different functions and are attributed to different causes in different cultural settings. In the West most interest has been shown in the inner-directed, subjective type of spirituality as a means to personal growth in a world that has seen the privatization of religion reach an advanced stage. In large parts of the Buddhist world and elsewhere the purposes and objectives are more informed by communal, societal concerns, although the individual dimension is increasingly important, especially in the major urban conglomerations, as the success of Falun Gong and similar movements in China in the 1990s indicates.

This study provides the opportunity to discuss reasons as to why the response to NRMs has been usually hostile, and such issues as why and how governments seek to control and shape religion in the modern world, the impact of NRMs on the secularization process, and, with the increase in Oriental spirituality in the West, the Easternization of the Western mind thesis. It also provides an opportunity to bring into the discussion NRMs that have received little attention to date, including Islamic-derived NRMs.

In addition to highlighting the variable nature of religious change, I hope I have been able to show that the dynamics of such change are complex and cannot be fully understood by using impact–response schemas, which is often the case when attempting to account for religious change in societies that have experienced colonial rule in the modern period.

In a volume such as this the problem of how much detail should be provided about a particular movement or topic always arises. Too much can obscure debate and discussion. An effort has been made in each chapter to provide enough information about particular movements to enable the reader to follow the theoretical issues raised, and there are many, by those NRMs that have begun to make an impact in recent times.

Overview of the contents

The chapters in this volume, with the exception of this introduction and the conclusion, which stand alone, are arranged in five parts. Part I consists of chapters on the global perspective, the New Age Movement (NAM) and society's response to NRMs. Although not a New Religion, the NAM is included in this section largely because of its role as the main vehicle for the worldwide dissemination of new forms of spirituality. In this sense it is a global spiritual movement. I also wanted to enter the debate concerning its very existence as a movement. A chapter on response to NRMs has also been included in this section principally for the reason that the reaction globally to these movements has been without exception hostile, creating in a sense a significant global movement in the form of the Anti-Cult Movement or ACM. Reasons, mostly of geography, history and culture, determine the composition of Parts II to V.

Chapter 1, which outlines the advantages of taking a global perspective of New Religious Movements, also explains the meaning of terms such as 'new religion' and attempts to account for the rise of NRMs and new forms of spirituality, including subjective and engaged forms found across the Middle East and Asia, which are not always as distinct as they might first appear.

Other themes addressed in this chapter include: the convergence of religions, new and old, and of new forms of spirituality; the shaping and reshaping of the religious landscape that this leads to; and the types of religious change generated by modernization and globalization, with particular reference to the emergence of NRMs.

This first chapter also looks at: the dynamics of religious change in different cultural contexts; processes of domestication and/or 'glocalization' (Robertson, 1992); the labyrinthine pathways across the globe taken by NRMs; the global character that some of the NRMs have taken on; and different understandings of religious change. This chapter also suggests that the unit of analysis for studying NRMs be enlarged to include religious change generally. Such a framework enables a clearer insight into the nature and impact of NRMs and NSMs. The chapter also emphasizes the importance of moving away from an impact–response framework in accounting for NRMs, for this tends to attribute too much to external factors in accounting for religious change and to overlook the creative, indigenous forces at work in society.

Chapter 2 addresses the question of whether such a movement as the New Age Movement exists, or has ever existed, or whether it is simply a media construct. It also looks at the debate regarding NAM claims in relation to self-improvement and improvement in one's social relations, and at questions of ideology in the sense of whether the beliefs the NAM expresses show a strong continuity with the past, in other words, are conventional, or clearly 'deviant' in the sense of esoteric and marginal. The response of

Buddhist groups and Christian churches to the NAM is also examined in this second chapter.

Chapter 3 discusses reasons for the universally hostile response to NRMs. The degree of hostility has varied. Australia, for example, has been less hostile than France and much of the rest of Europe, including Russia. The hostility can be best understood, it is suggested, if seen as a form of boundary maintenance.

Violence involving NRMs, which is also discussed in this chapter, has played a crucial role in generating global hostility in their regard, but cannot explain it since the hostility predates the violence. The question of NRMs and violence is also looked at in other chapters (see Chapter 7 on the Middle East and North Africa, Chapter 8 on Africa, Chapter 12 on Japan and Chapter 13 on China). Violence, it is argued, is for the most part interactive.

Chapter 4 considers the rise of NRMs in Europe, and in particular of NRMs that do not usually receive much attention, including Islamic and Sikh NRMs. The importance of both colonialism and immigration law are emphasized in accounting for NRMs in this part of the world. Developments in mainstream Christianity and such processes as the Europeanization of Buddhism and Islam, and their Gallicanization in the case of France, are discussed. The themes of subjective spirituality and of modern secular spirituality, in the form of Modern Yoga and of modern secular religions, are taken up in this chapter, as they are in several others, partly with a view to assessing the evidence for the Easternization of the Western mind thesis (Campbell, 1999).

This chapter also examines the core ideas of some of those thinkers who greatly influenced the form and content of contemporary New Religions and of the New Spirituality gaining ground in the West, as well as developments and changes within the older, mainstream religious traditions. The intellectual sources that motivate and move people to embrace alternative forms of spirituality have changed over time. In the 1970s, the writings of Pierre Teilhard de Chardin (1881–1955), the Jesuit paleontologist, were most frequently cited by Ferguson's (1982) respondents, that is the 181 'Aquarian conspirators' – those networking to bring about the 'Age of Aquarius' or of the mind's true liberation – as having had the most influence on their thinking. Teilhard de Chardin, himself greatly influenced by the philosopher Bergson's writing on Creative Evolution, described the world as a 'divine milieu'.

Chapter 5 also moves the discussion to North America and looks at NRMs from the beginnings of Transcendentalism in the early nineteenth century and this movement's influence on New Thought and the NAM until the 1950s, and from the 1950s to the present. Also addressed are: developments in mainstream Christianity; processes such as the Americanization of Buddhism; explanations for the increasing influence of Buddhism in the United States; the emergence of various forms of Sufism or Islamic mysticism;

the political dimensions of Neo-Paganism; and the response of NRMs to the destruction, allegedly by Al-Qaeda operatives, of the World Trade Center in New York on September 11th 2001. This chapter also provides a critical analysis of a number of theoretical perspectives, including that of the integrative hypothesis, which attempt to explain the rise of function of NRMs, and highlights, as does virtually every other chapter, the theme of millenarianism and NRMs, with particular reference to Native American religion. Millenarianism is probably one of the most common themes of modern New Religions. Considerable attention is also given to Sufi (mystical) movements, the Nation of Islam and Messianic Judaism. The history and aims of the North American Anti-Cult Movement are outlined in Chapter 3.

In Chapter 6 the rise of NRMs in Australia, New Zealand and Melanesia (particularly New Guinea) is the principal point of interest. Some of the limitations of the impact–response schema used to explain the rise of Cargo cults are identified and the 'commodity millenarianism' of these same movements is compared with other kinds of chiliastic expectancy (see Chapters 8, 9 and 10). The issue of the commodification of contemporary spirituality is addressed with special reference to modern Wicca, and the interaction between the NAM and Aboriginal Religion, and Traditional religion more generally, is also discussed here.

Chapter 7 on North Africa and the Middle East concentrates mainly on contemporary Islamist and jihadi movements and, in particular, the Muslim Brotherhood and Al-Qaeda. This discussion is situated in the wider context of the Wahhabi and Salafi reform movements, Islam's encounter with modernity and Gellner's Islamic exceptionalism thesis, and that of the Palestine–Israeli conflict. The notion that most of this innovation can be accounted for in terms of external forces provoking an internal response in the form of new jihād movements is shown once again in this chapter to be inadequate. The core ideas of those who inspired these movements, including Hassan al-Banna, Sayyid Qutb, Osama bin Laden and Ayman al-Zawahiri, are unpacked, as is the meaning of the term 'Islamic state' in the case of the Muslim Brotherhood. Also discussed is the modern secular salvation and messianic political 'religion' in Israel, Gush Emunim.

Chapter 8, in reviewing the developments in new and old religion (Christianity and Islam) in Africa, south of the Sahara, attempts to understand the dynamics of religious innovation there, and once again the limits of impact–response theory are highlighted, as they are in the section on Melanesia in Chapter 6, in the discussion of Islamic reform movements in North Africa (Chapter 7) and in the account of Neo-Hindu movements (Chapter 10). With the exception of East Africa and to a limited extent South Africa, much of the new religion in Africa, south of the Sahara, until recently was the product of the interaction of Traditional religion and either Islam or Christianity, or both. More recently there has been much more influence from Oriental religions, making for even more varied and original forms of new religion in Africa. It is argued in this chapter that the new African religions are best understood if seen as rational defences of Tradition under indiscriminate attack from outside.

Chapter 9 studies religious change in Latin America (mainly Brazil) and the Caribbean, and includes discussion of Neo-Pentecostal churches – such as the Universal Church of the Kingdom of God (Igreja Universal do Reino de Deus, or IURD), which has established branches in Europe, North America, Japan and Africa – and of new forms of Spiritist, Esoteric and Amerindian religion and spirituality. The chapter highlights some of the unique forms of millenarianism, and new unique practices that have developed from increasing interaction between Christianity and African-Brazilian religions, as well as Japanese New Religions, Shinto, older Buddhist traditions, and Spiritism in Brazil. The Caribbean section of this chapter is mostly devoted to the turbulent relations between African religious traditions, including Haitian Voodoo and Cuban Santeria, and Catholicism, and African-Catholic-Indian (Hindu) interaction. There is one detailed study of the New Religion, the Rastafarian movement.

Chapter 10 turns to South Asia and, in particular, looks at religious change and innovation in India, Pakistan and Sri Lanka, with special emphasis on: the emergence of applied spirituality including applied Sufism in India; Protestant Buddhism (Gombrich and Obeyesekere, 1988); Engaged Buddhism; more exclusive forms of Islam and the drift toward the use of jihād among Islamist movements; and the new versions of millenarianism that have been generated by the desire for world-transformation.

Chapter 11 covers only three of the eleven States of Southeast Asia: Thailand, Vietnam and Indonesia. But there is much here to examine and attempt to explain. The various types of Buddhism, Sufism and NRMs that have emerged could in themselves provide material for a volume on their own. We see old well-established interpretations of enlightenment (nirvana) turned upside down in a number of contexts, including Thailand, in pursuit of spiritual engagement and relevance.

Chapter 12 focuses on Japan and returns to some of the themes discussed in other chapters, including: the rise of New Spirituality Movements (NSMs) (Shimazono, 2004); religious violence and NRMs; and the Anti-Cult Movement both pre and post the Aum Shinrikyo affair of March 1995. Also considered are the negative connotations now attached to the concept of New Religion, Japanese NRMs overseas (see also Chapters, 6, 7 and 10), and the rise of 'unchurched' spirituality movements, a phenomenon also of European and North American society (Stark et al., 2005).

Chapter 13 on China, Taiwan and Korea provides some completely new versions of old Buddhism, new versions of millenarianism – the Won Buddhist version for example – and the rise of new spirituality groups including Falun Gong, and the Government's, at first positive, then completely hostile, response. It would appear that there is strong competition between the Government and the grass-roots in China to plug the ideological gap left by Maoism.

In the conclusion (Chapter 14), I draw further attention to the continuities and breaks in the modern history of religion, and compare and contrast NRMs and new forms of spirituality or New Spirituality Movements with Robert Bellah's (1969) ideal construct of modern religion. The defining characteristic of Bellah's ideal construct is the collapse of the hierarchical structuring of this and the other world and the consequent abandonment of the principle of mediated salvation in favour of the direct relationship between the individual and transcendent reality. While there are many similarities, there are also many significant differences between this version of modern religion and NRMs and NSMs, both of which display many traditional features.

The conclusion also critiques, in brief, controversial assessments of the impact of NRMs, such as the Easternization of the Western mind thesis developed by Campbell (1999) among others, contending that in the context of the porous pluralism of late modernity all religions have ceased to be regional or geographical facts and all are exposed to newer and more complex forms of hybridity, perhaps making for the most profound changes ever in their history of religions such as Buddhism and Hinduism.

Inevitably in the conclusion to a volume such as this, which looks at religious continuity and change and/or innovation, there will be some speculation about the future of both old and new religion. The conclusion, in addition to suggesting that the trend will be toward modern religion as defined by Bellah (1969), also speculates about this issue in the light of recent research by Heelas and Woodhead (2005) and Stark et al. (2005), which attempts to sketch a map of the future of congregational and/or mainstream, established religion in the context of the growth in unchurched spirituality and spirituality generally. I suggest that it is important to keep in mind in this discussion the extent of the overlap between congregational religion and alternative forms of being religious and spiritual, the former's potential for adaptation to modern trends, and the dependence of the new spirituality on old structures, points also made by Wuthnow and Cadge (2004). This notwithstanding, the most common way of thinking about religion is likely to be thinking about it for oneself, and this includes those committed to fundamentalist interpretations of their faith and can be seen for example even in the case of the *ijtihād* revolution in Islam (Chapter 7).

The conclusion suggests that the further opening up of China, Central Asia and other parts of the world, until recently sealed off from the rest, will doubtless increase the level of convergence among religions and between religions and humanistic systems of thought. This process and the corresponding collapse of monopolistic political ideologies will not only result in greater hybridity but will also stimulate the impulse to profusion, multiplication and replication of NRMs, which in turn will promote the basic, in-built features, so to speak, of modern religion.

References and select bibliography

Bellah, Robert (1969) 'Religious Evolution' in Roland Robertson (ed.) *The Sociology of Religion*, Baltimore, MD: Penguin Books, pp. 262–93.

Bromley, David G. and Melton, J. Gordon (eds) (2002) *Cults, Religion and Violence*, Cambridge: Cambridge University Press.

Campbell, Colin (1999) 'The Easternization of the West' in Bryan R. Wilson and Jamie Cresswell (eds) *New Religious Movements: Challenge and Response*, London: Routledge, pp. 35–49.

Ferguson, Marilyn (1982) *The Aquarian Conspiracy: Personal and Social Transformation in the 1980s*, London: Paladin.

Gombrich, Richard and Obeyesekere, Gananath (1988) *Buddhism Transformed: Religious Change in Sri Lanka*, Princeton, NJ: Princeton University Press.

Heelas, Paul and Woodhead, Linda (2005) *The Spiritual Revolution: Why Religion is Giving Way to Spirituality*, Oxford: Blackwell.

Hefner, Robert W. (1998) 'Mutliple Modernities', *Annual Review of Anthropology*, 27, 83–104.

Robertson, Roland (1992) *Globalization: Social Theory and Global Culture*, London: Sage.

Shimazono, Susumu (2004) *From Salvation to Spirituality*, Melbourne: Trans Pacific Press.

Stark, Rodney, Hamberg, Eva, and Miller, Alan S. (2005) 'Exploring Spirituality and Unchurched Religions in America, Sweden and Japan', *Journal of Contemporary Religion*, 20(1), 3–25.

Wuthnow, Robert (1982) 'World Order and Religious Movements' in Eileen Barker (ed.) *New Religious Movements. A Perspective for Understanding Society*, New York: Edwin Mellen Press, pp. 47–69.

Wuthnow, Robert and Cadge, Wendy (2004) 'Buddhists and Buddhism in the United States: The Scope of Influence', *Journal for the Scientific Study of Religion*, 43(3), 363–81.

Part I

Global perspective, New Age and society's response

Chapter 1

New Religious Movements (NRMs)

A global perspective

While the perspective on the phenomenon of New Religious Movements (NRMs) taken in this volume is global, the framework of discussion is religious change in a broad sense and includes change in the so-called older, mainstream religions. This should enable a better appreciation of the innovative character of NRMs or, which amounts to much the same thing, the degree of continuity between old and new religion. Criteria of innovation vary between religions and cultures, being centred more on doctrine in certain contexts and on changes in the performance and purposes of ritual and in orientation to the world in others.

A global perspective can shed much light on aspects of NRMs that might otherwise remain obscure, including their significance and impact. Such a vantage point also reveals the myriad forms, of what Robertson (1992) called 'glocalization', that NRMs have taken as they have attempted to embed themselves in different cultures. Also more clearly evident from this view-point are the different criteria of religious change and innovation adopted across the world, which have a bearing on why a particular movement is considered new. This standpoint too makes comparison possible in relation to the underlying reasons for, the variation in impact, and the different styles of NRMs in different parts of the world. Although I use the term 'NRMs', I also wish to apply what has been said to the new kinds of spirituality that have arisen, such as subjective spirituality in the West and applied and engaged spirituality in the Middle East, the East and elsewhere.

Working from a global perspective, it comes as no surprise to discover that subjective spirituality appeals more widely the more economically advanced society is, and applied and/or engaged spirituality in the form of engaged Buddhism (Queen and King, 1996), which closely resembles 'Protestant Buddhism' (Gombrich and Obeyesekere, 1988), engaged Hinduism (see Chapter 10), engaged Neo-Pentecostalism (Martin, 1990), or socially oriented Sufism, Islamic mysticism, and daw'a or Islamic missionary activity (see Chapter 7), where material conditions are less favourable. Where engaged spirituality exists in more economically advanced societies it is usually of a different kind to that found in the developing world. For example, an important part of the agenda of Engaged Buddhism in the United States is gender equality, which, although not absent, does not figure highly on the list of priorities of Engaged Buddhism in Thailand, Vietnam, Taiwan and elsewhere. Globalization is, however, partially offsetting the differences in the kinds of religious innovations that now appeal to North and South, East and West.

All of these engaged forms of religion and spirituality are about world transformation as self-transformation. They are based on the principle that to engage socially is not sufficient in itself. It is open to anyone to perform social service. However, when motivated by spiritual and religious belief or principles the result is the betterment both of the self and of society. Engaged Buddhism explains it this way. The showing of compassion in this world leads to the realization of one's Buddha nature, and helps toward the realization of the truth of the interconnectedness of all living things, of all sentient life.

It also becomes evident from a global vantage point how vast and varied is the range of spiritual resources and technologies that are now being drawn upon in every part of the world, and how this development is not only changing the content of belief systems but also creating a new cognitive approach to spiritual truth, a new way of knowing, described in a later section of this chapter, which gives a new meaning to faith, and a new understanding of the purpose of spiritual development. Many of those seekers who embrace this new spirituality are beginning to form a new class that neither *belongs* nor *believes*, in the sense that these terms are traditionally understood, at least in the West. This development correlates with new emphasis found everywhere on the role of lay actors in deciding their religious future. Indeed, there is a mood among these actors that the time has come to take back control once again of their religious heritage, which had been taken away by hierarchical religion. I will return to this issue later in this chapter.

The global perspective reveals not only the new forms of religious knowing but also the multiple meanings and understanding of the term 'new', and the new ways of religious belonging. Even where affiliation to one faith only is still considered important, doctrinal tenets are increasingly seen as matters of personal opinion. The emphasis is more on praxis.

There is no single highway or route across the world that is favoured by NRMs. They exist everywhere and move in all kinds of unexpected directions. Several Japanese NRMs, including Sekai Kyusei Kyo (Church of World Messianity), have arrived in parts of Africa, including Angola, Mozambique, South Africa and the Democratic Republic of the Congo, via the furthest point west of Japan, Brazil. The Brazilian NRM Santo Daime has travelled with Brazilian-Japanese migrant workers to Japan. Movements such as Subud have spread from Indonesia to Australia to Europe, others from Tibet to South Africa, others from India to Mauritius and the West Indies and yet others from the West Africa to Europe and the United States.

Older religions moreover have shed much more of their regional, geographical character and assumed a more universalistic image. The possibility of multiple belonging becomes much more likely as religions come to reshape each other. This reshaping is not, of course, a new development. One of the most effective globalizing forces, the Christian missionaries, has been involved in this process for many centuries. Kamstra (1994) gives an example of this in relation to Japan. He shows how a Japanese form of monotheism found in Shinto and Japanese Buddhism, and in many of the shin shukyo or new religions, including Tenrikyo (Religion of Heavenly Wisdom), and taken up by more than one third of the country's population, owes much to the preaching of the Jesuits and the influence of the Kakure-Kirishitan or Hidden Christians. At the same time, as Mullins (1998) shows, Christianity in Japan has undergone considerable domestication, as have both Christianity and Islam in Africa (Chapter 8). And in Europe, under the impact of Oriental religions, the New Age Movement (NAM), and NRMs of various kinds, for many being a Christian means something quite different from fifty years ago.

This process of shaping the local religion and being reshaped by it (a process previously referred to as glocalization) is also evident in contemporary Japanese NRMs both at home and overseas. In Japan itself, NRMs such as Kofuku no Kagaku (Institute for Research in Human Happiness) connect at several points with the European esoteric tradition, in particular Hermeticism and Theosophy (see Chapter 5), and after transforming their content, integrate them into their cosmology. Overseas, Japanese NRMs, as they attempt to adapt to cultures strikingly different from the ones in which they originated, have been highly reflexive in their relations with local religions. In Brazil this has meant integrating some of the rituals and beliefs of Brazilian Christianity, Spiritism and African Brazilian religions (see Chapters 9 and 12) (Clarke, 2000). Other examples of 'glocalization' include Zen Buddhism in the United States (Melton and Jones, 1994) and Yoga, particularly in the form of Modern Yoga (De Michealis, 2003)(see Chapter 4), which has undergone a process of secularization in Britain and elsewhere in the West.

But it is rare to find that one belief system has totally transformed another. For example, while Oriental religions have influenced the traditional Western idea of God, replacing the notion of a personal God with that of God as soul, many in the West proceed to gloss over the essential point that receives emphasis in the classical Indian yoga tradition that the soul of God is different from that of humans in not being affected by matter or nature.

Not all of the yoga performed in the West is secular Modern Yoga. What some in the West, and doubtless elsewhere, intend by taking up yoga as a spiritual discipline is to become God, but that has not been historically the goal. On the contrary, traditionally the aim has been to become like God not to participate in God. Furthermore, even those Westerners who retain this classical understanding of God are liable to introduce an element of worship into their practice, forgetting that there is no devotion to God in the classical

Christian sense of the term. The reason being is that God is seen as the divine exemplar of all human souls, and this makes contemplation of God useful rather than an act of worship.

Other examples of 'glocalization' and/or domestication include the reformulation of Zen in the United States by adepts including the composer John Cage (b. 1912). D. T. Suzuki (1870–1966), to whom Cage was greatly indebted, encouraged such reformulation by decontextualizing Zen and defining it as a universal form of heightening religious consciousness that could be found in any philosophy.

The process of 'glocalization' extends much wider than a few concepts or practices such as Yoga and Zen and includes the reformulation of core notions of Oriental systems of thought. As Anthony and Ecker (1987) point out:

> Since Eastern systems tend to see collective social reality as an illusion . . . salvation therefore involves the transcendence of society's moral rules, the socially conditioned notions of good and evil. But this Eastern idea of salvation tends to be interpreted from the standpoint of an 'American-utilitarian-individualist mentality'.

A global perspective, thus, sheds light on how various religious traditions are shaping, rather than displacing, each other's understanding of notions such as transcendence and faith, good and evil, of the meaning, purpose and functions of religion, of religious belonging and of attitudes toward, and methods of, disseminating religious beliefs. This perspective also sheds light on the different criteria of religious innovation that exist from one culture and religious tradition to another, although globalization is making for greater uniformity of outlook on this question (see Chapters 11 and 13). Broadly speaking, while the Jewish, Christian and Islamic traditions attach more importance to orthodoxy than orthopraxy, it is the converse in the case of the Oriental religions of Buddhism, Confucianism, Hinduism and Daoism.

Since it is seen as stimulating so much in the way of religious change, this seems an appropriate point to discuss briefly Robertson's (1992) idea of globalization itself as a new form of religion and/or spirituality.

Globalization as a new form of religion and/or spirituality

Robertson (1992) suggests that there is a religious dimension to global-ization, understood subjectively in the sense that the issues it raises are fundamentally important questions about self-identity and the meaning of being human, both of which are increasingly considered not from the perspective of particular religions but in the wider framework of a shared humanity. This is one way of attempting to explain the global character of the NRMs' phenomenon: by considering them as part of this quest for a sense of self-identity and self-understanding and as part of the project of constructing a global self for a global world. Their rise can also be related to the process of constructing global standards in ethics and human rights, as social relations increasingly take on a supraterritorial dimension through the proliferation of transnational bodies, and as the concern for what is happening to the planet ecologically and in terms of its bio-diversity widens and deepens. Moreover, in an endeavour to build consensus among people, certain NRMs also engage in developing commonly shared concepts of the transcendent (Clarke, 2005).

The widespread concern with the meaning and purpose of being human, with the interdependency of all things, with global ethics, and with common concepts, forms the traditional subject matter of the theology and philosophy of religion. Thus, when seen from this angle, the angle from which Robertson views it, religion in the contemporary world, including new religion, becomes part of the process of subjective globalization.

How significant a part is open to question. It is possible, if looked at from a single regional or geographical perspective only, to dismiss NRMs as marginal and inconsequential in terms of their impact on the shaping of religion in the modern world. However, not only are NRMs global in the sense of being a feature of virtually every society in the world but many are themselves, while others are becoming, global religions in their own right, and as such are major contributors, as we have already pointed out, to the shaping of the form and content of the religion and particularly of the spirituality of the modern world. Among the global NRMs is the Japanese NRM Soka Gakkai (Value Creation Society), which exists in every continent and in many countries in each continent. Another example of this kind of transnationalism, this time from Taiwan, is the Buddhist Compassion Relief Tzu Chi Foundation (Huang, 2005) (see also Chapter 13), whose vision of itself as a global movement is symbolized by the use of images of Shakyamuni Buddha overlooking the globe and the ritual of placing candles and lights on a world map, indicating that its teachings are being carried across the globe by its lay missionaries.

The growing demand for spirituality

The option for spirituality over religion and the stress on the need for a spirituality that pulls together, as it were, the world of the human and the divine, and that is relevant and self-empowering, are, clearly, developments promoted by the NAM (see Chapter 2), Indian-derived NRMs (Chapter 10) and the Self-religions and/or the Religions of the True Self, terms which are explained in more detail below.

Such spirituality, which turns doctrinal tenets into matters of personal opinion, is seen by the Catholic Church, some of the more theologically conservative Protestant churches, Islam and also some branches of Buddhism, to constitute a serious threat to 'authentic' religion. Official Catholicism and certain Buddhist communities have been particularly critical of the form and content of the new spirituality as it is found in the NAM (see Chapter 2). This official criticism notwithstanding, the influence of the NAM has penetrated most mainstream religions, and several of the so-called Traditional Religions, for whom it has become one of the principal means of their globalization (see Chapter 6).

While there is a growing interest in spirituality, often at the expense of established religion as traditionally practised, the nature and purposes of the former varies considerably within any one society and from one socio-economic and cultural context to another. Looking at the situation from West to East, one kind of spirituality that is increasingly sought after in the former context is the previously mentioned inner-directed or internally focused spirituality that gives rise to what, building on Heelas' (1991) concept of Self-religion, I prefer to describe as Religions of the True Self. The term 'Religions of the True Self' makes it clearer that the essence of this type of spiritual quest is to arrive at the deepest possible understanding and awareness of the authentic or real self, which, it should be stressed, is not necessarily regarded as the unique source of everything.

Religions of the True Self insist that it is the inner self that constitutes the authority for belief and practice, a Jungian principle and a leitmotif of the influential writings of those influenced by Jung, including the widely read German novelist Herman Hesse (1877–1962). It constitutes the central idea of the latter's novel *Damian*, which describes the path to one's true inner self, and is central to the teachings of George Ivanovitch Gurdjieff (see Chapter 4). Turning inwards brings together and harmonizes what are superficially perceived as opposites.

The direct nature of the religious experience that this new spirituality offers appears to be one of its more attractive features. It creates a new understanding of the historical space between the actual and potential state of an individual in that, in contrast with most long established religions, it brings the possibility of full self-realization within reach in the present. It makes it constantly available, the only hurdle to be overcome being that of ignorance about the nature of one's True Self. The distinction between earth and heaven is in this sense annulled. The former is no longer seen as a place of limitations and the latter one of unlimited potential.

Many seekers believe the process of introverting one's consciousness, which subjective spirituality promotes, can result in unmediated contact with the sacred in all its forms. From such contact comes the power to effect not only inner change but also to change the world. This spirituality, thus, does not of necessity entail a denial of the existence of spiritual beings, powers or forces, or of an Original Energy beyond the Self – that deep inner, divine reality as opposed to the ego – nor is it necessarily so inwardly focused as to be indifferent to, and unconcerned with, the social condition of the wider society.

It is worth noting at this point that the appeal of subjective spirituality, how it is understood and the purposes it is made to serve, will vary considerably from culture to culture, depending on the different conceptions of the self and of self-development that prevail. Some societies continue to assign greater priority to group values over individual values, and see self-identity in more sociocentric than individualistic terms. By way of contrast, there are societies where group and individual values form a continuum and are seen as complementary. Individual values are prized providing they are not seen to lead to dysfunctional, anti-social forms of self-centredness or selfishness.

Although there is evidence of a change in understanding, Japanese society, as Smith (1983) points out, tends to understand the self in an interactive rather than an individualistic sense. The 'I' is more of a relational, contingent concept than a substantive, detached, irreducible one, as is the case in, say, the United States and Europe. And while Shimazono (2004) sees a trend in Japan away from corporate toward a new, more personal, individualistic form of spirituality, these kinds of nuances in understanding of the self need to be kept in mind when discussing the nature of the self-transformation sought by practitioners of subjective spirituality. As we have seen in Asia, the overriding emphasis is on Engaged and/or Humanitarian Buddhist and Hindu NRMs (see Chapters 10, 11 and 13). The Brahma Kumaris movement (BK) (see Chapter 11) is one of several examples of Neo-Hindu movements that promote applied spirituality. A similar emphasis is found among Muslims in the Middle East, including the Ikhwan or Muslim Brotherhood (see Chapter 8), which makes a distinction between 'isolated' and 'social spirituality', and promotes the latter as being more in keeping with the teachings and aims of Islam. Engagement is also a central element in resurgent Sufism or Islamic mysticism in Indonesia (see Chapter 11) and a core element of the spirituality of the Senegalese Murid Brotherhood, now a global movement (see Chapter 8). All of this contrasts with the popularity of NRMs, such as Scientology, that promote subjective spirituality in the West.

The term 'new religion' has already been mentioned several times, and since it is used throughout this volume it is important at this point to define what is meant by it.

Identifying 'new' religion globally

As has already been noted, different, albeit converging, criteria are used to identify processes of religious change and innovation in different religious and cultural contexts. Often the terms 'sect' or 'cult' or, as in China, 'evil sect or religion (xiejiao)' (Chang, 2004: 7) are used to describe what in this volume are being referred to as NRMs. The term 'new' is used here in preference to such terms as 'cult' or 'sect', both of which have not only a descriptive but also a normative use, in the sense that they not only refer to empirical phenomena but also have acquired a negative value connotation. Nor is the term 'NRMs' itself free of negative connotations. It is sometimes used comparatively with older traditions to mean superficial or insignificant, and in certain contexts, such as Japan (Chapter 12), it has acquired a decidedly negative meaning, especially since the Aum Shinrikyo affair of March 1995 when this movement used sarin gas to kill and injure passengers on the Tokyo underground. It remains, however, less problematic than other available terms.

Focusing on the NRMs active in Europe and North America, Wilson (1993) identified a number of characteristics which set them apart from the older religions, and some of these characteristics are also evident elsewhere in the world. Among the more striking features of modern NRMs highlighted by Wilson was the stress they place on the central role of lay people in managing their own spiritual advancement and the consequent de-emphasis on the significance of the role of the clergy. Although there are countless gurus, they are generally perceived less as intermediaries whose role is essential to the spiritual advancement of their followers, and more as context setters. It does happen, of course, that some claim indispensability and in other cases disciples endow them with authority and power that they do not seek.

The growing 'protestantization' of religion, which Gombrich and Obeyesekere (1988) have described and analysed in the case of Buddhism (see Chapter 10), and Martin (1990) in the case of Latin America (see Chapter 9), shows how widespread this process of democratization has become. The catalysts that have triggered this greater 'protestantization' vary but almost everywhere they include increasing individualism and the declining importance of religion as the social cement of community due to ever-increasing institutional differentiation. Moreover, mainstream religion, associated in most people's minds with the old order to which it once gave give legitimacy, is increasingly regarded with indifference or seen as dysfunctional in terms of self-empowerment and progress. Furthermore, the conviction is gaining ground that being spiritual is no longer associated with being church-going or even belonging to a church (Davie, 1994), or, as we have seen, even with believing.

The new spirituality found in NRMs and the NAM is characterized, as we have already indicated, by its experiential approach to spiritual understanding and ultimate truth, and this sets it apart from creedal-based religion. Scientology provides but one of many examples of this turn away from faith toward evidence derived from personal experience. As the founder of Scientology, L. Ron Hubbard (1911–86), expressed it, what was important was 'the science of knowing how to know'. This he claimed:

> has taught us that man is his own immortal soul. And it gives us very little choice but to announce to the world . . . that nuclear physics and religion

have joined together and that we in Scientology perform those miracles for which Man, through all his search, has hoped. The individual may hate God or despise priests. He cannot ignore, however, the evidence that he is his own soul. Thus we have resolved our riddle (of the human soul) and found the answer simple.

(Hubbard, 1972: 36)

According to Ouspensky's recollections (1987: 228), Gurdjieff, on whose teachings the association known as The Work is based (see Chapter 4), was equally emphatic in his rejection of the traditional idea of faith and quotes him as saying:

In properly organised groups no faith is required; what is required is simply a little trust and even that only for a little while, for the sooner a man begins to verify all he hears the better it is for him.

The Friends of the Western Buddhist Order (FWBO) (see Chapter 4) and Soka Gakkai (Value Creation Society) (see Chapter 12 and *passim*) offer clear examples of the form this rejection of faith takes and the reasons for it among Buddhist-derived NRMs. In a seminar held at one of its centres the founder and leader of the FWBO, Sangharakshita (formerly Dennis Lingwood), in order to illustrate the differences between the Buddhist and Christian approaches to truth, raised for discussion the quotation from St Paul 'Now we see through a glass darkly, but then face to face'. He then went on to explain that:

According to Buddhism there is a distinction between seeing through a glass darkly and seeing face to face, but it is a distinction which can or does obtain within this life. You do not have to wait until you die. If you have to wait until you die then the whole theory, the whole content of faith becomes very uncertain because there is no possibility of verification ... but Buddhism makes the point that you can verify the content of faith in this life itself. One could even reverse the statement. If you cannot verify it (the teaching/doctrine) then it is not of the essential teaching.

(Sangharakshita, 1976: 86)

This kind of epistemology is clearly 'new' when compared with the traditional Christian understanding of the nature of faith and religious knowing. Buddhism does not have recourse to divine revelation or an external, divine source as the authority for what is believed or for a solution to the problem of meaning, most acute in the form of the problem of evil. The problem of evil is widely believed in new religious and new spirituality circles to be essentially a problem of ignorance or lack of awareness of the True Self within. While this new cognitive style draws those who espouse it closer intellectually to

Buddhism, and other religions of Oriental origin, it is not, however, being suggested here that this process has reached the stage where it has resulted in what Campbell (1999) terms 'the Easternization of the Western mind'.

NRMs generally, and Religions of the True Self and/or Self-religions, which include Scientology and the NAM, can be considered new in several other senses. They are new, as Heelas (1991: 167) points out, in that 'they fuse two domains – psychology and religion – which customarily were regarded as antagonistic'. This kind of religion, of which Scientology is a leading example, goes beyond the traditional purposes of psychology in that it alters the functions of psychological techniques, fashioning them in such a way as to make them serve to uncover the True Self. In this respect, and others, they contribute to the change in understanding of the notion of transcendence, as traditionally understood in the West, in that participants, instead of acknowledging and surrendering to a God who is other, seek God within. The Chinese Falun Gong (Law Wheel Cultivation) movement (Chapter 13) offers a striking example of this kind of self-referential spirituality. It teaches that humans who are functioning at present in a maze, if they wish to be saved, must return to their original true self (fanben guizhen), and become what they once were before the Fall, gods.

This understanding of one's self as divine and with limitless inner power, dynamism and strength assists, it is believed, not only with the resolution of existential problems, including the problem of mortality, but offers a way out of unhappiness, disappointment, unrest and even war. It is also believed to provide an antidote to what is referred to as the 'problem of work' that confronts many in modern society. In essence this last-mentioned problem is one of motivation, focusing on how to make work, which consumes most of our life, meaningful and fulfilling in a world in which the limitations of the Protestant work ethic as described by Weber (1978) have become only too obvious (Bellah, 1985). Tipton (1982) analysed the contribution of the ethics of *est* (Erhard Seminar Training)/the Forum to bureaucratic work and social relationships showing how this movement motivated its 'graduates' to lead their middle-class economic and social life effectively with an eye on both inner satisfaction and external success.

The increase in importance attached to intrinsic values such as mentally challenging work, work that leads to self-fulfilment, to the equivalent of what Maslow (1970) termed 'self-actualization', has become more notice-able since the 1980s. Evidence from industrial psychologists corroborates other evidence that many individuals are powerfully motivated by the desire for personal development through work. Sensitive to this growing interest in self-improvement through work, more than one company has encouraged employees to take courses, often offered by NRMs, with a view to increasing their motivation and improving their performance. Governments, including the Thai Government, have agreed, not without protest from Buddhist reformers as will be seen (see Chapter 11), to allow civil servants time off work for meditation (vipassana) so that their working life will become more meaningful and productive. The Chinese Government also ventured along a similar path until it began to fear that some of the movements it was encouraging were becoming so popular they could eventually threaten its ideological control over its citizens (see Chapter 13).

Differences, as we have already indicated, also exist between old and new religion over religious membership or belonging. Most NRMs resemble one or other form of client cult (Stark and Bainbridge, 1985) and accept multiple membership. It is not only possible to be a member of several NRMs simultaneously, but it is also possible to remain a member of the religion of one's birth. This gives rise to a whole new understanding of the meaning of conversion and is also of direct relevance to the brainwashing debate (see Chapter 3).

Modern NRMs are also organizationally different from those of the past, making greater use of more secular forms of management, administration and assembly, and of modern means of communication. Networking rather than a focus on religion as community also characterizes much modern religion. Indeed, many NRMs, including Scientology, mirror in so much of their style, ethos, organization, orientation and goals the wider society to the extent that Wilson (1990) describes them as modern 'secularised religions'.

Another point of contrast can be found in the different responses of previous and present-day NRMs to the Church and/or mainstream religion and to the society at large. While historically New Religions have been strongly opposed to both mainstream religion and the wider society, and while this response can still be found, most contemporary NRMs are both more inclusive and, while professing that they seek to transform it, more accommodating of the values of the existing social order. Japan's NRMs (see Chapter 12), and they are not alone in this regard, are frequently presented as offering benefits in keeping with the consumerist ethic of modern society and as providing religious legitimization for such benefits. In this they bear a striking resemblance to the American Theology of Success or Glory movement and, according to Ezzy (2001), to certain Wiccan groups in Australia.

With a few exceptions, the majority of which are fundamentalist movements – which incidentally are not as immune from mixing and managing beliefs and practices as is sometimes suggested – hybridity is rife in contemporary religions, and some observers, including Robertson (1991: 217–18; 1992: 171), have suggested that the future of religion is with those movements that seek to integrate different aspects of different traditions as well as the sacred and the secular. This 'harmonization' of faiths, and of faiths and secularity, has already produced much innovation, and this is nowhere more evident than in the NAM, which Hanegraaff (1999) describes as a 'secularist' movement (see Chapter 2).

While the NAM clearly has much in common with New Thought, Christian Science, Swedenborgianism, Theosophy and Mesmerism, it is more than simply a vehicle providing continuity for these ideas. It has also constructed what might be described as an original vision from all of these sources and others, and has not only introduced these to a wider public but has also changed their application. In making use of age-old techniques, such as channelling, the NAM employs these techniques for different ends than do movements such as, for example, Spiritualism.

The widespread usage of channelling in modern times dates from the 1970s with the appearance of the first series of books channelled through author Jane Roberts from an entity known as Seth, which described itself as 'an energy personality essence no longer focused in physical reality' (Melton, 1990: 101). Channelling is a fundamental part of many NRMs, including the Japanese NRM Kofuku no Kagaku (Institute for Research in Human Happiness) (see Chapter 12). As used by New Agers, contemporary channelling is particularly democratic in character, involving individuals from all walks of life and social backgrounds compared with the select few who performed it in the past. Unlike the Spiritualist the main concern of the modern day New Age channeller is to obtain advice and directives from an 'entity' or 'master'.

Parallel examples of 'innovation' using well-established rituals can be found in the new uses made of possession rituals by Omoto's (Great Origin) founder Deguchi Nao (1837–1918) (Ooms, 1993). Ooms contends (1993: 16) that Deguchi Nao's interpretation of the traditional ritual of possession (kamigakari) was profoundly novel and insists that her use of kamigakari should not be seen as mere borrowing or sterile imitation, for through her use this ritual:

> now represented not only a source of miscellaneous insights and immediate benefits, but also a source of a total and radically new view of the world and the individual's relation to the sacred.

Claims to newness are often based on having discovered the 'complete past', of having uncovered for the first time ancient and sacred foundational texts that enable for the first time a full understanding to be had of how things began. These discoveries allow the movement in question to contend that it is providing the first authentic interpretation of the teachings of a particular religion. An example is the above-mentioned Falun Gong movement, which, while acknowledging its debt to Buddhism, claims to be the most complete version of this religion. While, it maintains, Buddhism teaches two of the universe's fundamental moral principles – benevolence and compassion – it teaches all three: benevolence, compassion and forbearance (Chang, 2004: 73–4).

Several Japanese movements explain their originality in a similar way. Kofuku no Kogaku's for example, claims to be presenting for the first time the first full account of the true teachings of Buddha. Only written down 100 years after his death these were, it argues, wrongly interpreted. This movement also claims to be adding a new dimension – love – to Buddhism's traditional three jewels. Agonshu follows a similar line. Its founder Kiriyama Seiyu professed to have discovered new, hidden truths by reading early Buddhist texts known as the *Agama sutras*, texts that had been given little attention in Japan. Able to discern the hidden, inner meaning of these texts, Kiriyama uncovered a direct and rapid road to Buddhahood for the living and just as importantly for the dead. This discovery has resulted in even greater importance being attached to rituals for the pacification of the spirits of the dead and to those relating to their attainment of Buddhahood (jobutsu). As long as such spirits remained without jobutsu the living would not enjoy peace or secure well-being and prosperity (Reader, 1991: 211).

The Muslim world (see Chapter 7) has also seen significant changes introduced by such movements as the previously mentioned Muslim Brotherhood or Ikhwan, the most influential reform movement in modern Islamic history. Mention has already been made of this movement's novel emphasis on 'social' as opposed to 'isolated' spirituality. The movement was also persuaded, and it was not alone in this, that Islam could, and needed, to adapt to new situations rather than simply follow blindly the opinions of early religious authorities (taqlid). For this reason it claimed the right to reinterpret the sources of Islam; in other words it endorsed the principle of ijtihād or individual opinion. Some scholars have spoken of an ijtihād revolution in the contemporary Muslim, which the Muslim Brotherhood and similar 'new' movements have done much to foster.

A brief consideration of NRMs of Asian origin indicates that, while the notion of religious change is premissed on both ritual and ideological considerations, the former are more often the more important of the two. Orientation toward the world has also become increasingly significant. The previously mentioned Engaged Buddhist movements (see Chapters 10 and 11), and Engaged Hindu movements (see Chapter 10), struck the local communities in which they emerged as major religious innovations, principally for the reason that they involved changes in practice and response to the world. Of course, changes in practice can also mean changes in the way beliefs are understood and interpreted. Theorists of 'Engaged Buddhism' in Thailand, for example, insist, that enlightenment or nippan is not, and cannot be, the goal of Buddhism, but is simply a means to an end, which is social transformation (see Chapter 11). The founder of the Taiwanese Buddhist Compassion Relief Tzu Chi Foundation, the Venerable Zhengyan (see Chapter 13), made a similar point when she stated:

> In the past, Buddhism in this world had sounds but no forms, and was hardly practical (shiji). The so-called Buddhism saw only masters and temples speaking of texts [sic]. This was the image of Buddhism in the past 2,000 years, and the reason why most people misunderstood

Buddhism as only about chanting sutras and worshipping Buddha, a religion of old ladies . . .. I founded Compassion Relief for Buddhism and for all the living, with the hope that Buddhism shall not only exist on people's lips but also manifest itself – to demonstrate the spirit of Buddha through practical action; to pursue involvement (shi) (the spirit of Compassion Relief) and truth (li) (the spirit of Buddha) in tandem.

(Huang, 2005: 187–8)

Other examples of religious change involving beliefs, in the broad meaning of the term, practices and orientation toward the world include Foguangshan Buddhism (see Chapter 13). As Chandler (2004) has shown, this movement has evolved from a tradition that focused almost exclusively on personal salvation and the afterlife to one that in recent times has become preoccupied with establishing paradise on earth, a goal also pursued by Won Buddhism in Korea (see Chapter 13) and most of the Japanese and Indian NRMs (see Chapters 10 and 12). Indeed, millenarianism is a feature of almost all NRMs whatever their religious origins, which indicates among other things how widespread the belief is in the possibility of totally transforming life on earth through spiritual means. Millenarianism is also a most effective way of galvanizing support for a cause.

The dynamics of religious innovation are, thus, complex and variable, shaped as they are by differing sets of social and historical conditions, religious systems and cultures. As we have seen, the meaning of the term 'new' itself varies depending on the religious and cultural context being examined. Moreover, it is used not only to point to radical discontinuities or disconnections between the present and the past in terms of beliefs, rituals, and structures but also to examine the different uses made in the present of the religious past, the 'new' meanings given to the religious practices and teachings derived from that past, the new functions performed by religion and the changes in religious responses to the world.

Accounting for NRMs: rapid change or stagnation?

It is an important part of the mission of sociology to try to discover broad explanatory schemes that account in general and abstract terms for actual, empirical change. The concepts developed for this purpose, if not of universal application, should at least be capable of being applied to a wide range of cultural contexts rather than simply one or two. A study such as this illustrates how difficult it is to accomplish this task. Globalization in both its subjective and material or objective senses notwithstanding, the sociologist continues to remain the captive of, as Wilson (1982: 17) expressed it, 'the empirical circumstances of given cultures, of geography and history'. It was also Wilson's view (1982: 16) that the complexity of the situation is such that we should recognize the impossibility of providing, in terms other than the most abstract, any general theory of NRMs, including general explanations of their rise.

Nevertheless, some very general accounts have been offered. Wuthnow (1982), for example, suggested that modern religious movements are best understood if seen in conjunction with major changes in world order. By this he meant the transnational division of labour, which necessitates recurrent, patterned exchange, including cultural change across national boundaries.

Attention to the aims and objectives of NRMs can shed light on why they arose. For example, one cannot but be struck by the fact that virtually every single NRM, regardless of time or place, or religious and cultural background, from Tenrikyo, which was founded in Japan in 1838, to the Ikhwan or Muslim Brotherhood founded in Egypt in 1928, to Scientology founded in the United States in 1952 – and every movement founded since then – shares a common belief in the millennium, in the coming of a new world order or earthly paradise. All are concerned with world transformation, which clearly indicates a strong dissatisfaction with the way things are compared with what they could and should be like.

Reasons for this widespread desire for world transformation can include existential longing, which many believe cannot be attained in the world as it is and which may consist of improved self-understanding and understanding of others, and freedom from limitation and fragmentation. Following this line of thinking, NRMs can best be understood if seen as world transforming movements that express the human desire for betterment.

However, it is the concept of rapid social change leading to anxiety, stress and anomie that is most often used to account for modern NRMs. This is a highly problematic way of attempting to explain the phenomenon for the reason that rapid social change is a highly subjective notion that is difficult to measure. Moreover, it is not always in circumstances of rapid social change that NRMs arise but rather during periods of relative stagnation. Change or innovation can be seen as a saviour from such stagnation, which can be as threatening to the foundations of society as revolution. Wuthnow (1982) asks why rapid industrialization in the United States in the 1880s and 1890s failed to produce relatively fewer NRMs than the 1840s and why the disruption of the two World Wars in the twentieth century failed to produce more NRMs than the 1960s. Rapid social change theories also fail to explain the variability in the type, in terms of form, content and radical emphasis, of new religions of different periods.

There is something as inevitable about religious innovation as there is about other kinds of change. Mainstream religions, sometimes in collaboration with the political establishment, have often sought to acquire a monopoly over the religious life of a society and to impose their own system of religious belief and practice. These systems, however, generally fail to cater for the full range of human spiritual need. The result is that they leave openings for religious entrepreneurs to fill the gaps by founding new religions or by providing new spiritual associations or communities, methods and techniques to meet the demand from those who find the standard range of spirituality and ways of being spiritual too constricting. Evidence to support the theory of stagnation as a factor in the rise of NRMs can be found in many parts of the world, including China, where at present there would appear to be an ideological vacuum. This the government is attempting to fill, in competition with NRMs and new spirituality movements, through the construction of a new form of Confucianism.

The 'age of crisis' or 'age of anxiety' kinds of explanations of the rise of New Religion suffer from similar weaknesses to those associated with the rapid social change type. To take crisis: this term can mean so many different things to so many different people. For one it can mean unemployment, for another reading about the scale of environmental pollution, and for another the failure to attain a goal. As to the anxiety hypothesis resulting from stress and strain, these conditions are ever present and there is no way of knowing whether the modern period under review here has experienced more stress and strain than others.

Limiting their observations to the United States and Europe, many sociologists have followed Robbins (1988: 60) in referring to an acute and distinctively modern form of dislocation conducive to anomie, alienation, or deprivation. This, it has been suggested, led a minority of young Americans and Europeans to look for new structures, new meaning systems and new forms of community. NRMs moved in to meet these demands, which, as was pointed out above, often expressed themselves as demands for the total transformation of society. However, as Tipton's account (1982) of *est* illustrates, compromises had to be made in which the goal of transformation was commuted to that of reform.

Dislocation occurred in different spheres, including in the area of moral certainty. Bellah (1976) and Tipton (1982) are among those who have argued that the failure of political protest movements and of movements of cultural experimentation of the 1960s and 1970s led to disillusionment and disorientation. Tipton speaks of the 'ideological wreckage' that prevailed among those involved in many of these movements and in the counter-culture generally. In search of guidance and rules for living while continuing to be committed to the ideals of self-expression, many of the disillusioned turned to NRMs, which did not just happen to be there but reflexively sought to meet this demand. A similar situation emerged in post-independence Africa where the failure of politics often leading to military rule resulted in total disillusionment and a vast movement toward new forms of religion and spirituality (see Chapter 8).

As to the rise of NRMs in Africa under colonial rule (see Chapter 8) and in other colonized societies, including those of South and Southeast Asia (Chapter 10), the Middle East (Chapter 7) and Melanesia (Chapter 6), explanation is usually in terms of external impact–internal response theory.

I suggest that we question seriously this impact–response schema of analysis. As has already been pointed out, such a framework fails to do justice to the dynamics of religious innovation in these contexts and over-concentrates on external factors at the expense of internal ones. As we will see in Chapter 7, and as Gibb (1978) stresses, the rise of modern reform-minded Islam in North Africa and the Middle East cannot be explained according to impact–response theory. Nor can Neo-Hinduism in Asia (Sen, 2004) (see also Chapter 11) or Neo-Pentecostalism in Latin America (Martin, 1990) (see Chapter 10).

To return to the United States and Europe, other accounts of religious innovation tend to give more emphasis to structural factors rather than dislocation (Robbins, 1988). These include the search by the young for 'surrogate families', as society's traditional mediating structures, and particularly those institutions that bolstered the private sphere, such as the family, declined in strength. This had the effect of turning everything in the private sphere into a matter of choice, while the public sphere became increasingly institutionalized, bureaucratic and uniform. It was in these circumstances, it is suggested, that those NRMs that offered a more holistic sense of self, including the above-mentioned Religions of the True Self, and the NAM found their appeal.

At the core of other explanations of the rise of NRMs in the United States and Europe are the interconnected notions of secularization, pluralism and privatization (Berger, 1967; Wilson, 1982). The argument developed to account for the rise of NRMs based on these ideas takes different forms. One such contends that the ever-increasing rationalization of society and the consequent institutional differentiation that follows has consigned religion to the private sphere, leaving religious institutions with little social influence and even less social purpose. In this situation, as Berger points out (1967), the more public religion seeks to be, the more it lacks substance, and the more substance it seeks to retain in terms of its truth claims, the less communal it is. Free enterprise reigns, as beliefs, which can no longer be imposed, must instead be offered to potential clients, no longer obliged to purchase them, in a competitive religious market place. In was in this context of religious variety and competition that many NRMs were born.

Stark and Bainbridge (1985) see secularization not as a modern pheno-menon but as a feature of all societies whether modern or traditional, and go on to argue that where mainstream religions decline there is usually revival and innovation in the form of NRMs, which can result in the reversal of the secularization process. Wilson (1991) by contrast contends that the secular-ization process has now gone so far as to be virtually unstoppable. Moreover, NRMs would hardly be likely to stage a revival of religion as traditionally understood since they are in themselves no more than secular versions of religion, particularly in the way they seek to use instrumental rational techniques to advance non-empirical goals. Wilson (1991: 204) writes:

New religious movements, whether in the Christian, Buddhist or any other tradition, are not in the strict sense revivals of tradition: they are more accurately regarded as adaptations of religion to new social circumstances . ... In their style and in their specific appeal they represent an accommodation to new conditions and they incorporate many of the assumptions and facilities encouraged in the increasingly rationalised secular sphere. *Thus it is that many new movements are themselves testimonies to secularisation* [emphasis mine]: they often use highly secular methods in evangelism, financing, publicity and mobilisation of adherents.

Although, therefore, no universal explanation is available to account for NRMs as a global phenomenon, it remains the case, nevertheless, that valuable and interesting insights of a general kind can be had into the origins of modern NRMs worldwide by looking at them through the lens of world history, or modernization and globalization theory. As we have seen, Robertson (1992) views NRMs as part of a new, universal 'search for fundamentals' triggered by the relativizing effects of globalization. This is a view that I largely share (Clarke, 2005).

Conclusions

Whatever the problems associated with providing a general explanation of the emergence of NRMs and of the new forms of spirituality and/or New Spirituality Movements (NSMs), seen from a global perspective these developments provide a clear indication that the potential for innovation both in rituals and beliefs has grown exponentially in the modern world. Migration on a massive scale, increasing globalization, and the revolution in communication, including the development of Cyberspace as a place of encounter and discovery, have all contributed to increased pluralism and religious interaction and, thus, to the build up of such potential for innovation. In very recent times the Brazilians and Chinese have joined the Europeans, Japanese, North Americans and Australians and New Zealanders as significant contributors to the development of Cyberspace, not just as a tool but also as place of interaction with others.

These processes not only act as catalysts of religious innovation that takes shape in the form of NRMs and the new types of spirituality but have consequences for every religion, whether it be a religion from the so-called Traditional Religions, or World Religions category, in terms of their functions and goals. What Gregory (2000) has said of Buddhism – that the changes that have taken place in doctrine and in institutions since the onset of colonialism are likely to be as significant in the longer term as such developments in the past as the Mahayana tradition – could also be said of Christianity, Islam and Hinduism.

It is this broader context of religious change, which covers the old as well as the new religions, as I have already stated, that has been adopted in this volume. For this reason each chapter contains not only an account of the rise of the NRMs and new forms of spirituality of a particular region, say South Asia (Chapter 10), but also an overview of change in mainstream or standard religion. Without the latter it would be impossible to identify even the main features of the former.

References and select bibliography

Anthony, Dick and Ecker, Bruce (1987) 'The Anthony Typology: A Framework for assessing Spiritual and Consciousness Groups' in Dick Anthony, Bruce Ecker and Ken Wilber (eds) *Spiritual Choices: The Problem of Recognising Authentic Paths to Inner Transformation*, New York: Paragon, pp. 35–106.

Bell, Daniel (1977) 'The Return of the Sacred?', *British Journal of Sociology*, 28(4), 419–49.

Bellah, Robert (1976) 'New Religious Consciousness and the Crisis of Modernity' in Charles Glock and Robert Bellah (eds) *The New Religious Consciousness*, Berkeley: University of California Press, pp. 333–52.

Bellah, Robert, Marsden, Richard, Sullivan, William M., Swidler, Ann, and Tipton, Steven M. (1985) *Habits of the Heart: Middle America Observed*, London: Hutchinson Education.

Berger, Peter (1967) *The Sacred Canopy*, New York: Doubleday.

Campbell, Colin (1999) 'The Easternization of the West' in Bryan R. Wilson and Jamie Cresswell (eds) *New Religious Movements: Challenge and Response*, London: Routledge, pp. 35–49.

Chandler, Stuart (2004) *Establishing a Pure Land on Earth: The Foguang Buddhist Perspective on Modernization and Globalization*, Honolulu: University of Hawai'i Press.

Chang, Maria Hsia (2004) *Falun Gong*, New Haven, CT: Yale University Press.

Clarke, Peter B. (ed.) (2000) *Japanese New Religions: In Global Perspective*, Richmond: Curzon Press.

Clarke, Peter B. (2005) 'Globalization and the Pursuit of a Shared Understanding of the Absolute: The Case of Soka Gakkai in Brazil' in Linda Learman (ed.) *Buddhist Missionaries in the Era of Globalization*, Honolulu: University of Hawai'i Press, pp. 123–40.

Davie, Grace (1994) *Religion in Britain since 1945: Believing without Belonging*, Oxford: Blackwell.

Davie, Grace (2002) *Europe: The Exceptional Case: Parameters of Faith in the Modern World*, London: Darton, Longman & Todd.

Dawson, Lorne (1998) 'New Religious Movements and Globalization', *Journal for the Scientific Study of Religion*, 37(4), 580–96.

De Michaelis, Elizabeth (2004) *A History of Modern Yoga*, London: Cassell Continuum.

Durkheim, Emile (1915) *The Elementary Forms of the Religious Life*, London: Allen & Unwin.

Earhart, Byron (1989) *Gedatsu-Kai and Religion in Contemporary Japan*, Bloomington: Indiana University Press.

Ezzy, Douglas (2001) 'The Commodification of Witchcraft', *Australian Religion Studies Review*, 14(1), 31–45.

Gibb, H. A. R. (1978) *Islam*, Oxford: Oxford University Press.

Gombrich, Richard and Obeyesekere, Gananath (1988) *Buddhism Transformed: Religious Change in Sri Lanka*, Princeton, NJ: Princeton University Press.

Gregory, Peter (2000) 'Describing the Elephant: Buddhism in America', *Religion and American Culture: A Journal of Interpretation*, 11(2), 233–63.

Hanegraaff, Wouter J. (1999) 'New Age Spiritualities as Secular Religion: A Historian's Perspective', *Social Compass*, 46(2), 145–60.

Heelas, Paul (1991) 'Western Europe: Self-religions' in S. Sutherland and Peter B. Clarke (eds) *The Study of Religion: Traditional and New Religion*, London: Routledge, pp. 167–73.

Heelas, Paul and Woodhead, Linda (2005) *The Spiritual Revolution: Why Religion is Giving Way to Spirituality*, Oxford: Blackwell.

Hefner, Robert W. (1998) 'Multiple Modernities', *Annual Review of Anthropology*, 27, 83–104.

Hesse, Herman (1971) *Damian*, London: Panther Books.

Hexham, Irving and Poewe, Karla (1997) *New Religions as Global Cultures*, Boulder, CO: Westview Press.

Huang, C. Julia (2005) 'The Compassion Relief Diaspora' in Linda Learman (ed.) *Buddhist Missionaries in the Era of Globalization*, Honolulu: University of Hawai'i Press, pp. 185–210.

Hubbard, L. Ron (1972) *Scientology: A New Slant on Life* (2nd edn), Los Angeles: American St Hill Organization.

Iannaccone, Lawrence, R. (1994) 'Why Strict Churches Are Strong', *American Journal of Sociology*, 99(5), 1180–211.

Inoue, N. (ed.) (1991) *New Religions: Contemporary Papers in Japanese Religions (2)*, Tokyo: Kokugakuin University, Institute for Japanese Culture and Classics.

Kamstra, J. H. (1994) 'Japanese Monotheism and New Religions' in Peter B. Clarke and Jeffrey Somers (eds) *Japanese New Religions in the West*, Eastbourne: Japan Library, pp. 103–17.

Lambert, Yves (2004) 'A Turning Point in Religious Evolution in Europe', *Journal of Contemporary Religion*, 19(1), 29–47.

Martin, David (1990) *Tongues of Fire*, Oxford: Blackwell.

Maslow, Abraham (1970) *Motivation and Personality*, New York: Harper & Row.

Melton, J. Gordon (1990) *New Age Encyclopedia*, Detroit: Gale Research.

Melton, J. Gordon and Jones, Constance A. (1994) 'Japanese New Religions in the United States' in Peter B. Clarke and Jeffrey Somers (eds) *Japanese New Religions in the West*, Eastbourne: Japan Library.

Mullins, M. (1998) *Christianity. Made in Japan: A Study of Indigenous Movements*, Honolulu: University of Hawai'i Press.

Ooms, Emily Groszos (1993) *Women and Millenarian Protest in Meiji Japan*, Ithaca, NY: Cornell University, East Asia Program.

Ouspensky, P. D. (1987) *In Search of the Miraculous: Fragments of an Unknown Teaching*, London: Arkana Paperbacks.

Queen, Christopher S. and King, Sallie B. (eds) (1996) *Engaged Buddhism: Buddhist Liberation Movements in America*, Albany, NY: State University of New York Press.

Reader, Ian (1991) *Religion in Contemporary Japan*, Basingstoke: Macmillan.

Richardson, James (1996) 'Journalistic Bias Towards New Religious Movements in Australia', *Journal of Contemporary Religion*, 11(3), 209–303.

Robbins, Thomas (1988) *Cults, Converts and Charisma*, London: Sage.

Robbins, Thomas and Anthony, Dick (1978) 'New Religious Movements and the Social System: Integration, Disintegration or Transformation', *Annual Review of the Social Sciences of Religion*, 21, 1–28.

Robertson, Roland (1991) 'Social Theory, Cultural Relativity and the Problem of Globality' in Anthony D. King (ed.) *Culture, Globalization and the World System*, New York: Macmillan.

Robertson, Roland (1992) *Globalization: Social Theory and Global Culture*, London: Sage.

Sangharakshita (the Venerable) (1976) *The One Thousand Petalled Lotus*, London: Heinemann.

Sen, Amiya P. (ed.) (2004) *Social and Religious Reform. The Hindus of British India*, Oxford: Oxford University Press.

Shimazono, Susumu (1999) '"New Age Movement" or New Spirituality Movements and Culture?', *Social Compass*, 46(2), 126–34.

Shimazono, Susumu (2004) *From Salvation to Spirituality*, Melbourne, Trans Pacific Press.

Smith, Robert John (1983) *Japanese Society*, Cambridge: Cambridge University Press.

Stark, Rodney and Bainbridge, William Sims (1985) *The Future of Religion*, Berkeley: University of California Press.

Stark, Rodney and Bainbridge, William Sims (1987) *A Theory of Religion*, New York: Peter Lang.

Stark, Rodney and Finke, Roger (2000) *Acts of Faith*, Berkeley: University of California Press.

Stark, Rodney, Hamberg, Eva and Miller, Alan. S. (2005) 'Exploring Spirituality and Unchurched Religions in America, Sweden and Japan', *Journal of Contemporary Religion*, 20(1), 3–25.

Tipton, Steven M. (1982) *Getting Saved From the Sixties: Moral Meaning in Conversion and Cultural Change*, Berkeley: University of California Press.

Van Hove, Hildegard (1996) 'Higher Realities and the Inner Self: One Quest? Transcendence and the Significance of the Body in the New Age Circuit', *Journal of Contemporary Religion*, 11(2), 185–95.

Wallis, Roy (1984) *The Elementary Forms of the New Religious Life*, London: Routledge.

Weber, Max (1992) [1930] *The Protestant Ethic and the Spirit of Capitalism* (trans. Talcott Parsons, with an Introduction by Anthony Giddens), London: Routledge.

Werblowsky, R. J. Z. (1984) 'Religions New and Not So New: Fragments of an Agenda' in Eileen Barker (ed.) *New Religious Movements: A Perspective for Understanding Society*, New York: Edwin Mellen Press, pp. 32–47.

Wilson, Bryan R. (1979) 'The Return of the Sacred', *Journal for the Scientific Study of Religion* 18(3), 268–80.

Wilson, Bryan R. (1982) 'The New Religions: Some Preliminary Considerations' in Eileen Barker (ed.) *New Religious Movements: A Perspective for Understanding Society*, New York: Edwin Mellen Press, pp. 16–32.

Wilson, Bryan R. (1990) *The Social Dimensions of Sectarianism*, Oxford: Clarendon Press.

Wilson, Bryan R. (1991) 'Secularization: Religion in the Modern World' in Stewart R. Sutherland and Peter B. Clarke (eds) *The Study of Religion: Traditional and New Religion*, London, Routledge, pp. 195–208.

Wilson, Bryan R. (1993) 'Historical Lessons in the Study of Sects and Cults' in David G. Bromley and Jeffrey K. Hadden (eds) *Religion and Social Order*, Vol. 3, Greenwich, CT: JAI Press, pp. 53–73.

Wilson, Bryan R. and Dobbelaere, Karel (1994) *A Time to Chant: The Soka Gakkai Buddhists in Britain*, Oxford: Oxford University Press.

Wuthnow, Robert (1982) 'World Order and Religious Movements' in Eileen Barker (ed.) *New Religious Movements: A Perspective for Understanding Society*, New York: Edwin Mellen Press, pp. 47–69.

Wuthnow, Robert and Cadge, Wendy (2004) 'Buddhists and Buddhism in the United States: The Scope of Influence', *Journal for the Scientific Study of Religion*, 43(3), 363–81.

Chapter 2

The New Age Movement (NAM)

Alternative or mainstream?

Most aspects of the New Age Movement (NAM), including its existence, have been, and continue to be, the subject of debate. Moreover, the concept New Age Movement itself is such a slippery one that trying to locate it and capture its meaning is – to borrow the phrase used by the philosopher Gilbert Ryle to describe the difficulty of locating and identifying the soul – like trying to catch an eel using a knitting needle. The NAM cannot be easily isolated from the more general and increasingly widespread pursuit of self-realization by spiritual means.

These same questions regarding identity and related matters could be raised, albeit in a somewhat different way, about other spirituality movements and even about 'standard religions' in the post-modern, increasingly pluralist context. Using this comparative angle it is possible to compare the NAM with Confucianism (Yao, 2001). What Tu (1994) and Yao (2001) point out about Confucianism echoes much of the discussion about the existence and identity of the NAM. They insist, for example, that Confucianism is a very special religion partly because there is no Confucian religious community that one can join and, thus, that one becomes a Confucian 'through self-transformation'. As to Confucian identity in modern China this can be said to exist in 'everyone's daily life' (Yao, 2001: 320).

Other complex issues raised include Bainbridge's (2004) question concerning the extent to which we should think of the NAM as mainstream or alternative. While many of those involved in the NAM believe that it has by a process of osmosis become mainstream, the response of some Christian Churches, including Catholicism, and various forms of Buddhism to its ideas would suggest that it remains an alternative form of spirituality.

Regardless of the label used to describe it – leading New Agers such as William Bloom prefer the term 'Holism' – the New Age can be considered new and/or original, as I will attempt to show below, if looked at from the vantage point of history, and its vision and mass appeal. Prior to the 1970s when New Age Spirituality started to become a global pursuit it was largely an interest of a coterie of elite poets and intellectuals, most of whom lived on the East Coast of the United States or in the exclusive districts of Europe's capital cities. Today it is a mass movement on a world-wide scale.

There are also sound pragmatic reasons for using the term 'New Age'. It is, for example, a useful umbrella term to cover a vast array of groups, communities and networks, which everyone recognizes as in some sense distinctive, at least in terms of their objective, the transformation of human consciousness. Such a transformation it is believed will give rise to the Age of Aquarius or that period of history when the Sun will be in the sign of Aquarius at the Spring equinox. For some New Age practitioners this has already happened, for others it is still some hundreds of years away.

By pointing out this common objective, I do not wish to give the impression that there is a standardized New Age spirituality. As Rose (1998: 19) comments with reference to the Spirituality of the New Age 'it appears to have no fixed path in terms of institutions or dogmas in comparison to the more formalized religious traditions'. What Rose does make clear – and this is sometimes missed in academic discussions on the subject of the character of New Age spirituality – is its integrated concept of the inner spiritual and outer spiritual realms. Its understanding of the spiritual is, he writes, 'transpersonal, that is, both immanent and transcendent – a notion that is strongly linked to the concept of non-dualism' (1998: 19).

In discussing New Age spirituality a balance needs to be struck between presenting it as so heterogeneous as to defy all attempts to identify any common features or as a joined up, integrated system of spiritual ideas and practices. On the first point Heelas (1996) points to common features in relation to the issues that drive the spiritual quest of most New Agers, including the questions: why our lives do not work; what would count as a life that works; and where can the solution be found? Also common in most NAM circles, as Heelas (1996) also points out, is the belief that the Self, to be distinguished from the ego, is divine, evil is an illusion of the mind and Jesus is a 'way-shower'. I would add, and this is something that was discussed in Chapter 1, that most New Agers share a similar cognitive style, which is characterized by empathic knowledge rather than faith in relation to religious and spiritual reality and truth.

To see the commonalities from another angle, by adopting a via negativa approach, it becomes clear that many New Agers have a sense of what kinds of religious activities or approaches to spiritual development are not appropriate. Thus, however porous the boundaries that can be drawn between New Age ways of being spiritual and others, it can be said to have its own vision and methods and cognitive style of being spiritual.

The response from mainstream religions, including Christianity (see below), from the wider society, and even from some of the new Buddhist movements, has helped to create a New Age identity. Some Christian churches are clear that the NAM represents ideas, attitudes and trends that are in conflict with their fundamental tenets, and with the foundations of all religion based on faith and revelation. In research on this topic I have heard concern expressed in Catholic churches from Notre Dame Cathedral in Paris to the neo-Gothic Church of the Holy Name in Manchester about New Age spirituality and descriptions of it as 'the empty spirituality of a confused age'. These criticisms notwithstanding, Bainbridge (2004: 392) has recently suggested that there is considerable continuity between conventional religion and New Age beliefs. This, he suggests, makes the latter 'para-religious', 'comparable to religion and capable of becoming fully religious if it were to become embodied in formal organizations'. The principal reason for such a claim is that the NAM shares with conventional religion a belief in the existence of transcendent entities, such as the human soul or spirit, and the existence of a supernatural world, which can be accessed through prayer or meditation. Bainbridge argues, moreover, that the evidence shows that paranormal beliefs associated with the NAM are found not among people on the margins of religion but in the centre or middle of the religious spectrum, in other words, among those who are involved in what he refers to as 'standard religion'.

The NAM undoubtedly shares much in common with religion and spirituality generally. Nevertheless, it would seem to be too big a leap to infer from this that New Age spirituality, as it has become global, has brought with it nothing distinctive and new.

Historical overview

In attempting to show the creative side of New Age thinking about spirituality I do not want to suggest that it is not also highly derivative. The writings of Emmanuel Swedenborg (1688–1772) are among the principal sources of New Age thinking, in particular his metaphysical theology, which is an attempt to unravel the inner sense or spiritual sense of the Scriptures. According to Benz (2002: 351): 'He [Swedenborg] wanted to reveal the true nature of things' and believed that 'The Principles of true being are contained as an "inner sense" in the external words of Scripture'. This perspective and Swedenborg's doctrine or science of correspondences – the concordance between divine, spiritual and natural things and the consequent correspondence between their signs – have exercised a deep influence on New Age thought.

Franz Mesmer's (1734–1815) theory of healing known as 'animal magnetism' has likewise been extremely influential, as has the idealism of the New England Transcendentalist Ralph Waldo Emerson (1803–82) (see Chapter 5). Emerson, along with Emma Curtis Hopkins (1853–1925) and Phineas Parkhurst Quimby (1802–66), provided the New Thought Movement, a forerunner of the modern NAM, with one of its core idealistic perspectives, which contends that the highest reality and the basis of existence itself is mental.

New Thought ideas were to spread far and wide, and their influence can be seen in the development of twentieth-century Japanese spiritual writings, such as those of Masaharu Taniguchi (1893–1985), who in 1930 founded the Japanese movement Seicho no Ie (the home of infinite life, abundance and wisdom), and of Mokichi Okada (1881–1958), founder in 1935 of Sekai Kyusei Kyo (Church of World Messianity).

New Age thought also owes much to the co-founder of Theosophy, the Ukrainian-born Helena Petrovna Blavatsky (1831–91). At first a spiritualist who was preoccupied with communication with the dead, Blavatsky turned to receiving messages, written mostly on pieces of paper, from the mahatmas or masters of the Great White Brotherhood, the spiritual hierarchy that mediates between the human and divine realms. Blavatsky's goal was to ensure that the plans of these masters were fulfilled in preparation for the coming of the Lord or Bodhisattva Maitreya, the Future Buddha, whom she identified with the Christ of the Second Advent. Annie Besant (1847–1933), who after Blavatsky's death became the international president of the Theosophical Society, founded the Order of the Star of the East as the vehicle for launching Jidhu Krishnamurti (1895–1986) as the Lord Maitreya, who would initiate a new cycle in human evolution, the New Age.

Another integral part of the esoteric dimension of the New Age is the Association for Research and Enlightenment, Inc. (ARE), founded in 1931 by Edgar Cayce (1877–1945). The ARE, an open, unstructured movement characteristic of the New Age as a whole, has its headquarters in Virginia, from which it networks with several hundred inclusive, non-denominational study groups throughout the United States. There is no ritual nor is there a prescribed set of beliefs. There is, on the other hand, a common text in the form of 'A Search for God' (Books I and II) that proclaims the supreme ideal of love of God and love of neighbour. Personal transformation through the Christ-within can only be obtained by meditating on this ideal and acting accordingly. In a state of self-induced hypnosis, which explains why he is known as the Sleeping Prophet, Cayce produced his readings, invariably Christ-centred and expressive of what might be termed New Age Christianity or the Christian New Age.

The English-born Theosophist Alice Bailey made a significant contribution to the development of New Age thought. The stenographer of the Tibetan ascended master Djwhal Khul, who dictated through her nineteen lengthy volumes, the most widely read being *The Reappearance of Christ* (1948), Alice and her husband, established various organizations, including: the Lucis Trust (1922); the Arcane School (1923); the New Group of World Servers (1932); the Men of Goodwill, known since 1950 as World Goodwill; and Triangles, all with the purpose of bringing people of goodwill together.

Bailey's teachings speak of a 'divine evolutionary plan motivated by love' that can only work out through the efforts of human beings, of a World Teacher whom Christians call Christ, and others by other names, including

Imam Mahdi and Lord Maitreya. She also believed strongly in reincarnation, in karma, and in a spiritual hierarchy of mahatmas. Bailey's teachings also explain disease as disharmony and lack of alignment and control. Many of the above ideas are found in the writings of more contemporary NAM writers and practitioners, such as David Spangler (1976) and William Bloom (1991).

Other contemporary New Age writers speak of the infinite capacity within every individual for growth grounded on altruism, while others explore such core New Age themes as the lost world of Atlantis, the moral law of karma and the meaning and significance of the belief in reincarnation. Ruth Montgomery developed the concept of walk-ins, which became popular in New Age and UFO literature. Similar literature is published in Japan by the new, new religions and includes the widely read *The Laws of the Sun* by Okawa Ryuho (1990), founder of the Japanese new, new religion Kofuku no Kagaku (Institute for Research in Human Happiness) (see Chapter 12).

New Age teachings also derive from channelling spirit entities such as Seth. The latter is said to have been a deceased English teacher and described as 'an energy personality essence' that was channelled by the medium Jane Roberts (1929–84) from New York. The core Seth teachings stress that we create our own reality through the way we think, feel and anticipate the future. They predict that Christianity will fragment and die out by 2075 and be replaced by another system of thought. New Age channelling can be distinguished, as Spencer (2001) has shown from Spiritualist mediumship, principally by the fact that unlike the latter it relies solely on verbal communications.

Other formative New Age concepts include the version of the Gaia hypothesis expounded by the scientist James Lovelock, according to which the planet earth is a complete and self-regulating system that along with its inhabitants comprises a single, living organism. This supposition forms the basis of New Age holism. Other important theories that have had a formative impact on the development of the New Age understanding of the world and its future direction include those of Pierre Teilhard de Chardin (1881–1956) who, Ferguson (1982: 26) states, 'prophesied the phenomenon central to this book [*The Aquarian Conspiracy*]: a conspiracy of men and women whose new perspective would trigger a critical contagion of change'. Teilhard de Chardin's main thesis laid out in his *The Phenomenon of Man* (1955, translated and republished in 1999 as *The Human Phenomenon*), a widely read book in the 1960s and 1970s, speaks of the mind undergoing historically successive reorganizations until it reaches a crucial stage – the discovery of its own evolution. This awareness-evolving mind, which recognized the evolutionary process, was, he believed, the future natural history of the world. It would eventually become a collective phenomenon and crystallize as a species-wide enlightenment called the 'Omega Point'.

The affinity of much of Carl Jung's (1875–1961) thought with much New Age thinking is striking. Though there may be even greater reciprocity between the two in terms of the exchange of ideas than is as yet realized, what is clear is that New Agers, often with imperfect understanding, have appropriated several of Jung's ideas. His notions of the collective unconscious, synchronicity, archetype, the self, individuation, the union of opposites and the primacy of psychic reality have all interested New Agers concerned with the inner spiritual world, autonomous inhabitants of that world, the higher self, self-transformation, holism, the fundamental role of consciousness in the transformation of reality, and the importance and significance of the paranormal. The New Age thought has also been greatly influenced by the ideas of George Ivanovich Gurdjieff among others (see Chapter 4).

Although the New Age is not a Church or Community with a central bureaucracy and authoritative set of beliefs and rituals, a number of New Age communities have come to be recognized as exemplary centres of New Age thought and activity. Two of the longest established, most reputable and most widely known are Esalen in Big Sur, California, and the Findhorn Community in northeast Scotland (Sutcliffe, 2000). Other widely known New Age centres are the Naropa Institute in Boulder, Colorado, Interface in Newton, Massachusetts, Holy Hock Farm near Vancouver in Canada, the Omega Institute for Holistic Studies in Rhinebeck, New York, the Wrekin Trust in Malvern, Worcestershire, England, and the Skyros Centre on the Greek island of the same name. These centres offer a varied range of courses from 'Crystals, Magnets and Vibrational Healing', 'Cooking and Spiritual Practice', Kabbalistic Astrology', 'Aromatherapy' and 'The Joy of Self-Loving', to 'Know Your Car: Basic Automobile Preventive Maintenance'.

Although, as we have seen, the opinions of a number of its exponents, among them those of Baba Ram Dass (Richard Alpert), are widely respected and have acquired a form of scriptural authority, New Age individuals and communities constantly experiment to discover the most effective ways of realizing self- and world-transformation. What, however, more than anything else gives a degree of integration to the NAM is the goal aspired to by all participants, which is the transformation of the world through the awakening of every individual to the potential of the human self, to the capacity of one's psychic powers to heal both psychologically and physically. This will, as was previously mentioned, provide the trigger for a quantum leap of collective consciousness that will both usher in and constitute the New Age.

Ferguson (1982) uses the concept of paradigm shift to describe the way in which individual consciousness has begun to adopt a totally new way of thinking about old problems. The present time, she believes, is the most opportune age for this shift to occur. First of all, it is an age of unprecedented stress, which motivates people to seek for a new paradigm. It is also the age that has access to more liberating technologies than any other. Never before, Ferguson is convinced, has there been such an opportunity to explore the innate human capacity for mystical experience and never before has this occurred on such a large scale. A vast variety of aids or psycho-technologies exist to facilitate this exploration, among them, yoga, meditation and the martial arts, and there exists the material freedom to make use of these.

Thus, New Age salvation, or liberation, comes through the discovery of the transformative power of consciousness, a discovery facilitated by such practices as channelling – the ritual by means of which information is accessed and expressed by a source that is other than one's own ordinary consciousness – and by such alternative therapeutic techniques as acupuncture, acupressure (shiatsu), iridology, and reflexology. Alternative and/or complementary medicine is part of the bedrock of the New Age culture. This is an appropriate point at which to examine the relationship between the New Age and the Holistic Health Movement and the Human Potential Movement.

NAM, the Holistic Health Movement and the Human Potential Movement

While it is extremely difficult to unravel the precise origins of ideas, attitudes and practices, what is clear is that there exists a considerable degree of overlap on matters of healing between the NAM and both the Holistic Health Movement (HHM) and the Human Potential Movement (HPM).

The HHM, which emerged in the 1960s, is founded on the belief that the individual is responsible for her/his own actions, well-being, and quality of life and for discovering the path toward complete self-realization. From the outset there was a quasi-spiritual dimension to the HHM, symbolized in the layout and design of its temples, which were modelled on the Greek healing temples of Aesculapius, and in the healing practices, which included meditation. The Meadowlark Centre established in California in 1959 was designed in this way and emphasized meditation as an important element in physical and emotional healing. Important developments that influenced the growth of the HHM in Europe were the Westbank Healing and Teaching Centre in Fife, Scotland, which started in 1959, and the Research Society for Natural Therapeutics (formerly the Naturopathic Research Group), also founded in 1959 in Bournemouth, England. The Esalen Institute established in Big Sur in California in 1962 by Michael Murphy and Richard Price is perhaps the best-known centre and many of the HHM's healers were taught and trained there (York, 1995).

The HHM has made considerable headway in creating nationwide networks across the United States and a large number of professional associations have been formed to bring therapists and practitioners together, including the American Holistic Medical Association (AHMA), which was set up in 1978. An essential element of the teaching of the HHM is that a person is a whole system composed of mental, physical, emotional and spiritual dimensions. Health itself is viewed not merely as an absence of disease but as a positive condition, which everyone should aim to achieve. Illness for its part is also to be seen in a positive light as an opportunity for learning.

In contrast with the idea of medicine as the means to cure specific diseases by the use of drugs and surgery or to maintain the status quo where an individual's health is 'good', the holistic movement seeks to advance beyond this static and passive view of health and healing to an approach that might be termed pro-active and largely non-intrusive.

The HHM sees most illnesses as resulting from a loss of equilibrium between the various elements that make up the individual. The lack of harmony between the individual and her/his environment, whether this be their social, cultural or natural environment, is also considered to be an important causal element. This general understanding of sickness and health is found in 'traditional' societies and the HHM not only endorses the theory but also incorporates both the healers and the healing practices and techniques, such as acupuncture, of these societies into its programmes.

There is no clear-cut dividing line between the HHM and the Human Potential Movement (HPM), founded by Abraham Maslow (1908–70) and also known as the Growth Movement. The HPM emerged in part because of a growing dissatisfaction with the narrow ends of psychoanalysis and behaviourism as practised. It became popular in the mid-1960s with the spread of Encounter Groups, Gestalt Therapy, Primal Therapy, Bioenergetics and myriads of other groups that sought to enable people to experience the deepest levels of their consciousness and being in a self-directed way. These groups were motivated by the belief that human beings, though born perfect, became warped by their existence in society, and particularly through its chief agent of socialization the nuclear family, an idea that dates back to Rousseau and the Age of Enlightenment and beyond.

Initially, those who frequented HPM centres showed little concern for spiritual development in itself. But a change occurred, the reasons for which are a subject of debate. Many of those who were to eventually join such new religions as the Rajneesh movement were involved at first in the HPM, which, as already pointed out, conceived of human health and wholeness in natural terms and pursued what were largely natural ends.

Many NRMs began as HPMs, among them The Process, Synanon, Scientology and Silva Mind Control. Their goals were essentially naturalistic. While the ultimate objective was, as previously noted, the realization of the greatest possible amount of one's potential at every level, movements also claimed that their techniques would enable recruits to reap such this-worldly and natural rewards as greater success in examinations, in business, in personal relationships and in other practical, 'materialistic' goals (Wallis, 1991).

While the extent of the shift varied from one group to another, many essentially Growth groups moved beyond the human potential stage into a more spiritual realm where a new understanding of the self and its development was cultivated. There are those who maintain that this change in orientation was in part a result of the frustration generated by the fact that the rewards movements claimed to be able to provide were very often not forthcoming (Stark and Bainbridge, 1985: 263–83). Moreover, their repeated failure to provide the benefits promised gave rise to a stock of counter evidence that could be used against these movements and the only way to avoid this was to offer what are termed 'compensators' of a less tangible, less verifiable kind, in other words, supernatural or spiritual rewards (ibid.).

It would appear that it was not only the failure – and there was failure in the case of Synanon and other movements – of the HPM to supply the 'natural' rewards sought that motivated people to move into spiritual groups. The commercialization of the movement was also a factor in turning people away from the HPM to more identifiably spiritual movements, although the latter were in time to be charged with the same failing. HMP goals were often perceived as worthwhile, but it was a loose, diffuse movement that shunned any idea of limits on growth while encouraging continual experimentation. It was this outlook and spirit as much as anything else that created the demand for something more profound and deeper and facilitated the move by practitioners from an overriding concern with the natural to a deeper involvement in the spiritual.

The pursuit of more spiritual or supernatural goals did not, however, mean that the 'natural' HPM aim of realizing one's full potential was dismissed as worthless. It was a stage on the path that led beyond full self-development to radical self-transformation, the realization of which required a change in perspectives and techniques. The spiritual techniques made available by the NAM and a host of NRMs were designed to achieve this end, and this brought these movements into conflict with the psychological professions in particular (see Chapter 3). Many of these healing movements went on to develop a recognizably religious belief system drawing mainly on Eastern religious ideas.

Jung, Fromm and Maslow, among others, had seen the possibility of a fruitful dialogue and exchange between Western psychology and Eastern spirituality long before the new religions of the 1970s began to attempt to create a synthesis between the two. As already noted, early HHM centres and Scientology sought to integrate the two. These were followed in the early 1970s by radical self-transforming movements such as the Rajneesh movement. The latter developed a psycho-spiritual therapeutic system founded on ideas of, and ways of realizing, the True Self, derived from Eastern spirituality, and on the 'new' and as yet fringe developments in psychotherapy in the West. Other similar movements include: Transcendental Meditation; Erhard Seminar Training and/or *est* (also known as the Forum) (see Chapter 5); Insight; The Life Training and Silva Mind Control, which is based largely on New Thought; and Mind Dynamics, an offshoot of Silva Mind Control.

Several of these movements claim to have evidence that their courses have changed for the better the attitudes and outlook of top executives, scientists, researchers, laboratory assistants, personnel managers and secretaries of such companies as the giant pharmaceutical manufacturers Hoffmann-La Roche (Silva and Miele, 1980: 140ff.). Whether there is any substance to these claims is a matter of debate. What impact the NAM has had on its clients' lifestyle is also a controversial topic.

Questioning the personal and social role of the NAM

Some observers speak of the NAM as a new way of being spiritual, and this is a view I would endorse, but not exactly in the same way and for all of the same reasons as others (see Chapter 1). For Heelas (1998) the NAM is essentially a new way of being spiritual in that it looks to the 'Self' as the repository of all the means and power necessary for self-realization, rather than to a Source or Being or Force outside the 'Self' whose liberating, salvific 'energies', so to speak, are mediated objectively to individuals. This is perhaps the principal reason why the present age is unique and why it is seen as the foundation for the cataclysmic, mystical revolution in consciousness that is shortly to occur. Although they may use different techniques, New Age participants believe that every individual has access to the same source of spiritual power, which will unite the world in the same understanding.

The vision is not without its practical side. The New Age focuses on improving the quality of life, on caring, on improving the environment and on personal health. Some believe 'sin' to be the cause of sickness, while others attribute the cause to incorrect ways of understanding, most commonly those which are disconnected from the spiritual realm, from the Divine Mind or the Truth within.

The extent to which New Age belief and practices influence behaviour and commitment to the values it espouses has been debated, with Heelas suggesting the existence of a strong link (1996: 207). He writes:

> the New Age can be highly effective in communicating and fuelling commitment to values . . . nature, humankind's equality . . . (egalitarianism being an aspect of New Age perennialism), authenticity, love and so on.

Heelas' conviction about the efficacy of New Age ideas is related to the general point he makes about New Age perfection, which consists in moving beyond the 'socialized self to the true inner self' (1996: 19). Without this transformation its effects will be limited.

Bruce (1998) is not convinced. He is concerned that the New Age does not provide any details on what becoming one's true inner self might entail in the way that Fundamentalist conservative Christianity, for example, does. In other words there are no identifiable, visible signs of change. Bruce's (1998) perusal of the literature of some prominent New Age lives leads him, moreover, to seriously question whether any of them have had their lives improved and empowered by their experiences. He finishes by making a more general criticism of New Age claims to improve and empower lives, which is that it benefits from the 'psycho-social problems of instability, uncertainty and restlessness' that are at the heart of the problem of modernity (Gehlen, 1980) and, rather than providing a cure for these, 'promotes vigorously the individualism, relativism and cultural diversification which are the essential preconditions for its existence' (Bruce, 1998: 35). What concerns Bruce most of all as a sociologist is the New Age idea that life can be lived virtuously independently of social order and in the absence of social authority. Authenticity in terms of self-authenticity, he believes, must be informed by demands that arise from outside the self, so to speak.

While not wanting to disagree with Bruce over the importance of social order, it is worth making the point that this importance is relative, and that the New Age may well have arisen in part in response to its failure to provide anything more than materialistic values and a materialistic vision of the purpose of life. It may also have arisen in response to the way spirituality is perceived to have come under the control of church institutions and to be managed top down by ecclesiastical bodies, thus depriving individuals of any significant role in their own self-growth or spiritual development. It is worth recalling how frequently mysticism, and, in the Islamic context, Sufism, have been marginalized and even attacked by institutionalized religion, as have most practices concerned with the culture of the self that did not have approval from above.

Furthermore, there are, and have been, numerous, long-lasting, largely leaderless and loosely organized societies and groups, including the Quakers, in which people have displayed great virtue and reached high levels of self-development. Moreover, several major religions, including Buddhism, have understood the path to transcendence as a journey inward without necessarily undermining social order to any greater extent than religion that focuses most of its attention on society.

This debate could be had in relation to any religion and is one that is virtually impossible to resolve according to objective criteria.

Other more theologically based objections to the NAM have been made by a number of branches of Buddhism and Christianity.

Some Buddhist and Christian responses to the NAM

Generally, the religious response to NAM varies from cultures based on relatively strict monotheism to those based on more immanentist conceptions of the divine. When a monotheistic religion such as Christianity opposes the NAM it tends to do so mostly on doctrinal grounds, while an immanentist religion such as Buddhism does so mostly on grounds of superficiality. During my research on a Japanese Buddhist-based NRM, which defines itself as New Age in Thailand and Sri Lanka, Theravada Buddhist monks, many of whom made use of its healing practices in their temples, informed me that they found both New Age ideas and practices unproblematic. The reasons behind this response varied. For some NAM ideas were all contained in the Sutas and the practices raised no difficulties since they posed no threat to Buddhist philosophy. Others replied that they were simply using the ritual while either rejecting the spiritual principles on which the practices were based or underpinning them with their own.

Cush's research (1996) on Buddhist attitudes to the New Age in the United Kingdom shows a more varied response among Buddhists in a Western setting. Among Tibetan Buddhists in the United Kingdom the reactions were mixed, some positive and some opposed. The New Kadampa tradition (see Chapter 4) regards New Age practices as superficial and the application of its techniques, such as the expression of anger, as completely the opposite to those of Buddhism. Moreover, the idea of experimenting until you find your own path was not the Buddhist way (Cush, 1996: 201). On the other hand, Cush found other Tibetan Buddhist groups – especially those dedicated to dialogue and with interests in ecology and alternative therapies, such as the Gelugpa Federation for the Preservation of the Mahayana Tradition (FPMT) – much more tolerant of the NAM. Soto Zen practitioners in the United Kingdom tend not to become involved with the NAM and do not regard it as a threat.

Like the Tibetans, Thai Theravada Buddhist groups also differ in their response. While Thai Buddhists of the Forest tradition (see Chapters 4 and 11) in the United Kingdom found New Age ideas to be in practice very old ideas, the response of the House of Inner Tranquility, whose aim was to return to the purity of the Pali Canon, was 'definitely critical of the New Age' (Cush, 1996: 199). This group's criticism focused on what it regarded as the futile attempt of the New Age to bring together at a popular level two cultures, the result being a failure to fully understand 'deep and subtle teachings' and 'a serious misunderstanding and corruption of Ancient truths' (ibid.: 199–200).

The most critical of the Buddhist responses has come from the Japanese Buddhist movement, Soka Gakkai (Value Creation Society). This movement is opposed in particular to the 'provisional and partial' character of New Age teachings, which it believes are incapable of being compared with those 'superior, broader, deeper teachings of Nichiren Buddhism on which its own philosophy rests'. Involvement in NAM practices is referred to as 'dabbling' and discouraged for the reason that it is a wasteful use of valuable energy, while, as some members were apparently doing, adorning one's butsudan [Buddhist shrine kept in the home] with crystals was described as 'slandering the gohonzon [the sacred mandela housed in the shrine]' (Cush, 1996: 200).

A New Age response would be to say that what, to some, appears as 'dabbling', to others is necessary experimentation, experimentation to which there is a logic. As it is not only a vision but also an approach to spiritual development, a democratic approach, it follows that the NAM will of necessity provide space for individuals to independently seek out and test and try techniques that can further that higher spiritual growth and understanding for which humans are, it is believed, by their nature destined. Such an approach inevitably results in the emergence of a vast laboratory of techniques and practices, which have for theoretical justification different philosophies, derived from different traditions.

From the perspective of the Christian Churches, or at least some of them, including the Catholic Church, the problem of the New Age, as we have already indicated, is not so much its 'superficiality' – at least it has never been officially presented in this way – but the doctrinal threat it poses to the fundamentals of Christian teaching and, indeed, to the fundamentals of monotheistic religions. The NAM from an official Catholic standpoint undermines two such doctrines in particular: belief in a personal, creator God and belief in the doctrine of original sin. And more generally it is believed to encourage doctrinal relativism. Official Catholicism regards the NAM as a vehicle for the advancement of elitist Gnostic, Pelagian, Pantheist and Occult ideas, a narcissitic philosophy of the self, and one that leads to the abandonment of human reason (Dinges, 2004).

What they see as New Age immanentism has prompted not only the Catholic Church but also other Christian Churches to attack the movement as a form of modern paganism. While many Christians have adopted New Age ideas (Kemp, 2004), many Christian Churches have opposed its beliefs in reincarnation, its portrayal of Jesus as a 'way-shower' rather than as a Saviour, and its occult and psychic emphases. What also clearly sets the NAM apart from doctrinally based religions such as Catholicism and many other Christian denominations is its basis in experience rather than belief. New Agers seek to discover a relationship with the divine or Self (see Chapter 1) that is unique for every individual. Jesus and Buddha and other eminent religious masters are revered and respected as 'way showers' and no one path or method is encouraged to the exclusion of any other. This inevitably leads to great diversity.

What, thus, appears to be particularly problematic about the NAM for a Christian Church, such as the Catholic Church or an Evangelical Protestant Church, and less difficult perhaps for most Buddhist movements to tolerate is its relativism, which is seen to undermine the whole notion of objective truth.

The NAM interacts with all kinds of religions and spiritualities and this seems an appropriate point at which to address its interaction with Indigenous spiritualities, with special reference to Aboriginal and Native American spiritualities.

The NAM and traditional and/or indigenous religions: the Australian case

Most Australians involved in the New Age, although they do not accept being called New Agers, draw upon much the same sources as New Agers elsewhere and pursue the same goals. Possamai (2001: 86–7) interviewed thirty-five individuals in Melbourne who 'would commonly be called New Agers' and found that 91 per cent were monists in the sense of holding to the belief that a single unifying principle underlay all reality, 97 per cent believed in what he defined as the 'human potential ethic' – the process of operating on the self with the help of various techniques, such as meditation, to discover the higher self – and 94 per cent were involved at some level in the pursuit of gnosis. Since the term 'New Age' was unacceptable, Possamai proposed as a replacement the label 'perennism', which he defines as 'spirituality which interprets the world as monistic, and whose actors are attempting to develop their human potential ethic by seeking spiritual knowledge, mainly that of the self' (ibid.: 93).

Australian New Agers are not all in pursuit of the same kind of self, some being interesting in discovering or constructing the 'indigenous self'. The sources accessed in this case tend to be more North American Indian, less recourse being had than might be expected to Aboriginal cosmology (Mulcock, 2001).

Mulcock has sought to explain the interest shown by Australian New Agers in Native American religion and their comparative relative lack of interest in Aboriginal religion, while Pecoti (2001) focused on the equally interesting question of Aboriginal responses to the NAM. Mulcock interprets this pursuit by contemporary New Agers as the pursuit of their pre-modern, non-Western self, as a longing to be 'other' in the sense of being closer to nature, and consequently less individualistic, less selfish, less materialistic. It is a search, Mulcock believes, for an 'eco-spiritual rebirth', which involves the individuals who embark on it in 'a global process of spiritual evolution' (Mulcock, 2001: 49).

Why Australian New Agers in their search for closer ties with their pre-Christian ancestors believe this can be accomplished more effectively through means of Native American religion than Aboriginal religion is difficult to explain. Among the reasons Mulcock advances is that of distance in terms of time and space, and also politics. It is easier to romanticize about and idealize that which is less familiar and makes fewer demands of a political and economic kind, than about that which is close and challenging. It is also possible that they are more aware of the claims to 'otherness' made by Aboriginal religionists, claims that directly contradict some of the idealized representations of Native cultures that the New Agers have come to depend upon in their endeavour to discover indigenous qualities within themselves. Mulcock does not, however, wish to create the impression that

Australian New Agers do not consciously make clear-cut distinctions between one type of indigenous religion and another, stating:

> As bearers of this primal wisdom Indigenous people become role models for those 'Westerners' who believe they can change the world and themselves by 'getting in touch' with their 'inner indigene' . . . . here there is no need for cultural specifics because this indigene is present in all of us, is universal, is original.

What appears to be happening, thus, is the development of a perception of indigenous religions as essentially the same. The specific, distinguishing characteristics of the spirituality of each one are ignored by the New Age, as all are fused into a single source of primal wisdom. Indigenous religions do not, of course, remain passive in this situation as the 'outsider' fundamentally alters their cosmologies.

In contrast with New Age thinking, Aboriginal cosmology is radically pluralist. As Pecoti (2001: 70) writes, 'Aboriginal understandings do not recognize the cosmos as a unified arena in which events occur; one cannot speak of space of any kind in the singular'. By contrast, Holism and the gaia hypothesis are at the heart of much New Age philosophy. This difference has not, however, prevented borrowing between the two at times for other than purely spiritual reasons. As Pecoti points out (2001: 77) there are Aboriginals who are prepared to accommodate Holism into a fundamentally pluralist religious world view in order to appropriate the New Age powerful cultural critique, in other words to use the New Age as a vehicle for telling their story and reconstructing their culture and religion.

Here, once again, we have a striking example of 'glocalization' (Robertson, 1992).

Conclusions: the future of the New Age

Opinion on the future of the NAM varies. Some (Sutcliffe and Bowman, 2000) have already discussed the next stage of spirituality after the NAM, while practitioners and spokespersons such as Bloom (2004) now prefer to talk about Holistic spirituality as the spirituality of the future.

While Bainbridge (2004: 392) also writes about the time after the New Age, he sees the NAM as persisting as a 'para-religious' movement in the sense of a movement comparable to religion, unless, that is, it becomes institutionalized or 'churchified'. Against this it can be argued, as Wuthnow and Cadge (2004) have suggested, that the NAM already enjoys considerable structural support in the wider society, in, for example, the bookstores, colleges, business centres and even religious organizations that either sponsor or accommodate its activities, and this could well sustain it and extend its influence at least in the area of spiritual and religious orientation and behaviour.

Moreover, the increasing growth of 'unchurched' spirituality of the subjective kind (Lambert, 2004; Shimazono, 2004; Heelas and Woodhead, 2005; Stark *et al.*, 2005) could ensure the NAM a steady supply of practitioners for the foreseeable future.

Whatever its future impact on individuals and society, few will deny that the NAM has clearly acted as a catalyst in changing the way spirituality has come to be understood and practised in the contemporary world. It has been an important vehicle in inspiring and creating a new spiritual mood and outlook that has become increasingly global in character since the 1970s, as other chapters in this volume show.

References and select bibliography

Bainbridge, William Sims (2004) 'After the New Age', *Journal for the Scientific Study of Religion*, 43(3), 381–95.

Benz, Ernst (2002) *Emanuel Swedenborg. Visionary Savant in an Age of Reason*, (translated with an introduction by Nicholas Goodrick-Clarke), West Chester, PA: The Swedenborg Foundation.

Bloom, William (2004) *SOULution*, London: Cygnus Books.

Bloom, William (ed.) (1991) *The New Age: An Anthology of Essential Writings*, London: Rider.

Bruce, Steven (1998) 'Good Intentions and Bad Sociology: New Age Authenticity and Social Roles', *Journal of Contemporary Religion*, 13(1), 23–37.

Cusack, Carole and Digance, Justine (2003) 'Religious, Spiritual, Secular: Some American Responses to September 11th', *Australian Religion Studies Review*, 16(2), 153–72.

Cush, Denise (1996) 'British Buddhism and the New Age', *Journal of Contemporary Religion*, 11(2), 195–209.

Dinges, William, A. (2004) 'The New (Old) Age Movement: Assessing a Vatican Assessment', *Journal of Contemporary Religion*, 19(3), 273–98.

Ezzy, Douglas (2001) 'The Commodification of Witchcraft', *Australian Religion Studies Review*, 14(1), 31–45.

Ferguson, Marilyn (1982) *The Aquarian Conspiracy: Personal and Social Transformation in the 1980s*, London: Paladin.

Gehlen, A. (1980) *Man in the Age of Technology*, New York: Columbia University Press.

Hanegraaff, Wouter (1999) 'New Age Spiritualities as Secular Religion: A Historian's Perspective', *Social Compass*, 46, 145–60.

Heelas, Paul (1982) 'Californian Self-Religions and Socializing the Subjective' in Eileen Barker (ed.) *New Religious Movements: A Perspective for Understanding Society*, New York: Edwin Mellen Press, pp. 69–85.

Heelas, Paul (1996) *The New Age Movement*, Oxford: Blackwell.

Heelas, Paul (1998) 'New Age Authenticity and Social Roles: A Response to Steve Bruce', *Journal of Contemporary Religion*, 13(2), 257–65.

Heelas, Paul (2002) 'The Spiritual Revolution: From "Religion" to "Spirituality"' in Linda Woodhead, Paul Fletcher, Hiroko Kawanami and David Smith (eds) *Religion in the Modern World*, London: Routledge, pp. 357–77.

Heelas, Paul and Woodhead, Linda (2005) *The Spiritual Revolution: Why Religion is Giving Way to Spirituality*, Oxford: Blackwell.

Hermansen, Marcia (1998) 'In the Garden of American Sufi Movements: Hybrids and Perennials' in Peter B. Clarke (ed.) *New Trends and Developments in the World of Islam*, London: Luzac, pp. 155–77.

Hill, Michael (1987) 'The Cult of Humanity and the Secret Religion of the Educated Classes', *New Zealand Sociology*, 2(2), 112–27.

Höllinger, Franz (2004) 'Does the Counter-Cultural Character of the New Age Persist? Investigating Social and Political Attitudes of New Age Followers', *Journal of Contemporary Religion*, 19(3), 289–311.

Hume, Lynne (1997) *Witchcraft and Paganism in Australia*, Melbourne: Melbourne University Press.

Hume, Lynne (1998) 'Creating Sacred Space: Outer Expressions of Inner Worlds in Modern Wicca', *Journal of Contemporary Religion*, 13(3), 309–21.

Hume, Lynne (2002) *Ancestral Power: The Dreaming, Consciousness and Aboriginal Australians*, Melbourne: Melbourne University Press.

Jervis, James (1998) 'The Sufi Order in the West and Pīr Vilāyat 'Ināyat Khān: Space-Age Spirituality in Contemporary Euro-America' in Peter B. Clarke (ed.) *New Trends and Developments in the World of Islam*, London: Luzac, pp. 211–61.

Kemp, Daren (2004) *The New Age: A Guide*, Edinburgh: Edinburgh University Press.

Lambert, Yves (2004) 'A Turning Point in Religious Evolution in Europe', *Journal of Contemporary Religion*, 19(1), 29–47.

Melton, J. Gordon (1990) *New Age Encyclopaedia*, Detroit: Gale Research.

Mulcock, Jane (2001) '(Re)-discovering our Indigenous Selves: The Nostalgic Appeal of Native Americans and Other Generic Indigenes', *Australian Religion Studies Review*, 14(1), 45–65.

Mullins, Mark (1992) 'Japan's New Age and Neo-New Religions' in James R. Lewis and J. Gordon Melton (eds) *Perspectives on the New Age*, Albany, NY: State University of New York Press, pp. 232–47.

Okawa, Ryuho (1990) *The Laws of the Sun*, Tokyo: IRHH Press.

Pecoti, David (2001) 'Three Aboriginal Responses to New Age Religion: A Textual Interpretation', *Australian Religion Studies Review*, 14(1), 65–82.

Possamai, Adam (2001) 'Not the New Age: Perennism and Spiritual Knowledges', *Australian Religion Studies Review*, 14(1), 82–97.

Possamai, Adam (2003) 'Alternative Spiritualities, New Religious Movements and Jediism in Australia', *Australian Religion Studies Review*, 16(2), 69–87.

Robertson, Roland (1992) *Globalization: Social Theory and Global Culture*, London: Sage.

Rose, Stuart (1998) 'An Examination of the New Age Movement: Who Is Involved and What Constitutes its Spirituality', *Journal of Contemporary Religion*, 13(1), 5–23.

Shimazono, Susumu (2004) *From Salvation to Spirituality*, Melbourne: Trans Pacific Press.

Silva, Jose and Miele, Philip (1980) *The Silva Mind Control Method*, London: Granada.

Somers, Jeffrey (1994) 'Whirling and the West: The Mevlevi Dervishes in the West' in Peter B. Clarke (ed.) *New Trends and Developments in the World of Islam*, London: Luzac, pp. 261–77.

Spangler, D. (1976) *Revelation: The Birth of a New Age*, San Francisco: Rainbow Bridge.

Spencer, Wayne (2001) 'To Absent Friends: Classical Spiritualist Mediumship and New Age Channelling Compared and Contrasted', *Journal of Contemporary Religion*, 16(3), 343–61.

Stark, Rodney (1996) 'Why Religious Movements Succeed or Fail: A Revised General Model', *Journal of Contemporary Religion*, 11(2), 133–47.

Stark, Rodney and Bainbridge, William Sims (1985) *The Future of Religion*, Berkeley: University of California Press.

Stark, Rodney, Hamberg, Eva and Miller, Alan S. (2005) 'Exploring Spirituality and Unchurched Religions in America, Sweden and Japan', *Journal of Contemporary Religion*, 20(1), 3–25.

Sutcliffe, Steven (2000) 'A Colony of Seekers: Findhorn in the 1990s', *Journal of Contemporary Religion*, 15(2), 215–33.

Sutcliffe, Steven and Bowman, Marion (eds) (2000) *Beyond New Age*, Edinburgh: Edinburgh University Press.

Teilhard de Chardin, Pierre (1999) *The Human Phenomenon* (trans Sarah Appleton-Weber), Brighton: Sussex Academic Press.

Tipton, Steven M. (1982) *Getting Saved from the Sixties*, Berkeley: University of California Press.

Tu, Wei-ming (1994) *The Living Tree: The Changing Meaning of Being Chinese Today*, Stanford, CA: Stanford University Press.

Vatican Congregation for the Evangelization of Peoples (2003) 'Jesus Christ the Bearer of the Water of Life: A Christian Reflection on the "New Age"'.

Wallis, R. (1991) 'New Religions: North America' in Stewart R. Sutherland and Peter B. Clarke (eds) *The Study of Religion: Traditional and New Religion*, London: Routledge, pp. 154–67.

Wuthnow, Robert and Cadge, Wendy (2004) 'Buddhists and Buddhism in the United States: The Scope of Influence', *Journal for the Scientific Study of Religion*, 43(3), 363–81.

Yao, Xinzhong (2001) 'Who is a Confucian Today? A Critical Reflection on the Issues Concerning Confucian identity in Modern Times', *Journal of Contemporary Religion*, 16(3), 313–28.

York, M. (1995) *The Emerging Network: A Sociology of the New Age and Neo-Pagan Movements*, Lanham, MD: Rowman & Littlefield.

Chapter 3

Accounting for hostility to NRMs

The response to New Religious Movements (NRMs) across the world from governments, the media and mainstream society, although not always of the same intensity, has almost without exception been hostile. This is particularly, although by no means exclusively, the case where the New Religion is of foreign origin. In the past, Christian churches and sects, as is well known, were persecuted all over Europe and many were obliged to take refuge abroad in countries such as the United States. And in present day China, both indigenous movements such as Falun Gong and foreign-derived Christian movements are persecuted. Moreover, the Anti-Cult Movement (ACM) in the United States began as a response to the activities of the American Christian movement then known as the Children of God and now as The Family.

Historically, it has been the pattern for societies to greet New Religion with suspicion and even to persecute its adherents, especially when it comes from abroad. It was the case with Buddhism in China many centuries ago (Harvey, 1990), with Christianity in the Roman Empire and in Japan, and it is the case with Islam in the West in modern times. These are but a few of many examples that could be given of hostility to an incoming New Religion. Even where the ruling elite has been the vehicle for the introduction of New Religion, as was the case with Buddhism in Japan, the religion in question is usually obliged to reconstruct itself in the image of the indigenous religious tradition. This has also happened in modern times, as many Asian NRMs, which began as anti-religions, felt it necessary to assume many of the characteristics of the Christian religion with a view to finding acceptance in the West.

This chapter surveys the responses to NRMs in the United States, Europe, Australia and Japan, while other chapters examine in some detail the response of governments and churches, and of the media and the general public to NRMs and to older, increasingly influential religions such as Buddhism and Islam in new geographical and cultural contexts. Chapter 2, for example, examined the response of the Churches to the New Age Movement (NAM), Chapter 4 considers the response of the French Government to

Islam, Chapter 11 that of the Indonesian Government to NRMs such as Subud and Sufi mystical movements, Chapter 13 the response of the Chinese Government to Falun Gong, Zhong Gong and other qiqong-derived movements, and Chapter 12 looks at Japan with special reference to the situation post the Aum Shinrikyo affair.

In the countries under review in this chapter the response to NRMs has largely been orchestrated by the media and voluntary organizations formed by parents of recruits to NRMs. Where governments have intervened, as, for example, in Australia and France (see below), there have been some differences in the tone and nature of their responses. The Australian response, albeit somewhat more ambiguous and inconsistent, has been more nuanced than the French, which has been much more forthright and condemnatory. NRMs themselves have not always responded democratically to criticism, some of which has been justified. Some have used threatening behaviour, calumny, demonization and other unsavoury means to silence or punish critics (Chang, 2004).

Much of the response from mainstream religions, especially from conservative and fundamentalist churches, has also been negative. As was pointed out above, aspects of the religious response are considered in the discussion on the New Age Movement (NAM) (see Chapter 2). As a broad generalization it can be said that mainstream religion's concern, even where the mainstream religion in question is non-creedal, is with preserving the distinction between what it perceives as the 'deviant' spiritual knowledge of sectarian and cultic religion and spirituality and the authenticity and purity of its own ancient truth. NRMs, such as Agonshu (see Chapter 12), have often countered this attempt to discredit their teachings by claiming to be doctrinally even older than the so-called historic religions.

It is more difficult to generalize about the response of academics to NRMs, particularly psychologists and sociologists. In Robbins' (1988) opinion, the latter have tended to be more sympathetic than the former, and have tended to question the use of such terms as 'normal' and 'abnormal', 'sect' and 'cult' when applied to members of NRMs. The opposition to the use of these terms and sociological definitions of religion, which are increasingly used in court cases – a development that points to a more religiously plural society and a shift away from the traditional reliance on monotheistic definitions – is among the reasons why sociologists are suspect in ACM circles, as they are seen to lend support to the claims made by so-called cults to be religions. But the most important cause of suspicion and mistrust has been the sociologists opposition to such terms as brainwashing, menticide and thought control, used by the ACM to account for conversion and continued belonging to NRMs. We will look at this question in detail below.

Although consistently hostile, society's response to NRMs follows no logical pattern, leaving one to conclude that there is no acceptable way for these movements to act in order to gain the trust and respect of the public at large. If an NRM's response to society is in Wallis' (1984) terminology 'world-denying', it risks being criticized for encouraging its members to withdraw from society in a socially irresponsible way, a criticism that is rarely made in the West of enclosed monastic orders, although it is one that Islam would make in general terms. If an NRM diplays a 'world-affirming' orientation, the accusation is that its main aim is to infiltrate society and take over. If an NRM is 'world-indifferent', then it risks being condemned for encouraging passivity. All of this led Wilson (1998: 188) to conclude that the principal reason for treating NRMs with hostility was because they are new. If this is the case then it raises pertinent questions about the contemporary understanding of religion, about the kind of religion society is prepared to tolerate and about what society has come to expect from religion.

The history of the ACM

In the following overview of the history and objectives of the ACM in a number of different countries, it is well to keep in mind, as was already pointed out, that this is not a homogeneous movement. Sectors of it can and do vary in terms of the degree of opposition they display to NRMs within countries and from country to country, as Arweck (1997) has shown in the case of France, Germany and the United Kingdom, and as is evident from a comparison of Australia and New Zealand with other Western countries.

The United States

Although wrongly regarded as the main exporter of NRMs to the rest of the world, there can be little doubt about the global impact of the American ACM. The beginnings of this movement in the United States date back to the early 1970s when concerned parents began to voice their objections to the tactics and lifestyle of NRMs that had begun to attract their teenage sons and daughters. Jewish leaders were also concerned at a plan developed by Christian evangelical groups known as 'Key 73' to announce to every household in the United States the Christian gospel. Also committed to proselytizing at this time were numerous Jesus People groups, among them Jews for Jesus and the Children of God (later to become known as The Family), that engaged in conversion campaigns that targeted Jewish communities among others. Jewish converts to NRMs were widely seen among Jews as abandoning their Jewish identity. In Israel itself, the first ACM, founded in Haifa in 1980 and known as Concerned Parents Against Cults, was modelled on similar associations in the United States (Beit-Hallahmi, 1992: 37).

The first of the ACM organizations to be formed in the USA was in response to the Children of God (The Family) and was known as The Parents Committee to Free Our Sons and Daughters from the Children of God, later simply Free the Children of God (FREECOG). This movement was set up in

1972 by David Berg, a former holiness minister, and initially attracted many of the street people who spent much of their time surfing on Huntingdon Beach in southern California. In 1973 FREECOG became the more broadly based Volunteer Parents of America (VPA), which was superseded in turn by the Californian-based Citizens Freedom Foundation (CFF).

Without its own resources, at the beginning this organization depended for information on existing hostile literature produced mainly by Protestant Christianity. And very early on it adopted the tactic of deprogramming, which it justified on the grounds that the NRMs, or cults as they were called, were exploiting recruits through the use of mind-control techniques (Melton, 1999). The psychologist Robert Jay Lifton in his *Thought Reform and the Psychology of Totalism* (1961) maintained that the tactics of various social groups, including religious revival groups, could be compared with the methods of thought control used by the Chinese on American POWs in Korea, and, as we shall see, by the mid-1970s the term 'brainwashing' had become widely used in ACM circles to explain participation in NRMs.

The ACM was keen from the very early days to make the 'cult problem', as it was called, a political problem but met with little success until the tragedy struck in the form of the People's Temple mass suicide in Jonestown, Guyana, in 1978 (Hall, 1987). Congressman Leo Ryan and those who accompanied him on a fact-finding mission to Jonestown, Guyana, the headquarters of the People's Temple, in November 1978 were killed just before leaving. Following on their death, over 900 members of this movement, including its founder, the preacher Jim Jones, either died tragically by committing suicide on the orders of their leader, or were murdered. This calamitous event did more than anything else to reinforce in the ACM, the media and political circles the existing negative stereotype of NRMs (Anthony and Robbins, 1992: 7).

After Jonestown, professionals – deprogrammers, clergy, psychologists, psychiatrists, lawyers and sociologists – took charge of the ACM, as parents gradually moved to the wings. Morever, at this point the movement began to reorganize around the revitalized Citizens Freedom Foundation (known from 1984 as the Cult Awareness Network). In time, a central office was established in Chicago under professional management. While the CFF was being reorganized, the American Family Foundation (AFF) took over the activities of the Return to Personal Choice group, which consisted mainly of psychologists and psychiatrists whose purpose was to assist parent groups in their attempt to 'rescue' their children from the 'cults'. Under the direction of the psychiatrist John Clark, an adjunct professor at Harvard University, the AFF, likewise composed mostly of professional psychologists and psychiatrists, began to publish its research into the 'cult problem' in the *Cult Studies Journal* founded by Clark.

The tactics adopted by some ACM groups, in particular deprogramming and kidnapping, always put them at risk of going out of business through actions against them in the courts. This happened in the case of that most efficient of ACM networks the Cult Awareness Network (CAN). For some time previously, but more frequently during the 1990s, a number of NRMs in the United States, including Scientology, went on the offensive against the ACM, documenting among other things incidences of deprogramming. One deprogramming case, that of Jason Scott, a member of the United Pentecostal Church International, was taken up by a Scientology lawyer and resulted in a multi-million dollar judgement against both the deprogrammer and his assistants, and CAN. The case led to the virtual collapse of CAN and seriously undermined the whole ACM in the United States.

Australia and New Zealand

Where the response to NRMs is concerned Australia both resembles and differs from the United States and other Western countries (Bouma, 1999; Hill, 2001; Richardson, 2001) (see Chapter 6). However, while acknowledging that there has been less hostility to NRMs from government in Australia than, for example, in parts of Western Europe, and in particular France, researchers are of the opinion that protection is still inadequate. Moreover, some scholars (Possamai and Murray, 2004), using a 'fear of crime theoretical perspective' to examine the response of government to NRMs, believe that the country's intermediary position between the United States and Western Europe could change and become increasingly intolerant.

Hill (2001) argues, as we will see later in this section, that the Australian Government's response to NRMs has been inconsistent, moving from a more liberal position at one time to a more conservative stance at another.

While there is no nationwide Anti-Cult network as in the United States, for example, the views of Australian society as expressed through the media and other public institutions indicate considerable suspicion and intolerance of NRMs, at least of certain kinds of NRMs, and in particular of what are perceived as political movements. Among the latter is the Ananda Marga movement. So-called therapeutic movements, including Scientology, and 'morally unconventional' movements, such as the Rajneesh movement, are also suspect.

One of the first incidents to condition the way the media, the police and the public in general came to respond to NRMs was the association of the Ananda Marga movement – a Yoga-based movement founded in Bihar, India, in 1955 by former railway clerk, Praphat Ranjan Sarkar – with the famous Hilton bombing case in Sydney in 1980 (Richardson, 1995). A political and a religious movement based on Praphat's political ideology known as Progressive Utilization Theory, Ananda Marga had attempted to organize the lower classes in India against the ruling government and the Communists. When in 1975 the then Prime Minister of India, Indira Gandhi, declared a state of emergency, the Ananda Marga was banned on grounds of having been involved in violence.

While members of Ananda Marga may not have had anything to do with the Sydney hotel bombing, the movement had protested against the presence of the Indian prime minister at the conference being held in that hotel and had become known for its radical political views and actions. Several members, including at least one Australian, had engaged in violent acts, including suicide by self-immolation, in protest against the imprisonment of their leader in India, who was eventually found not guilty and set free. All of this undoubtedly helped to promote the image of Ananda Marga as a violent movement and helped to give rise to considerable public hostility towards it and other NRMs in Australia.

The media did much to generate countrywide suspicion of the above-mentioned so-called 'therapeutic cults' through the interest it showed in the book *Dangerous Persuaders* written by the Melbourne therapist Louise Samways and published by Penguin in 1994. This short book, highly critical of a range of therapies and 'cults', was widely reviewed by the media. Most reviews were positive, which suggests, Richardson (1995) believes, that the book itself reflected the thinking of much of the media on the question of NRMs.

Although the Seventh Day Adventist Church is not usually seen as an NRM, the dingo incident, in which Lindy Chamberlain, a member of that Church, claimed her child had been taken by a wild dog (dingo), also reinforced the negative stereotype of NRMs. A second inquest into this mysterious case concluded that the child was probably murdered by her mother and this led to Chamberlain being imprisoned for life. Although the forensic evidence was found to be weak and Chamberlain was released after two and a half years, Richardson (1995) is convinced that the case aroused great hostility against minority religions. Moreover, along with other analysts, he is of the opinion that the media was largely responsible for the way this case developed and for the further misrepresentation of NRMs that followed.

Australian opinion towards NRMs like opinion elsewhere has been greatly affected by the various tragedies that have occurred, from Jonestown, Guyana, in 1978 to Aum Shinrikyo in 1995 (see Chapter 12). Moreover, Phipps and Possamai (2003), Cahill and Phipps (2003) and Bouma (2003) are concerned that the September 11th 2001 attack by Al-Qaeda on the twin towers in New York and the Bali bombing of October 2002, in which the majority of the over 200 who died were Australians, will also have heightened fear and increased government, media and public suspicion of both the stranger and strangeness in relation to religious groups.

Prior to these tragic events and even prior to any large-scale violence involving NRMs, various state governments in Australia clashed with NRMs, including the Government of the State of Victoria, which set up a board of enquiry into Scientology in the early 1960s. This board produced a report that in Wallis' (1976: 215) words 'led to an 'international moral panic'.

The Government reports on NRMs mentioned above of 1998 and 2000 differ from each other in several respects. The 1998 report (Commonwealth of Australia, 1998, see Hill, 2001) is somewhat more tolerant and liberal in attitude than the latter, acknowledging as it does the bias that is created by the use of the term 'cult'. It also accepts that it is not always easy to distinguish the religious character of mainstream religion from that of NRMs (Hill, 2001: 114–15). On the other hand it is inconsistent in that it uses the term 'cult' itself from time to time. Moreover, it is weak in its analysis of the evidence frequently used in allegations of coercion, brainwashing and menticide where recruitment to NRMs is concerned. Moreover, while recommendations were made that a Federal Religious Freedom Act be enacted, the Government decided against this on the grounds that since NRMs posed few problems in this field there was no real necessity.

By contrast the 2000 report commissioned by the Minister for Foreign Affairs consistently uses the term 'cult' to describe NRMs and not in a value neutral sense (Hill, 2001). Moreover, it relies on poor evidence mostly derived from hostile sources in its analysis of the recruitment activities of NRMs. Overall this report, and to a lesser extent the 1998 report, made inadequate use of the sound evidence available to make assessments and formulate policy regarding NRMs. It is these failures and the belief that the protection of religious freedom in Australia is not as comprehensive as in the United States that has prompted the above-mentioned scholars to speculate about future responses of Australian governments when under pressure from the media and the public at large, should fear of new religious crime increase. However, as Bouma (1999) has pointed out, Australia has so far witnessed less hostility between and toward NRMs than most other countries. This happens to be the case despite the fact that in Australia, as elsewhere, there tends to be over reliance by government and the media on Anti-Cult organizations for information. The situation is similar in New Zealand.

Although NRMs in New Zealand have also encountered hostility from the media and the public at large, the overall reception has possibly been less hostile than elsewhere. Why this should be so is a matter for speculation. Wallis (1986) suggests that since the outset the country has imported culture and has become accustomed to innovation. He believes that there is, therefore, less stigma attached to belonging to something culturally and religiously different than in more homogeneous societies. The boundaries between 'purity' and 'danger' in this sphere are not so clearly defined as, for example, in Japan. On the contrary. In culturally pluralist societies the new beliefs and the lifestyles that go with them have little difficulty in acquiring legitimacy.

Ellwood (1993: 198), who is in broad agreement with Wallis, points out that almost every aspect of White New Zealand culture since 1840 is an import and that the settlers, who came mostly from denominational societies, were from the outset accustomed to a pluralist model of religion. Moreover, the period when settlement was at its peak – the mid- to late nineteenth century – was also the period when alternatives to Christian denominations, such as Spiritualism and Theosophy, were beginning to become known to settlers and the indigenous Maori people alike. A Maori tohunga or shaman-priest was, Ellwood (1993: 199) informs us, one of the first Theosophists in New Zealand. These observations on the openness of settler societies to new forms of religion do not appear to apply so well to other settler societies, including the United States.

Europe

A number of differences exist in the ACM in Europe both within and between countries and between governments. There has also been a response to NRMs from the European Parliament prompted by the ACMs across Europe and which for this purpose became a single European-wide movement.

The campaign in the European Parliament for legislation against NRMs in the early 1980s resulted in a report in 1984, which had the strong support of the British Euro MP Richard Cottrell who acted as rapporteur. Page 3 of the Introduction to the Report speaks of the 'explosive growth' of the NRM phenomenon, which it described as 'one of the remarkable social developments in the last decade'. The ACM campaign, media coverage and outbreaks of violence involving NRMs had made what was numerically a relatively minor social development in Europe into a 'remarkable social development'.

This report, which came to be known as the Cottrell Report, revealed as much about mainstream concerns and values as it did about the purposes of the movements it was intended to shed light on. While avoiding the unequivocal language of the more stridently hostile branches of the ACM, this report made little effort to distinguish between one movement and another, a trait noticeable in such sentences as:

> Almost all have inspired controversy in one form or another, with accusations of fraud and other fiscal improprieties common, and in the social sphere, frequent criticism on the grounds of causing distress within families and psychological harm to recruits.
>
> (Cottrell, 1984: 8)

However, education not legislation – apart from the recommendation that charity status regarding tax exemption for religious bodies be harmonized throughout Europe – was recommended as the most effective means of countering the 'cults'.

A report compiled shortly before the Cottrell Report, by the French parliamentarian Alain Vivien in 1983 and published as *Les Sectes en France* in 1985, illustrates clearly that NRMs were seen as invasive and dangerous.

NRMs in France, it claimed, posed a serious threat to the integrity of French culture and society. The Vivien report went on to propose that a high-level functionary be appointed to co-ordinate, under the supervision of the French Prime Minister, the activities of an interministerial committee that would oversee the activities of NRMs, which were undermining the very fabric of French culture and society. It also recommended that impartial information be circulated to the general public and that a more robust defence be made of the French doctrine laïcité, which was not, as it had been allowed to become, merely a doctrine of neutrality with regard to reflection on and teaching about religion (Cottrell, 1984: 111).

Little action was taken by the French Government and another report was commissioned by the French National Assembly in 1996 in the wake of the Solar Temple tragedy, which involved loss of life in France, nearby Switzerland and Canada. Once again the emphasis was on the need to use the weapon of laïcité to protect the State and society from dangerous forms of religion. The report 'Cults in France' listed 172 'dangerous sects' from Buddhist to Evangelical Christian to Occult groups. Although its findings were questioned by academics among others, the publication of 'Cults in France' resulted in such organizations as ADFI (Association for the Defence of the Family and the Individual) receiving more funding, and in the tightening and enforcing with greater rigour the law on holding public meetings of a religious kind in hotels, leisure centres and educational establishments.

In Germany Youth Religions (Jugendreligionen), the term used for NRMs, have come under strong criticism from Church and State since the 1970s (Arweck, 1997). As in the United Kingdom, the intensity of the hostility shown to NRMs by these institutions has varied and some sections of the Church in Germany, including the Evangelische Zentralstelle für Weltanschauungsfragen (EZW), have pubished what can only have seemed to other more conservative church bodies positive accounts of NRMs. One such by Reinhart Hummel (1981) concluded that the established church could learn a great deal from the activities and communal lifestyle of the four Indian 'guru movements' that he had researched.

By contrast Pastor Thomas Gandow in Berlin took an almost exclusively negative line toward NRMs and, to give concrete expression to his views, founded in 1992 the 'Programme for Parents and Victims for Mental Liberation from Psychic Dependency' (Usarski, 1999: 242). Other clerics engaged in 'cult watching', among them Pastor Haack in Munich and the Catholic priest Hans Löfflemann, compared the 'bosses' of NRMs to drug dealers who, although they may not be able to ruin their members physically, 'could cause incalculable psychic damage' (ibid.: 243).

Tension in Germany between government and NRMs has been most acute in relation to Scientology, which has likened its situation to that of the Jews during the Nazi era. In 1996 the Bavarian Government attempted to ban all Scientologists from taking up employment in the public services and particularly as teachers. In the same year the Federal Parliament set up a committee to look into 'so called cults and psycho groups'.

Relations between the authorities and Scientology further deteriorated in 1997 when the Federal ministry of the interior ordered state security officials to monitor this movement's activities.

Other governments and Church bodies in Europe have been influenced by the tactics of governments in France and Germany and have displayed even greater hostility to NRMs (Melton, 1999). In 1984 the Russian Duma declared several NRMs, including ISKCON, the International Society for Krishna Consciousness, better known as Hare Krishna (see Chapter 10), to be totalitarian sects that use psychological techniques to recruit their members, and even destroy their libido. Morover, in Russia, Greece and Bulgaria the Orthodox Church remains privileged in law at the expense of minority religions.

Thus, although they have frequently exchanged information and collaborated through meetings and conferences, there are, nonetheless, clear differences between the European governments on the question of NRMs and how to deal with them, as there are between the Anti-Cult organizations in different countries. In Germany and France governments have been more inclined to become involved than in the United Kingdom, and with regard to the ACM this has been influenced much more by the clergy in Germany, and in particular the Lutheran clergy, than in either France or the United Kingdom.

Moreover, the ACM response is not a uniform one even within the same country, as has been pointed out already with regard to Germany. In the United Kingdom the organization known as Family, Action, Information, Rescue (FAIR), which later changed its name to Family Action Information and Resource, and the Deo Gloria Trust differ in their response to NRMs. The former displays a more nuanced approach than the latter, which is unambiguously and consistently critical.

FAIR's change of name indicates a change in how this ACM understands its role in the twenty-first century. It is essentially a resource base that aims to provide the world of medicine, politics, education and that of mainstream religion with information about 'cults'. Its concern is more with the place of these cults in public life than with the issues of recruitment and brainwashing, although these remain important.

The need for reliable, unbiased information about NRMs was the reason for the establishment of such institutes as the ISAR, the Institute for the Study of American Religion, founded in 1969 in Evanston, Illinois, by J. Gordon Melton. In 1985 Melton's Institute became associated with the University of California, Santa Barbara, to which the Melton collection of more than 40,000 volumes was transferred from Illinois. The Institute's book collection has since become the 'American Religion Collection' at the Davidson Library of the University of California, Santa Barbara.

From its base at Santa Barbara, California ISAR co-operates with similar institutes and scholars from around the world, and although primarily a research institute, it supplies information to the media and to governmental authorities on a regular basis. Some of ISAR's recent publications include its four-volume encyclopaedia *Religions of the World*.

The Centre for New Religions was established at King's College, University of London, in 1982. For fifteen years this centre held conferences annually on various aspects of NRMs, including the brainwashing controversy in which researchers, parents, members of NRMs, politicians and others participated. The Centre at King's College also founded the journal *Religion Today* to facilitate discussion of these and related issues, and in 1995 this journal assumed its present form with a wider brief as the *Journal of Contemporary Religion*.

From 1984, King's College also began to offer one-year courses on NRMs at undergraduate level and from 1990 an option on NRMs in its MA programme in the Anthropology and Sociology of Religion. The research under the aegis of the Centre resulted in twenty-five doctoral theses and over one hundred MA dissertations on NRMs, covering the New Age (York, 1991; Kemp, 2000), Gender and New Religions (Puttick, 1994; Ionescu, 1998), Gurdjieff's Tales of Beelzebub (Wellbeloved, 2000), the Law and New Religions (Hanson, 2004), the ACM (Arweck, 1997), a comparative study of NRMs and Altruism (Inaba, 2000), the Buddhist Compassion Relief Association (Tzu Chi) (Yao, 2001), and Japanese NRMs as millenarian movements, the case of Kofuku no Kagaku (Fukui, 2004). Other activities included a four-year research project on Japanese NRMs in North America, Europe, Brazil, Australia and Taiwan.

Other academic centres of information and research that provided a sociological understanding of NRMs in the United Kingdom include Inform founded by Eileen Barker in 1988 and based at the London School of Economics (Barker, 2002). In Italy CESNUR was founded by Massimo Introvigne in Torino in the 1980s and in Denmark the Research Network on New Religions (RENNER) fulfilled a similar function.

Japan also has research centres on NRMs, including one at Kokugakuin University in Tokyo. In Japan, as in much of Europe, the Unification Church and/or the Moonies was the prime target of the ACM for a considerable number of years, uniting in a way nothing else could all shades of political and religious opinion.

Japan

Although millions of Japanese joined the new religions (shin shukyo) and new, new religions (shinshin shukyo) – only the first of these terms will be used in the rest of this chapter – the public response, as in other countries, has been generally hostile, bringing together the centre, the left and the right of the political and religious spectrum, including Communist Trades Unionists, politicians and evangelical Christians. This would seem to indicate that whatever one's political views there is a common consensus concerning what constitutes 'authentic' religion.

As in Australia, New Zealand, the United States and Europe, the ACM in Japan was composed initially of parents taking action to prevent their offspring joining new religions. As was previously mentioned, particular hostility was shown in Japan initially and throughout the 1970s and 1980s to the Unification Church (UC) or Genri Undo (Principle Movement) from Korea, known widely in the West as the Moonies. Of course, prior to and during World War II, many NRMs, including Omoto (Great Origin) and Soka Gakkai (Value Creation Society), were persecuted by the Government and their leaders imprisoned for crimes of lèse-majesté.

Post-World War II, it was parent groups, branches of the medical and legal professions, the media, trades unions and churches, among other associations and organizations, that drove the ACM. The *Asahi Shimbun* newspaper was among the first of the media to take up the concerns of parents over the Moonies, describing it as 'the religion that makes parents weep' for the part it played in the break-up of families. The parent group known as the 'Parents of Victims of the Unification Association', which was formed in 1973, received support from the Japanese Communist Party. The latter became an implacable opponent of the UC, largely on account of the latter's anti-Communist ideology and tactics, and campaigned against what it declared to be its tactics of brainwashing and kidnapping. An idea of how deeply opposed the Communist Party was to the UC can be gleaned from the fact that its newspaper, *Akahata*, launched a daily attack on the movement for a whole year (1978). During this campaign it alleged that, among other things, the UC had been founded by the Korean Secret Service and was, therefore, interfering in the internal affairs of Japan. It also linked the movement to the scandal known as 'Koreagate', which erupted in the United States in 1978.

Other Anti-Cult groups formed in the 1970s, which focused their attention on the UC included the 'People Concerned About the Principle Movement'. This movement's tactics raised serious questions about religious freedom and mental health. Composed of professionals, many of whom were academics, this group sought to ostracize the UC whose members it regarded as mental patients. 'People Concerned', with the collaboration of doctors, had recruits kidnapped and confined to mental hospitals, where they were disoriented by drug treatment before being rehabilitated by professional deprogrammers. Some of the victims managed to escape while others were freed through writs of habeas corpus obtained by the UC, which claimed that some 300 of its members were deprogrammed annually between *c*.1978 and 1985.

Several Churches, church associations, church newspapers and clergy were equally strongly opposed to the UC and engaged in deprogramming its recruits. Catholic bishops published a lengthy statement in 1985 claiming that the UC was not a Christian organization and informed Catholics that they should not associate with the movement. A year later a statement of the United Church of Christ in Japan (UCCJ) disassociated itself from the Moonies on grounds of faith, spoke of the rapid personality changes that occurred in its members and criticized the movement for its 'deceptive sales tactics'. In 1987 the Japan Bar Association likewise attacked what it referred to as the movement's 'Spiritual Sales Method', which included its high-pressure sales tactics and the fraud that resulted from its use of psychic mediums. The Japan Consumer Information Centre also published innumer-able complaints about UC sales. All of this activity invigorated the ACM and led to further deprogramming efforts, which received support from new church foundations such as the National Liaison Committee for Christians Opposing the Principle Movement, another widely used name, as we have already seen, for the UC.

While kidnapping and deprogramming continued, opposition to both tactics began to grow from the late 1980s. This was no surprise as the evidence was clearly suggesting that such tactics were having little effect on recruitment. Moreover, they gave the impression of an ACM that was no different in essentials from what it was attacking. The Government and the judiciary for their part showed little enthusiasm for these sorts of methods until the Aum Shinrikyo affair of March 1995 (Shimazono, 1995; Reader, 2000) (see also Chapter 12). Since this point in time the ACM has had little difficulty in galvanizing support (Watanabe, 1997). The violence perpetrated by Aum and the information concerning Aum's methods and aims that came from the long trials of its leader, Shoko Asahara, and his close associates, and the coverage given to these events in the media, did more to undermine confidence in the NRM phenomenon in Japan than anything done previously by the ACM. Indeed, today the term 'NRM' has acquired many of the same negative connotations as the term 'cult'.

Of course, long before Aum, the Japanese public was aware of the links between NRMs and violence. The public generally placed the blame for tragedies like the previously mentioned mass suicide in Jonestown, Guyana, in 1978 on the movements involved, as they did in the case of Aum Shinrikyo. However, the evidence suggests that both internal and external factors were at play in at least some of these violence episodes.

NRMs and violence

While the incidents of violence involving NRMs occurred at different times and in very different contexts, it is possible nonetheless to identify some common characteristics without implying direct links between the tragic events. For example, all the movements were to a greater or lesser degree hostile to the wider society. All, moreover, were driven on by an apocalyptic, millenarian vision, not that a direct link can be made between millenarianism and violence. As is stressed elsewhere (see Chapters 5, 6, 8 and 9), many millenarian movements have espoused pacificism, a point sometimes overlooked in discussions of NRMs and the roots of violence. The movements, further, were under the control of a charismatic leader and this in itself, as Wallis (1984: 1993) and Robbins (2002) have shown, can be a source of volatility. Focusing on the leader, however, as Dawson (2002) points out, can obscure the real causes of violence and can fail to address the question why so many people were prepared to entrust themselves to the leader in question. Although it can be manipulative and highly unstable, charismatic authority is by definition relational and demands an act of faith on the part of the follower in the claims made by or on behalf of a leader.

Common elements are one thing; direct links between the tragedies are another. There is one incident where one of the movements that came to a violent end, the Solar Temple, viewed the actions of another, at Waco, which it does not appear to have fully understood, as a challenge to engage in even greater horrors (Mayer, 2003: 208). As far as is known, the Waco tragedy was not intentional, but the result of mistakes by both the movement and the authorities, the United States Bureau of Tobacco, Alcohol and Firearms. The latter used tactics that backfired in trying to get the members to leave their compound. These included, among other things, the threat of the use of weapons, armed incursion and even siege music. External pressures on the Solar Temple were far less frightening, although this movement, as Robbins (2002: 60) points out, 'did experience agitation by apostates, and anti-cult activists, negative media attention and a governmental investigation prior to the violence'. The right to investigate cannot be denied, but it is the manner in which an investigation is carried out that can push leaders and communities, which feel under serious threat from a world they have rejected and demonized, to prefer death to surrender.

While in the Waco case account needs to be taken of both internal and external factors when explaining the violence (Hall, 2002), external influences were largley absent in the case of the Heaven's Gate mass suicide in 1997 (Balch and Taylor, 2002). Given the complexity of the issues involved, it would seem that any research involving NRMs and violence could do no better than to begin with the principle formulated by Bromley and Melton (2002: 241) that 'violent episodes are fundamentally interactive in nature. That said, it is equally true that the primary impetus toward violence may either emanate from movement or control agents.'

While the ACM's accusation that NRMs brainwashed recruits seemed to be supported by Jonestown, Waco, the Solar Temple, Heaven's Gate and the Aum Shinrikyo tragedies, it remains the case that such a claim was never substantiated by solid evidence. When the brainwashing thesis eventually lost much of its credibility, other highly emotive allegations came to the fore, including the abuse of children. Both allegations suggest that the ACM and those who supported it saw NRMs as posing a threat to the very foundations of society.

The brainwashing hypothesis and child abuse allegations

In arguing against the brainwashing thesis as a general explanation of recruitment to NRMs, it is being suggested that the ACM did not identify a number of serious problems, including abuse of disciples by the leadership (Jacobs, 1984), or that recruitment tactics were necessarily beyond reproach. Similar problems and abuses and others, as Beckford (2003) has shown, have been found to exist in 'older' religions and in some religious orders, but are rarely the subject of a co-ordinated national or international campaign, in which the media, politicians, lawyers and medical professionals and academics all play a leading role. The desire to protect established boundaries is part of the explanation for the selective nature of this response.

Where the ACM is concerned, it also has to be kept in mind that parents and relatives and close friends of recruits often underwent great emotional turmoil, anger, frustration, even despair, at the way their complaints were nonchantly dismissed by certain NRMs. Parents in particular have had to try to understand the radical change in behaviour in their offspring, sometimes amounting to a radical reorganization of identity, without the help of any kind of meaningful explanation. Hence the attraction of ideas such as coercive persuasion and/or brainwashing.

Events in the wider society appeared to lend further plausibility to the brainwashing thesis and, in particular, the trial in 1975 of the newspaper heiress Patty Hearst, who had been kidnapped by a radical political group and subjected to indoctrination. Hearst 'converted' to the group and went on to take part in a bank robbery. Her defence argued that she had been brainwashed and was, therefore, not responsible for her actions, an argument rejected by the jury.

Involved in that trial was the psychologist Professor Margaret Singer, who was later to write a number of highly influential articles in relation to the mental and emotional health of ex-members of NRMs, including 'Coming out of the Cults' (*Psychology Today*, January 1979). Singer also testified in several trials concerning members of NRMs, including that long, widely publicized and expensive libel case brought in 1981 against the British newspaper the *Daily Mail* by the then leader of the Unification Church (Moonies) in Britain, Mr Orme, for publishing articles in which it accused the Unification Church of brainwashing its recruits (Barker, 1984). The *Daily Mail*'s accusations were implicitly endorsed by the jury's verdict and the consequences of this for the Church were a vast amount of adverse publicity and parliamentary moves to remove it from the Charities' Register, a move dropped in February 1988 (Robillard, 1984: 10–11).

It should be noted, however, that judgments by the courts and pronouncements by judges on NRMs are not all of a kind. Judges can and do vary in the verdicts they recommend and the language they use, which Hanson (2004) argues can often reveal an implicit Christian 'bias'. This language can range from outright condemnation of a New Religion to positive approval. Justice Latey's open-court verdict following a private hearing in which he declared Scientology to be 'corrupt, sinister and dangerous' (*The Times*, July 24th 1984) provides an example of the former.

The conclusions of the judgment of Lord Justice Ward of the High Court in London on October 19th 1995 on The Family (formerly the Children of God) was, in terms of its tone, much different. This case concerned an application by a grandmother to make her grandson a ward of court and to have care and control of the child taken away from his mother who was a member of The Family, a communalistic movement that lives separately from society and against which allegations of child abuse had been made in different parts of the world.

Although this judge was convinced that The Family had made several important improvements that reduced the risk of harm to children being reared in the movement, he still felt there was a need for further progress (Bradney, 1999). However, he did not demand that the child be withdrawn from his mother, whose ability to rear her son had never been questioned by her mother. What he did require for the child to stay with his mother was that the movement should agree to implement a list of suggestions that he made.

The Family saw this judgement as a victory and was quick to make known the unusually encouraging tone of the judge. In its summary of Ward's conclusion on its fitness to raise children, it reports him as having written:

> One cannot have listened, as I have, to over thirty members of the Family without being impressed by and in many ways filled with admiration for their total dedication to their discipleship, to their beliefs in the teaching of their master, Jesus Christ, and to their spreading of His Gospel. Believing, as they do, in an active Satan, their inclination is, as Berg (their founder) expresses it: 'For God sake, speak the truth'.
>
> (Summary, p. 31 – author's copy)

An additional excerpt selected by The Family from its summary of Ward's conclusions bears upon the question of brainwashing under discussion here. Ward, who was aware of the negative past history of the group and recognized that important changes had been made, reportedly stated:

> There is no evidence whatsoever to suggest that NT [the child's mother in the case] – or CT [the child's maternal uncle] for that matter – were put under any improper pressure to join the family. Far from it. They went into it voluntarily and happily. The letters of NT are eloquent of the new found happiness in finding Jesus.
>
> (Document in the author's possession)

By contrast, Singer (1979) claimed in her defence of the brainwashing thesis that the intense allegiance of the 300 ex-members to the 'cults' they once belonged to could be reasonably accounted for in terms of the ideological arguments of the groups and the social and psychological pressures and practices that, intentionally or not, they were under from these groups. These amounted to conditioning techniques that constricted attention, limited personal relationships and devalued reasoning.

Singer also claimed to have identified negative effects brought on by the long hours of prayer, chanting or meditation (in one Zen sect, 21 hours of meditation on consecutive days, several times a year) and by 'lengthy, repetitive lectures day and night'. Also mentioned as potentially harmful was the exclusion of family and other outside contacts, rigid moral judgements of the behaviour of the unconverted in the outside world or the demonizing of the rest of humanity, and restrictions on sexual behaviour, all of which formed part of a strategy to increase followers' commitment to the goals of the group and in some cases to its powerful leader (ibid.).

Furthermore, most ex-members of 'cults', according to Singer, struggled with one or other of several problems, including depression, attendant on the meaninglessness that followed on from leaving a movement that once regulated one's whole life and gave one a sense of purpose. The depression also resulted from the realization of having been used by the movement to which one wrongly surrendered one's autonomy. There was also the loneliness consequent on leaving friends, which was reinforced by being unable to relate to outsiders whom one formerly despised and from whom one was previously cut off. Ex-members were also said to slip in and out of altered states as a result of the tension, anxiety and indecision they experienced on leaving the movement. Indecisiveness resulted from having been totally regulated for so long. According to Singer there was also a blurring of mental acuity in the form of 'subtle cognitive inefficiencies and changes that take some time to pass' and this means that some 'have to take simple jobs until they regain former levels of competence' (ibid.).

Uncritical passivity was another problem experienced by ex-members, Singer noted, and this took the form of 'almost total acceptance of all one hears, pre-cult skills for evaluating and criticising being in relative abeyance' (1979). There was also the fear factor in the form of 'warnings of heavenly damnation, harassment and the use of force to make members return' (ibid.). Another 'serious' problem highlighted by Singer was the agony that accompanied any explanation of the difficulties of leaving to those unfamiliar with the 'cults', as well as the guilt arising from having practised deception while a member, especially with regard to fund-raising and recruitment. She also identified the problem of coming to terms with the loss of elite status, for leaving a movement meant that the individual had to cope with no longer being one of a select band of world savers.

All of these emotional and psychological problems notwithstanding,

Singer somewhat surprisingly concluded that most ex-members were 'neither grossly incompetent or blatantly disturbed', a conclusion that would seem to contradict the view that NRMs indulge in 'menticide', 'thought reform', 'mind control' and even brainwashing itself (1979).

The previously mentioned Boston consultant psychiatrist Dr Clark, the Berkeley, California-based clinical psychiatrist Dr West, and the Irish psychiatrist Dr Anthony Clare, reached similar conclusions to those expressed by Professor Singer. However, Clark and others (1981), though they used the terms 'brainwashing' and 'mind control', preferred the phrase 'unethical methods of persuasion' to describe the process whereby recruits are inducted into new religions. 'Unethical methods of persuasion' include isolation, group pressure, denigration of critical thinking, physical debilitation, induction of trance-like states, and extensive control of information for the purpose of recruiting and holding on to converts and for the exploitation of converts financially and psychologically (ibid.).

While admitting that it is difficult, if not impossible, to demonstrate 'with rigorous scientific methodology', Clark and others concluded by acknowledging that not all the harms associated with NRMs derived from membership of these organizations. Clark speaks of six varieties of personal harm found in, though not exclusive to, NRMs: physical harm, including child abuse; psychiatric problems such as speaking rather slowly; diminished personal autonomy where the person is unable to exercise her/his capacity to make decisions by choosing from a set of alternatives without undue interference from others in the movement; diminished critical thinking in the sense of an individual's inability to discriminate, to ask pertinent questions, to formulate and test hypotheses and to analyse the logic of a perceived relationship; impaired psychological integration where the person cannot, without great difficulty, order her/his memories, values, beliefs, heritage and so on into a unified whole because they are persuaded by the leader to reject significant 'chunks' of themselves, such as family and personal goals; and financial exploitation (ibid.).

Despite these conclusions by psychologists and psychiatrists, many sociologists remained far from satisfied that the brainwashing/mind-control hypothesis could be made to account for conversion to NRMs. Above all, they questioned testimony that was provided by outsiders only, and from their own research with 'insiders' found little or no evidence of coercive persuasion, brainwashing or menticide (see, for example, Barker, 1984). It was principally on the basis of this kind of evidence that most sociological research argued that there was no basis for legislation or for government intervention as demanded by the ACM. Such legislation would undermine a basic tenet of a free society: that the law knows no heresy and that citizens have the right to practise their beliefs providing they do not run counter to the law of the land or, as is the case in Britain, to 'paramount social concerns' (see Robilliard, 1984: x). This notwithstanding, the administrative measures taken by the British Minister of Health in 1968 to discourage the propagation and growth of Scientology were taken not because there was evidence of criminal offences committed by the movement but were justified on the grounds that that particular movement was alleged to have negative effects on the minds of its adherents (ibid.: 106–7).

Not only was there a lack of empirical evidence in support of the brainwashing/mind-control hypothesis but the hypothesis also suffered from numerous other methodological and theoretical defects. It displayed, for instance, an inadequate knowledge of comparative religion in that the characteristics it attributed to NRMs could also be said to exist in some of what might be termed the 'legitimate' older religions or churches. Some Catholic monks, for example, would want to point to basic similarities in their own training and that of members of the Hare Krishna movement. Moreover, although there have been developments in understanding and interpretation in recent times of the vow of obedience in, for example, the Catholic tradition, the abandonment of one's own will and intellectual convictions through the vow of obedience was for long regarded as an integral part of the process of becoming a religious virtuoso, and essential to the eradication of all trace of self-esteem and self-pride.

It is clear, thus, that the 'problems' identified by Singer, Clark, West and others were by no means peculiar to these movements. Moreover, the loss of a sense of one's own identity, of self-motivation and purpose in life, and of enthusiasm and interest in what was once regarded as important, a sense of helplessness and even disorientation, can follow on from breakdown in other circumstances. This can occur, for example, among those who abandon relatively highly integrated, small-scale communities or societies in which person-to-person encounter is the norm, for more open, more anonymous, more impersonal groupings whose ethos, mores and rules, both implicit and explicit, are unfamiliar and alien.

Other methodological and theoretical objections to the brainwashing thesis concern the nature of the concept itself. Brainwashing is clearly a 'spongy', 'imprecise', and 'highly emotive' term that greatly increases the difficulties of arriving at a value-free, objective assessment of the evidence. Furthermore, it is capable of being easily used as an ideological weapon and more likely, therefore, to motivate people to become actively involved in ill-thought-out, ill-considered schemes and activities on behalf of members – including kidnapping and deprogramming.

A further, somewhat incomprehensible problem arises over the evidence put forward by Singer and others in defence of brainwashing and that is their failure to examine with greater thoroughness the opinions of existing members. Equally incomprehensible was their failure to recognize the problems NRMs were experiencing in retaining those they recruited. These are perhaps the two most compelling arguments against Singer's evidence in particular. By the end of the 1980s many scholars were of the same mind as the psychologist Dick Anthony, who argued that Singer had postulated a 'robot' theory of brainwashing that lacked scientific support (1990). Other psychologists, including Galanter (1978), in contrast to Singer, pointed to the positive effects of participation.

The Unification Church was often cited in the context of the debate on NRMs as a total institution that brainwashed its recruits. However, as Lofland (1978) and Barker (1984) have shown, the first encounters of potential recruits with the movement through workshops and seminars in the United States and Britain rarely led to conversion. Writing of this movement's efforts at evangelization in the 1960s in the United States, Lofland described them 'as thoroughly inept' (Lofland, 1978: 8). Admittedly, the position was to change dramatically in the 1970s as tighter control over the social environment of recruits was introduced by, among other things, isolating them at workshops and seminars, along with greater emphasis on 'love bombing' and the involving of recruits in activities such as fund-raising. Even this approach failed to prevent recruits from dropping out.

Thus, with all the contrary evidence available, brainwashing continued to be presented as an explanation for joining NRMs, partly, I suspect, for the reason that it had become an article of faith rather than a matter of scientific evidence. To have rejected the brainwashing explanation would have meant accepting that those who joined NRMs – often relatives and close friends, and sometimes deprogrammed recruits to the ACM itself – had knowingly and voluntarily surrendered to what were considered to be the immoral, anti-social activities of the cults.

Many in society at large continued to have serious reservations about the credibility of sociological and other research that undermined the brainwashing hypothesis. The outbreaks of violence ensured that this should be so, as did the narrow focus of most of this research, which concentrated exclusively on the flaws of the brainwashing hypothesis without examining charges of manipulation and deception. Moreover, the sociological perspective depended greatly on close contact with NRMs, which often appeared more like fraternizing with the enemy than objective research.

The divide was further exacerbated by the sociological preference for such models of conversion to NRMs as the 'drift model', which suggested that conversion was a gradual, sometimes inadvertent process that resulted not from the use of manipulative and persuasive techniques but that came about primarily through pre-existing social networks and interpersonal bonds: friends recruited friends, family members recruited each other and neighbours recruited neighbours (Bromley and Richardson, 1983; Barker, 1984; Robbins, 1988; Anthony, 1990).

Research on conversion by Lofland and Skonovd (1981) found little evidence of coercive persuasion among recruits to NRMs and instead highlighted intellectual conversion as one of the most frequently reported motifs in conversion narratives. The majority of my own random sample of fifty interviews carried out over a period of three years (referred to below as author's interviews, 1984/85/87/88) with converts to NRMs in the mid- to late 1980s found that the majority were 'active' as opposed to a passive converts. Over half had experimented with one or more NRMs before opting for the movement they belonged to at the time of interview.

The intellectual component took various forms. In the case of Scientology, reading brought several to the movement in the first instance, including a twenty-four-year-old, middle-class convert, without higher educational qualifications, who read *Dianetics* and found it 'fascinating'. He went on to take a Scientology course with the intention of becoming 'clear' and after some time at the movement's British headquarters he revealed that, while he discovered from his reading of *Dianetics* and other Scientology manuals that the movement possessed a relatively simple technique 'which appeared to work', he was somewhat disturbed by the 'lack of evidence of clears'. His intention was to remain in the movement only as long as he felt he was deriving benefit. If he ceased to do so, he would look elsewhere.

Other recruits to Scientology also encountered the movement initially through reading *Dianetics*, some finding that it 'tied in' with other literature they had read. It spoke to one in a way similar to that in which Conrad and Lawrence spoke to him, in that it rejected the idea of depraved humanity and stressed that there could be no real happiness and fulfilment unless individuals became their 'natural' and/or real self (see Chapter 1 on Religion of the True Self). For another, a nurse who 'lapped it up', *Dianetics* presented the most convincing theory of psycho-somatic illness that she had so far encountered in her reading and, she added, 'experience had since shown it [*Dianetics*] to be correct'. The committed Baptist who joined Scientology at the age of 58, did so two weeks after reading *Dianetics*, which he stated 'had answers and solutions to the ills of the present, confused and disoriented world' (author's interviews, 1984).

I also found the intellectual mode of conversion common among converts to new Buddhist movements such as the Friends of the Western Buddhist Order (FWBO) (see Chapter 4). Several members of the FWBO recalled that they had first come to know about Buddhism through reading about it. One, a Cambridge graduate and former Roman Catholic, abandoned his Catholic faith at the age of thirteen explaining that he felt 'isolated' at school because of his Catholicism. Later, while at University, where he read several books on Buddhism, he found this religion culturally alien and difficult to separate from its Eastern origins, a problem that was resolved when he heard of the FWBO, which provided him with a Western perspective on Buddhism.

Reading was the beginning of the path to the FWBO for another former Roman Catholic. This convert, dissatisfied with his faith because 'It never answered any of the important questions I was asking and in particular it had no answer for the problem of evil which is disastrous for Christianity' (author's interviews, 1984), 'stumbled upon' Alan Watt's *The Way of Zen*.

This, together with Suzuki's essays on Zen Buddhism, aroused his interest in Buddhism and eventually led to his ordination in the FWBO. Older Catholic converts to this and other Buddhist movements often appear to have a serious obstacle to overcome in the form of abandoning belief in God. While two young members of the FWBO, sixteen and seventeen years of age, insisted that they had no problem at all in rejecting this belief, another, aged thirty-five, a former soldier, spoke of grappling with this problem from first encountering the FWBO in 1967 until 1985. It was only then that he was able to commit himself, 'with conviction', to joining.

The writings of Gurdjieff (see Chapter 4) have proved to be an important trigger in the conversion of others. Cases include converts to Subud, a movement founded by Bapak Muhammad Subuh Hadiwidjojo in Samarang, Indonesia, in 1924 and established in Britain in 1957 (see Chapter 11). Recruits to several other NRMs, including the Emin Foundation, Transcendental Meditation, Exegesis and the now officially defunct Rajneesh movement, also recalled how they had been strongly influenced in their spiritual search by Gurdjieff.

Some converts read for a very long time before committing themselves. Examples include the former Catholic turned Marxist who spent fifteen years studying the writings of the Worldwide Church of God (author's interviews, 1988). Another, who was deeply interested in Sufism, read and sought 'specialist' advice on the works of Idris Shah for 'at least a decade'. These relatively long drawn out conversion processes were by no means the exception. A convert to the previously mentioned FWBO, aged thirty-five at the time of our interview with him, and a former landscape gardener, spoke of his 'slow' conversion over a period of fifteen years and of his having, before he finally committed himself, 'no illusions about the hypocrisy that can exist in the movement' (author's interviews, 1987).

An interest in music, art, meditation, ecology, spiritualism and alternative medicine have also influenced people to search for a faith. Many of the white, Caucasian converts to the Rastafarian movement have been attracted initially by reggae, some also by drugs and others by the Rasta hairstyle, dress and outlook on life. A concern for the environment brought several recruits into contact for the first time with Neo-Paganism, and the Brahma Kumaris and Soka Gakkai movements, which organized discussion groups and activities on this subject.

Dramatic conversion experiences seem to be rare. Only in very few cases do converts appear to have experienced any sudden flash of inspiration. When they do occur, it would seem that cathedrals are among the places most conducive to sudden, life-transforming insights, which is somewhat counter-productive as far as holding fast to the Christian faith is concerned. A convert to a Buddhist new religion recalled how the 'light came' in Salisbury Cathedral, when, as he explained, 'I rejected the creed [Anglican] lock, stock and barrel and immediately experienced a tremendous sense of liberation'.

Then followed a 'difficult period of searching for three or four years' before this seeker eventually found what he was looking for in Buddhism, a religion 'without a God figure imposing rules, regulations and restrictions' (author's interviews, 1985).

Another former Anglican, also a convert to the new Buddhist movement Soka Gakkai (Value Creation Society), recalled how he found himself in Hong Kong Cathedral 'thinking things over'. While there was no 'blinding light', he remembered 'wandering outside from that dark atmosphere into the brilliant sunshine and seeing people everywhere, and then', he recalled, 'something inside me clicked'. He continued, 'This is what religion should be all about, I thought. It's about the very basics of everyday life. And so my decision was made' (author's interviews, 1985). Through his work, which took him frequently to Japan, he encountered Buddhism and came to realize that this was his path. Thus, 'mystical' conversion – the term used to describe a sense of sudden understanding of the spiritual path one should follow, accompanied by a feeling of elation, a feeling of change within the self, associated with a sense of presence – does not appear to be a common form of conversion to NRMs.

While most of my informants stressed the developmental nature of conversion, they also saw it as a new start, a new beginning, a rebirth. A substantial minority spoke about their desire to recover an experience of childhood – the closeness and strong feeling for God variously defined – was the most common experience they sought to recapture. Other spoke of their desire to make sense of and develop the ideas and beliefs they had begun to think about as teenagers but felt obliged to shelve for fear of family or social disapproval, or peer group pressure. For others, it was a question of returning to the moral and spiritual values that their parents stood for but which they had unwisely rejected. The latter often remarked that their parents rarely if ever recognized this element in their conversion, mistaking the outward appearance – Hare Krishna dress and hair style – for the reality underneath.

Other studies of conversion also point to the prevalence of active seekers among recruits to NRMs. For example, in her study of the Rajneesh movement, Puttick (1994) concluded that none of her thirty-five respondents could have been described as simply drifting into sannyas (discipleship) or as being coerced against their will. She states: 'Apart from three who joined as children, they all made a conscious choice, usually preceded by experiences of alternative spiritual and social options' (1994: 56).

This kind of evidence notwithstanding, the tendency remains for researchers from different disciplines to reach different conclusions about the effects of recruitment to NRMs. The traditional concern of psychology and psychiatry with individual deviance and/or pathology might offer an explanation as to why the professionals from these disciplines are more inclined to give priority to the brainwashing model than those involved in sociological research, which strongly opposes what it sees as 'psychological reductionism'. Moreover, there is a tendency in psychology and psychiatry to view religion from a rather narrow angle, seeing it almost exclusively in terms of emotional and mental well-being, both of which states are measured in terms of their own 'scientific' and 'secular' paradigms of the healthy individual. The extent to which these models conform to reality is of course highly debated. The psychological professions' view of NRMs may also be affected more than that of social scientists by the growth of an unscientific, even harmful psychotherapeutic subculture (Beit-Hallahmi, 1992) – of which NRMs are an important component – which makes claims that directly impinge on the former's sphere of competence. Many NRMs tend to fuse psychology and religion, claim to understand the innermost depths of the human personality and to have the tools to enable individuals to reach their full potential.

Thus, the NRMs can be seen as stepping over boundaries and invading the space of the psychological sciences. There is less overlap and competition with sociology. The sociological perspective, based as much on wishful thinking as hard fact, has tended to see NRMs as clearly demarcated, small, manageable groups, with a view to furthering theoretical understanding of how and why these and similar communities emerge. The ultimate aim has been to improve social understanding of the workings of the wider society that gave rise to NRMs in the first place.

As it began to prove difficult to find 'scientific support' for the brain-washing hypothesis, attacks on NRMs switched toward accusations of child abuse. Allegations of this kind created panic and alarm across France, Argentina and in other countries, leading to police raids on communes and the taking of children into care. Moreover, resort was had to the courts to have children removed from the custody of members of NRMs and to be made wardens of court. The previously mentioned High Court case in London in 1995 against members of The Family is but one example of several such cases. Research from health education experts was often used in support of claims that parenting in NRMs was inadequate. Such reports spoke of digestive as well as mental and emotional problems as a result of participation in NRMs, and alleged that a substantial minority of children were either physically disadvantaged, even disabled, or hurt, and that punishment was either life-threatening or required the care of a physician (Gaines et al., 1984).

These negative views of the effects of NRMs on the personality and physical and emotional well-being of children came to form the basis of opinion among professionals, including politicians, and of the population at large, and, like brainwashing, were used to justify such unlawful measures as kidnapping and deprogramming as a means of extricating people from what they saw as the clutches of NRMs. These methods were used mostly on adults and were defended on the grounds that NRMs had deprived them of their freedom, and that the temporal restriction placed on the physical liberty of the individuals in question were necessary to restore to them their natural and moral right of freedom of choice. In certain cases judges advised juries against finding those accused of kidnapping guilty when the evidence strongly suggested they were.

Space limits the amount of attention that can be given here to this important and controversial issue of allegations of child abuse. The wider question of children in NRMs is explored in depth in Palmer and Hardman (1999) while here I suggest, without denying the possible existence of abuse, that the allegations raised by the ACM on this count also can likewise be interpreted as another boundary maintenance strategy. This is particularly so if seen from the perspective of mainstream society's increasing dependence on education in the contemporary Western world as a means of socializing the young.

Conclusions

The brainwashing and child abuse allegations, while extremely important in themselves, have not been solely about these specific issues but have been part of a wider debate. As Beckford (1985) suggests, the NRM controversy has acted as a barometer of the changes taking place in society and, in particular, the change in relationship between the individual and society. As he points out, the NRMs can be said to have in a sense forced society to become involved in their activities legally, politically and medically by challenging secular assumptions about its boundaries. Elsewhere, the main issue has been of a different nature. In China, for example, it has been mostly about ideological control and stability (see Chapter 13).

References and select bibliography

Anthony, Dick (1990) 'Religious Movements and Brainwashing Litigation: Evaluating Key Testimony' in Thomas Robbins and Dick Anthony (eds) *In God We Trust*, New Brunswick, NJ: Transaction Books, pp. 295–344.

Anthony, Dick and Robbins, Thomas (1992) 'Law, Social Science and the "Brainwashing" Exception to the First Amendment', *Behavioral Sciences and Law*, 10(1), 5–25.

Arweck, Elisabeth (1997) 'A Comparative Study of Responses to New Religions in Britain and Germany', PhD Thesis, King's College, University of London.

Balch, Robert W. and Taylor, David (2002) 'Making Sense of Heaven's Gate' in David G. Bromley and J. Gordon Melton (eds) *Cults, Religion and Violence*, Cambridge: Cambridge University Press, pp. 209–29.

Barker, Eileen (1984) *The Making of a Moonie: Choice or Brainwashing?* Oxford: Blackwell.

Barker, Eileen (2002) 'Watching for Violence: A Comparative Analysis of the Roles of Five Types of Cult-Watching Groups' in David G. Bromley and J. Gordon Melton (eds) *Cults, Religion and Violence*, Cambridge: Cambridge University Press, pp. 123–49.

Beckford, James, A. (1985) *Cult Controversies: The Social Response to the New Religious Movements*, London: Tavistock Publications.

Beckford, James, A. (2003) 'The Continuum Between Cults and Normal Religion' in Lorne L. Dawson (ed.) *Cults and New Religious Movements*, Oxford: Blackwell, pp. 26–33.

Beit-Hallahmi, Benjamin (1992) *Despair and Deliverance: Private Salvation in Contemporary Israel*, Albany, NY: State University of New York Press.

Bouma, Gary (1999) 'From Hegemony to Plurality: Managing Religious Diversity in Modernity and Postmodernity', *Australian Religion Studies Review*, 12(2), 7–27.

Bouma, Gary (2003) 'Globalization, Social Capital and the Challenge to Harmony of Recent Changes in Australia's Religious and Spiritual Demography: 1947–2001', *Australian Religion Studies Review*, 16(2), pp. 55–69.

Bradney, Anthony (1999) 'Children of a Newer God: The English Courts, Custody Disputes and NRMs' in Susan J. Palmer and Charlotte E. Hardman (eds) *Children in New Religions*, New Brunswick, NJ: Rutgers University Press.

Bromley, David G. and Melton, J. Gordon (eds) (2002) *Cults, Religion and Violence*, Cambridge: Cambridge University Press.

Bromley, David G. and Richardson, James T. (eds) (1983) *The Brainwashing/Deprogramming Controversy: Sociological, Psychological, Legal and Historical Perspectives*, New York: Edwin Mellen Press.

Cahill, Des and Phipps, Peter (2003) 'After September 11th: Religion, Diversity and Social Cohesion under Globalization', *Australian Religion Studies Review*, 16(2), pp. 8–19.

Chang, Maria Hsia (2004) *Falun Gong*, New Haven, CT: Yale University Press.

Clark, John G., Langone, Michael D. and Schecter, Robert E. (1981) *Destructive Cult Conversion: Theory, Research and Treatment*, Weston, MA: American Family Foundation.

Cottrell, Richard (1984) (rapporteur) The European Parliament Draft Report on 'The Activity of Certain New Religious Movements in the European Community'.

Dawson, Lorne L. (2002) 'Crisis of Charismatic Legitimacy and Violent Behaviour in New Religious Movements' in David G. Bromley and J. Gordon Melton (eds) *Cults, Religion and Violence*, Cambridge: Cambridge University Press, pp. 80–102.

Ellwood, Robert (1993) *Islands of the Dawn: The Story of Alternative Spirituality in New Zealand*, Honolulu: University of Hawai'i Press.

Fukui, Masaki (2004) 'A Study of a Japanese New Religion with Special Reference to its Ideas of the Millennium: The Case of Kofuku-no-Kagaku', PhD Thesis, King's College, University of London.

Gaines, M. Josephine, *et al.* (1984) 'The Effects of Cult Membership on the Health Status of Adults and Children', *Update*, Sept./Dec., pp. 9–17.

Galanter, Marc (1978) 'The "Relief Effect": A Sociobiological Model for Neurotic Distress and Large Group Therapy', *American Journal of Psychiatry*, 135, 588–91.

Galanter, Marc (1980) 'Psychological Induction into the Large Group: Findings From a Modern Religious Sect', *American Journal of Psychiatry*, 137, 1574–9.

Hall, John H. (1987) *Gone From the Promised Land: Jonestown in American Cultural History*, New Brunswick, NJ: Transaction Books.

Hall, John H. (2002) 'Mass Suicide and the Branch Davidians' in David G. Bromley and J. Gordon Melton (eds) *Cults, Religion and Violence*, Cambridge: Cambridge University Press, pp. 149–70.

Hall, John H. (2003) 'The Apocalypse at Jonestown' in Lorne L. Dawson (ed.) *Cults and New Religious Movements*, Oxford: Blackwell, pp. 186–208.

Hanson, Sharon (2004) 'Rumours of Angels in Contemporary English Texts and

Law: A Narrative Exploration of the Range of Forms of the Secularization Thesis', PhD Thesis, King's College, University of London.

Harvey, Peter (1990) *An Introduction to Buddhism. Teachings, History and Practices*, Oxford: Oxford University Press.

Hill, Michael (2001) 'Cult Busters in Canberra? Reflections on Two Recent Government Reports', *Australian Religion Studies Review*, 14(1), 113–22.

Hubbard, L. Ron (1950) *Dianetics: The Modern Science of Mental Health*, Los Angeles: American St Hill Organization.

Hummel, Reinhart (1981) 'Jugendreligionen-missionieren Gemeinschaften?' *Zeitschrift für Mission* [Basle], pp.135–40.

Inaba, Keishin (2000) 'Altruism in New Religions: The Jesus Army and the Friends of the Western Buddhist Order', PhD Thesis, King's College, University of London.

Introvigne, Massimo and Mayer, Jean-François (2002) 'Occult Masters and the Temple of Doom: The Fiery End of the Solar Temple' in David G. Bromley and J. Gordon Melton (eds) *Cults, Religion and Violence*, Cambridge: Cambridge University Press, pp. 170–89.

Ionescu, Sanda (1998) 'Women in New Religions: Soka Gakkai and Seicho-no-Ie in Germany', PhD Thesis, King's College, University of London.

Jacobs, Janet (1984) 'The Economy of Love in Religious Commitment: The Deconversion of Women from Non-traditional Movements', *Journal for the Scientific Study of Religion*, 26(3), 294–308.

Kemp, Daren (2000) 'The Christaquarians? A Sociology of Christians in the New Age', PhD Thesis, King's College, University of London.

Lifton, Robert (1961) *Thought Reform and the Psychology of Totalism: A Study of 'Brainwashing' in China*, New York: Norton.

Lofland, John (1977) *Doomesday Cult*, New York: Irvington (original version, 1966).

Lofland, John (1978) 'Becoming a World-saver Revisited' in James Richardson (ed.) *Conversion Careers*, Thousand Oaks, CA: Sage.

Lofland, John and Skonovd, Norman (1981) 'Conversion Motifs', *Journal for the Scientific Study of Religion*, 20(4), 373–85.

Mayer, Jean-François (2003) '"Our Territorial Journey is Coming to an End": The Last Voyage of the Solar Temple' in Lorne L. Dawson (ed.) *Cults and New Religious Movements*, Oxford: Blackwell, pp. 208–27.

Melton, J. Gordon (1999) 'Anti-Cultists in the United States: An Historical Perspective' in Bryan R. Wilson and Jamie Cresswell (eds) *New Religious Movements: Challenge and Response*, London: Routledge, pp. 213–35.

Palmer, Susan (1996) 'Purity and Danger in the Solar Temple', *Journal of Contemporary Religion*, 11(3), 303–19.

Palmer, Susan and Hardman, Charlotte (1999) *Children in New Religions*, New Brunswick, NJ: Rutgers University Press.

Phipps, Peter and Possamai, Adam (2003) 'After September 11th: Religion, Diversity and Social Cohesion under Globalization', *Australian Religion Studies Review*, 16(2), 8–19.

Possamai, Adam and Murray, Lee (2004) 'New Religious Movements and the Fear of Crime', *Journal of Contemporary Religion*, 19(3), 337–53.

Puttick, Eizabeth (1994) 'Gender, Discipleship and Charismatic Authority in the Rajneesh Movement', PhD Thesis, King's College, University of London.

Reader, Ian (2000) *Religious Violence in Contemporary Japan: The Case of Aum Shinrikyo*, Richmond, Surrey: Curzon Press.

Richardson, James (1993) 'Concept of "Cult": From Sociological-Technical to Popular-Negative', *Review of Religious Research*, 34, 348–56.

Richardson, James T. (1995) 'Media Bias Toward New Religious Movements in Australia' (unpublished paper).

Richardson, James (1996) 'Journalistic Bias Towards New Religious Movements in Australia', *Journal of Contemporary Religion*, 11(3), 289–303.

Richardson, James (2001) 'New Religions in Australia: Public Menace or Societal Salvation?', *Nova Religio: The Journal of Alternative and Emergent Religions*, 4(2), 258–65.

Richardson, James T. (2003) 'A Critique of "Brainwashing" Claims about New Religious Movements' in Lorne L. Dawson (ed.) *Cults and New Religious Movements*, Oxford: Blackwell, pp. 160–7.

Robbins, Thomas (1988) *Cults, Converts and Charisma*, London: Sage.

Robbins, Thomas (2002) 'Sources of Volatility in Religious Movements' in Temple' in David G. Bromley and J. Gordon Melton (eds) *Cults, Religion and Violence*, Cambridge: Cambridge University Press, pp. 57–80.

Robbins, Thomas (2003) 'Constructing Cultist Mind Control' in Lorne L. Dawson (ed.) *Cults and New Religious Movements*, Oxford: Blackwell, pp. 167–81.

Robilliard, St John A. (1984) *Religion and the Law: Religious Liberty in Modern English Law*, Manchester: Manchester University Press.

Shimazono, Susumu (1995) 'In the Wake of Aum: The Formation and Transformation of a Universe of Belief', *Japanese Journal of Religious Studies*, 22(3&4), 381–415.

Singer, Margaret (1979) 'Coming out of the Cults', *Psychology Today*, 12(Jan.), 72–82.

Usarski, Frank (1999) 'The Response to New Religions in East Germany after Re-unification' in Alain Vivien (1985) *Les sectes en France*, Paris: La Documentation Française.

Wallis, Roy (1976) *The Road to Total Freedom: A Sociological Study of Scientology*, London: Heinemann.

Wallis, Roy (1984) *The Elementary Forms of the New Religious Life*, London: Routledge & Kegan Paul.

Wallis, Roy (1986) 'Figuring out Cult Receptivity', *Journal for the Scientific Study of Religion*, 25(4), 494–503.

Wallis, Roy (1993) 'Charisma and Explanation' in Eileen Barker *et al.* (eds) *Secularization, Rationalism and Sectarianism*, Oxford: Clarendon Press, pp. 167–81.

Watanabe, Manubu (1997) 'Reactions to the Aum Affair: The Rise of the Anti-Cult Movement in Japan', *Bulletin of the Nanzan Institute for Religion and Culture*, 21, 32–48.

Wellbeloved, Sophia (2000) 'Gurdjieff, Astrology and Beelzebub's Tales', PhD Thesis, King's College, University of London.

Wilson, Bryan R. (1998) 'New Religions: The Problems They Encounter', *Journal of Oriental Studies*, 8, 185–202.

Wilson, Bryan R. and Cresswell, Jamie (eds) (1999) *New Religious Movements: Challenge and Response*, London: Routledge, pp. 237–55.

Yao, Yu-Shuang (2001) 'The Development and Appeal of the Buddhist Compassion Relief Movement in Taiwan', PhD Thesis, King's College, University of London.

York, Michael (1991) 'The Emerging Network: A Sociology of the New Age and Neo-pagan Movements', PhD Thesis, King's College, University of London.

Part II

New religions in the West

Chapter 4

Europe

This discussion of New Religious Movements (NRMs) in Europe is set in the context of developments in Christianity, Buddhism, Hinduism and Islam. While the doctrinal content of Christianity is becoming increasingly influenced by its interaction with other faiths, the other three religions are undergoing a process of Europeanization, initiated both by internal forces and by state-sponsored initiatives designed to shape and mould their emerging structures. Among other new developments highlighted here is the growing interest in Europe in Yoga, and particularly in what has become known as Modern Yoga, a largely secular practice, which, as such, asks questions of both Campbell's Easternization of the Western mind thesis (Campbell, 1999) and the spiritual revolution thesis (Heelas and Woodhead, 2005).

The chapter also focuses on the themes of 'Engaged religion' and applied spirituality, both of which are also discussed elsewhere in this volume (see Chapters 1, 7, 11 and 12). With regard to NRMs, the concentration in this chapter is on those movements that have been, and continue to be, influential but that are relatively rarely discussed. These include various kinds of Sufi and Islamist movements, Buddhist movements and alternative movements such as The Work, a movement, based on the teachings of Gurdjieff, that has greatly influenced the 'new' cognitive style previously mentioned and the method and content of the new spirituality. This movement concerns itself with, among other things, the question of how to raise the present state of human consciousness – described as a sleeping, trance-like state – and transform what is a dysfunctional self into a powerfully effective being capable of achieving immortality. There is more on Gurdjieff's ideas and those of other leading thinkers linked to NRMs and the New Age Movement (NAM) in a separate section below.

But, before examining the core ideas and practices, and the orientation of the new movements and the changes occurring in the old religions, it is worth looking at the overall context of religious change, with special reference to the unchurched but spiritual who are not necessarily believers. Their spirituality is holistic, mostly self-focused and based not on faith but on experience.

Religious change in modern Europe: some general comments

With increasing globalization bringing with it ever higher levels of economic migration, modern Europe has witnessed the growth during its recent history of new kinds of religious pluralism, which has influenced the way many of its inhabitants now believe and the content of what they believe. Berlin now has over 400,000 Muslims, most of whom arrived as guest workers from Turkey beginning in the 1960s. There are also more Germans becoming Tibetan Buddhist monks than Jesuit priests.

Many more Europeans now than forty years ago draw on Oriental sources of belief and shape and adapt these to their own particular circumstances. Reincarnation, widely understood in Europe in the positive sense as providing the opportunity for continuous spiritual growth and advancement, in contrast with the potentially negative implications with which it is traditionally associated in Oriental traditions, is an example of this domestication. Modern Yoga (see below) is another case of this. As practised in Europe it has acquired a largely therapeutic purpose compared with the mainly soteriological function of yoga in the classical Indian tradition. Adaptations of this kind are commonplace.

What the repeal in 1965 of the Asian Immigration Exclusion Act did to increase religious pluralism in the USA, various pieces of restrictive legislation enacted by the European governments in the 1960s have done for religious pluralism in Europe. In the case of the United Kingdom, the principal effect of legislation, introduced in 1962 and 1968 to curb immigration, was its contribution to the creation of more permanent and stable Asian communities, which from then on began to abandon the idea of returning 'home'. Fearing that the rest of their families still living in Asia would be excluded by the legislation, these communities resettled them in the United Kingdom before the legislation was enforced, and with whole families now together, it became necessary to establish the religions that they professed on firmer foundations.

Thus, Buddhism, Hinduism, Islam and Sikhism in the British context and in most of Western Europe quickly began to change their status from the 1960s onwards from religions that were little more than exotic appendages on the margins of society to religions more deeply embedded in the religious life of the society as a whole, and much more widely accessible to all sectors of the population. Similar developments took place among Caribbean and African immigrant communities, leading to the growth in African-Christian churches such as the Ghanaian Musamo Christo Disco Church and the Aladura (praying) churches from Nigeria (see Chapter 8). By the 1990s there were over 1,000 mosques in the United Kingdom, compared with less than twenty in the 1970s, and many more Hindu, Sikh and Buddhist temples, colleges and/or seminaries for the training of clerics, qur'ānic schools, and African-Christian and African-Caribbean churches.

Similar developments also began to take shape over roughly the same period in France, Germany and Holland. A new phenomenon also appeared, that of new religions or churches founded in Europe by Asians and Africans, one example being the True Teachings of Christ Temple founded in Amsterdam by the Ghanaian immigrant Daniel Himmans-Arday (Ter Haar, 1998). Others include the New Testament Assembly, established in London by West Indian immigrants in the 1970s, and the Ruach Ministries established in London in 1997, and which by 2004 had over 8,000 active members and is growing rapidly.

Many Black-led churches such as these began in people's homes, in parlours or basements, and later moved to Community Centres and Town Halls. Inspired by Pentecostalism they emerged in opposition to the discrimination Caribbean and African immigrants experienced in the mainstream churches. They also helped to compensate for the status deprivation felt by many of these immigrants whose dignity and self-esteem were undermined by the discrimination they encountered in the wider society. Pentecostalism tends to thrive among migrants and in the case of the Caribbean and African migrants to Europe it was no different.

These Churches gave direction and a sense of stability, and facilitated networking. Moreover, their emphasis on engaged Christianity in the form of service to the community, on Gospel music, their use of the 'hooping tradition' where the preacher sings and talks at the same time as the music is playing, and the call and response style of preaching, all of these features resonated with their experience of church life. By contrast, the Rastafarian movement, which originated in Jamaica and found a following in Britain in the aftermath of colonization and immigration sparked by the British demand in the 1950s for West Indian labour (Clarke, 1986), disowned all established forms of institutional religion but for that of the Ethiopian Orthodox Church.

The emergence of countless numbers of NRMs has increased the level of religious pluralism. In the European context, NRMs from South Asia, Southeast Asia, Africa and Latin America have, for reasons of colonialism, culture, language, immigration, family and ethnic bonds, first established themselves in the capital city and other larger cities of the former colonial power, using these locations as launching pads to the rest of Western Europe, Eastern Europe, Russia, the United States, Africa and Latin America. For example, the Portuguese colonization of Brazil and its cultural impact explains in part the route taken to Europe and to Africa by many Japanese NRMs who have arrived there via their bases in Brazil.

Most Brazilian NRMs, including the Igreja Universal do Reino de Deus (the Universal Church of the Kingdom of God or IURD) (see Chapter 9), have entered Europe through Portugal. Likewise the cultural, linguistic and economic effects of Dutch colonization on, for example, Surinam facilitated the spread of the Winti cult to Holland in particular (Van Wittering, 1998).

The Santo Daime movement from Brazil took a somewhat different route to Europe, entering via Amsterdam and not Lisbon.

NRMs from countries not colonized by European nations have generally found Europe extremely difficult to penetrate and have concentrated their attention instead on what they regard as the more spiritually aware and receptive countries of the developing world. Several Japanese NRMs are cases in point, making Brazil rather than Europe their main sphere of missionary activity outside Asia, claiming that the level of spiritual awareness and receptivity there is much higher than in the West.

À la carte Christianity and the growth of the unchurched but spiritual

Lambert's (2004) analysis and interpretation of the data from the European Values Studies in 1981 and 1990 and the survey of 1999 suggests that the Christian religion in Europe rather than being in terminal decline appears to be regaining some ground, at least in several areas including that of confidence in the Church's capacity to give adequate responses to the 'spiritual needs of individuals'. This has improved from 44 to 52 per cent during the period 1981–91. There is also evidence of an increase in the number of those who believe in a personal God, up from 44 to 52 per cent over the same period, and in Hell, which has risen from 22 to 25 per cent also over the same period. At the same time decline continues in some areas, although, if its pace during the periods 1981–90 and 1990–9 is compared, it appears to be slowing down, and as we have just seen even to be in reverse where certain beliefs and practices are concerned (Lambert, 2004: 33).

This minor revival in orthodoxy is accompanied by an increase in believing without belonging and a growth in the percentage of those who have never belonged to a religion (Lambert, 2004: 33). There is also a remarkable decline in knowledge about Christian history and beliefs amounting to a condition akin to a loss of memory. This has clearly to do with problems over transmission – increasingly fewer parents and future parents do not regard it as their obligation to pass on their religious beliefs (Ashford and Timms, 1992). Many are committed to the principle of freedom of choice in religion for all, including their offspring. The choices on offer have become increasingly varied and include a vast array of alternative religious sources once thought of as alien or widely shunned as deviant forms of knowledge. This increased religious pluralism has impacted upon Christianity making à la Carte Christianity the dominant form of Christianity in Europe (Lambert, 2004: 39).

The increase in belief without belonging mentioned above is variable across Europe and is more in evidence in Belgium, Britain, France, the Netherlands and Sweden than in other countries. The growth in the number of unchurched who are spiritual adepts is also variable, reaching higher levels in Sweden than elsewhere. According to research (Stark *et al.*, 2005) many of these adepts in Sweden, and possibly elsewhere, still describe themselves as Christians 'but in their own way'. However, only 4 per cent of Swedes attend church once a week, while 6 per cent attend once a month. A far higher percentage – 38 per cent – prays regularly and only 20 per cent have no belief in God, although they have great difficulty in defining what this means.

While unchurched spirituality is gaining ground this is not always at the expense of every form of Church-based religion. It is not a unilateral develop-ment that is structurally and ideologically independent of what Bainbridge (2004) refers to as 'standard religion'. It is even promoted by the latter – at least by some mainstream denominations – while at the same time introducing its members to various elements of holistic spirituality leading to what Kemp (2004: 136 and *passim*) has described as the emergence of Christaquarians and/or New Age Christians. Many New Agers with no formal Christian links find valuable spiritual materials in the writings of Christian monks and priests such as Bede Griffiths and Thomas Merton.

Wuthnow and Cadge (2004) also point to a number of mainstream institu-tions in the United States, some of them well-established churches, that act as vehicles for the spread of Buddhist ideas and practices that appeal to alter-native spiritual groups and associations. There is, therefore, no watertight dichotomy between unchurched spirituality and all forms of 'standard' religion. Some of the former can even be said to be theistic after a fashion, including Christian Meditation, a world-wide Catholic initiative, that attempts to pull together inner-directed, subjective spirituality and belief in a transcendent, independent source of all being. Practitioners of this form of meditation use various types of Yoga, among other disciplines, in their search for the true or authentic Self and the divine Source of everything.

The growth in holistic spirituality does not necessarily provide evidence to refute those who support the secularization thesis. Wilson (1991) and Hanegraaff (1999) have argued against this in the case of Scientology and the NAM, respectively. De Michaelis's (2004) research on Modern Yoga could also be used to support the secularization thesis. What the future of unchurched spirituality might be is hard to predict. From a historical and sociological perspective its prospects do not appear to be good without further institutionalization, a process that the Nonchurch movement in Japan eventually had to accept in order to survive (see Chapter 12 and Mullins, 1998). Stark and others (Stark, 1996; Stark *et al.*, 2005), moreover, point out that the lack of creeds and structures could seriously reduce the social and moral impact of unchurched spirituality and facilitate the spread of superstitions of all kinds.

Not only has the established Christian church experienced a small revival in a limited number of areas in recent times, but a number of 'new' versions of Christianity have also enjoyed considerable success in attracting participants, including the Alpha Course or fifteen-session evangelizing programme designed in the late 1980s by Nicky Gumbel, the pastor of Holy Trinity Church, Brompton, in London. It is interesting to note, in the light of what has been said about the character of the new personal-experience-based spirituality gaining ground, that Alpha's success comes in part from the fact that it seeks to initiate participants into a particular kind of religious experience, a felt, embodied experience. It avoids being overly dogmatic and traditional – although it holds the first century of the Christian Church as described in the Acts of the Apostles as the model for the Church today – and places the emphasis on experiencing the good news of God in the here and now. As Watling (2005: 104) describes it: 'Alpha is in a sense a ritual a doorway . . . into a "new" "charismatic" worldview. The idea is to reject previous "secular" . . . existence and to enter into a "new" charismatic Christian existence.'

Other new developments related to Christian churches include the House Church Movement (HCM), which began in the 1950s. As Walker (1985) has shown, this movement stands apart from the Charismatic Renewal movement of the mainstream churches, maintaining that denominational Christianity is contrary to God's intention to build the 'Kingdom of God' or Church. It follows from this that the principal goal of Christians is to restore the Kingdom or Church according to the model of church life given in the New Testament. This interpretation provides the basis on which communities are structured under the leadership of apostles and elders.

A large number of churches organized along these lines sprang up across Britain in the 1960s and 1970s. Only very imprecise estimates can be given of their size but by the end of the 1970s there were between 2,500 and 3,000 members, most of whom came over from mainstream Protestant churches, and a disproportionate number of these were university graduates.

The community-based 'new' conservative Christian churches are another new development. These churches began to emerge around the same time as the HCM and include the Jesus Fellowship Church, also known as the Bugbrooke Jesus Fellowship, which has for its evangelical wing the Jesus Army. Started in the village of Bugbrooke in Northamptonshire, England, in the 1950s as a community that placed a high premium on celibacy, this conventional village-based Baptist church underwent a transformation in the 1960s. With the appointment of Pastor Noel Stanton important changes were made to the Bugbrooke fellowship, which led to its rapid expansion in the 1970s. While retaining the movement's commitment to spiritual and social engagement with the poor and deprived, Stanton made community life optional and introduced a 'divide, grow and plant policy', which led to the establishment of satellite communities nationwide. Strong commitment is demanded, particularly of those referred to as 'covenant members' who promise at baptism to give generously of their time to the social outreach programmes and to the study and observance of the Scriptures.

In an effort to improve their outreach, both spiritual and social, among the poor and the marginalized, the movement established the previously mentioned Jesus Army in 1987. With over 2,000 members, many of whom practise community living and celibacy, these 'combatants', recognizable by their military style uniforms and by their general lifestyle, go into a daily battle for souls in Britain's main cities. Alcohol and smoking are prohibited, and the use of television and radio is discouraged. Gender roles follow traditional norms and the boundaries between the sexes are clearly delineated. Women are obliged to dress modestly, and are not supposed to wear trousers, are assigned traditional roles in the communities, and can only associate with men with the permission of the elders.

A similar concern with community and social outreach is evident in several new Catholic movements, including Opus Dei, the Neo-Catechumenate and the Focolare movements. For example, the last-mentioned, founded in Trento in Italy in 1944 by Chiara Lubich, consists of 'little towns' or small communities. This movement, which includes both Catholics and non-Catholics, focuses its activities on social action, inter-religious dialogue – according to some, in order to convert others to Catholicism – and world peace.

While Christianity has been in decline Islam in Europe has been expanding rapidly in recent times and undergoing a process of Europeanization and it is to this and the rise of new Islamic-related movements that I now turn.

Toward a European Islam

Islam in Europe is a diverse phenomenon. Most Muslims are Sunni or followers of the way of the Prophet; others are Shi'ites, that is, of the party of Ali, cousin and son-in-law of the Prophet Muhammad. There are a variety of forms of Shi'ism, including a number of Ismaili groups, among them the followers of the Aga Khan who are known as the Ismaili Khojas. Other Muslim bodies include the Armadiyya movement (see Chapter 10), which, like certain branches of Ismailism, is widely considered among Muslims to be heretical.

Most Shi'ite Muslims, like Sunnis, subscribe to a basic set of teachings, which include belief in the oneness and unicity of Allah/God, in the Prophet Muhammad as his final messenger, and in the Qur'ān as Allah's/God's final revelation to mankind. They also accept the obligation to perform what are usually referred to as the five pillars of Islam: the profession of faith or kalimat; the pilgrimage or hajj once in a lifetime, if possible; the five daily prayers or salat; fasting or swam; and alms-giving or zakat. Holy war, one form of jihād, is not an individual but a community obligation. These common beliefs and practices notwithstanding, Islam in Europe is as varied as Christianity, in terms of its history, culture and interpretations of beliefs and practices.

Over a period of some forty years Islam has become the second largest religion in several of Europe's most populated countries. The first generation of Muslims, mainly migrant workers who had left their families 'at home', remained closely attached to the culture of their upbringing, and the Islam they practised remained heavily influenced by that culture. By contrast, later generations born and educated in Europe tend to look in two directions simultaneously, to the culture of their parents and grandparents, and to the local, European one.

While, even among European-born Muslims, criticism can be heard of the corrosive influence of Western influence on Islam, there is at the same time a move to create a European version of this faith. This is seen as important by the majority of those who favour it because, as they argue, for Islam to be seen as a universal faith it must be able to show that it has the capacity to implant itself in European soil and grow and flourish therein, in the same way as it has in African, Middle Eastern and Asian cultures. The argument continues that without Europeanization the Asiatic way of life will be mistaken for the Islamic way of life, consequences of which would be the relativization of Islam and the negation of its universality. Moreover, European Muslims, far from being integrated into the Umma or worldwide community of Muslims, would remain isolated without Europeanization. These views have been strongly expressed by young European Muslims:

> The Asiatic way of life that exists in some countries should not be mistaken for the Islamic way of life proper . . .. Unfortunately there is a tendency to Asiaticise [sic] European society by holding fast to a fossilized, allegedly Islamic way of life. This is a sterile undertaking, harmful in particular for Muslim Youth in Europe because it robs them of all religious support.
>
> (Clarke, 1998: 16–17)

Alongside this demand from Muslims themselves for Islam to identify more with the European culture, governments, particularly the French Government, are concerned about what they perceive as the rise of militant Islam and its threat to the secular character of the state. As a result they have begun to attempt to fashion what is best described as 'moderate' Islam. Conservative Islamist Muslims in particular, but not exclusively, see this attempt to create a 'moderate Islam' as a strategy designed to empty it of its real content. This kind of conservative Islam is also totally opposed to secularism, although the meaning it gives to this term differs from its constitutional meaning. To the former it is an anti-religious ideology, while in the latter context it means religious neutrality.

In France the term 'secularism' or 'laïcité' is a concept rooted in nineteenth-century anti-clericalism. More recently its purpose has become that of ensuring the equality of all religions by excluding them from the public arena.

This line of thinking was behind the hijab or headscarf affair (l'affaire du foulard) in 2004, when the Government passed a ruling banning the wearing of Muslim headdress and other conspicuous symbols of religious belonging in publicly funded schools.

Of even greater concern to the French Government than what are seen as symbolic infringements of laïcité are the potentially subversive consequences of radical preaching by Imams in mosques, a concern also of other governments. Indeed, this was among the main reasons why the Finsbury Park Mosque in London was closed in 2002. In France, the Government has identified Islamist Imams preaching jihād (struggle) or holy war as the major threat, after terrorists, to security. Many of the country's over 1,500 Imams are originally from North Africa and a substantial number of these are neither well trained in the Islamic sciences, including theology and philosophy (kalam), nor do they possess an adequate grasp of the French language. A similar situation exists across much of Western Europe, including Britain, and has been criticized by, among others, many young European-born Muslims educated in the Western system.

In France it has been decided that the solution to the 'Imam problem' is to be found in educating Imams to 'the standard required by the Republic'. This means in effect that Western subjects including Western philosophy will be added to the traditional Islamic curriculum, which consists of studying the Qur'ān, Shari'a (Islamic law) and the Hadith or Traditions, principally the sayings attributed to the Prophet Muhammad. Where this education is to be given and who will fund it has been the subject of much debate, since the State, given its commitment to the policy of laïcité, cannot offer financial support for religious education. The French Ministry of the Interior has proposed that a way round the question of laïcité in this case might be found through the setting up of a Foundation of Islamic Works, which would distribute funds, including donations from foreign sources, to new mosques and to institutes for the training of Imams. This appears to have met with the approval of the Imam of the Central Mosque in Paris.

There already exist in France, as in Britain, institutes for the training of Imams. In France there is the European Institute of Human Sciences (IESH) in Burgundy, widely regarded as a radical organization, which is headed by an Iraqi teacher and has an international body of students training to be Imams. The curriculum consists of Islamic subjects and Arabic, and the institute insists on the veiling of women and separate living areas for male and female students. A more broadly based curriculum is in use in the Grand Mosque in Paris and this aims at taking into account what it describes as the realities of French life. The Grand Mosque school not only teaches Western philosophy alongside Traditional Islamic Sciences but also attempts to explain the reasons behind and the purposes of laïcité in the context of French history.

As was pointed out above, Islam in Europe displays considerable diversity, not all of it welcomed by mainstream groups, and it is to a discussion of this that I now turn.

Islam: new developments and movements

While almost all of the new Islamic movements discussed elsewhere in this volume, including the Jama'at-i-Islami and the Deobandi movements (see Chapters 7 and 10), have a presence in Europe, here most attention is given to Islamic movements of European origin, a description which includes Turkey. Some of these movements are missionary for like Christianity there is a growing number of young Muslims who no longer frequent the mosque and who refuse to follow the guidance in religious matters of their religious leaders or their parents.

Many modern Islamic movements are described as Islamist movements for the reason that they stress 'the importance of the construction of an Islamic state as a prerequisite for any successful realization of an Islamic society'. Islamist movements are political in that for them Islam is an ideology. Their appeal, Roy contends, is largely to 'a modern intelligentsia or to new professional groups and social strata whose upward social mobility is thwarted by the conservative elite, whether traditional or secular . . .' (1998: 54).

There are, however, 'liberal' Islamist movements, including the Turkish movement Fethullah Gulen, named after its founder, which insists that Islam is a privatized religion. Given space to develop by the liberalization measures of the 1980s and influenced by the notion of 'Turkish Islam', Fethullah Gulen's philosophy has been greatly influenced by the writings of Said Nursi, known as the Risale-i-Nur, which highlight the links between Islam and reason, science and modernity.

Fethullah Gulen's mission is to promote modernism, tolerance and democracy without abandoning the principles on which Islam rests. He is opposed, for example, to the state applying Shari'a law, on the grounds that most Islamic law applies to the private sphere of life and this in a sense makes Islam a mostly private matter. According to Gulen, who bases his argument on Said Nursi's teachings, there is clear compatibility between Islam and Republicanism in that the former accords with the Islamic insistence on consultation. What is important, Gulen argues, is that all Muslims, and in particular Muslim leaders, live their lives in accordance with Islamic precepts.

The number of those influenced by Fethullah Gulen's ideas is unknown but rough estimates place it anywhere between a quarter of a million and four million. Many are town dwellers and many are professionals. One of the most effective means used to promote Fethullah Gulen's thoughts has been education – schools, universities, cultural centres and organizations, such as the Turkish Teachers' Foundation, which organizes national and international conferences. This attempt to reconcile traditional Islamic values with modernity has gained for the movement a large following, not only in

Turkey but in many other countries, and has led to the building of schools around the world, especially in the Turkic republics, which support the model of a secular state.

Gulen's relations with other Islamists, such as the Turkish Refah party and its successor, the Fazilet (Virtue) party, have not been cordial, mostly for the reason that he is as strongly opposed to the creation of an Islamic state as the latter is in favour of it. Thus, where Fethullah Gulen's philosophy differs from that of other Islamists is in its conviction that the way forward for Muslims is not by separating out from the existing political order and creating an Islamic state but in creating a self-disciplined Islam, an Islam not unlike Weber's Protestant movement of the sixteenth century, that can create a viable fit between its traditions and the demands of modernity (Aras and Caha, 2000).

Among other Islamist movements recently established in Europe is the Islamic Party of Great Britain, founded in 1989 to represent the interests of Muslims, which the Rushdie affair, it was maintained, made clear were not being advanced by any of the mainstream political parties. It is the first Islamic party to be formed in a non-Muslim country. The principal mover in the formation of the Islamic Party was Sahib Mustaqim Bleher, a German convert to Islam who believed that the time was appropriate for greater political action by Muslims in Britain. Very often, by way of contrast, conversion to Islam in Europe does not result in a radically new cultural outlook. The second major reason for the Party's existence is daw'a or mission (Kose, 1993: 45).

The Party has so far failed badly in both local and national elections, even in what are relatively densely populated Muslim areas. The prominence of European converts to Islam in the executive branch of the Party has been seen as a weakness by some life-long Muslims and leaders of the Muslim community. Sardar severely criticized the position of converts in the Party:

> In following the Sunna, example of Muhammad, the converts came to see themselves as personifying the Prophet; only they could interpret Islam for other Muslims. So they sought to impose their often authoritarian version of Islam and the Sunna.
>
> (Kose, 1993: 45)

Others expressed their concern that such leadership was incapable of understanding the real problems of Asian Muslims and, in particular, the problem of racism.

Although they receive much attention in the media, Islamist and similar ideological tendencies in Europe have little active support and tend to function for the most part as pressure groups. Research in the Netherlands, for example, has shown that, whatever their professional or educational background, economic status or gender, a majority of Muslims, while they may have sympathy for the aims of certain radical Muslim groups such as the Algerian Islamic Salvation Front (FIS), do not become actively involved in such groups (Kemper, 1996: 204). Nor can such sympathy be interpreted as antipathy toward, and disenchantment with, Western society.

Turning to Sufi or mystical Islam, this has considerable appeal among Westerners and at the same time is often the prime target of Islamist movements. The clear-cut distinction sometimes made between Sufi or mystical groups and radical Islamist movements can be misleading, as it wrongly suggests that the former are in principle pacifist and tolerant of non-Muslim cultures, while the latter are totally intolerant of both. Sufi *turuq* (brotherhoods), including the Sanusiyya in nineteenth-century North Africa, have shown themselves to be as militant as any type of Islamic reform movement, especially when faced with colonialism. The tension between scholarly, orthodox Sunni Islam and Sufism, nonetheless, persists and militant jihadis continue to reserve their strongest criticism for, and use their force against, popular, unscholarly Sufi or mystical Islam for its practice of what they consider to be impure Islam (Zahab and Roy, 2002).

A recent Sufi development, the Darqawiyya movement, represents an introverted form of Sufism that is primarily concerned with the restoration of European Islam. It was founded by the former writer and actor Ian Dallas, who turned to Islam in 1967, taking the name Abd al-Qadir. Plagued with the same disillusionment that beset many of the younger generation of the 1960s, Dallas set out in 1968 on a search that took him to Marrakech. There he met Shaykh Muhammad ibn Habib al-Darqawi, who, after initiating him into the order, allegedly appointed him a muqaddam (representative) of the Darqawiyya tariqa or brotherhood, giving him the name of as-Sufi and ordering him to go forth and call people to Islam.

Abd al-Qadir renamed his movement the 'Murabitun European Muslim Movement', claiming that centuries ago in Spain Islam had in fact become a European phenomenon, and that the Muslim communities to come closest to the Medinan model of the Prophet had been formed in Granada and Cordoba during the Muslim rule of Spain. His mission became the rediscovery of the authentic, Western form of Islam, stressing that to become Muslim it was not necessary to look to North Africa, the Middle East or beyond Europe. The purpose of da'wa or mission was 'not to make everybody a Pakistani or Egyptian, but to allow the natural genius of the people to express itself in embracing Islam' (Kose, 1993: 46).

Other versions of Sufism with a presence in Europe include the highly tolerant Beshara and Naqshabandiyya movements. The Beshara movement, founded in Gloucester in the United Kingdom in 1971 by an unknown Turkish citizen, is based on the teachings of Jalal al-Din Rumi (1207–73), the great Persian mystic and author of the classical work of poetry the *Mathnavi*. Often referred to as the 'Qur'ān of the Persian language', the *Mathnavi* is a storehouse of mystical lore expounded in stories and lyrical poetry, and has as its principal theme the exploration of the relationship between the Self and the One God. Also of great importance to Beshara are the writings of the Spanish-born mystic Muhyiddin Ibn Arabi (1165–1240), who took for his sole guide his 'inner light' with which, he believed, he had been illuminated in a special way. He also believed that he had seen the beatified Prophet Muhammad, knew the greatest name of Allah, and had acquired a knowledge of alchemy by divine revelation. Ibn Arabi held that all being is essentially one, as it is all a manifestation of the divine substance. His most important treatise, *al-Futkūhāt al-Makkīya,* was intended to provide a complete system of mystic knowledge.

The Beshara movement, which attracts a disproportionate number of graduates and makes no great effort to proselytize, not surprisingly remains small. The movement seeks to avoid all forms of dogmatism and sees its mission as that of enabling adepts to return to, and merge with, the source of everything, God. The principal methods used for this purpose are dhikr, the ritual of the remembrance of the many names of God – no particular form is imposed – study, and service to others, which brings one closer to God. There are clear parallels between the spirituality of this movement and the subjective spirituality that is spreading widely in the West (Heelas and Woodhead, 2005), as there is between the spirituality of the Sufi Order in the West (see below) and subjective spirituality.

Naqshabandiyya circles of the Cypriot Shaykh Nazim have been formed in a number of European countries and the United States (Hermansen, 1998). Shaykh Nazim began visiting Britain during the month of Ramadan in 1973 and followers include many different nationalities: Turkish, English, Pakistani, Malay, and African, among others. American and European, especially German, converts to Islam travel to London to attend his Ramadan sessions. During his absence followers tend to separate into subgroups along lines of ethnicity, geographical location and gender.

Unlike Islamist movements the Naqshabandiyya movement is tolerant of Western culture and this tolerance has prompted critics to suggest that Shaykh Nazim's success can be attributed largely to his having turned Islam into a soft option for Westerners, in the manner that some Indian gurus have been accused of 'packaging' Vedanta for the West. Shaykh Nazim's own conviction is that religions must take into account the differences in the conditions people face. This can involve concessions, and in practice the Shaykh insists that Westerners should not be overburdened with instructions on the full requirements of worship, fasting and dress, which come more easily to those born and educated within the Muslim tradition (Kose, 1993: 185–206). Also permitted is what Islamists would describe as 'bida' or innovation, including the presence of women alongside men at dhikr gatherings at which the many names of Allah are chanted. This mixing of the sexes would be condemned not only by fundamentalist but even by traditionalist Muslims. As for members' dress, the robe is rarely worn and the turban only during dhikr and salat or prayers.

What is referred to as 'perennial' Sufism (Hermansen, 1998) present in Europe draws on a variety of religious traditions for inspiration. The Sufi Order in the West, founded in 1910 by Pir Hadrat 'Ināyat Khān (1882–1927), and later reconstituted by his son Pir Vilāyat 'Ināyat Khān, is among the main vehicles for the spread of perennial Sufism and New Age esotericism (Jervis, 1998; Wilson, 1998). This movement acknowledges that 'perennial' Sufism is 'heretical' and 'non-Islamic', even according to traditional Sufi criteria. Doctrinally, for example, it holds views, anathema to Sunni, Shi'ite and Sufi Muslims, that the nature of Allah/God is changeable, that Allah/God and human beings are essentially one and that the human being is divine. It also gives qualified acceptance to the belief in reincarnation, and endorses and promotes the idea of a feminine dimension of the sacred. The Order has established a 'Committee for the Divine Feminine' and the 'Chrysalis Connection: The Feminine Council of the Sufi Order', an institution that has been undergoing reform. Men and women are said to enjoy equal rights in the movement, both participating in all activities on the same footing and both occupying positions of authority. These 'deviations' or 'innovations' are deemed to be compatible with Sufism, which the founder of the Sufi Order insisted was not essentially an Islamic tradition but a 'Universal message of the time' (Jervis, 1998: 234).

Pir Vilāyat 'Ināyat Khān's notion of Sufism has much in common with that of Idris Shah. The latter has been highly successful in attracting Westerners to his type of 'perennial' Sufism through his writings and his Society for Sufi Studies. Reading, he believes, is just the first step on the path to Sufism and he regards his numerous writings on this theme as purely introductory. These writings are purposely packaged in the language of psychology rather than theology to enable contemporary society, which he regards as culturally underdeveloped and, therefore, unable, at the stage it is at, to comprehend notions such as God or the Infinite or the Divine, or to relate to them.

This inclusive characterization of 'perennial' Sufism is also evident in the Golden Sufi Centre (Hermansen, 1998: 168), which was inspired by the teachings and writings of Irena Tweedie, a disciple of a Hindu Naqshabandi. Tweedie's Sufism is best expressed in her *Daughter of Fire*, where she relates her Hindu guru, Bhai Sahib's, understanding of the phenomenon: 'Sufism is a way of life. There are Hindu Sufis, Muslim Sufis, Christian Sufis . . .. My revered Guru Maharaj was a Muslim' (Sviri, 1993: 79). Inclusive movements such as these suggest a concern among participants to discover a form of being spiritual that transcends cultural and religious differences.

As will be seen below, Islam's experience of adapting to European society is not unique. Buddhism and Hinduism in Europe are also undergoing similar processes of domestication, although in these cases there is little government intervention.

Buddhism and Europeanization

Buddhism became a new religious option for Europeans in the nineteenth century. Initially, converts came to Buddhism through reading philosophical and philological treatises such as those of Schopenhauer (1788–1860) and the French philologist Burnouf (1801–52). Others joined Buddhist communities abroad. There was, however, little in the way of Buddhist practice in Europe until the 1920s, when centres and 'parishes' were first started. Small coteries of intellectuals and professionals, and specific ethnic groups, were the main practitioners and belonged mostly to the Theravada (Doctrine of the Elders, and/or the Lesser Vehicle) tradition, whose principal meditation practice is *vipassana*.

From the 1960s a much greater interest was shown in Zen Buddhism, which uses the *kōan* and *mondo* to attain enlightenment or *satori*, and stresses the importance of applying meditation to work and art. Mahayana (Greater Vehicle or Great Way) Buddhism, the final goal of which is complete Buddhahood, the perfection of wisdom and compassion, was introduced by Japanese NRMs, including Soka Gakkai (Wilson and Dobbelaere, 1994), in the 1960s. Later, in the 1980s and 1990s, a widespread interest developed in Vajrayana (Thunderbolt or Diamond Way) Buddhism, which involves the use of ritual magic to achieve both Buddhahood itself and this-worldly benefits.

An idea of the increasing interest in Buddhism in Europe can be gleaned from the growth rates in certain countries over a fifteen-year period beginning in the mid-1970s. In Germany there was a fivefold increase in the number of Buddhist centres and communities during the period *c.*1975–*c.*1990, and in Britain over roughly the same period the increase was similar, with the number of centres rising from 91 in 1979 to 213 in 1991 (Baumann, 1995: 62). With expansion came attempts to indigenize this old 'new' religion, an attempt strongly supported by the founder of the Friends of the Western Buddhist Order (FWBO), the Venerable Sangharakshita (formerly, Dennis Lingwood). The FWBO, established in London in 1967, has an estimated 500 ordained members and 5,000 'lay' associates in Britain, retreat centres in Wales, France Italy and Spain, and social welfare projects in India. Its primary aim is to create the appropriate kind of new Buddhist communities and institutions that will change the environment and social milieu to enable the Dharma to be practised in the West.

Due largely to higher levels of immigration from majority Buddhist countries, France is presently the European country with the largest number of Buddhists and Buddhist educational institutions and centres. Buddhism in France remained, to all intents and purposes, an immigrant religion until the 1970s, when its ethnic make up, social composition and orientation toward society began to change. The effect was that by the early 1990s there were an estimated 600,000 Buddhists in France, 150,000 of whom were of French origin or French nationality, who were attracted in the main to Zen and Tibetan forms of Buddhism (Gira, 1991: 1).

These statistics do not convey the full extent of the Buddhist impact on France in recent times. Even more significant and influential for the intellectual, cultural and religious life of the country than the actual numbers of Buddhists are the many Buddhist institutes, pagodas and retreat centres throughout the country. Some 80 per cent of these organizations form part of the Buddhist Union of France (UBF), which came into existence in 1986 to facilitate, among other things, dialogue between the different forms of Buddhism active in the country.

Much Buddhism in Europe, as elsewhere (see Learman, 2005), is missionary. The aim of the Buddhist establishments in France is to change the spiritual and cultural climate not only of that country but also of the West. One such centre is the Buddhist International Cultural Centre of Linh Son, known as Dharmaville, established at Joinville on the outskirts of Paris in 1988. This centre's objective, which it is accepted will not be realized for another quarter of a century, is to make Dharmaville a Buddhist Institute of Higher Studies with some 250 monks and 150 nuns. The various Zen schools are also gaining in popularity. Although many practice Zen independently in smaller centres, the three principal institutes are the International Zen Association (AZI) in Paris, which is comprised of some fifty dojos or meditation halls, the Tai Sei Bukkyo Dai Ichi Zen temple in the Loir-et-Cher region and the Taille Zen Centre in the Ardèche. Among the well-established, community-based Tibetan centres is the Kagyu-Ling monastic community founded in 1974 at the old chateau of Plaige-La Boulaye, which provides long retreats for those wishing to become lamas. It also specializes in the translation of Buddhist texts, and this is in line with the UBF policy of indigenization, which regards the establishment of centres of translation as an important element of its strategy in adapting Buddhism to French society.

Another example of a successful Tibetan community in France is the Dhagpo Kagyu Ling, established on the Côte de Jor in Dordogne in 1977. Since 1988 this community has enjoyed the same legal status as Christian monasteries, and dependent upon it are a number of other communities, including the community of Kundreul Ling in Le Bost, Auvergne, headed by Lama Gendun, who spent more than thirty years in secluded meditation. There have been as many as a hundred Western monks at this monastery at any one time making three-year retreats, and across Europe as many as 300 will be undergoing the Kagyu training programme. While most of these communities and centres are under Tibetan leadership, a number are now headed by native French lamas, among them the scholarly community of Karma Ling, established in 1980 at the old Chartreuse monastery of Saint Hugon-Arvillard near the town of Pontcharra, Rhônes-Alpes.

In France, as elsewhere in Europe and the West where it has found a following, the Buddhist way of facilitating self-understanding and an under-standing of the world by starting from personal experience sets it apart from the mainstream Islamic and Christian approach. Moreover, the Buddhist notion of inner transcendence is gaining ground and is promoting the growth of subjective spirituality, while a belief in a personal God, particularly among the young, is in decline (Lambert, 2004: 41). Engaged Buddhism (see Chapters 5, 10 and 11) is also an important dimension of Buddhism in France. One of the principal agents in the advancement of this kind of Buddhism is the Vietnamese monk Thich Nhat Hanh. From his compound in Plum in France where he founded the Église Bouddhique Unifiée – a branch of the United Buddhist Church of Vietnam, which was formed in Vietnam in the 1960s (see Chapter 11) – Thich Nhat Hanh, through his writings, such as *Being Peace*, and his retreats and seminars, advocates the message of Engaged Buddhism, which is essentially the non-violent engagement through Buddhism with all aspects of life.

Institutions such as the European Buddhist Union (EBU), established in 1975 and composed of over thirty member organizations from eleven countries, were founded to promote the case for a European form of Buddhism in order to widen its appeal. EBU congresses are organized on a regular basis to facilitate dialogue and assess the methods of disseminating Buddhism in a European setting, with discussion focusing on what teachings, practices and institutions are to be retained as essential to Buddhism and what can be regarded as no more than cultural accretions and, therefore, to be discontinued. It is of great interest to learn by observing an exercise such as this what issues and by whom are considered to be of culture and what of the essence of the religious tradition (see Clarke, 2000).

While almost all agree that the notion of the Buddha nature in everyone is one central tenet that is believed to transcend all traditions and cultures and is, therefore, 'essential', there are those who would like to see other concepts retained but modified in the light of European reality. For example, it has been suggested that the Buddhist concepts *prajna* (wisdom) and *karuna* (compassion) might be presented to a European audience as action and 'engaged Buddhism', respectively. Stress has also been placed on the need to develop institutions appropriate to the European context, the FWBO suggesting the establishment of 'residential spiritual communities' and team-based co-operatives and/or 'right livelihood businesses' (Baumann, 1995: 66).

Others pursue the possibility of creating less hierarchical, more egalitarian communities where the distinction between ordained and lay members and between male and female members is less pronounced than is the case in practice in Asia. While the search continues for greater integration and further adaptation, the general view is that diversity is not in itself undesirable nor should it be eliminated simply for the purpose of presenting a united front.

New Buddhist communities and movements

Several of the New Buddhist communities in Europe, including the FWBO mentioned above, are committed to creating a form of Dharma for the West. There are others, however, whose aim is to turn the West into a Buddhaland modelled on Tibet or some other Buddhist heartland.

Throssel Hole Priory, a Zen monastery founded in 1972 by an English female convert to Buddhism, Jiyu Kennett Roshi, is an example of the first of these two orientations. The Priory is a member of the Order of Buddhist Contemplatives whose headquarters are at Shasta Abbey at Mount Shasta, California (Morgan, 1994) and it has affiliated groups in many parts of the British Isles. Most Zen centres in Britain have branches in several parts of Europe and other parts of the world and are also affiliated to other centres abroad. For example, the International Zen Association in Bristol is affiliated to the Association Zen Internationale (AZI) in France. The Kanzeon, the Zen Practice Centre Trust, also a Soto Zen group, has founded centres in France, Holland and Poland, as well as the United States. Other Zen groups in Britain directly connected to Japan include the Chester Zen centre under the spiritual guidance of the Japanese Soto Zen teacher Master Hogen Daido, who visits Britain regularly. Rinzai Zen centres are mainly concentrated in London and are under the spiritual direction of Japanese monks.

The British Forest Sangha, an innovation from Thailand, began in 1977 when the Thai forest monk Ajahn Chah, founder of the well-known hermitage monastery Wat Nong Pah Pong in northeast Thailand, visited Britain with three Western disciples. After starting the Hampstead Vihara and the Cittaviveka residence in Chithurst in Sussex, the forest monks opened in 1984 the Amaravati Centre near St Albans in Hertfordshire. Bell (1998: 155) tells us that most British converts are attracted to the Forest Sangha 'by a strong desire for self-help and self-cultivation that leads them to learn meditation'. Most do not subscribe to the theory of merit and 'pay little or no attention to merit making', which is associated with benefits in this life. Their refusal to subscribe to the theory of merit contradicts customary practice in much of Buddhist Southeast Asia (see Chapter 11).

The older Japanese schools of Buddhism present in Europe have tended, with few exceptions, to remain culturally Japanese, and include the Shingon school founded by Kobo Daishi (774–835), the Jodo shu or Pure Land school, which owes its origins in Japan to Honen (1133–1212), and the Jodo Shinshu or True school of the Pure Land, founded in Japan by a disciple of Honen, Shinran (1173–1262). The thirteenth-century Nichiren tradition has been widely established in Europe principally by Soka Gakkai, which is now active all across Europe. Among the principal goals of this and other Japanese Buddhist movements both old and new in Europe, as elsewhere, is the advancement of peace within and between nations, religions and communities (Kisala, 1999). This agenda is promoted by seminars, research, and exhibitions and by the annual ceremony in August at the Myohoji Peace Pagoda in London, which is performed in remembrance of the victims of the atomic bombs dropped on Nagasaki and Hiroshima.

Although the Chinese presence in Britain dates back to the nineteenth century, there has been little practice of Chinese Buddhism either within or outside the Chinese community until relatively recently. Since the 1980s a number of Chinese Buddhist Temples and Associations have been founded in Britain and elsewhere in Europe, among them the Guanyin Temple in Chorley, Lancashire, England. In the nearby city of Lancaster there is the Ch'an Association and in London there exists a branch of the Real Gold Society of Great Britain. Among the Taiwanese Buddhist organizations with a presence in Europe are the Buddha's Light International Association (BLIA), founded in 1967 in Taiwan, which opened the Foguang Temple in London in 1992, and the International Buddhist Progress Society. Both groups follow the Pure Land Buddhist tradition and both are headed by the Taiwanese Master Hsu Yun. The BLIA, in addition to its Taiwanese and British centres, has opened centres in France, Japan, Hong Kong, Singapore, Malaysia, Indonesia, the Philippines, North and South America and South Africa.

Compared with the generally negative response to Islam and to NRMs (Beckford, 1985), there has been relatively little public opposition to Buddhism in Europe to date. What negative criticism there has been has been directed at the FWBO, Soka Gakkai and one or two prominent figures in Tibetan Buddhism. Regarding the latter, a main cause of controversy in the past was the lifestyle of the late Tibetan lama Chogyam Trungpa (1939–87), an exponent of the Kagyu tantric tradition. It is commonly thought that this tradition was started by Marpa (1012–96), who had once been recognized by the influential spiritual leader Karmapa (man of action) as the eleventh Trungpa Tulku, or reincarnated lama. A former student of comparative religion at Oxford University, Chogyam Trungpa, with the assistance of his colleague Akong Rimpoche, opened the first Tibetan monastery in Europe, Samye Ling, in Dumfriesshire in Scotland in 1968. A year later he abandoned his monastic vows and eagerly embraced the counter-culture. While this action, and his erudition, attracted many young students keen to break away from traditional moral and religious values and attitudes, it alienated many others, even among the young, many of whom were more conventional in their attitudes and style of life than was widely thought. Samye Ling itself acquired a reputation locally and nationally for decadence.

By 1970 Chogyam Trungpa had left Samye Ling for North America where, without any change in behaviour, he succeeded in setting up a number of Buddhist rural retreat centres and several Buddhist study centres or Dharmadhatus, all overseen by the a co-ordinating body the Vajradhatu. He also set up the Naropa Institute, a liberal arts college, and the Maitri Institute for psychotherapeutic care. Meanwhile, several of his European disciples established training centres under his patronage in Germany, Holland and England, modelled on those in North America.

The New Kadampa Tradition (NKT) (Kay, 1997) is another controversial Tibetan Buddhist NRM, this time for reasons of a doctrinal rather than of a moral kind. Although it was formally established in Britain in 1991, its roots go further back to the setting up by Tibetans and Westerners in the 1970s of the Foundation for the Preservation of the Mahayana Tradition (FPMT). Its opening by Geshe Kelsang Gyatso Rimpoche in 1991 was hailed by one enthusiast as 'a wonderful new development in the history of the Buddhadharma' (Kay, 1997: 283). Geshe Kelsang Gyatso Rimpoche had been the resident teacher at the British Branch of the FPMT, the Manjushri Institute, established at Conishead Priory in 1975. However, he eventually resigned after a long running dispute between himself and the founder of this monastery, Lama Yeshe. The latter, who died in 1984, was less of an intellectual and more eclectic and ecumenical in his opinions and outlook than Geshe Kelsang Gyatso Rimpoche. He was also inclined to centralize authority at the expense of local community initiatives.

Another serious bone of contention with international, if not global, repercussions since it involved disagreement between Geshe Kelsang Gyatso Rimpoche and the Dalai Lama, was the question of the status of the Dharma-Protector. While the former maintains that he is a divine being who merits to be worshipped as a Buddha, the latter regards him merely as a worldly protector and undeserving of any special veneration or spiritual practices.

The purpose of the launching in 1991 of the New Kadampa Tradition (NKT) was to unite those centres that opted to be under the spiritual tutelage of Geshe Kelsang Gyatso Rimpoche for the purpose of teaching to the West 'pure' Tibetan Mahayana Buddhism as taught by the Tibetan scholar Je Tsongkapha. The New Kadampa tradition, thus, represents the replacement of the inclusive approach, followed by Lama Yeshe and his supporters, with a rigid, exclusive one. By following this course, Geshe Kelsang Gyaso Rimpoche believes he has reintroduced Kadampa Buddhism to the West in its pristine, authentic form, which he describes, paradoxically, as an autonomous, modern, Western tradition (Kay, 1997: 286).

Similar developments giving rise to much the same debates take place among Hindus in Europe.

New Hindu and Sikh movements

The presence of Hinduism and Neo-Hindu NRMs (see Chapter 10) in Europe dates back to the first part of the nineteenth century (Knott, 1997: 756ff.). Among the first arrivals was Raja Rammohun Roy, the founder of the Brahmo Samaj movement, who came to England in the 1830s to discuss issues of common concern with Unitarians. A century later members of the Ramakrishna mission founded in India in 1897 by Swami Vivekananda (1863–1902) (see Chapter 10), also one of the founders of 'Modern Yoga' (De Michaelis, 2004), came to study in England and this was followed by the establishment in 1947 in London of the Ramakrishna Vedanta Centre. Earlier in 1911 a Sikh gurdwara had been built in London, and earlier still, in 1861, the Religious Society of Zoroastrians of Europe had been started.

Hindus, less congregational-based than either, proved to be slower than Muslims and Sikhs in establishing permanent institutions in Britain. However, spurred on by the arrival of East African Asians in the 1960s, they began the construction of purpose-built temples, the first of which was erected in Leicester, England, in 1969. With the construction of temples in many of the major cities of the United Kingdom (Nye, 1996), attempts began to be made by such organizations as the National Council of Hindu Temples to unite what still remains a very diverse Hindu community and one that is increasingly, as are the Muslim, Sikh and Buddhist communities in Britain and elsewhere in Europe, having to face the challenges posed by second- and later generation members educated entirely in the Western system of education.

Its obvious diversity notwithstanding, some researchers have detected in the Hindu communities in Britain and among Hindu diaspora communities generally the growing influence since the 1980s of the Hindutva movement, whose core philosophy is based on Vinayak Damodar Savokar's treatise of 1923 'Hindutva – Or Who is a Hindu?'. A nationalist movement that also focuses its attention on gender and sexual politics with a view to re-creating Hindu tradition in these areas, Hindutva's broader aim is the establishment of a common Hindu nation and civilization (Bhatt and Mukta, 2000).

Among the Hindu NRMs in Europe with the highest profile are the International Society for Krishna Consciousness, more popularly known as the Hare Krishna movement, the Sathya Sai Baba, the Sahaja Yoga, the Rajneesh and/or Osho and the Brahma Kumaris movements, all of which are discussed in some detail in the chapter on South Asian NRMs (see Chapter 10). The Rajneesh movement, once the most sought after of the Hindu NRMs in Europe, despite having undergone a complete transformation since the death of its founder the Bhagwan Shree Rajneesh (1931–90), continues to attract a large numbers of seekers, mainly through its impressive literary output (see Chapter 10).

The Sathya Sai Baba movement, whose founder is considered to be the universal Godhead, emphasizes, somewhat paradoxically, that all religions are but different paths to the Truth. This inclusiveness is reflected in his movement's ethnic and social composition to a degree rarely seen in other Neo-Hindu movements and NRMs generally, and indeed in older religions in Europe. This image of ethnic, social and religious diversity makes the movement attractive to second- and third-generation Asians of different faith traditions who are seeking to bridge two cultures, and also exercises a strong appeal in Latin America.

Also ecumenical in approach is the Sikh-derived Namdhari (meaning the one who has adopted God in her/his life) movement founded in 1857 by Ram Singh (1816–85) (see Chapter 10). A vegetarian movement that differs from mainstream Sikhism by acknowledging a lineage of human gurus after Gobind Singh, the founder of Khalsa, and regarded by a majority of Sikhs as the last of the lineage of human gurus, its tenets are: meditation on the name of God; earning a living through honest work; and sharing with the poor. Among the reforms its founder sought to promote were women's rights, the ending of infanticide practices on females, the selling of girls into slavery and the system of dowry, which the movement itself no longer practises. The founder also campaigned against the slaughtering of cows, sought to promote higher standards of literacy and pursued a policy of non-co-operation with British rule in India, which resulted in his being exiled to Burma. Art, music and sport are activities that are given high priority by Namdharis.

Modern 'secular' Yoga

As was previously mentioned, Wilson (1990) has written of 'secularized' religion with reference to Scientology and Hanegraaff (1999) has described the NAM (see Chapter 2) in the same terms. Here we consider the phenomenon of Modern 'secular' Yoga (De Michaelis, 2004).

De Michaelis uses the term 'Modern Yoga' in a precise, technical sense and traces its origins back to the Indian guru Swami Vivekananda (see Chapter 10), whose book *Raja Yoga* (1896) consists of a highly original blend of Western esotericism, psychology and yoga. These provide the core ingredients of Modern Yoga, a secularized form of yoga in the sense of its being detached from its spiritual roots which lay in classical Indian religion. From this point on Yoga began to be promoted as a way of life that anyone, believer or not, could usefully practise, and this is how it is seen by most people in Europe today.

Versions of Modern Yoga are endless and its popularity widespread. This popularity can be explained in part by its having become conflated with Western therapy and transformed in the process from its classical purpose, which was to provide the spiritual means to liberation, into a 'secular' technique for coping with the stresses and strains imposed by modernity or for promoting relaxation. Contrasting Modern Yoga as practised in the West with the classical Yoga of India, Hardy (1984: 17) writes:

> The classical formulation of the raison d'etre of yoga refers to the heightening of one's awareness and perceptive faculties, the polishing of one's mind like the sharpening of a knife, and the eventual looking into the deeper nature of things . . . classical meditation wants to free it (the mind) from the clutterings that already exist in it and quite confidently leaves it to generate its own insights . . . the very flavour of classical Indian culture derives from such insights having been made socially and culturally available, made subject to reflection and arguments over their significance, and thus giving rise to some of the most sophisticated philosophical systems.

Hardy (1984: 17) asks:

> What about features like 'integration of the whole person', 'intensified concentration', 'greater job efficiency' – features which are often included in the offer made by Indian groups to the West? The classical indologist cannot provide an answer if it concerns the efficacy of meditation in these areas. But what he can say is that classical India did not connect yoga with day-to-day life. To draw on yoga for greater job efficiency could hardly arise when the yogi had actually renounced society; the Renaissance ideal of the whole person did not exist but in pockets of Indian culture other than classical yoga.

There are few if any contemporary Yoga manuals that do not offer the benefits of relaxation and relief from stress. Offering such benefits can, of course, be interpreted as providing the means to a kind of salvation. The Foundation Course Syllabus of the British Wheel of Yoga, for example, contains much advice and information that can be readily traced to Western relaxation therapy in general and to Annie Payson Call's system of relaxation developed in Massachusetts in the 1880s (Singleton, 2005). Of course, 'salvation through relaxation' is something that William James understood (1971: 121).

Meditation practices such as vipassana are undergoing a similar transformation in Southeast Asia but not without growing opposition from monks and lay people alike, who strongly object to the progressive instrumentalization of the discipline (see Chapter 11). Such a shift in purpose does not generate anything like the same concern in the West, where Buddhist meditation is often valued solely for its this-worldly, non-spiritual effects.

It hardly needs to be said that Modern Yoga and Buddhist meditation are not always used in secular ways. Raja Yoga, having undergone a process akin to denominationalization, has become the main practice of several Neo-Hindu movements, including the Hare Krishna and Brahma Kumaris movements (see Chapter 10). It has also been taken up as a spiritual discipline by a number of mainstream and alternative religions. It is the case, nonetheless, that much of what is widely practised in the West as yoga often bears little relation to any extant classical Indian tradition of the discipline. This development poses a further challenge to the theory that a new spirituality, which relies heavily on techniques such as yoga, is emerging that could eventually replace congregational religion.

Neo-Paganism is another important ingredient of that new spirituality.

Neo-Paganism

Across Europe, from North to South and East to West, interest in the phenomenon widely referred to as Neo-Paganism and/or Contemporary Paganism has been growing (Pearson *et al.*, 1998). There is no need to look for a complete break between contemporary and traditional Pagan practice and belief. Butler (2003: 8) sees the new dimension as consisting of 'an interplay of re-interpretative and inventive elements'. With regard to practice she writes:

> Rituals may have been carried out with the intention of reconstructing the rituals that are believed to have occurred at certain sites in the distant past. Some practitioners build their own versions of these ancient structures on the landscape.

> (ibid.)

Neo-Paganism in Greece provides a variation on this theme of the re-interpretative and inventive as the basis of the new. As Papalexandropoulos (1999) points out, Greek Neo-Paganism, a phenomenon that has become increasingly popular since the 1970s, is 'new' in that its practitioners impose 'new' religious ideas on Ancient Greek religion and eliminate from the latter all traces of dualism. All the Ancient Greek gods, some of whom were traditionally considered as personal gods, are turned into expressions, or manifestations, or forms of the Absolute. Moreover, all that is negative about Ancient Greek religion is either screened out or given a positive interpretation, including death, which is interpreted as blissful for all. In Ancient Greek religion death was blissful only for certain heroes. Greek Neo-Paganism, thus, offers a non-historical reformulation and reinterpretation of Ancient Greek religion.

New Age (see Chapter 2) links with Neo-Paganism and the links of both with Wicca are often debated (Pearson *et al.*, 1998). Albanese (1990), writing with reference to the North American context, interprets New Age religiosity and Neo-Paganism as representative of a certain kind of Nature Religion, affirming an optimistic vision both of the universe and of human nature. Both are used as umbrella terms for a range of specific traditions concerned with the sacralization of the person and the world.

Pearson *et al.* (1998), however, point out, regarding New Age–Wicca connections, that these are often assumed rather than proved. Keeping to the description of the NAM as an optimistic vision of the world's future and of human nature as its defining feature, Wicca, by contrast, adopts a more pragmatic, more realistic, more critical view of human nature, or to use York's metaphor (1995: 147) it tends more than the New Age, which fixates on the 'White Light', to incorporate 'the interplay between light and dark'. Moreover, while the NAM has no clear position on social engagement, an important development in Wicca that Crowley (1994) emphasizes is its engagement with the world and, in particular, with the environment. Starhawk's Reclaiming movement (see Chapter 5) considers this dimension indispensable to 'authentic' Paganism, which also includes as an essential part of its remit the empowerment of women.

The importance Wicca attaches to engagement is shared by most Neo- and/or Contemporary Pagans, at least in theory. However, their main contribution to modern spirituality has been the wider awareness they have created of the earth as a sacred and sacralizing force. They have contributed much to the development of Creation spirituality, which Matthew Fox, among others, has applied to Christian theology.

Satanism is sometimes associated in popular discussion with Paganism of every kind, and by evangelical Christians with the New Age also. Satanists are a disparate group. Some may organize themselves in 'churches' or 'temples', while the practice of others is mostly ad hoc. While the objectives of organized Satanist movements are not always easily identifiable, Harvey's (1995) study points to a concern with the 'Self' and with 'Self-expression' as a principal goal. He comments (1995: 295) that the Satanism he researched was 'neither an inversion of Christianity nor a development of Paganism. Nor is there a single ecological or political platform to which all Satanists are committed.' He continues:

> Contemporary Satanists are committed to their own Self, its development and expression. Satanism in contemporary Britain does not require belief in the Satan of the Christian pantheon . . .. The reality is a series of techniques for allowing individuals to affirm themselves . . . in the context of spirituality.

Thus, close comparisons of the New Age with Neo-Paganism and of Satanism with the latter seem inappropriate. The outlook of Satanism and its orientation to the wider world are not only more pessimistic but lack the broader, 'transcendental' and transformative dimensions of both these groups.

Influential thinkers and the new spiritualities: the case of Gurdjieff

The list of thinkers that have greatly influenced the form and content of contemporary alternative spirituality and the developments and changes within the older, mainstream religious traditions is endless, and makes the decision to focus here on George Ivanovitch Gurdjieff (1866/9–1949), the inspiration behind the movement known as The Work, somewhat arbitrary.

Moreover; the intellectual sources that motivate and move people to embrace alternative forms of spirituality have changed over time. In the late 1970s, according to Ferguson (1982: 462), the writings of Pierre Teilhard de Chardin (1881–1955), the Jesuit palaeontologist, were among the most often named by her respondents, the 181 'Aquarian conspirators' – those networking to bring about the 'Age of Aquarius' or of the mind's true liberation – as having had the most influence on their thinking. Teilhard de Chardin was himself greatly influenced by the philosopher Bergon's writing on Creative Evolution, which he spoke of as having enabled him to see the world in a totally different light, as the evolving heart of God, animated by the risen Christ and, therefore, as a 'divine milieu'. Of Teilhard de Chardin's own writings the most widely read, and the most difficult, is *The Phenomenon of Man* (1938, translated and republished in 1999 as *The Human Phenomenon*).

In Ferguson's survey Carl Jung (1875–1961) followed Teilhard de Chardin as the second most influential thinker and writer of the time. Jung's concept of synchronicity, defined variably by the author as 'meaningful coincidence' or 'acausal parallelism', or 'an acausal connecting principle' or 'the simultaneous occurrence of a certain psychic state with one or more external events which appear as meaningful parallels to the momentary subjective state' is, as Main (2003: 2) points out, but one of his many notions that have greatly influenced New Age thought in the sense of reinforcing, among other things, its notion of non-causal relationships. The NAM, for example, finds support in Jung for its idea of correspondence – an idea developed much earlier by the Swedish scientist Emmanuel Swedenborg (1688–1772) – according to which non-causal relationships exist between different levels of reality simply by virtue of their inner affinities, even where there is no plausible causal connection.

While the impact of an idea is often difficult to measure, there can be little doubt about the formative influence on a number of contemporary types of alternative spirituality in the West, and beyond, at different times in modern history, of the astrological theories of Swedenborg. These include: the notions of 'influx' and of a universal magnetic fluid, notions refined by the Austrian physician Franz Mesmer (1733–1815); the idea of a hidden tradition underlying all religions expounded by Helena Petrovna Blavatsky (1831–91), the Theosophist (see Chapter 5); and the concept of self-culture – the development of one's mind and capacities through one's own efforts. This last-mentioned aim is a major theme of contemporary, subjective spirituality, and among its other major advocates were Gurdjieff, as we shall see, and in the United States, the Transcendentalist Ralph Waldo Emerson (see Chapter 5).

To return briefly to Swedenborg and Mesmer. The former's 'realized eschatology' (he believed the Second Coming of Christ had begun in the spiritual realm in 1757), his interest in healing associated with his above-mentioned theory of correspondences between the spiritual and material realms summarized in the adage 'as above so below', his depiction of the Afterlife in his Heaven and Hell (1758), his liberal moral views, and his search for ancient wisdom are all echoed in New Age and/or Aquarian discourse. While he himself did not found a church, his disciples established the Church of the New Jerusalem in London in 1787, also known as the Swedenborgian Church or New Church, for the purpose of preserving his teachings. Swedenborgian and Mesmerian ideas fused over time to form the basis of Spiritualism as it took shape from the 1840s.

It would be difficult to overestimate the impact of the opinions of the humanistic psychologist Abraham Maslow (1908–70), founder of the Human Potential Movement (HPM), on contemporary subjective spirituality and modern holistic psychology and environmentalism. His notion of unused human potential and his insistence on the importance of going beyond mere subsistence to real needs have been particularly influential. Also crucial to the development of much modern spirituality, including Creation Spirituality, are the theories on the organic unity of all terrestrial life developed by atmospheric biochemist James Lovelock, one of the authors of the *gaia* hypothesis, the all-encompassing system that acts as if it were a single organism to control weather and temperature and air and sea and soil and other dimensions of the biosphere, indeed all living things.

The growing popularity of contemporary witchcraft owes much to the writings and activities of Gerald Gardner (1884–1964). The ideas developed by Aleister Crowley (1875–1947), a prominent member of the Hermetic Order of the Golden Dawn, and later of the Ordo Templi Orientis, a German system of the Occult, have also been highly influential in magical and occult circles. Crowley formulated what has come to be accepted in such circles as a fundamental principle of behaviour and is known as the Law of Thelema – 'Do what thou wilt be the whole Law; Love is the Law, Love under Will'.

The ideas of Marcus Garvey (1887–1940) on the biblical roots of Black people inspired the creation of many African-derived movements, including the Rastafarian movement, while those of Abdul Ala Maududi (1903–79), Hassan al-Banna (1906–49) and Sayyid Qutb (1906–66) have had a profound impact on the many modern Islamist movements dedicated to the restoration of 'authentic' Islam and the creation of an Islamic Shari'a-based society. This last-mentioned objective, and other developments, including the debate on the eventual entry of Turkey into the European Union, has led to a wide-ranging discussion concerning the compatibility of Islam and Western democracy (Abou El Fadl, 2004; see also Chapter 7). Jiddhu Krishnamurti (1895–1986), Swami Vivekananda (1863–1902), Swami Paramahansa Yogananda (1893–1953), Sri Aurobindo Ghose (1872–1950) and the Bhagwan Shree Rajneesh (1931–90), also known as Osho, are but five of modern Hinduism's most prominent figures whose teachings (see Chapter 10) have been widely read both in India and abroad, and who have made a significant contribution to, among other developments, the emergence of 'Modern Yoga'.

Other writings that have attracted a worldwide readership are those of the Vietnamese Buddhist monk Thich Nhat Hanh (b.1926), whose publications and addresses have been among the most effective vehicles for the promotion of 'Engaged Buddhism'. The 'mystical' novels of the Brazilian author Paulo Coelho are among the most widely read books of modern times, while the writings of the founder of Scientology, L. Ron Hubbard (1911–86), in particular his *Dianetics: The Modern Science of Mental Health* (Hubbard, 1950) have influenced the development of modern therapeutic religion in general and more specifically what I referred to in a previous chapter as Religions of the True Self (see Chapter 1).

George Ivanovitch Gurdjieff's writings, along with those of his student and recalcitrant collaborator, Pyotr Demainovitch Ouspensky (1878–1947), provide the basis of what is known as 'the System', 'the Fourth Way, 'The Gurdjieff Work', or simply 'The Work', which was established in London in 1955. As Wellbeloved (2002) notes, Gurdjieff's influence continues to widen through the various Gurdjieff Foundations, and through foundations that have been greatly influenced by his and Ouspensky's writings, included among which are the School of Economic Science, the Fellowship of Friends, the Emin Foundation, and the Arica Institute. The essential teachings of Gurdjieff are to be found in his three-volume work *All and Everything*, published posthumously in 1950, which includes the controversial Beelzebub's Tales to His Grandson, described by some as a hotchpotch of nonsensical meandering on the occult, and by others as profound and illuminating. Among Ouspensky's best-known work is his *In Search of the Miraculous: Fragments of an Unknown Teaching* (Ouspensky, 1950).

The Gurdjieffian scholar James Moore describes *Beelzebub's Tales* as a 'book of revelation and mystery: a book of rustic simplicity and Hegelian opacity; a book so plain it could be read in working men's clubs, and yet so deep it would attract a formidable premium of attention and pondering' (1991: 222). Wellbeloved's much needed study (2002) provides the reader with a structure of the *Tales* that brings a degree of order to the work and enables the reader to pull together its varied, diverse and disparate strands of meaning.

According to the Gurdjieffian model of consciousness, human beings are asleep, react mechanically and have only a very limited sense of who they are, of their 'real' self. Human beings, Gurdjieff believed, were 'unfinished' and, as a consequence, were led unconsciously by their automatic conditioning under the pull of external stimuli. The transition Gurdjieff sought to encourage people to make was from this state to ordinary waking, to self-remembrance and ultimately to the rare state of objective consciousness. The immediate goal was to escape from this sleep by leaving behind the states of consciousness referred to as sleep, and start the process of self-remembering which would lead to awakening.

This emphasis on the necessity of awakening from sleep, of separating the True Self from the socialized, dysfunctional self that manifests as one's ego, is found in one form or another throughout the Religions of the True Self and/ or the Self-religions, across the whole range of NAM spirituality, and is a feature of most modern ideas on alternative spirituality. Gurdjieff went on to develop a specific method for the development of consciousness, by which he meant, as de Salzmann (1987) pointed out, something more than mental awareness or functioning. The capacity for consciousness required, Gurdjieff taught, a harmonious blending of mind, feeling and body, which alone could ensure the realization of those activities within human beings of the higher influences usually referred to as 'nous', 'bodhi' or 'atman'.

At the Institute for the Harmonious Development of Man, which he opened at Fontainebleau near Paris in 1922, Gurdjieff continued to develop his Fourth Way as the path to objective consciousness; the first way being that of the fakir which consists of physical discipline, the second the taming of the emotions, which is the way of the monk, and the third the way of the yogi, who develops inner knowledge or awareness. By contrast the Fourth Way as taught by Gurdjieff involved: silent meditation; breathing control; rhythmic exercises; hard, physical and sometimes demeaning work; performances of Sacred Dances attended by among others Diaghilev; and the 'Science of Idiotism', the purpose of which appears to have been to provide students with a mirror in which they could see themselves (Wellbeloved, 2002: 24).

Inextricably, but nonetheless controversially, linked with Gurdjieff's name is the Enneagram, or nine-sided figure, which he extolled as 'a universal glyph, a schematic diagram of perpetual motion' (Moore, 1991: 344). The Enneagram has been freely adapted as a diagram by both mainstream and alternative teachers of religion and religious guides, and by secular organizations, a use which highlights the process of interfacing and even the merging of the marginal and the mainstream in late modern society, a process that can be shown to have occurred, or to be occurring, in many other areas of contemporary spirituality including Modern Yoga and the New Age Movement (see Chapter 2).

Gurdjieff, Moore (1991) informs us, applied this 'dynamic model' specifically to synthesizing, at macrocosmic and microcosmic level, his 'Law of Three' and 'Law of Seven'. The former, Moore (1991: 44) points out,

> lays down that each phenomenon from cosmic to sub atomic, springs from the interaction of no more than three forces: the first, or Holy Affirming, being active; the second, or Holy Denying, passive, and the third, or Holy Reconciling, neutralizing.

The process involves the higher blending with the lower to actualize the middle. The Law of Seven is much more complex and though it defies easy summary can be said to be grounded on the principle that there are seven discrete phases, construed as notes or pitches, to every completing process, which develop irregularly in either an ascending or a descending scale. This Law of Seven, illustrated in the Ray of Creation, enabled Gurdjieff, among other things, to position the earth in terms of the Universe as a whole and explains the Fall of Mankind.

Although, as we have seen, Gurdjieff's cosmological reflections are sometimes dismissed as full of absurdities and contradictions, many have found in them answers to such crucially important existential questions as the significance of life on earth, the purpose of the earth itself, and the core moral issue of freewill. Commenting on the Ray of Creation as a philosophical model Moore (1991: 45) contends that it 'comes as near as is humanly possible to reconciling the irreconcilable: involution, evolution, determinism and freewill, entropy and negative entropy, suffering and God's benignity'.

Gurdjieff's depiction of the human condition is dualistic in that he believed that it was defined by a titanic struggle between the personified forces of darkness and light. There is, nonetheless, a strong note of optimism, which is most pronounced in the conviction that through 'conscious labour and intentional suffering' individuals might slowly perfect themselves to the level of what is called 'Objective Reason' and, thus, attain immortality by reintegrating with their source, the Divine Sun (Moore, 1991: 48).

Conclusions: a changing paradigm

As we saw in Chapter 2, the questions are often asked: who is a New Ager and are there any defining characteristics of the New Age Movement? It was also pointed out there that the same questions have been asked about Confucianism in modern times by Yao (2001) and could also now be asked about Christianity, at least in the European context.

The religion of the majority in Europe remains Christianity, but à la carte Christianity or 'Christianity of my own kind'. As we have seen, Buddhism, Hinduism, Islam and the other older, more recently arrived, religions are slowly undergoing domestication or 'glocalization' (see Chapter 1). At the same time, New Religious Movements and a new kind of holistic, inner-directed spirituality have introduced a new cognitive religious style, which appeals to a growing number of 'unchurched' in particular. This is a style that places the emphasis on experience not on faith. One can, thus, be spiritual or religious without faith. Indeed faith, it is argued, is completely unnecessary.

What the future of the religious past in Europe will be, and what the future of religion in general will be, is difficult to predict with any accuracy at this juncture. There have been, as we have noted, a few signs of Christian renewal among the young in particular. As for the new holistic spirituality, the most that can be said of that is that while it is not a majority pursuit it signals a major shift away from congregational religion. It was, however, pointed out not only that the new spirituality is varied but that it should not be regarded as the polar opposite of congregational religion. Bainbridge (2004) and Stark *et al.* (2005) make the same point regarding the United States. Moreover, it is not always entirely free of all theistic notions or of all forms of reliance on external forms – be they texts or Tradition – for its legitimacy. Nor is it always spirituality without a social purpose. It is, however, largely a spirituality without faith and without an institutional base, and this must cast doubt about its long-term future prospects.

Regarding Buddhism, Hinduism and Sikhism, these religions are all, as we have seen, undergoing a process of Europeanization. The rise of radical Islamist groups and Imams has led to government-driven policies to create 'moderate Islam' for purposes of social harmony, in a way not dissimilar to the monotheisms created by the Indonesian Government for a similar purpose (see Chapter 11). If we use Fethulah Gulen and Sufism as a guide, the stronger trends, however, are not toward radicalism but toward greater inclusiveness, less rigid forms of religious membership, less concern with right doctrine and more with applied spirituality, with the positive effects personal and social of the spiritual or religious.

The religious space of Europe, in particular Western Europe, is post-Christian. Within it a new religious paradigm is presently being constructed, the stuff of which is derived from a range of diverse sources, including Oriental religions, Sufism and the new holistic spirituality, much of which is now mainstream but which, initially, was largely disseminated through the NAM (see Chapter 2) and the NRMs from South Asia (see Chapter 10).

References and select bibliography

Abou El Fadl, Khaled (2004) *Islam and the Challenge of Democracy*, Princeton, NJ: Princeton University Press.

Albanese, Catherine L. (1990) *Nature Religion in America: From American Indians to the New Age*, Chicago: University of Chicago Press.

Andrews, Ahmed (1998) 'South Asian Sunni Reform Movements in the West: The Lang Scots Miles from Delhi to Dundee' in Peter B. Clarke (ed.) *New Trends and Developments in the World of Islam*, London: Luzac, pp. 59–74.

Aras, Bulent and Caha, Omer (2000) 'Fethullah Gulen and his Liberal "Turkish Islam" Islam Movement', *Middle East Review of International Affairs*, 4(4), 1–11.

Ashford, S. and Timms, N. (1992) *What Europe Thinks: A Study of Western European Values*, Aldershot: Dartmouth.

Bainbridge, William Sims (2004) 'After the New Age', *Journal for the Scientific Study of Religion*, 43(3), 381–95.

Baumann, Martin (1995) 'Creating a European Path to Nirvana: Historical and Contemporary Developments of Buddhism in Europe', *Journal of Contemporary Religion*, 10(1), 55–70.

Beckford, James, A. (1985) *Cult Controversies: The Social Response to the New Religious Movements*, London: Tavistock Publications.

Bell, Sandra (1998) 'British Theravada Buddhism: Other Worldly Theories and the Theory of Exchange', *Journal of Contemporary Religion*, 13(2), 149–71.

Berger, Peter L. (ed.) (1999) *The Desecularization of the Modern World*, Grand Rapids, MI: Eerdmans.

Berzano, Luigi (1998) *Damanhur: Popolo e Communità, Leumann*, Turin: Elledici.

Bhatt, Chetan and Mukta, Parita (2000) 'Hindutva in the West: Mapping the Antinomies of Diaspora Nationalism', *Ethnic and Racial Studies*, 23(3), 407–41.

Bruce, Steve (1995) *Religion in Modern Britain*, Oxford: Oxford University Press.

Butler, Jenny (2003) 'Ireland's Neo-Pagan Community: Worldview and Ritual', paper presented to the International Conference on Alternative Spiritualities and New Age Studies, the Open University, UK, May/June.

Campbell, Colin (1999) 'The Easternization of the West' in Bryan R. Wilson and Jamie Cresswell (eds) *New Religious Movements: Challenge and Response*, London: Routledge, pp. 35–49.

Clarke, Peter B. (1986) *Black Paradise: The Rastafarian Movement*, Wellingborough: Aquarian Press.

Clarke, Peter B. (1998) 'Islam in Western Europe: Present State and Future Trends' in Peter B. Clarke (ed.) *New Trends and Developments in the World of Islam*, London: Luzac, pp. 3–39.

Clarke, Peter B. (2000) 'Modern Japanese Millenarian Movements: Their Changing Perception of Japan's Global Mission with Special Reference to the Church of World Messianity in Brazil' in Peter B. Clarke (ed.) *Japanese New Religions: In Global Perspective*, Richmond, Surrey: Curzon Press, pp. 129–81.

Crowley, Vivianne (1994) *Phoenix from the Flame: Pagan Spirituality in the Western World*, London: Aquarian Press.

Davie, Grace (1994) *Religion in Britain since 1945: Believing without Belonging*, Oxford: Blackwell.

Davie, Grace (2002) *Europe: The Exceptional Case: Parameters of Faith in the Modern World*, London: Darton, Longman & Todd.

De Michaelis, Elizabeth (2004) *A History of Modern Yoga*, London: Cassell Continuum.

de Salzmann, Michel (1987) 'Gurdjieff. G. I.' in Mercia Eliade (ed.) *The Encyclopedia of Religion*, Volume 6, New York: Macmillan, pp. 139–40.

Ferguson, Marilyn (1982) *The Aquarian Conspiracy: Personal and Social Transformation in the 1980s*, London: Paladin.

Gira, Denis (1991) 'La Présence Buddhiste en France' in *Documents Episcopat*, Paris: Secretariat General de l'Episcopat, pp. 1–16.

Hanegraaff, Wouter (1999) 'New Age Spiritualities as Secular Religion: A Historian's Perspective', *Social Compass*, 46, 145–60.

Hardy, Friedhelm E. (1984) 'Indian New Religions in the West', *Religion Today*, 1(2/3), 15–19.

Harvey, Graham (1995) 'Satanism in Britain Today', *Journal of Contemporary Religion*, 10(3), 283–96.

Heelas, Paul (1996) *The New Age Movement*, Oxford: Blackwell.

Heelas, Paul and Woodhead, Linda (2005) *The Spiritual Revolution: Why Religion is Giving Way to Spirituality*, Oxford: Blackwell.

Hermansen, Marcia (1998) 'In the Garden of American Sufi Movements: Hybrids and Perennials' in Peter B. Clarke (ed.) *New Trends and Developments in the World of Islam*, London: Luzac, pp. 155–78.

Hervieu-Leger, Danielle (2001) 'France's Obsession with the "Sectarian Threat"', *Nova Religion: the Journal of Alternative and Emergent Religions*, 4(2), 249–57.

Hubbard, L. Ron (1950) *Dianetics: The Modern Science of Mental Health: A Handbook of Dianetic Procedure*, Los Angeles: American St Hill Organization.

James, William (1971) *The Varieties of Religious Experience*, London: Fontana.

Jervis, James (1998) 'The Sufi Order in the West and Pir Vilāyat Ināyat Khān: Space Age Spirituality in Contemporary Euro-America' in Peter B. Clarke (ed.) *New Trends and Developments in the World of Islam*, London: Luzac, pp. 211–61.

Kay, David (1997) 'The New Kadampa Tradition and the Continuity of Tibetan Buddhism', *Journal of Contemporary Religion*, 12(3), 277–94.

Kemp, Daren (2004) *New Age: A Guide*, Edinburgh: Edinburgh University Press.

Kemper, E. (1996) 'The Impact of Radical Islam on the Political Attitudes of the First Generation Muslims in the Netherlands' in W. S. Shadid and P. S. Van Koninsveld (eds) *Political Participation and Identities of Muslims in Non-Muslim States*, Kampen: Kok Pharos, pp. 190–204.

King, John (1998) 'Tablighi Jama'at and the Deobandi Mosques in Britain' in Peter B. Clarke (ed.) *New Trends and Developments in the World of Islam*, London: Luzac, pp. 75–92.

Kisala, Robert J. (1999) *Prophets of Peace: Pacifism and Cultural Identity in Japan's New Religions*, Honolulu: University of Hawai'i Press.

Knott, Kim (1997) 'The Religions of South Asian Communities in Britain' in John Hinnells (ed.) *A New Handbook of Living Religions*, Oxford: Blackwell, pp. 756–75.

Kose, Ali (1993) 'Conversion to Islam: A Study of Native British Converts', PhD Thesis, University of London.

Lambert, Yves (2004) 'A Turning Point in Religious Evolution in Europe', *Journal of Contemporary Religion*, 19(1), 29–47.

La Raison (2003) 'Laïcité en Europe ou Europe cléricale?', Sept./Oct., 3.

Learman, Linda (ed.) (2005) *Buddhist Missionaries in the Era of Globalization*, Honolulu: University of Hawai'i Press, pp. 162–85.

Main, Roderick (2003) 'New Age Thinking in the Light of C. G. Jung's Theory of Synchronicity', paper presented at the International Conference on Alternative Spiritualities and New Age Studies, the Open University, UK, May/June.

Moore, James (1991) *Gurdjieff: The Anatomy of a Myth*, Shaftesbury: Element Books.

Morgan, Daishin (1994) 'Soto Zen Buddhism in Britain' in Peter B. Clarke and Jeffrey Somers (eds) *Japanese New Religions in the West*, Eastbourne: Japan Library, pp. 132–48.

Mullins, M. (1998) *Christianity: Made in Japan/A Study of Indigenous Movements*, Honolulu: University of Hawai'i Press.

Nielsen, Jorgen (1991) *Muslims in Western Europe*, Edinburgh: Edinburgh University Press.

Nye, Malory (1996) *A Place for Our Gods: The Construction of a Temple Community in Edinburgh*, London: Curzon Press.

Ouspensky, P. D. (1950) *In Search of the Miraculous: Fragments of an Unknown Teaching*, London: Routledge & Kegan Paul.

Papalexandropoulos, S. (1999) 'Greek Neo-Paganism as a New Religion', *Syntaxe*, No. 69, pp. 23–8 (trans. Maria Petsani).

Pearson, Joanne, Roberts, Richard H. and Samuel, Geoffrey (eds) (1998) *Nature Religion Today: Paganism in the Modern World*, Edinburgh: Edinburgh University Press.

Roy, Olivier (1998) 'The Divergent Ways of Fundamentalism and Islamism Among Muslim Migrants' in Peter B. Clarke (ed.) *New Trends and Developments in the World of Islam*, London: Luzac, pp. 41–58.

Singleton, Mark (2005) 'Salvation through Relaxation: Proprioceptive Therapy and its Relationship to Yoga', *Journal of Contemporary Religion*, 20(3), 289–305.

Stark, Rodney (1996) 'Why Religious Movements Succeed or Fail: A Revised General Model', *Journal of Contemporary Religion*, 11(2), 133–47.

Stark, Rodney and Bainbridge, Williams Sims (1985) *The Future of Religion: Secularization, Revival and Cult Formation*, Berkeley: University of California Press.

Stark, Rodney, Hamberg, Eva, and Miller, Alan S. (2005) 'Exploring Spirituality and Unchurched Religions in America, Sweden and Japan', *Journal of Contemporary Religion*, 20(1), 3–25.

Sutcliffe, Steven J. and Bowman, Marion (eds) (2000) *Beyond New Age*, Edinburgh: Edinburgh University Press.

Sviri, Sara (1993) 'Daughter of Fire by Irene Tweedie' in Elizabeth Puttick and Peter B. Clarke (eds) *Women as Teachers and Disciples in Traditional and New Religions*, Lampeter: Edwin Mellen Press, pp. 77–90.

Teilhard de Chardin, Pierre (1999) *The Human Phenomenon* (trans. by Sarah Appleton-Weber), Brighton: Sussex Academic Press.

Ter Haar, Gerrie (1998) *Halfway to Paradise: African Christians in Europe*, Cardiff: Cardiff Academic Press.

Van Wittering, Ineke (1998) 'Some Thoughts on Syncretism in Suriname Creole Migrant Culture, as Reproduced by Migrant Women in the Netherlands', in Peter B. Clarke (ed.) *New Trends and Developments in African Religions*, Westport, CT: Greenwood Press, pp. 223–45.

Walker, Andrew (1985) *Restoring the Kingdom: The Radical Christianity of the House Church Movement*, London: Hodder & Stoughton.

Wallis, Roy (1977) *Road to Total Freedom*, New York: Columbia University Press.

Watling, Tony (2005) 'Experiencing Alpha: Finding and Embodying the Spirit and Being Transformed – Empowerment and Control in a ('Charismatic') Christian Worldview', *Journal of Contemporary Religion*, 20(1), 91–108.

Wellbeloved, Sophia (2002) *Gurdjieff, Astrology and Beelzebub's Tales*, New York: Solar Bound Press.

Wilson, Bryan R. (1990) *The Social Dimensions of Sectarianism*, Oxford: Clarendon Press.

Wilson, Bryan R. (1991) '"Secularization": Religion in the Modern World' in Stewart Sutherland and Peter B. Clarke (eds) *The Study of Religion: Traditional and New Religion*, London: Routledge, pp. 195–208.

Wilson, Bryan R. and Dobbelaere, Karel (1994) *A Time to Chant: The Soka Gakkai Buddhists in Britain*, Oxford: Clarendon Press.

Wilson, Peter (1998) 'The Strange Fate of Sufism in the New Age' in Peter B. Clarke (ed.) *New Trends and Developments in the World of Islam*, London: Luzac, pp. 179–210.

Wuthnow, Robert and Cadge, Wendy (2004) 'Buddhists and Buddhism in the United States: The Scope of Influence', *Journal for the Scientific Study of Religion*, 43(3), 363–81.

Yao, Xinzhong (2001) 'Who is a Confucian Today? A Critical Reflection on the Issues Concerning Confucian Identity in Modern Times', *Journal of Contemporary Religion*, 16(3), 293–313.

York, Michael (1995) *The Emerging Network: A Sociology of the New Age and Neo-Pagan Movements*, Lanham, MD: Rowman & Littlefield.

Zahab, Miriam Abou and Roy, Olivier (2002) *Islamist Networks: The Afghan–Pakistan Connections*, London: Hurst.

Chapter 5

North America

The religious culture of North America shares much in common with Europe (see Chapter 4), with the settler societies of Australia and New Zealand (see Chapter 6), and increasingly with parts of Central and Latin America (see Chapter 9). However, notwithstanding the continent's global character and the ever-increasing pace of globalization, it remains distinctive and invites comparison with these cultures and many others.

Perceptions of North America are often lumpish and based as much on myth as on hard fact. One such is the widespread view of the continent, and in particular of the United States, as the world's main provider of New Religious Movements (NRMs). The reality is Europe (see Chapter 4), Africa (see Chapter 8) and parts of Asia, including India (Chapter 10) and Japan (Chapter 12), have been even more prolific in this regard.

North America remains, nonetheless, both the original home of, and host to, a range of NRMs and new types of spirituality, some of which have had a global impact. As we will see, many are highly derivative and marked by continuity, while others are strikingly original and have acted as catalysts for the creation of new religious structures, forms of membership, and styles of believing and practising religion.

In what follows, this theme of continuity and change will be discussed with reference to a select number of NRMs and new forms of holistic spirituality. Some of the NRMs considered are usually given only a brief mention in the literature and this is one reason for their inclusion here. Among these is Transcendentalism, which, while it derived many of its ideas from Emanuel Swedenborg (1688–1772) (see Chapters 4 and 6), was a major influence on the development of Positive Thinking, New Thought and New Age and the ever-increasing concern with religion as a tool of self-culture.

The rarely mentioned NRMs included in this chapter are also worth discussing for the light they shed on such important issues as the social and political causes of millenarianism, as will be seen in the sections on the Native American-, Islam- and Jewish-related NRMs. These include the Peyote cult, the Nation of Islam, and Messianic Judaism, respectively. We also examine how the belief in the coming of the millennium can sometimes become part of the intellectual ingredients of religious violence. This development is discussed in the section on Ufology with special reference to Heaven's Gate. Here we can identify not only a change in the traditional Ufological understanding of this belief but also how it was used to legitimate collective suicide (Balch and Taylor, 2002). Although the circumstances were different, a similar process unfolded in other movements, including the People's Temple and the Aum Shinrikyo movement (Chapter 12).

Scientology does not fit into the category of NRMs not usually discussed in the literature but is chosen here to illustrate, on the one hand, the continuity in ideas between nineteenth-century movements such as Christian Science, which developed the concept of religion as a tool for self-improvement, and, on the other, the therapeutic NRMs of the post-1950s era. While its core ideas on the nature of being human resemble those in circulation in nineteenth-century NRMs, Scientology at the same time innovated by rationalizing the path to salvation and in this respect moving away from 'standard religion' (Wilson, 1990: 273). Moreover, by examining the role this movement sought to play at Ground Zero after the September 11th tragedy (see below), Scientology also provides an example of how a highly controversial alternative religion comes to stand side by side in the public arena with mainstream religion.

In this chapter, as in others, the unit of analysis is not just new religion in isolation, for this would obscure its innovative characteristics. The framework of discussion has been extended, therefore, to include an examination of developments within the more established, 'standard' religions. Some of these, as in the case of Engaged Buddhism, parallel developments in, for example, Neo-Paganism and make for an interesting comparison between the two, the latter being represented here by the Reclaiming movement (see below).

Although within every religion there are movements dedicated to the preservation of the purity of the tradition that often mistake cultural elements for authentic religious ones, most of the older religions that have relatively recently established themselves in North America are undergoing, albeit at differing rates, a process of glocalization (Robertson, 1992) and the example given here of this process is the formation of American Buddhism (Queen and King, 1996). This development notwithstanding, Ethnic Buddhism still remains a part of the religious landscape. Within other religions, for example Judaism, there is a strong desire to adapt to the modern world and this has led to the emergence of such movements as Reconstructionist and Humanistic Judaism (see below).

The issue of religion and hegemony is also addressed briefly in this chapter – and in Chapter 9 – with reference to new forms of conservative Christian churches, including the Faith Ministries, and more generally with respect to the global spread of Neo-Evangelical and Neo-Pentecostal Christianity, which Berger (1999) believes is making for a world that is 'furiously religious'.

But is this happening primarily in the interests of religion or in the interests of the North American Capitalist way of life? Martin (1990) argues that this would be a simplistic way of explaining the appeal of the neo-Evangelicalism sweeping Latin America (see Chapter 9). The same question has been asked about Japanese NRMs (Cornille, 2000) and about certain Indian NRMs (see Chapter 10).

Historically, many of North America's NRMs were Christian and came from Europe (Wilson, 1990). They included pietist, introversionist groups that were seeking refuge there and, as segregated communities, were able to preserve much of the style, form and content of European spirituality. By contrast, North American NRMs in Europe and elsewhere, which were mostly Christian, have tended to be centralized and to attach great importance to recruitment, to the role of the laity and to the use of modern means of communication. If in the past Europe was the principal supplier of NRMs to North America, more recently Asia has taken over that role. As Wuthnow (1986: 1) has remarked:

> In the first three decades following the Second World War the United States and Canada witnessed the founding of more religious movements than at any other time in these nations' histories. It was the repeal of the final sections of the Oriental Exclusion Act in 1965 that turned the United States in particular into the principal mission territory in the Western world for many NRMs of Asian origin.

The nineteenth and first half of the twentieth century were also times of religious innovation, although on a smaller scale, and in certain respects can be said to have laid the foundations for many of the new developments in religion and spirituality of *c.*1950 to the present period, including therapeutic religion, religion of self-culture, and New Age religion and spirituality (Jenkins, 2000). Too much stress should not, however, be placed on the element of continuity for, although the seminal ideas of contemporary spirituality can be shown to have been present in the nineteenth or first half of the twentieth century, this does not mean that these more recent forms are not in any sense new. Contemporary New Age spirituality is far more widespread among the general population than was the case in the nineteenth century, and this and the manner in which it is now lived out, the enlargement and diversification of its philosophical and ritual content, and the purposes it is made to serve also differ greatly from the past. From these angles the New Age Movement (NAM) can be said to be new.

The 'new ethic' (below) that began to take shape in the period *c.*1950 to the present and that many of the NRMs and alternative forms of spirituality endorsed was an ethic which, if it did not entirely ignore, then greatly played down the long held understanding that 'divinity' or spiritual advancement could only be attained through suffering. Even fundamentalist or conservative

Protestantism of the 1940s and 1950s cannot be compared in every detail with that of, say, Jerry Falwell's Moral Majority of the 1980s. As Harding (2000: 163) has pointed out, the fundamentalist and conservative Protestants under Billy Graham, Carl Henry, Harold Okenga and others when they turned to public life 'disavowed their militancy as well as various forms of separation', while 'Jerry Falwell and his co-belligerents, on the other hand, took their militancy with them'. For Falwell it was time to 'speak harsh language, to make people mad' (ibid.).

NRMs are not only vehicles for and sometimes even producers of change, but also undergo change themselves. Some of the NRMs established in the 1960s would hardly be recognizable today by those who encountered them then. Some have taken on a completely new ethos and world view, turning from religious to secular or humanist movements, while others have gone in the opposite direction. As the history of movements such as the Nation of Islam indicates, frequent shifts in orientation toward the world are common. Moreover, multiple and apparently irreconcilable orientations are espoused simultaneously.

NRMs (c. 1820–c. 1950)

The period covered in this chapter – the early nineteenth century to the present – is best described from the perspective of religion as one of ever-increasing complexity and diversity with regard to the historic, mainstream Christian tradition, the more recently arrived Oriental religions and Islam and Judaism, Native American religion and alternative religion and spirituality.

The nineteenth and the first half of the twentieth century witnessed the emergence of several indigenous NRMs and new spirituality movements, some of which were influenced by European, Asian, and African movements. Several of these were to have an important impact on the religious life of North America and abroad, and include: Transcendentalism; Theosophy; Christian Science; New Thought; Mormonism; Millerism; Seventh Day Adventism; a variety of forms of the Native American Ghost Dance religion, Peyotism; the Nation of Islam; and the Worldwide Church of God and/or Armstrongism.

Transcendentalism, though never a numerically large movement, has been described as 'the single most provocative spiritual movement in American history' (Ahlstrom, 1985: 29). It is one of the most important nineteenth-century sources of, among other developments, the NAM, Positive Thinking and more generally holistic spirituality.

Transcendentalism arose out of Unitarianism as an anti-materialist, anti-rationalist, anti-enlightenment movement, under the inspiration of the former Unitarian minister and poet Ralph Waldo Emerson (1803–82). As Cole (1998) has shown, Emerson was greatly influenced by the talented religious innovator Mary Moody Emerson (1774–1863), through whom he came to know about the many and varied spiritual influences that were in vogue in alternative circles at the time. These included: mystical Catholicism; Oriental religions; Swedenborg's (1688–1771) teachings – in particular his doctrine of correspondences, according to which Nature is a symbol of the spirit; the Neo-Platonism of Jacob Boehme (1775–1642); and the Hermetic and/or Secret Traditions. All of these sources offered alternatives to the biblical orthodoxies with which Emerson and his friends had become increasingly disenchanted. The more he read, the more Nature became for Emerson a holy thing.

In his own mind a seer, prophet and teacher, Emerson was determined not to replace the biblical orthodoxies that he had rejected with a new set of dogmas and for this reason, and to encourage self-reliance, he adopted an aphoristic style of teaching and lecturing that was rich in metaphor and paradox. This led to frequent misunderstanding and confusion. Gurdjieff and Rajneesh (see Chapters 5 and 10), among other thinkers who have greatly influenced the development of contemporary forms of religion, adopted a similar rhetorical style, contradicting the day after what they had stated categorically to be true the previous day.

As was previously mentioned, Emerson's thought has greatly influenced several important currents in modern American alternative spirituality. For example, his lectures and seminars on the gnostic and esoteric aspects of religion, and on Eastern religions, proved a valuable source for such movements as Theosophy. His stress on self-realization, on the importance for individuals of fulfilling their potential, places him in the long tradition of 'Positive Thinking', which also influenced Christian Science and New Thought and concerned itself essentially with health, happiness and human well-being. Moreover, his critique of the rational and the instrumental culture of the time, which he believed was the main reason for the growing disenchantment and disillusionment that many felt so strongly, and for the alienation and disaffection arising from the pursuit of materialism, which he believed was undermining the relationship between human beings and Nature, all resonated with many who joined the Counter-culture or sought an alternative lifestyle in the world-transforming NRMs and New Age Movement of the 1960s, 1970s and 1980s.

A very different kind of movement, the Holiness movement, also a nineteenth-century phenomenon, arose out of Methodism and gave rise in its turn in the early years of the twentieth century to one of the most dynamic and global forms of contemporary Christianity, Pentecostalism. The mid-nineteenth century also witnessed the rise of Spiritualism, while also growing in popularity were movements teaching the power of mind over matter, including Christian Science, a system of thought developed by Mary Baker Eddy (1820–1910). The latter was a disciple of Phineas Parkhurst Quimby (1802–66) of Belfast, Maine, whose ideas and practices evolved into the New

Thought Movement, more a type of teaching than a religion. Quimby himself was greatly influenced by Franz Anton Mesmer's (1734–1815) theory of animal magnetism and/or electro-biology, which was concerned with the nature and causes of sickness. Mesmer's theory attributed illness to the obstruction of the putative magnetic field surrounding the body, while Quimby believed that the source of health was in the mind and it was from there that cures must begin.

Christian Science and similar movements are evidence of what Wilson (1990: 269) describes as 'the burgeoning of a more utilitarian approach to religion'. Good religion could be demonstrated to be good for the individual and then marketed as a commodity that could provide immediate salvation. Such religions shifted the emphasis away from the contemplative, devotional, congregational and communitarian aspects of religion to the harnessing and application of spiritual power to everyday problems of an emotional, physical and even material kind. The idea of religion as a means of progress and self-improvement became attractive and as material conditions improved the content and focus of salvation changed from a concern with life in the next world to life in this world. This nineteenth-century shift in emphasis became more pronounced after World War II (1939–45) and is one of the core characteristics of NRMs such as Scientology (see below). It is also a feature of Oriental spirituality.

Oriental religions and spirituality in North America date back to the nineteenth century. They began to spread more widely during the last quarter of that century through NRMs such as Theosophy, founded in New York in 1875 by Helena Petrovna Blavatsky (1831–91), Henry Steel Olcott (1832–1907) and William Q. Judge (1851–96). Theosophy's size today is around 5,000–10,000 members worldwide, and this is small compared with its membership in the last quarter of the nineteenth century when the movement was perhaps the most important channel in the spread of Eastern spirituality to the West. While the results of scholarly research on Indian religions was confined to the few, Theosophy made Hinduism and Buddhism much more accessible to a much larger number of Western seekers of Oriental spirituality. Also by facilitating access to esoteric ideas it played a key role in their modern revival.

The goal of making Oriental spirituality more accessible notwithstanding, Theosophy has long been regarded as a secretive movement, partly on account of its symbolism, drawn from Eastern mysticism and Western occultism, and for the reason that its core teachings are open only to a select few. The existence of a subgroup known as the Esoteric section strengthens this view of Theosophy. On the other hand, its teachings have been published in various books, including Blavatsky's *Isis Unveiled* (1877) and *The Secret Doctrine* (1889). In the latter volume, Blavatsky wrote of a common hidden core to all the world's religions and of the establishment of a universal brotherhood that would abolish all distinctions of creed, race, class, caste or gender. The volume also reveals her deep interest in exploring the paranormal powers inherent in individuals.

Theosophy began as a millenarian movement that was looking to discover the Maitreya or the future Buddha, whom it looked to as the one who would come as the World Teacher, and around 1900 it was believed that he had come in the person of a young Indian, Krishnamurti (1895–1986). When the latter publicly refused to be associated with this role, the millenarian dimension became less pronounced and a decline in influence and fall off in the membership followed.

Theosophical doctrine, which Blavatsky claimed to have channelled from the Ascended Masters and Mahatmas of Tibet, particularly Kuthumi and El Morya, both regarded as representatives of the wisdom of the ages, integrates Hindu and Buddhist mysticism with Western occultism. Blavatsky was later to claim that these Masters and Mahatmas formed the Great White Brotherhood that mediated between the divine and human spheres, and from time to time became incarnate for the purpose of creating new forms of religion and spirituality.

It was chiefly through Blavatsky and Olcott that the religious doctrines of karma and reincarnation became more widely known in the West, and today they are adhered to by over 20 per cent of the population of Europe. Theosophy's most important objectives are the formation of an inner core of the universal brotherhood of humanity in which everyone would be equal in every respect, the furtherance of the study of comparative religion, philosophy and science leading to an explanation of the unexplained laws of nature, and the uncovering of vast reserve of powers that lie hidden in human beings.

Among the new movements that owe much to Theosophy's ideas is Rudolf Steiner's (1861–1925) Christian Occult group, Anthroposophy, which broke away in 1913 for the reason that Theosophy attached too much importance to Eastern ideas and reduced the status of Jesus Christ to an avatar when in reality he was the central event of history.

The World Parliament of Religion held in Chicago in 1893 also provided an opening for Indian religions to reach the West. For example, it provided the Indian guru Swami Vivekananda (see Chapter 10) with a launching pad for the teaching of Vedanta in North America and the West. Few movements, however, exercised as much influence as Theosophy in the late nineteenth and early twentieth centuries in opening up Eastern spirituality to the West. Once regarded as revolutionary in this regard and with regard to its main objectives, Theosophy now exercises very little influence, and is considered to have lost its way.

New religious ideas were emerging in every area of North American life in the second half of the nineteenth century and early part of the twentieth century and I now turn to a consideration of how the indigenous peoples of North America altered their conception of salvation and became increasingly messianic, as Native lands came under pressure from white intrusion.

Native American New Religions

Native American religion through the New Age Movement has become something of a global phenomenon in recent times (see Chapter 2). Never static, it was undergoing new kinds of change in the late nineteenth century, changes brought about by the disruption of North American Indian society by white outsiders. That resistance movements should form was inevitable given, among other things, the overriding importance Indians attached to their sense of identity, first as members of a particular tribe and second as Native Americans. New resistance movements – many of them founded by prophets and inspired by a millenarian dream – emerged among the Wanapum Indians of eastern Washington, including that led by the Catholic-educated prophet Smohalla (b.1815?), who claimed visionary and healing powers. Smohalla's was a pacific resistance movement with a clear millenarian vision that protested against the transfer of Indian lands to whites and the removal of Indians to reservations. He predicted a cataclysm after which the ancestors would return to rid the land of the whites and ensure the restoration of the Indian way of life, at the centre of which was a prohibition against any form of violation of the earth, including the practice of agriculture.

Successive waves of Ghost Dance movements sprang up in different Indian communities in the 1870s, 1880s and 1890s also promising an early return of the dead and the restoration of the traditional way of life, in some cases after a catastrophe had wiped out the whites. Such movements attached great importance to the pursuit of more effective means of curing and the seeking of deeper personal relationships with the sacred through vision. The Ghost Dance, which originated in 1890 with the prophet Wovoka, who beheld God in a vision, is typical of others. This millenarian movement combining Christian and Native American notions swept across the Great Basin and Plains areas in the 1890s. Its message was that both the old way of life and the dead would return if Indians regularly performed dances. The movement ended with military action against the Sioux, which resulted in the death of Chief Sitting Bull and many of his soldiers.

The Peyote Cult arose in very similar conditions, espoused the same aims and used similar tactics of resistance to white encroachment on Indian land. This movement's principal object of ritual and devotion is the hallucinogen peyote, the small, juicy, turnip-like cactus button that grows in southern Texas and northern Mexico, which members consume and from which the movement takes its name. Although this kind of religious activity dates back many centuries, the spread of Peyotism among North American Indians does not appear to have started until the last quarter of the nineteenth century. Peyote became a new means of power and an important shamanistic weapon in the struggle against the intrusion of the more technologically advanced and militarily better-equipped white intruder. Peyotism, however, was not simply a desire to preserve the status quo or a negative reaction to all and every kind of change. As Wilson (1973) explains, 'It was a new reassertion of the Indian way, but it was also an adaptation of it to new conditions.'

From the 1870s, peyote rituals began to be developed – the main one being the all-night ritual in a tipi around a crescent-shaped earthen mound (a moon) and a ceremonial fire – and from the 1880s adepts of the new faith, among them the Kiowa and Comanches, spread the rituals and ideology from Oklahoma to the Plains. Healing, welfare, security, and hospitality were all good reasons for holding a ceremony. Peyote was the teacher, the guide to knowledge and wisdom, and as it created a mystical bond between adepts it at the same time fostered self-reliance. Peyote became a vehicle for the expression of a new sense of what it was to be Indian. On its travels it encountered various Christian denominations and, influenced by them, came to use the Bible and Christian prayers and to teach a version of Christian ethics. Known to have been practised in sixteen tribes by the end of the nineteenth century, by the 1960s Peyotism was considered to be the 'major religious cult of most Indians of the United States between the rocky Mountains and the Mississippi . . . and additionally in parts of southern Canada, the Great Basin and east-central California' (Wilson, 1973: 424).

Through millenarianism, Peyotism and similar movements offered an ideology of change that proved highly persuasive and attractive to communities whose social solidarity, status symbols and power over their own lives were being undermined mainly by modernization and outside forces with superior technology. Parallels to the peyote response to outsiders and modernization can be found elsewhere, including in late nineteenth-century Japan, which saw the rise of the highly influential millenarian movement Omoto (Great Origin), founded by the peasant woman Deguchi Nao in 1892 (see Chapter 12). The Melanesian Cargo cults are another example, and in Africa a plethora of pacific millenarian movements, some of them Islamic, arose during roughly the same period under the impact of colonial rule (see Chapters 6 and 8).

NRMs c.1950 to the present: anxiety in the midst of prosperity

While in the period prior to the 1950s much of the religious and spiritual innovation came from the northeast of the United States, in the period since 1950 there has been more variability. The areas most affected by NRMs in this second period have been the West Coast of the United States and Canada. These are the areas where membership of churches and of voluntary organizations is lower than elsewhere (Stark and Finke, 2000: 250–1). Reasons given for this are greater mobility and the consequent weakness of those kinds of family, social and cultural ties that usually limit the possibility of religious conversion. All of this suggests there is a strong link between a fall off in churchgoing among members of the mainstream denominations and religious innovation in the form of the rise of NRMs. However, Wuthnow's point (1982) should not be lost sight of that NRMs began to flourish in the United States from the 1950s to the 1980s, a period during which some of the more historic mainstream religions such as Catholicism, and well-established nineteenth-century sects such as the Seventh Day Adventists and the Mormons, were continuing to expand.

As we saw in a previous chapter (Chapter 1) numerous attempts have been made to account for the rise of these post-Second World War NRMs and earlier ones. Long before the 1950s, that perceptive, acute observer of American democracy and society Alexis de Tocqueville, writing in the 1830s, had commented on 'the restlessness of America in the midst of prosperity' (1969), a restlessness that was to grow and affect increasing numbers of individuals. Later in the same century others were to identify the same pheno-menon, albeit using different terms to describe it, including 'nervousness' (Beard, 1881). The reasons given for this restlessness were many, including the severe strain placed on relationships by the constant striving to do well, a striving which entailed a great deal of energy-sapping work. Among other reasons given are rapid change in every sphere of life including that of ideas and beliefs, the fragmentation of local communities and the consequent need for individuals to meet challenges in the national arena, largely unaided, for which they were very mostly unprepared. As in post-Second World War Japan, success was to be found in 'disembedding' (Giddens, 1991) from the local and moving away and on to the escalator.

It seemed that little was being done to cure this restlessness in a world in which a basically economic understanding of human life, utilitarian individualism, clashed with the pursuit of self-realization grounded in the notion of expressive individualism, which insisted that each person possesses a unique core of intuition and feeling that needs to be allowed to unfold and be expressed if that person is to reach fulfilment. In these conditions therapy assumed increasing relevance (Bellah et al., 1985) and it is no coincidence that one of the most successful of the post-1950s American NRMs, the Church of Scientology, began as an applied system of mental health.

Scientology began in the early 1950s when the therapeutic view of religion, discussed above in relation to Christian Science and similar movements, and the utilitarian and instrumentalist understanding of it were becoming more widespread, as was the interest in Oriental religions and spirituality. This therapeutic and instrumentalist view was evident in Christian theological circles such as the Theology of Glory and/or Success movement.

Scientology's founder, L. Ron Hubbard (1911–86), a former naval officer and science fiction writer, developed a prescription for a new type of therapy, which was called *Dianetics: The Modern Science of Mental Health*, com-pleted in 1950. Dianetics is but one example of many NRMs that did not actually begin as religions. There are also examples of movements that did start as religions only to become in time secular or purely humanistic enterprises, one example of which is the Ethical Society and another, Synanon.

Scientology became a Church in Los Angeles, California, in 1954, and in 1959 Saint Hill Manor in England became the worldwide headquarters of the movement. While it believes that human beings are basically good, Scientology, like Christian Science, does not accept that a person is her/his body. Its elaborate metaphysical system speaks instead of the individual as being occupied by a thetan, or being or soul, that is immaterial and immortal and potentially in possession of infinite creative powers. Scientology's purpose is to discharge those engrams, or impediments to rational thought, which arise from traumatic and painful experiences. The methods used – principally auditing – will, it is claimed, have the effect of enhancing an individual's capacity for effective communication with oneself and enable the thetan to function with increasing effectiveness. Eventually, with the thorough cleansing from engrams, the condition of 'exteriority', which is one of complete self-determination, is reached. This is in essence the salvation that Scientology claims to be able to provide. It is, of course, a this-worldly, 'secular' version of salvation in that it is acquired by the use of rational procedures and techniques, or in Scientology's language by 'standard tech'. We will return to Scientology later and to its application of its teachings at Ground Zero after September 11th 2001 (see below). For the time being it is sufficient to say that similar kinds of movement, with the same mission of improving health, sustaining and even heightening levels of motivation and guaranteeing success, have emerged since the 1950s.

NRMs are not all of an exact type. Others pursue more obviously world-transformation through self-transformation, among them Soka Gakkai, and yet others like Erhard Seminar Training or *est*, a number of Zen Buddhist associations and Pentecostal Christian Fellowships (Tipton, 1982) have enabled their members or clients to resolve the widely felt conflict experienced between instrumental and expressive individualism. For example, *est* proposed to its members, many of whom had joined the counter-culture of the 1960s, which had enthroned expressive individualism and dethroned instrumental individualism, 'a unified model of interaction – affectively expressive yet detached, therapeutically poised and engaging, and assertively self-interested' (ibid.: 208). Thus, the strategy consisted in utilizing these personally fulfilling and expressive ends to justify the routine work and goal achievement of mainstream public life. The *est* formula was 'work hard and achieve your goals', a formula which, according to Tipton, justified 1960s youth in dropping back into middle-class economic and social life and, while aiming for 'external success', retaining an interest in and concern for inner satisfaction.

What is most striking about North American NRMs is their variety. Although movements such as Soka Gakkai (Value Creation Society) had already begun to make ground in the United States before then, the increase in NRMs was greatly assisted by the repeal of the Asian Exclusion Act in 1965. This had the effect of opening up a new laboratory replete with techniques and methods for achieving personal wholeness and success in every walk of life, and for alleviating the stresses and strains imposed by the new economic order. The thinking that misleadingly associated religions with regions – Buddhism with Asia and Islam with the Middle East – changed with the greater internationalization of religions, even ethnic, non-proselytizing religions. Many ceased to associate particular religions with particular ways of life or political and cultural regions, and began to evaluate the psychological and social, as well as the philosophical and spiritual dimensions of religions, independently of their place of origin.

Soka Gakkai (Value Creation Society) offers one of the clearest examples of this process of disembedding. Virtually unknown in most of the West other than by name, this movement spread rapidly across the world from the 1960s with Japanese economic expansion, and within a decade of its establishment in North America Soka Gakkai had 'converted' large numbers of Caucasian Americans (Hammond and Machacek, 1999). Its capacity for efficient organization, its concern to be inclusive – the movement set up a national diversity committee 'to sensitize its leadership to gays, minorities, and other marginalized groups' (Chappell, 2000: 324) – its emphasis on social solidarity, and its enthusiasm for disseminating its message of human revolution all contributed greatly to this success.

Ufology and Occultism

Modern Ufology, whose beginnings date back to the late nineteenth century, is a diverse phenomenon containing specific kinds of Ufological vision. Writings about UFOs appeared in the nineteenth century and included *Oahspe* (1882), by John Ballou Newbrough, which provides a description of celestial angels living in spiritual universes who travel the skies in ethereal ships. The first popular sighting of UFOs in North America occurred in 1947, and with this began claims by those interested that they had been the recipients of telepathic messages from spiritually and technologically advanced 'star brothers'. Some of these beings are intent on giving earthlings advice about how to prevent catastrophe resulting from the mismatch between the high level of technological advance made compared with the low level of spiritual achievement. Reports spoke of alarm and the possible catastrophe that could result from humankind's access to atomic and nuclear power and its lack of the necessary spiritual resources to handle this power safely.

Much of the thinking behind Ufology resembles that found in esoteric movements such as Theosophy. It is debated as to how widespread such thinking is. While Wuthnow (1986) detected a decline in interest in the occult and more generally the esoteric in North America, others have observed a remarkable flourishing of what they term occult belief systems since the 1950s. This development was apparently so evident in literature that it prompted the author and critic George Steiner to conclude about the mentality of the late twentieth century:

> In terms of money and time spent, of the number of men and women involved to a greater or lesser degree, in terms of the literature produced and the institutional ramifications, ours is the psychological and social climate most infected by superstition, by irrationalism, of any since the Middle Ages and perhaps, ever since the time of crisis in the Hellenistic world.
>
> (citation in Clarke, 1992: 4)

Support for this view comes in various forms including the seemingly unquestioning belief in countless theories about all aspects of human life and civilization that go unsupported by empirical evidence. Daniken's theory that traces the origins of our present social system to the biochemical aptitudes and skills of advanced sophisticated aliens is one such theory. The existence of countless numbers of occult belief systems in addition to Ufology, including various 'schools' of witchcraft, of Hermetic and Eastern lore, dowsing, palmistry, magical healing, astrology, and of other forms of involvement in magical and supernatural phenomena, including channelling, Wicca and Satanism, furnishes further support for Steiner's opinions.

Occult and Satanist beliefs are sometimes linked in several different ways, from small groups, who become involved for highly questionable, even nefarious, ends, to church-like organizations with their own biblical sources such as Anton Szandor LeVey's Church of Satan, which is based on his *The Satanic Bible*. While the latter type in particular gained in popularity in the 1960s and 1970s, the degree of interest and involvement in this phenomenon was much less than the Anti-Cult Movement (ACM) and several Christian organizations, particularly the Evangelical and Fundamentalist Christian churches, contended (Richardson *et al.*, 1991).

An apocalyptic, millenarian element is present in many Ufological movements, some of which await an imminent 'Big Beam' unto the Star Brothers' ships before the earth is according to some destroyed, or according to others cleansed, and yet according to others restored to its pristine state of wholeness and integrity. Movements of this kind and others are often an attempt to respond to contemporary anxieties. From this vantage one can understand the preoccupation of some Ufology groups with the apocalyptic and millenarian theme of the Earth suffering from excessive human pollution which will result in a series of disasters in the form of earthquakes, floodings and meltdown at the poles. Before this happens, it is intended that an 'Evacuation' or 'Lift off' will be organized so that earth can be returned to the state of a perfect garden ready to be inhabited for a period of a thousand years by the spiritually transformed, who will inhabit an 'ethereal' or 'half-ethereal body' invisible to normal sight.

Some contemporary Ufology movements hold to a different vision of the apocalypse and the millennium, including the previously mentioned Heaven's Gate, which was distinguished chiefly by its lack of optimism about the future. This movement came to the world's attention on March 22nd 1997 when all thirty-nine members from their base in an exclusive suburb of San Diego, California, returned by means of a carefully planned suicide to what they described as 'Level Above Human in Distant Space'.

Hybridity is clearly a feature of this movement, as it is of Ufology movements generally, and this can be seen from its teachings. Founded in the 1970s by Marshall Applewhite (1931–97), Heaven's Gate taught a unique blend of Ufology and Christianity, the essentials of which speak of a race of beings who lived at a higher level, the 'Next Evolutionary Level Above Human'. This race interacted periodically with humans and had sent Jesus, its 'Captain', as its representative to earth. 'Adversarial space races', known as Luciferian, exterminated the Captain, whose message was corrupted by his Church. However, those belonging to the 'Next Evolutionary Level' remained intent on raising those on earth to the next level.

Thus, like other Ufology groups, Heaven's Gate placed great stress on the imminent advent of the millennium but unlike others it gave little or no importance to the notion of 'Heaven on Earth', or to the earth as a venue where spirtual beings from the celestial spheres would come for reasons of spiritual advancement. Further, with its exclusive focus on leaving a disintegrating planet, it paid no heed to the arrival of extra-terrestrial cargo. Balch and Taylor (2002) offer a detailed historical analysis of the 'process of progressive, deliberate disconnection from society' that led this 'totalistic movement' to the conviction that the body was merely a suit of clothes and that suicide would mark the beginning of new lives.

It became extremely important to escape this earth by the end of the millennium (2000), as it was not only believed to be collapsing but was thought to be about to be 'spaded over' or annihilated by the next level inhabitants who, Applewhite was convinced, would arrive when the Hale-Bopp, trailed by a spaceship, was sighted. The collective suicide previously mentioned followed in line with the belief that the Next Level – a genderless world without desire – could not be accessed in the physical body, whereas it had originally been held that the only way to enter the Kingdom of Heaven was in a 'living physical body' (Balch and Taylor, 2002: 209). A new kind of body would be provided instead for the incoming soul. In all of this anticipation there is a complete absence – and this is unusual – of a belief in a restored Earth or millennial paradise where the spiritually refined would dwell in perfect happiness.

Although they differ in detail, the vast majority of Ufology movements in North America and elsewhere display a concern for the creation of a viable synthesis of science and/or technological and spiritual and/or religious knowledge.

Reclaiming as politically engaged Wicca/Witchcraft

The inclusive nature of the NAM (see Chapter 2) means that it shares much in common with a whole range of religious and spirituality movements, including Wicca and/or Witchcraft and Neo-Paganism. The spirituality of some Wiccans and Neo-Pagans, however, tends to be more Goddess centred than that of the New Age and criticizes what is seen as the patriarchal character found in some of the latter's ideas and expressions. Moreover, the New Age belief that 'darkness' is evil and to be eradicated conflicts with the Neo-Pagan view that it is necessary for life. Neo-Paganism is also critical of what it sees as New Age rejection of matter and of its concentration on the discarnate, the pure, that which has been unsullied.

It would, however, be wrong to create the impression that Neo-Pagan and Wiccan movements are rigidly exclusive on matters of belief and practice. Nor does one Wiccan/Witchcraft movement necessarily think of itself as in full possession of the truths of that belief system. For example, the Wiccan movement Reclaiming, founded by the well-known American Witch Starhawk, while claiming to be a separate Wiccan tradition, does not claim to have a monopoly of Wiccan truth. Moreover, it encourages members to look outside the movement for knowledge and enlightenment. Many of its teachers belong not only to Reclaiming but also to one or more different movements, and some of its practitioners also belong to such movements as Santeria (see Chapter 9). What Reclaiming tends to do is adapt, where it believes this can be of benefit, the techniques learnt from other movements and to incorporate them in its own repertoire. A Goddess-based witchcraft movement, it leaves the question of the reality or otherwise of the deity up to the individual practitioner. Reclaiming theology teaches that myriads of both female and male deities arose from the act of creation. However, rather than focusing on its own theology, it places the stress on what it shares in common with the rest of the Wiccan tradition.

As an eco-feminist version of the Witchcraft movement, Reclaiming appeals strongly to feminists, environmentalists and humanists. It had its beginnings in a civil action in the 1970s known as the Diabolo Canyon protest, which attempted to prevent the construction of a nuclear power plant. It continues to attach great importance to political activism and regards this as an important bonding element. It teaches magic to political activists and political activism to the practitioners of magic. Spiral dances, one of Reclaiming's principal techniques, have been performed at protest meetings against the World Trade Organization (WTO) and other agencies of globalization, and classes are provided for cells such as Earth First on the issues in locations where political protests are envisaged. Literature is also made available, including such writings as Starhawk's *Dreaming the Dark* and *Webs of Power*, which offer a Reclaiming explanation of the notion of individual empowerment and a faith-based critique of the current practice of Capitalism. This political activity is seen to flow from faith and also to act as a form of social cement, in that it binds the Reclaiming community together and the community to the wider society.

The discussion now turns briefly to the rise of NRMs and their response to September 11, 2001.

NRMs and September 11th 2001

The attack by Al-Qaeda (see Chapter 7) on the World Trade Center on September 11th 2001 gave rise to diverse responses from religions both old and new, at least in the sense of providing different interpretations of the meaning and significance of that tragic event. The message put out by many of the former was one of peace. This was also the message of non-conventional religions including Scientology, while the Earth Link Mission (ELM) (Cusack and Digance, 2003) offered a type of New Age interpretation of the event, which presented it as the dissemination of negative energies which would have in time a positive outcome. The New Age guru David Spangler spoke of humans contributing to hatred and violence and the channelled being the 'Soul of America' taking on, in a sacrificial way, a portion of the negative energy generated by such hatred and violence and transmuting it, hopefully, although not necessarily before revenge had been taken, into a spirit of love and healing. Such responses contain no thoughts of a clash of civilizations or religions but of conflict between negative and positive energies.

While Scientology, New Age and other NRMs saw a silver lining in September 11th 2001, it is their practical response to the tragedy that has received most attention. That response, as Cusack and Digance (2003) have shown, took on, in the case of Scientology, one of the very few NRMs to become directly involved practically, the provision of therapy and solace to those directly affected. Elsewhere, for example, in Japan at the time of the Kobe earthquake in 1995 when 5,000 people died, NRMs likewise became engaged and sought to provide various kinds of material and spiritual relief.

Scientology decided to become involved directly in the relief operation at the site of the World Trade Center by offering through its Volunteer Minister Programme (VMP), formally established in 1976 and open to all including non-members, a counselling service and a specific Scientology kind of therapy known as 'assists' for the police, firemen and all those engaged in clearing the site at Ground Zero. Assists consist of two basic types, contact and touch assists, which are similar to the laying on of hands and have as their purpose to help individuals confront physical and emotional difficulties. While Scientology emphasized that the most valuable help it could offer was Scientology technology in the form of assists, it also, through the VMP, whose members could be recognized by their yellow uniforms, set up aid centres to supply food and water to the rescued. As Cusack and Digance point out, this kind of involvement by a non-conventional, new, 'secular' religion placed Scientology in the company of long established major Christian denominations, and other mainstream religions, all of which, following their traditional practice in times of tragedy and disaster, offered spiritual, psychological and material help to the victims, their relatives and friends, and the police, fire service and ambulance staff at Ground Zero.

Scientology's involvement at Ground Zero was not appreciated by everyone. Opportunism was one word used to describe it, and the National Mental Health Association (NMHA) in one of its news releases of September 17th 2001 tried to warn people to beware of the Church's claims to be mental health professionals and spoke of it using the tragedy to recruit new members. For its part, Scientology posted on its own website letters received from the police and fire brigade services acknowledging the contribution it had made at Ground Zero.

I now turn to new developments within mainstream religions.

New Christian and Christian-related movements and the expansion of Western interests

The discussion that follows regarding New Christian and Christian-related movements and the spread of Western interests could be had regarding Japanese or Chinese or South Asian NRMs and the spread of Japanese, Chinese, or South Asian material and cultural interests, and indeed has been. As we will, Cornille (2000) has discussed the question of the role of Japanese NRMs in the spread of Japanese nationalism. Here for reasons of space, most of the comment is limited to Christian NRMs and Christian-related movements in North America.

One of the most significant religious changes in North America during the period under review, and particularly since the mid-1980s, has undoubtedly been the re-enfranchisement of conservative, evangelical Christianity, which is essentially Neo-Conservative Evangelical Christianity. Paradoxically, this development gathered strength at a time when fears were mounting that civil liberties were being endangered by post-September 11th 2001 concerns with security. Such Christianity is not, of course, a homogeneous grouping. Although the oratorical styles vary greatly, what above all else creates the impression of its unity is the all-pervasive, conservative Christian moral rhetoric. In reality the movement is characterized by hybridity and fluidity and offers many distinct ways of being born again, from those advocated by the Moral Majority to those of the Christian Coalition. As to sources of unity, Harding (2000: 274) identifies several including 'a shared, yet variously inflected folk theology of Jesus' and 'the multifarious and shifting field of millennial theories'.

Positing a causal link between moral rectitude and political, economic and social well-being and security – as do Muslim Fundamentalists – Evangelicals and Fundamentalists in the United States use the most advanced technology and all the conventional means available to acquire huge sums of money, including national telecasts, door to door fund raising campaigns and direct mail solicitations. These methods have raised large amounts of money for the building of schools and the distribution of literature in order to promote Evangelical values and to oppose liberal causes such as the Equal Rights Amendment (ERA) proposals of the 1980s, abortion, same sex unions, and the right to rely on medical opinion to end the life of the terminally ill (the Sciavo case of March 2005 offers a graphic illustration of this last point). All of these measures are seen as weakening, if not destroying, America.

Evangelical and Fundamentalist Christianity not only produced the already mentioned Moral Majority Movement but several others, including the Toronto Blessing – a global movement inspired by John Wimber's Vineyard Ministry (Hunt, 1995), which began in a church, the Airport Vineyard Church, at the end of the runway in Toronto (Richter, 1996) – and the Faith Movement, which consists of numerous ministries that have acquired a wide influence beyond the United States in many and different cultural conditions. The Airport Vineyard Church in Toronto, a charismatic church, is based on the notion of a 'time blessing' from God such as that referred to in Acts 3:19.

The early growth of this movement was unprecedented. In 1994 alone it was visited by over 4,000 clergy, many of whom arrived from outside Canada, and it soon became associated internationally with such uncontrolled, ecstatic experiences as 'spiritual drunkenness', frantic running on the spot that included head-shaking, jerking and bowing, sobbing and weeping, and collapsing to the ground after being 'slain in the Spirit'. This charisma of the Spirit, while attractive to many, has generated, not unexpectedly, considerable tension with those who believe in the fundamental importance to spiritual devotion of order and decorum. As Percy (2005) has shown, although this charismatic fellowship has lost much of its popularity and influence, it continues to offer a viable spiritual resource within global revivalism.

This global success, and that of Neo-Evangelical Christianity generally, has been interpreted as part of the expansion of what Bourdieu (1977) termed 'cultural capital'. The advance and success of Christianity during the era of European imperialism has been interpreted in a similar way, that is, in terms of its role as the harbinger of Western political domination, civilization and progress.

This line of interpretation locates movements, such as those Neo-Evangelical movements engaged in missionary activity overseas, within what is termed 'the hegemonic model'. It sees them as a vital part of the process of advancing Western cultural domination and indirectly promotes its economic, political, military and scientific supremacy. A similar argument has been developed as was previously mentioned with respect to Japanese New Religions (Cornille, 2000). The teachings and activities of Evangelicals and Fundamentalists are, thus, to be read as justifying all those essential elements of Capitalism that 'Christian' America, and the materially successful and prosperous 'Christian' West generally, stands for: the free market, the ethic of consumerism, and the entrepreneurial spirit.

Much criticism can be made of the 'hegemonic model', including its tendency to treat local cultures as passive, easily manipulated recipients of outside influences. The reality is that Evangelical and Fundamentalist perspectives are just as likely as any other religious ideology to be, if not turned on their head, then substantially modified by local conditions. The global is localized to produce 'glocalization' (Robertson, 1992). In Brazil, in this writer's experience, members of movements of Evangelical churches provide some of the sharpest and most lucid critiques of the free-market economy from a local perspective, and of its failure to advance the material well-being of their communities and country.

Another example of 'glocalization' – this time in reverse – is the rise of 'Americanized' Buddhism.

'Americanized' and other 'new' forms of Buddhism

The influence of a religion can be much greater than its numbers might suggest. The research, already mentioned, by Wuthnow and Cadge (2004) examined some of the broader influences of Buddhism in the USA and considered, in particular, those factors that made for contact with Buddhism, those that led to people's thinking of religion or spirituality being affected by Buddhism, and those that made people receptive to Buddhism. As to the number of Buddhists in the United States, the question with which Wuthnow and Cadge begin their account, they suggest that between 0.7 and 1.9 per cent of people in the United States 'might be sufficiently affiliated with Buddhism to qualify as Buddhist' (2004: 364). That translates numerically as between 1.4 and 4 million. Of these, many are immigrants or descendants of Asian immigrants, although a large number of native-born Americans became involved with Buddhism in the 1960s, 1970s and 1980s, and even before then many of the more highly educated Caucasian Americans had become involved with Zen Buddhism (Melton and Jones, 1994). While they accept that the number of Americans who claim to be very or somewhat familiar with the teachings of Buddhism is difficult to estimate, Wuthnow and Cadge (2004: 365) report from the national survey they conducted in 2002 that '14 per cent of the public claimed to have had a great deal or fair amount of "personal contact" with Buddhists and that 30 per cent claimed to be very or somewhat familiar with Buddhist teachings'. Thus, between 25 and 30 million Americans have either had contact with Buddhists or Buddhist teachings and have therefore been influenced by Buddhism.

Moreover, the impression of those who are familiar with Buddhism is 'generally favourable' (2004: 365).

Wuthnow and Cadge were concerned, as we have seen, to understand the processes whereby such influence has come about and to question theories that explain religious success and failure (Stark and Finke, 2000) by emphasizing the role of rational choices made by consumers, and claims based on such theories as strict religions are the most successful in a competitive religious market. They suggest that this approach to explanation tends to overemphasize demand and the importance of strictness. In examining the growing influence on American society of Buddhism, what they deem to have been of greater significance than either demand or strictness is Buddhism's relationship in the United States to existing institutional structures that mediate its teachings or some aspect of them to the rest of society. Being non-doctrinal and inclusive, Buddhism is capable of being embedded, piecemeal, in numerous institutions, including churches, synagogues and holistic and alternative health movements, and of making use of the personnel of these institutions, and in this way its influence spreads across society.

While this institutional approach to understanding the spread of Buddhism's influence offers a corrective to existing theories that highlight the role of markets and the rational choices made by consumers who use those markets in accounting for patterns of religious growth and decline, it would seem to need further refinement by, in particular, introducing the question that would invite respondents to state whether or not they perceive Buddhism to be a religion. Research elsewhere (Carpenter and Roof, 1995) shows that either ambiguity or uncertainty about a new movement's self-definition – whether it is a religion or simply a philosophy – can greatly assist its chances of success in a new environment. Moreover, certain Buddhist schools in Brazil (Clarke, 2000) define themselves not as religions but as humanistic philosophies, partly for the reason that they are found to be less threatening and consequently evoke a more positive response from outsiders. A second point that can be made in relation to the research by Wuthnow and Cadge, which their account of the reasons for Buddhism's growing influence ought perhaps to consider, is the highly active missionary dimension – not necessarily carried on through the use of aggressive proselytizing techniques – of much of the new Buddhism in America and elsewhere (Learman, 2005).

These qualifications notwithstanding, there can be little doubt that, as Wuthnow and Cadge (2004) conclude, Buddhism in the United States, and, we can add, in North America as a whole, exercises an ever greater influence. Moreover, it is generally seen as consisting of two main forms, one Asian and the other American (Prebish and Tanaka, 1998), a distinction based mainly on the tendency for ethnic factors to determine the composition of the practitioners in the various temples. Recently this situation has been changing.

Several attempts have been made to create unity and co-operation among Buddhist schools and churches themselves, including the founding of the association of Buddhist Churches of America (BCA) in 1944 for this purpose. But little was achieved.

The major inroad into mainstream American society was made by D. T. Suzuki's (1870–1966) writings and by Zen. This was followed in the 1960s by the previously mentioned Nichiren Buddhist lay movement Soka Gakkai (Value Creation Society), the largest Japanese NRM in Japan, and also in North America, Europe and elsewhere. As we have already seen, Soka Gakkai enjoyed most of its success in the United States in the 1960s and 1970s, though it probably never reached anything like the 200,000 members it is often said to have attracted during those decades. At present there are between 50,000 and 70,000 members across North America. Several of the Tibetan or Vajrayan schools of Buddhism established in North America, including those founded by the previously mentioned Chogyam Trungpa (see Chapter 4), are multi-ethnic in composition. Others are still mainly composed of a single ethnic group, and among these are the Taiwanese lay Buddhist movements Foguangshan and Tzu Chi (see Chapter 13).

This very mixed picture notwithstanding, Queen (2000a) nevertheless contends that an authentic form of 'American Buddhism', which is 'not merely a composite of the many Buddhisms-in-America', is evident. He writes:

> The marks of this new Buddhism transcend both the plurality of traditions that co-exist here – that is virtually all of the Asian schools and lineages living side by side – as well as the great divide that Charles Prebish called the 'two Buddhisms' twenty years ago, that is the religion of Asian American Buddhist immigrants and the religion of Euro-American converts and sympathizers.
>
> (Queen, 2000a: 20)

Queen maintains that the main stimulus behind the development of this new form of Buddhism has been the worldwide emergence of 'Engaged Buddhism', the three principal features of which are: democratization, pragmatism and engagement. The first, also a marked feature of the new Buddhism of Japan (see Chapter 12), consists of a de-emphasis on hierarchy and the importance of the role of monks, and a stress on lay practice and gender equality. By pragmatism is meant the relatively greater importance attached to ritual practices, ethical activities, and meditation, and their benefits to the individual, than to belief – 'in essence', says Queen (2000a: 21), 'a new agnosticism'. By engagement is understood the widening of the meaning of spiritual practice to include 'service and activism' of an altruistic kind that is directed at the greater well-being of family, friends and society as a whole, including its institutions and the environment. This definition of engagement contains the core features of 'Engaged Buddhism', a global phenomenon, and described as 'a new vehicle for Buddhist spirituality' or, according to Queen, citing Ambedkar, a '*Navayana*' or 'fourth *yana*' or path/vehicle (2000a: 18).

Queen accepts that, while this and other evidence exists for his notion of American Buddhism, there is also evidence to support the continued existence of Prebish's 'two Buddhisms' thesis. Queen perhaps underestimates how ethnic Buddhism in the United States, whether it be of Japanese, Chinese or South Asian origin, remains. This is suggested by studies of the ethnic composition of the *sanghas* or communities, many of which are predominantly either Asian or Caucasian American. On the ethnic composition of the Taiwanese movement Foguangshan, a movement with more temples around the world than any other Buddhist movement, Chandler (2005: 167) states: 'It is safe to say that ninety nine per cent of the members of BLIA [the Buddha Light International Association, a lay branch of the movement] are ethnically Chinese.' And Huang, writing of another international Taiwanese Buddhist movement, Tzu Chi (Compassion Relief Merit Society) (see Chapter 13), notes that, of its 50,000 members in the USA, the majority of members by far are from Taiwan and the next largest number from China (2005: 195). The point to note here is that these are by comparison with most Buddhist movements in the United States numerically large movements.

Moreover, a number of what were once relatively highly integrated temples have felt it necessary to facilitate greater choice for different ethnic groups of the same temple, permitting separate worship if so desired. Even those movements such as Soka Gakkai, with an established track record in integrating its membership ethnically, and widely perceived as an 'American form of Buddhism' both philosophically and organizationally, have had to make certain allowances for situations in which different ethnic groups prefer to practise separately. Differences, seemingly small, over, for example, the position adopted for chanting – whether it was essential to recite the *gongyo* sitting on the ground, the Japanese way, or whether seated on a chair was permissible, the preferred the American way – led to the use of separate temples in San Francisco (Clarke, 2000: 283). In this case, as in others, religious divisions rarely seem to begin with major doctrinal or philosophical disagreements, although these may well underlie the divide or be brought in to justify it.

Islam and new Islam-derived movements

Estimates of the number of Muslims in North America, like those of Muslims in Western Europe, vary. A reasonably reliable estimate for the United States is around 6 million (Stone, 1991: 29). This total is made up mainly by African-American, Middle-Eastern, a majority of whom are Iranian, and Eastern European Muslims. The largest concentrations of Muslims in the United States are in California, Illinois and New York, and of the many Muslim organizations, including organizations that call themselves Muslim, the largest is the Nation of Islam (NOI). This is the only organization to generate mass appeal based on its own version of Islam's teachings, its championing of black nationalism, and the unity of all black people and their distinctiveness from, and superiority to, whites (Taylor, 1998: 177).

The NOI has historical links with several earlier religious movements that preached the message of Black Nationalism, including the Moorish Science Temple founded in 1913 in Newark, New Jersey, by the African-American Noble Ali Drew (1866–1922) from North Carolina. Drew believed that connections could be established between African-American and Oriental peoples, and claimed that he was a reincarnation of the Prophet Muhammad, an event heralded by Marcus Garvey among others. In 1927, after moving to Chicago, he produced the Holy Koran of the Moorish Temple of Science.

Drew, who died in mysterious circumstances, was succeeded by Wallace D. Fard (pronounced Fa-ROD) (c.1887–1934), whose ethnic origins and rise to the leadership remain largely unknown, but who claimed to come from Mecca. Fard used the Bible, which he saw as a stepping-stone to the Qur'ān, as the basis for persuading his African-American listeners that Islam not Christianity was the true religion of Africa and Asia.

The NOI under Fard began organizationally as a House Church until a temple in the form of a hall was hired in Detroit and named the Allah Temple of Islam. Fard's rhetoric became increasingly anti-white as he encouraged African-Americans to study and get to know what he described as the glorious history of the African-Asian races. The end of Fard's leadership was as mysterious as its beginnings. He was arrested, imprisoned in relation to the conviction of a sacrificial killing by a member in 1932 and then ordered out of Detroit. He eventually disappeared. After his death, Fard was deified by the members as Allah.

Elijah Muhammad (1897–1975), son of a Baptist minister from Georgia and one of Fard's officers, controversially assumed the leadership and took the title of Prophet and 'sole messenger of Allah'. A leadership struggle soon followed and the movement split, some members moving with Elijah Muhammad to Chicago, where he became known as 'Spiritual Head of Muslims in the West', 'Divine Leader' and 'Reformer'. His ministers referred to him as 'The Messenger of Allah to the Lost Found Nation of Islam in the Wilderness of North America'. He named his faction 'Muhammad's Temples of Islam'.

In 1942, Elijah Muhammad was imprisoned for preaching that African-Americans had an obligation not to serve in the armed forces, and, while in prison, he began what became one of the NOI principal activities, the conversion of prisoners and former prisoners. In was in prison that Malcolm Little, alias Malcolm X Shabazz, from Omaha, Nebraska, also son of a Baptist minister, was converted and recruited in 1947. A former follower of Marcus Garvey (see Chapter 9), Malcolm X experienced the worst of racism as he witnessed the Ku Klux Klan burn down his father's home when he was six years old. He later encountered his father's dead body mangled by a train on the railway tracks near where he lived.

Although Malcolm X was later appointed by Elijah Muhammad to be his personal assistant, the two men did not always agree. While Elijah Muhammad aimed his message mainly at African-Americans, Malcolm X sought to turn the NOI into a thoroughgoing Black Nationalist movement by involving Africans worldwide. Then a long running dispute with Elijah Muhammad concerning the propriety of the comment Malcolm X made on the assassination of President John F. Kennedy in 1963 eventually led to the latter withdrawing and founding the Mosque Inc. and its secular counter-part, the Organization of Afro-American Unity. Malcolm X's perception of whites changed as a result of his travels to Mecca and elsewhere, which convinced him that they were not intrinsically racist. He was assassinated in February 1965, one of the assassins being a member of the NOI.

The transition to a more orthodox Muslim community by the NOI came with the confirmation, after much wrangling and opposition, of Wallace D. Muhammad as the successor to Elijah Muhammad, who died in 1975. The changes involved giving the NOI a new name, the 'World Community of al-Islam in the West', calling ministers imams, and reducing Fard's status from Allah to that of an ordinary mortal. Wallace also placed less stress on the ideology of Black Nationalism. These reforms created further division, with Louis Farrakhan (b.1933), then an imam, from the Bronx, New York, leaving the movement with the intention of reconstituting the old NOI. Though other factions also emerged to restore the NOI, Farrakhan, who has acquired a reputation for anti-Jewish rhetoric and who is strongly opposed to Christianity, though not to Black Christians, has done most to refashion the movement in line with the teachings of Elijah Muhammad.

NOI teachings are many and complex, and the following is but the briefest of summaries. The teachings given here are those that were formulated under Elijah Muhammad. The NOI believes in a cyclical notion of God, whom it does not consider to be immortal. Every 25,000 years one God dies and passes on his knowledge and 'godship' to another. There is a 'God of gods' and different gods perform different functions, one creating the sun, another the moon, and so on. Gods resemble human beings and like the Greek gods and the Traditional gods of Africa they marry, enjoy normal human pleasures and make mistakes, such as marrying a non-African woman. The first God was a man and all Gods are 'Blackmen' (Taylor, 1998: 190). Human beings are divided into two races, one black and one white, the former being self-created, and the 'Original Man' and the 'maker and owner of the universe'. The authentic, original religion of the Black race was Islam, and all Black men are 'god'. Allah is the supreme Blackman and, therefore, God of gods. Black people are believed to be the 'descendants of the Asian black nation and of the tribe of Shabazz' (ibid.). The beginning of all of this creative activity was 60 trillion years ago. Whites, who are evil by nature, were invented by a Dr Yakub, of the black race, and were taught to rule that race. Their religion is one of self-interest, and their rule will last for 6,000 years.

White rule will end with the arrival of a prophet sent by Allah – prophets are sent frequently by Allah – to predict 'the coming of God', who will appear at the 'end of the world', which is understood by NOI to mean the 'end of the white race'. Allah is believed to have come to Wallace Fard from Mecca on July 4th 1930, and from that point on Fard took the place of Allah, and Elijah Muhammad became his prophet in the place of the Prophet Muhammad. It was Elijah's mission to teach Africans the 'knowledge of Self', which is the essence of their redemption, their real identity as members of the Nation of Islam, their true place of origin, Asia/Africa, their true God, Allah, and their true religion, Islam. In authentic millenarian fashion, all of this is taught in relation to this world, with little speculation about the afterlife.

As NOI became more orthodox there was an increase in membership. It has grown from a small group of some 8,000 African-Americans in the 1950s to around 2 million members today.

Other growth areas – again the groups involved are not always orthodox Muslim – include various forms of Sufism or Islamic mysticism. Hermansen (1998) has divided Sufi groups into 'hybrids' and 'perennials', the former having a direct and exclusive relationship with Islam, and the latter interpreting Sufism in much wider and more general terms as predating Islam and including many religious, spiritual and even humanistic traditions. The 'hybrid' movements attract on the whole non-Euro-Americans and are more recent than the 'perennials', which appeal more to the Euro-American population. The former include the African Sufi brotherhoods, such as the Tijaniyya, which originated in Algeria in the late eighteenth century, the Murid (see Chapter 8) founded in Senegal by Ahmadu Bamba in the early years of the twentieth century, and active in France and Italy, and the Bawa Muhaiyaddeen Fellowship founded in Philadelphia in the United States in 1971 by the elderly, French-speaking Senegalese Shaykh of the same name. Other 'hybrids', some of which are also present in Europe, include the Turkish Helveti-Jerrahi Order, a dervish order, of Shaykh Muzaffer Ozak, one of whose disciples, Tosun Bayrak, began teaching in New York in 1980. Later, centres were opened in San Francisco and in other American cities. This movement, like the Mevlevi dervish order, spreads its message not only through teaching but also through music and dance.

Most of these 'hybrid' Sufi Orders belong to Sunni or orthodox Islam. There are also Shi'ite movements founded by Iranians and Iraqis in the United States. An example is the Nimatullahi order of Iranian origin, which was started in the United States in the early 1970s by the Iranian physicist Dr Javad Nurbakhsh. Now a worldwide movement, the Nimatullahi has centres in some dozen American cities and appeals mainly to intellectuals, a majority of them Anglo-American, and the rest Iranian. The Uvaysiyya is another, smaller Iranian Shi'ite Sufi order, active in the United States since the 1980s and which chairs the International Association of Sufism, established in 1983 to bring Sufi groups into closer contact and co-operation with each other.

Two of the most active of the 'perennial' groups are the Sufi Order led by Pir Vilāyat Ināyat Khān and Idris Shah's Society for Sufi Studies. Shah purposely targeted Westerners and, according to Hermansen (1998: 169), with some considerable success. However, there remains room for Sufism to continue to expand among the Euro-American Muslims, of whom there are about 40,000, or just under (ibid.), and among the far larger African-American Muslim population, and the Turkish, Iranian and other ethnic-based Muslim communities in the United States. With regard to the future of the Sufi Order in North America and Europe, some (Jervis, 1998: 244) are of the opinion that 'it is well prepared to move into the twenty first century' and will prove to be a viable choice for those seeking an alternative to dogmatic, highly systematized and ritualistic forms of religion. Women in particular, it is implied, could find in this movement certain attractions other than the mysticism, including the emphasis on equal rights (ibid.: 235).

Judaism and new movements derived from Judaism

A variety of new and old forms of Judaism are to be found in North America and these include Reform, Neo-Orthodoxy, Conservative, Humanistic, Reconstructionist and Messianic Judaism, and Black Jewish movements.

Judaism grew slowly in North America until the arrival of Jews from Europe, mainly from Germany, in the nineteenth century, after the failure in Europe of the liberal, anti-monarchist revolutions of 1848, which left in their wake much social turmoil and insecurity. Many of the new Jewish arrivals belonged to Reform Judaism, a movement started in Germany by Abraham Geiger (1810–74) from Frankfurt in the first half of the nineteenth century. The changes introduced by Reform Judaism included the modification of Synagogue practice, such as the simplifying and shortening of the liturgy, the use of the vernacular, the playing of organ music, the sanctioning of women and men sitting together, and the modification and even discarding of some of the dietary laws. The purpose of these reforms was to enable Jews to actively participate in the modern world by offering a rational alternative to total assimilation. Inevitably, a counter movement emerged in the form of Neo-Orthodoxy begun by Samson Raphael Hirsch (1808–88) also from Frankfurt, which, while recognizing the need to participate in society, strictly upheld traditional Jewish practices. But the response to Reform Judaism did not end there. Later in the nineteenth century, in the United States, Conservative Judaism emerged under the leadership of Solomon Schecter (1847–1915) to offer a middle way between Orthodox and Reform Judaism, by retaining the rabbinic tradition while modifying worship.

Humanistic Judaism tries to move away from these concerns and provide a home for Jews who no longer have faith but seek to remain culturally Jewish. Its philosophy of life is the satisfaction of human needs, and it holds that this world exists independently of any other world or source of existence, and is committed to the resolution of all problems by recourse to human reason. Humanistic Judaism originated in 1965 when the Birmingham Temple in Detroit, Michigan, began to publicize its philosophy in the journal *Humanistic Judaism*, a philosophy which affirmed that Judaism should be governed by empirical reason and human needs (Cohn-Sherbok, 2005).

After several more temples were founded, the movement the Society for Humanistic Judaism was established in Detroit 1969 to provide a basis for co-operation among members. It soon became a national movement under a National Federation, and then an international movement with a membership of around 30,000 and currently consists of nine organizations in the United States, Canada, Britain, France, Belgium, Israel, Australia, Argentina and Uruguay.

The essentially human dimension of everything is stressed and valued as such. Jewish history is human history, Judaism is the civilization of the Jews, Jewish identity is an ethnic fact, and Judaism is the creation of Jewish people and will change as different generations construct it in their own way in the pursuit of the satisfaction of their human needs. Its agenda is modern, insisting on human rights and equality for all, the separation of religion from the State, and democratic government for all. One of the principal theorists of Humanistic Judaism is Rabbi Sherwin Wine, who believes that the traditional conception of Jewish history is mistaken. At the same time, he is said to question the existence of Abraham, Isaac and Jacob. The Exodus account is also mythical, as is the idea that Moses was not the leader of the Hebrews and the one who composed the Torah. What the Bible offers is a human account of the history of the Israelite people, with a view to strengthening the faith of the Jewish nation.

Reconstructionist Judaism, which derives its teachings from the ideas of the Lithuanian Mordecai Kaplan, from Vilna, who arrived in New York City as a child in 1889, also believes that for Judaism to survive and remain relevant it must divest itself of the spiritual dimensions of the faith and reformulate its teachings in humanistic and naturalistic terms. Reconstructionism began as a movement in 1922 when Kaplan launched a programme for creating a form of Judaism that would meet the demands of modern life. In 1934, in the publication of *Judaism as a Civilization*, Kaplan offered an assessment of the main religious groupings of American Jewry and endorsed the notion of the evolving character of Judaism. On the other hand, he criticized those who overlooked the social basis of Jewish identity as well as the organic nature of the Jewish people. He found Neo-Orthodoxy wanting insofar as, while it acknowledged Judaism as a way of life and provided an intensive programme of Jewish education, it held to the idea of an unchanging Jewish religion. As for Conservative Judaism, he regarded this as being too closely bound to traditional Jewish legal teaching and, thus, unable to respond to new circumstances. It was Kaplan's conviction that a definition of Judaism as an evolving religion and civilization was essential if this necessary accommodation was going to be possible without destroying Judaism.

Despite its intentions to remain within the Orthodox fold, by the 1960s the Reconstructionist movement had acquired all the features of a separate denomination and was training its own rabbis in its own philosophy. It also claimed that the ultimate source of authority lay with the Jewish people, as opposed to the rabbis, and instituted a process whereby each congregation was allowed to evolve its own customs. It also permits mixed marriages and recognizes the offspring as Jewish if brought up as Jews.

The new movement known as Messianic Judaism has given rise to perhaps even more controversy than the above two movements whose main teachings have just been outlined. Messianic Judaism regards the present period of history as the 'end days'. It sees catastrophe befalling the human race before the Messiah returns to reign with the faithful, the Jewish people, and those Gentiles who have turned back to God's truth as revealed in the Old and New Testaments, and have accepted Yeshua (Jesus) as the Messiah.

Messianic Judaism is a revivalist movement that sees the present as a period of rebirth for the Jewish people and cites in support of this belief various biblical texts stretching across the Old and New Testaments. These include Deuteronomy 30:1–5, Jeremiah 30–31, and in the New Testament references are made to Romans 11 and Luke 21:24. Furthermore, events in modern history are believed to lend support to the belief in a revival of the Jewish people and offer proof of the fulfilment of scriptural prophecy. The retaking of Jerusalem by Israel in 1967 is widely seen as the fulfilment of Luke 21: 24.

Messianic Judaism is also about a return to roots, Jewish roots. During the strong revival in its fortunes in the 1960s and 1970s many of the new converts stressed that in professing faith in Yeshua they were not becoming Christians but more fully and completely Jewish. They maintained further that to be fully Christian it was necessary for a Gentile to become a Jew. Ultra Orthodox and Orthodox Judaism have tended to see things differently and in certain contexts Messianic Jews have suffered discrimination for their beliefs (Beit-Hallahmi, 1992: 134).

While Messianic Judaism possesses no systematic theology and liturgy, there is a core belief or central tenet which all adhere to: the belief in Yeshua (Jesus) as the Messiah. The movement is concerned to point out that belief in Jesus does not mean that it is a Christian movement. Rather, it interprets this belief as 'biblical' Judaism. Consequently, Jewish believers in Jesus are not abandoning Judaism for another faith, but actually upholding the true faith of Abraham, Isaac and Jacob, which was brought to fulfilment in Yeshua, the Messiah.

The term 'biblical' is important to Messianic Jews who, like Humanistic and Reconstructionist Jews, are critical of rabbinic Judaism. This notwithstanding, Messianic Jews are strict observers of the holy days of the Old

Testament – for example Yom Kippur – believing that these have been fulfilled in Jesus. At the same time they are opposed to the celebration of Christmas, which is regarded as a pagan festival. The negative aspects of Christian history in relation to the Jewish people are also exposed, particularly the Crusades and Christian anti-Semitism generally.

Messianic Jewish parents, furthermore, would expect their children to receive a thorough grounding in their faith and to be aware of its distinctive features. Some would teach their children Hebrew and have them formally trained in Jewish culture. On the other hand, they are inclined to be inclusive rather that exclusive in matters regarding their children's relations and contacts with people of other faiths.

Black Jewish movements have existed in North America for over 100 years. With their roots in the experience of slavery, their central message has been one of messianic nationalism. These share much in common in terms of their understanding of their biblical past with, for example, the Rastafarian movement (see Chapter 9). They see themselves as heirs of the ten lost tribes of Israel, while white Jews are the result of miscegenation with Christians. Both New York and Chicago have been major centres of Black Judaism, some of which intend, and at least one has, to migrate to Israel. More contemporary Black Jewish movements and churches have tended to repudiate all Christian influences, to insist on being called Ethiopian Hebrews, and to place strong emphasis on the theme of returning to Africa, a return that is often more psychological and metaphorical than a practical goal.

Conclusions

Although Christianity is the dominant religion of North America, its dominance is sometimes exaggerated, as by contrast, is the low level of religion in Japan (see Chapter 12). Wuthnow and Cadge highlight what they refer to as the 'relatively broad and almost certainly growing impact of Buddhism on American culture' (2004: 377), while Stark *et al.* (2005) point to the growing number of unchurched in the United States – a phenomenon also seen in Europe (see Chapter 4) – who, nevertheless, define themselves as spiritual. While active participation in Christianity is declining and there is some evidence of a trend towards spirituality, Stark *et al.* are not prepared to support the hypothesis that there is in progress a decisive switch from one to the other (2005: 13).

Bainbridge's (2004) analysis of the relationship of conventional religion to the New Age spirituality is also interesting in this respect, in that it suggests that if the New Age were to acquire formal organizations it might well become fully religious, and by implication a strong competitor of what he refers to as 'standard religion' in the USA. While, as he shows, subjective religiousness and personal prayer or meditation among those who never attend a church correlate strongly with New Age spirituality, 'standard churches' may well be facilitating New Age ideas and practices. At the same time, Bainbridge points to the necessity for researchers to consider more seriously the growing absence of religion in the United States, evidenced by the increasing number of Atheists and Agnostics (2004: 393).

There can be little dispute as far as most of North America is concerned, and most of the West, about the growing fit between the holistic spirituality disseminated by many NRMs and by the NAM (see Chapter 2) and a world in which therapy becomes the model for relationships. As Bellah *et al.* (1985: 123) point out, the therapeutic attitude of self-realization and empathic communication has become increasingly relevant to the interpersonal nature of the work now undertaken, as more and more of the workforce engage in occupations for which therapy is a model. This new spirituality, which is engaging increasing numbers of the unchurched in particular, along with the embedding and growth of Oriental religions and Islam, particularly since 1965, has the potential to reshape the American religious landscape. Evangelical Christianity in particular is responding to this threat to the position of Christianity at the centre of the religious paradigm. The future, however, of 'standard religion', while it has not as yet been decided, is no longer as certain as it once was in North America.

The new spiritual influences from Oriental religious sources and their potential to reconfigure the religious pace of North America notwithstanding, what remains striking about the new religious and spiritual developments of recent times (since the 1950s) is the extent to which they derive so many of their core ideas from the past, and principally from such early nineteenth-century movements as Transcendentalism.

References and select bibliography

Ahlstrom, Sydney E. (1985) 'Ralph Waldo Emerson and the American Transcendentalists' in Ninian Smart *et al.* (eds) *Nineteenth Century Religious Thought in the West*, Volume II, Cambridge: Cambridge University Press, pp. 29–67.

Albanese, Catherine (1977) *Corresponding Motion: Transcendental Religion and the New America*, Philadelphia, PA: Temple University Press.

Bainbridge, William Sims (2004) 'After the New Age', *Journal for the Scientific Study of Religion*, 43(3), 381–95.

Balch, Robert and Taylor, David (2002) 'Making Sense of Heaven's Gate Suicides' in David Bromley and J. Gordon Melton (eds) *Cults, Religion and Violence*, Cambridge: Cambridge University Press, pp. 209–28.

Beard, George M. (1881) *American Newness*, New York: Arno Press.

Beit-Hallahmi, Benjamin (1992) *Despair and Deliverance*, Albany, NY: State University of New York Press.

Bellah, Robert, *et al.* (1985) *Habits of the Heart: Middle America Observed*, London: Hutchinson Education.

Benz, Ernst (2002) *Emanuel Swedenborg: Visionary Savant in an Age of Reason* (trans. with an introduction by Nicholas Goodrick-Clarke), West Chester, PA: Swedenborg Foundation.

Berger, Peter L. (1999) 'The Desecularization of the World: A Global Overview' in Peter L. Berger (ed.) *The Desecularization of the World: Resurgent Religion and World Politics*, Grand Rapids, MI: Eerdmans, pp. 1–19.

Bourdieu, Pierre (1977) *Outline of a Theory of Practice*, Cambridge: Cambridge University Press.

Bromley, David G. and Melton, J. Gordon (eds) (2002) *Cults, Religion and Violence*, Cambridge: Cambridge University Press.

Bruce, Steven (1999) *Choice and Religion: A Critique of Rational Choice Theory*, Oxford: Oxford University Press.

Carpenter, Robert T. and Roof, Wade Clark (1995) 'The Transplanting of Seicho no Ie from Japan to Brasil: Moving Beyond the Ethnic Enclave', *Journal of Contemporary Religion*, 10(1), 41–54.

Casanova, Jose (1994) *Public Religions in the Modern World*, Chicago: University of Chicago Press.

Chandler, Stuart (2005) 'Spreading the Buddha's Light: The Internationalization of Foguang Shan' in Linda Learman (ed.) *Buddhist Missionaries in the Era of Globalization*, Honolulu: University of Hawai'i Press, pp. 162–85.

Chappell, David (2000) 'Socially Inclusive Buddhists in America' in David Machacek and Bryan R. Wilson (eds) *Global Citizens: The Soka Gakkai Buddhist Movement in the World*, Oxford: Oxford University Press, pp. 299–326.

Clarke, Peter B. (1992) 'The Occult and Newly Religious in Modern Society', *Religion Today*, 7(2), 3–6.

Clarke, Peter B. (2000) '"Success" and "Failure": Japanese New Religions Abroad' in Peter B. Clarke (ed.) *Japanese New Religions: In Global Perspective*, Richmond, Surrey: Curzon Press, pp. 272–312.

Cohn-Sherbok, Dan (2005) *Encyclopedia of New Religions*, London: Routledge.

Cole, Phyllis (1998) *Mary Moody Emerson and the Origins of Transcendentalism: A Family History*, Oxford: Oxford University Press.

Cornille, Catherine (2000) 'New Japanese Religions in the West: Between Nationalism and Universalism' in Peter B. Clarke (ed.) *Japanese New Religions: In Global Perspective*, Richmond, Surrey: Curzon Press, pp. 10–35.

Cusack, Carole and Digance, Justine (2003) 'Religious, Spiritual, Secular: Some American Responses to September 11th', *Australian Religion Studies Review*, 16(2), 153–72.

Davie, Grace (2002) *Europe: The Exceptional Case: Parameters of Faith in the Modern World*, London: Darton, Longman & Todd.

Ferguson, Marilyn (1980) *The Aquarian Conspiracy*, Los Angeles, CA: J. B. Tarcher.

Giddens, Anthony (1991) *Modernity and Self-Identity: Self and Society in the Late Modern Age*, Cambridge: Polity.

Hammond, Philip E. and Machacek, David (1999) *Soka Gakkai in America*, Oxford: Oxford University Press.

Harding, Susan Friend (2000) *The Book of Jerry Falwell: Fundamentalist Language and Politics*, Princeton, NJ: Princeton University Press.

Hardy, Freidhelm E. (1984) 'How "Indian" are the New Indian Religions in the West?', *Religion Today*, 1(2 and 3), 4–8.

Heelas, Paul and Woodhead, Linda (2005) *The Spiritual Revolution: Why Religion is Giving Way to Spirituality*, Oxford: Blackwell.

Hermansen, Marcia (1998) 'In the Garden of American Sufi Movements: Hybrids and Perennials' in Peter B. Clarke (ed.) *New Trends and Developments in the World of Islam*, London: Luzac, pp. 155–77.

Huang, C. Julia (2005) 'The Compassion Relief Diaspora' in Linda Learman (ed.) *Buddhist Missionaries in the Era of Globalization*, Honolulu: University of Hawai'i Press, pp. 185–210.

Hunt, Stephen (1995) 'The "Toronto Blessing": A Rumour of Angels?', *Journal of Contemporary Religion*, 10(3), 257–73.

Jenkins, Philip (2000) *Mystics and Messiahs: Cults and New Religions in American History*, New York and Oxford: Oxford University Press.

Jervis, James (1998) 'The Sufi Order in the West and Pīr Vilāyat Ināyat Khān: Space-Age Spirituality in Contemporary Euro-America' in Peter B. Clarke (ed.) *New Trends and Developments in the World of Islam*, London: Luzac, pp. 211–61.

Learman, Linda (ed.) (2005) *Buddhist Missionaries in the Era of Globalization*, Honolulu: University of Hawai'i Press.

Martin, David (1990) *Tongues of Fire*, Oxford: Blackwell.

Melton, J. Gordon and Jones, Catherine A. (1994) 'New Japanese Religions in the United States', in Peter B. Clarke and Jeffrey Somers (eds) *Japanese New Religions in the West*, Eastbourne: Japan Library, pp. 54–77.

Melton, J. Gordon, Clark, Jerome and Kelly, Aidan A. (eds) (1990) *New Age Encyclopaedia*, Detroit: Gale Research.

Percy, Martyn (2005) 'Adventure and Atrophy in a Charismatic Movement: Returning to the "Toronto Blessing"', *Journal of Contemporary Religion*, 20(1), 71–91.

Prebish, Charles S. and Tanaka, Kenneth K. (1998) *The Faces of Buddhism in America*, Berkeley: University of California Press.

Queen, Christopher S. (2000a) 'An Emerging Global Buddhism: Hybridity, Alienation and Engagement', unpublished paper presented at the conference on Globalization and Buddhism, Boston University, April 2000.

Queen, Christopher S. (ed.) (2000b) *Engaged Buddhism in the West*, Boston: Wisdom.

Queen, Christopher S. and King, Sallie B. (eds) (1996) *Engaged Buddhism: Buddhist Liberation Movements in America*, Albany, NY: State University of New York Press.

Richardson, James T., Best, Joel and Bromley, David (eds) (1991) *The Satanism Scare*, Hawthorne, NY: Aldine de Gruyter.

Richter, Philip (1996) 'Charismatic Mysticism: The Toronto Blessing' in Stanley E. Porter (ed.) *The Nature of Religious Language*, Sheffield: Sheffield Academic Press.

Robertson, Roland (1992) 'Globalization or Glocalization', *Journal of International Communication*, 1, 33–52.

Roof, Wade Clark (1993) *A Generation of Seekers: The Spiritual Journeys of the Baby Boom Generation*, San Francisco: Harper San Francisco.

Sharot, Steven (2002) 'Beyond Christianity: A Critique of the Rational Choice Theory of Religion from a Weberian and Comparative Religions Perspective', *Sociology of Religion*, 63(4), 427–55.

Stark, Rodney (1996) 'Why Religious Movements Succeed or Fail: A Revised General Model', *Journal of Contemporary Religion*, 11(2), 133–47.

Stark, Rodney and Bainbridge, William Sims (1985) *The Future of Religion*, Berkeley: University of California Press.

Stark, Rodney and Bainbridge, William Sims (1987) *A Theory of Religion*, New York: Peter Lang.

Stark, Rodney and Finke, Roger (2000) *Acts of Faith*, Berkeley: University of California Press.

Stark, Rodney, Hamberg, Eva and Miller, Alan S. (2005) 'Exploring Spirituality and Unchurched Religions in America, Sweden and Japan', *Journal of Contemporary Religion*, 20(1), 3–25.

Stone, Carol L. (1991) 'Estimates of Muslims Living in America' in Yvonne Y. Haddad (ed.) *The Muslims of America*, New York: Oxford University Press, pp. 25–39.

Taylor, Mike (1998) 'The Nation of Islam' in Peter B. Clarke (ed.) *New Trends and Developments in African Religions*, Westport, CT: Greenwood Press, pp. 177–221.

Tipton, Steven M. (1982) *Getting Saved from the Sixties*, Berkeley: University of California Press.

Tocqueville, Alexis de (1969) *Democracy in America* (trans. George Lawrence, ed. J. P. Mayer), Garden City, NY: Doubleday.

Wallis, Roy (1976) *The Road to Total Freedom*, London: Heinemann.

Werblowsky, R. J. Zwi (1984) 'Religions New and Not So New: Fragments of an Agenda' in Eileen Barker (ed.) *New Religious Movements: A Perspective for Understanding Society*, New York: Edwin Mellen Press, pp. 32–47.

Wilson, Bryan R. (1973) *Magic and the Millennium,* London: Heinemann Educational.

Wilson, Bryan R. (1990) *The Social Dimensions of Sectarianism*, Oxford: Clarendon Press.

Wilson, Bryan R. (1991) '"Secularization": Religion in the Modern World' in Stewart Sutherland and Peter B. Clarke (eds) *The Study of Religion: Traditional and New Religion*, London: Routledge, pp. 195–208.

Wilson, Bryan R. (1992) 'The Changing Functions of Religion: Toleration and Cohesion in the Secularized Society', IOP EC Lecture Series. The Wisdom of the East in Modern Society, Maidstone: Institute of Oriental Philosophy.

Wuthnow, Robert (1982) 'World Order and Religious Movements' in Eileen Barker (ed.) *New Religious Movements: A Perspective for Understanding Society*, New York: Edwin Mellen Press, pp. 47–69.

Wuthnow, Robert (1986) 'Religious Movements and Counter-movements in America' in James Beckford (ed.) *New Religious Movements and Rapid Social Change*, London: Sage, pp. 1–29.

Wuthnow, Robert (1993) *Christianity in the 21st Century*, Oxford: Oxford University Press.

Wuthnow, Robert and Cadge, Wendy (2004) 'Buddhists and Buddhism in the United States: The Scope of Influence', *Journal for the Scientific Study of Religion*, 43(3), 363–81.

York M. (1995) *The Emerging Network: A Sociology of the New Age and Neo-Pagan Movements*, Lanham, MD: Rowman & Littlefield.

Chapter 6

Australia, New Zealand and Melanesia (New Guinea)

A new kind of religious diversity promoted by old and new religions from Asia is the main new feature of the religious landscape of Australia and New Zealand.

While Australia, New Zealand and New Guinea are no strangers to religious diversity, the contemporary form that it takes differs from that of the past, as is the case in Europe (Chapter 4), North America (Chapter 5) and in other parts of the so-called West. Kerkhove (2004: 88) contends that at least parts of Australia such as the Sunshine Coast (the North Coast Region) 'were probably always multi-faith in that every area has had some representative of diverse groups whose religious beliefs were . . . sharply distinguished from one another, whether denominationally, tribally/ethnically or as distinct world faiths.' Moreover, for much of their modern history both Australia and New Zealand have been home to many and varied kinds of alternative spirituality.

What Hill (1987) said of New Zealand, that it occupies a position of 'world prominence in terms of cultic geography', applies equally, if not more so, to Australia (Bouma, 1999). And as Stark and Bainbridge have shown (1985), in terms of Eastern and Indian cult centres per million of the population, New Zealand with 5.2 is second only to Australia with 5.3 per million. Inward immigration from Asia, in particular, since World War II accounts for this advancing Easternization of the religious culture of these two countries.

Although no direct causal link has been established between the two processes, it is, nonetheless, the case that the established religions of Asian origin and NRMs, which derive from a vast array of spiritual and religious traditions, have been growing while several of the mainstream Christian churches, excluding Roman Catholicism, have been declining in both Australia and New Zealand. This process provides further material (see Chapter 4) for testing what I describe as the Stark and Bainbridge (1985) and the Stark and Finke (2000) steady-state theory of religion, a theory that implies that the fundamental social condition of religion is unvarying, and is maintained by the constant creation through competition of new forms of the phenomenon.

Stark and Finke (2000: 249) refer to the 'very first proposition ever formulated about "religious economies": "Cults will abound where conventional churches are weakest" (Stark and Bainbridge, 1980).' By 'cults' these authors mean here 'all new religious firms, whether within the conventional religious culture or not' (2000: 250). Associated with this proposition are the formal statements that the degree of competition in a religious economy will be an overall stimulus to the degree of religious vitality in that economy and that rational choices made by consumers in religious markets account for religious growth or decline. Iannaccone (1995) also focuses on these issues and elsewhere (1994) attempts to show that what makes for growth in the contemporary context is strictness and competition. By contrast, where there exist powerful religious monopolies there tends to be stagnation or decline. As will be seen below, the history of New Religious Movements (NRMs) in Australia and New Zealand, while lending some support to these theories, also suggests that other considerations such as the openness of settler communities to cultural and religious innovation are also an important part of the explanation for their rise.

Wallis (1986) contended that, although NRMs may increase with declining Church attendance, their proliferation is particularly high in Anglo-Saxon, Protestant-dominated, and immigrant-based communities. Ellwood's response (1993: 185) is to point out that where the situation in New Zealand is concerned both Stark and Bainbridge and Wallis rely 'excessively on a small number of recent groups – the Hare Krishna, Scientology, the Unification Church, the Children of God (now The Family) – and on sometimes questionable statistics provided by the groups themselves'. The section below on New Zealand follows Ellwood (1993) in attempting to provide a fuller picture that incorporates more longstanding alternative religious groups.

NRMs in Melanesia are widely associated with numerous movements, collectively referred to as Cargo cults, founded on what Wilson (1973) describes as 'commodity millennialism'. These movements can be interestingly compared with modern Maori millenarian movements in New Zealand (see below) and other messianic movements that emerged in Africa (see Chapter 8), Latin America (see Chapter 9), North America (see Chapter 5) and South Asia (see Chapter 10) and East Asia (see Chapters 12 and 13) in the nineteenth and twentieth centuries.

The case of Melanesian millenarianism provides a further opportunity to examine the limitations of the impact–response framework for analysing religious change (see, for example, Chapters 8 and 10) and the extent to which its primary goal is the defence of the traditional way of life (see Chapter 5).

Australia: the ending of the 'white only policy' and a new kind of religious diversity

The ending after World War II of the 'White Australia Policy', a policy introduced in 1901, did for the religious diversity of Australia what the repeal of the Asian Exclusion Act in 1965 did for religious diversity in the United States (Chapter 5). This policy had in effect excluded non-whites and gave Christianity an almost total monopoly of the official religious life of the country. Its end saw the arrival of increasing numbers of immigrants from Asia and elsewhere, making Australia one of the most religiously diverse countries in the world.

Diversity did not begin at this point, as we have already indicated. Moreover, the mid-nineteenth century saw a growing interest in alternative religious and spirituality movements such as Theosophy and the Liberal Catholic Church. There existed, however, only the merest trace of Oriental religion. Immigration from Asia, which began as a trickle in the nineteenth century, had reached a total of only 2,100 persons by 1933. By 1991 this figure had risen to 61,602. By 1995 there were an estimated 125,000 South Asians and people of South Asian origin living in Australia (Bilimoria, 1997: 733).

By 2001 the complexity of religion in Australia had changed markedly. In 1947 Anglicanism was the largest Christian denomination with 39 per cent of the population declaring itself members of that church. However, according to the 2001 census some 26.7 per cent of Christians identified with the Catholic Church and only 20.7 per cent with Anglicanism (Bouma, 2003: 58). Pentecostalism has experienced steady growth in Australia since 1996 rising from 175,000 in that year to 195,000 in 2001.

Buddhism has made the most remarkable advance. In the very short period between 1996 and 2001 Buddhism experienced a 79 per cent growth rate increasing its following from 200,000 to 358,000, or 1.9 per cent of the population according to the 2001 census. Hinduism also grew rapidly over the same period from 67,000 to 95,000 and Muslims from 201,000 to 282,000. The Jewish population likewise increased, although by much less, from 80,000 to 84,000. Sikhs who numbered around 7,000 in 1996 had reached 17,401 by 2001. On the other hand the history of Aboriginal religion is one of decline from around 7,000 in 1996 to 5,000 in 2001. There was a sizeable increase in the numbers of Agnostics from 9,000 to 18,000 over the same period and in Atheists, from 7,000 to 24,000; the number of Rationalists was 24,464.

Among the New Religions the Baha'i faith was the largest in 2001 with membership of around 11,000, while the number of Paganists was also in the region of 11,000, with Wiccans at 9,000, Spiritualists at 9,000, Theosophists at 1,700, Chinese religionists at 4,000, and Japanese religionists, Scientology, and Rastafarians all at around 1,000. There were some 3,000 members of the predominantly Maori Ratana Church (see below). Only very few of the South and East Asian NRMs were singled out by name and among those that were the Vietnamese-derived movement Caodaism (see Chapter 11) was listed as having 819 members, and the Japanese movement Sukyo Mahikari, 513. The 2001 census counted close on 19 million believers and of these women were in the majority but only marginally so.

Buddhism had not only expanded exponentially but had also developed organizationally. According to Spuler (2000: 30), 308 Buddhist associations had been established by 1998 representing the whole range of Buddhist traditions – Theravada, Mahayana, Vajrayana and Triyana (Friends of the Western Buddhist Order). The first Buddhist association was founded in Melbourne in 1925 by an Australian convert who had been influenced by Burmese Buddhism. A significant number of these associations are multi-ethnic and over thirty of the groups are 'ecumenical' in the sense of inclusive and non-sectarian. The ethnic diversity of Buddhism in Australia is another of its striking features. Classified in terms of their place of birth, the majority of Buddhists in Australia come originally from Vietnam (31%) followed by Australia (19.7%), Malaysia (7.5%), Cambodia (6.8%), Thailand (6.2%), Sri Lanka (5.2%), China (4.6%), Laos (3.4%), Taiwan (2.5%) and Indonesia (2.2%) (Hughes, 1997: 17). Diversity on such a scale owes much to the arrival of immigrants from Southeast Asia after the ending of the Vietnam and/or American War (1974–5). Efforts by ecumenical Buddhism in Australia have not, in Spuler's opinion (2000: 37), achieved the same successes as in the United States and Europe in integrating the various ethnic groups.

This notwithstanding, Buddhism in Australia does share a number of characteristics with Buddhism in the United States and Europe (Spuler, 2000; 2003) including emphasis on lay practice, also a feature of modern Japanese forms of Buddhism (see Chapter 12), and emphasis on engagement with environmental and social issues. Also noticeable in Australian Buddhism and in Buddhism globally is the interest in its therapeutic value, many finding in its meditation techniques a means of relieving stress and improving concentration.

Women have played a crucial role in the development of Buddhism in Australia. An American-born Buddhist nun was instrumental in establishing the Buddhist Society of New South Wales in 1952, while Natasha Jackson, editor of *Metta: the Journal of the Buddhist Federation of Australia*, has been described as the dominant voice in Australian Buddhism from 1951 to 1977 (Spuler, 2000: 35). The type of Buddhism promoted in this period was both highly intellectual and socially committed or engaged. High on its list of priorities was its concern with showing that, unlike Christianity, Buddhism and modern scientific thought were compatible. It also defended Aboriginal land rights, campaigned against poverty and illiteracy and opposed the Vietnam War.

Hindus, though a numerically smaller group than Buddhists, are among the most highly organized immigrant communities in Australia. A sizeable minority of them – some 30 per cent – belong to the strict, orthodox Arya Samaj movement (see Chapter 10), which rejects the use of printed images and sculptured icons. Most Hindus have sought to continue to practise the entire range of their religious rituals, some of which are highly elaborate, only to find that the secular context of Australia has made this difficult.

Many of the present-day Muslims in Australia arrived, at least originally, from Afghanistan, Turkey, the Middle East, Fiji, Indonesia and South Asia, including Sri Lanka. Over time Islam has gradually taken on a more 'protestant' form, as has, for example, Buddhism in Sri Lanka, a trend the exclusive, reformist Tablighi Jama'at movement (see Chapter 10) is attempting to counteract. The Sikh presence in Australia dates back to the nineteenth century. Most come from the Punjab and are more traditional in observance than a minority from Malaysia who tend to be more liberal.

The decline of Aboriginal religion, like the decline of Maori churches such as the Ratana Church, can be attributed in part to modernization. A diverse people, a majority of the Aboriginal population now lead a Western style of life and few speak any of the Aboriginal tongues. Considerable numbers have converted to Christianity and according to the 2001 census there are only some 5,224 Aboriginal Traditional Religionists. Hume (2002) puts the figure higher saying that at around 10,000 could be considered adherents of the traditional Aboriginal belief system. This is a complex system about which there is much debate. Most scholars agree, however, the notion of 'Dreaming' or 'Dreamtime' expressed in various indigenous terms is the one fundamental feature of all Aboriginal religion. It contains several distinct albeit interconnected meanings, including a narrative myth of the foundation and shaping of the world by uncreated, eternal ancestor heroes and the belief that the power of these ancestor heroes is embodied in the land, in certain sites, and in certain species of flora and fauna.

New Religions from East and South Asia

A number of Japanese NRMs have a presence in Australia but have not so far attracted many followers, their combined total being around 10,000 only.

One of the relatively more successful movements is Mahikari, which defines its mission as one of purification by *okiyome* or the transmission of the Divine Light of Su-God, the supreme deity. This deity it is believed embodies simultaneously the deities of all religions. A millenarian movement, Mahikari believes that a new 'sunshine civilization' is about to break through but will only come about after a series of cataclysms. Prayers such as the *Butsumetso no yo* are recited by adherents to bring on the time when by a 'baptism of fire' the world will be purified. Women make up the majority of those who attend Mahikari dojos (training places) in Australia, as they do in Japan.

Like many other Japanese religions Mahikari gives expression to various themes and preoccupations which have long been important in Japanese culture: a strong concern with purification; belief in the continuing presence among and influence of the ancestors and the spirit world generally on the living; and belief in the need to ensure through ritual action that they exist in a state of contentment. The movement places the emphasis on purification in the wide sense of the term and stresses that healing at the individual level is a by-product of the power of True Light to uplift and improve the spiritual, mental and physical realms.

Regarding its approach to other religions, Mahikari adopts a position not unlike that of Japanese Buddhism and Shinto. For example, it is not a prerequisite that new members leave the religion of their birth in order to practise and benefit from *okiyome*. Its ecumenical outlook can be seen in its teachings, which contain elements of what it describes as the 'five major religions', Buddhism, Daoism, Christianity, Confucianism and Islam. This notwithstanding, its rituals remain distinctively Japanese. For example, members are requested to erect ancestral altars and to peel the fruit placed thereon to be consumed by the ancestral spirits. Such practices are not considered by the movement itself as Japanese but rather as inculcating 'Divine Principles', which are described as universal.

Mahikari in Australia appears to have made little attempt to adapt, nor interestingly has there been much demand for it to do so (Bouma *et al.*, 2000: 90). Being other in the sense of not adapting may well constitute an attraction for those non-Japanese Australians, including not only Caucasian but also Chinese members, who join Mahikari. The Japanese character of Mahikari is evident on first sight of a dojo. Its divine emblem incorporates the six-pointed star and the sixteen-petalled crest symbolic of the Japanese Imperial family, kneeling is performed in the Japanese style, as is bowing, and the ancestors are venerated daily using Japanese rituals. Another important factor in attracting Australian members, and this in part explains their indifference to extensive adaptation at least at the intellectual level, is the movement's emphasis on experiencing the divine as opposed to a stress on its doctrinal content (ibid.: 91).

Other NRMs from abroad include the Brahma Kumaris movement (BK), which is widely seen as championing gender equality and as promoting feminine spirituality (Palmer, 1993, 1994). My own research suggests that, while some of the BK's women leaders in Britain would accept the use of the label feminist as a way of characterizing the movement, others in India tend to be much more cautious. Informants at Mount Abu, the Indian head-quarters of the movement, in January 2000 left me with the impression that female authority and power over men was not the central issue where leader-ship was concerned. What appeared to be of the utmost importance in terms of an individual's suitability for leadership was not gender but knowledge derived from association with the teachings, ethos and spirit of the move-ment's male founder, Dada Lekhraj (see Chapter 10). What mattered most was the 'chain of memory' that linked the leaders of today with those that had had close contact with Lekhraj or his immediate entourage, most of whom were women. Also important in appointing women in particular but not exclusively to the role of teachers was the Indian tradition according to which, I was informed at Mount Abu, it was customary for women to take responsibility for passing on society's mores and culture. Women, it was believed, were endowed with a special gift of patience and good judgement necessary for the effective performance of this role. Whatever interpretation the West might want to put on it, the BK, I was informed, was following tradition in charging women with the task of teaching. But this did not exclude men (brothers) from such a role or from performing important administrative functions. Indeed, the most senior adviser to the present leader is a brother who had direct contact with the founder.

Howell's research (1998) on the BK movement shows that the leadership role of women can vary depending on social contexts and conditions. This research compares and contrasts the position of women in the BK movement in Western settings, particularly Australia and Britain. It argues that gender relations in this movement cannot be assumed to follow the early Indian model, where the founder gave 'special encouragement to women to develop their spiritual lives and take leadership positions' (1998: 454). Howell's contention is that there will be differences in gender relations within the movement according to the pattern of gender relations in the wider society in which it establishes itself. In both Britain and Australia, unlike in India, there tended to be a convergence of male and female roles in the early history of settlement in these countries, making for a shift in gender practices. In Australia men accounted for the majority of the first wave of recruits to the movement and founded the majority of its first centres and, it followed, were more prominent in leadership positions. However, as women recruits came to outnumber men the situation in Australia changed, although in New Zealand male leaders continue to outnumber female leaders.

Why the BK movement attracted so many male recruits early on in its history in Australia and New Zealand is an interesting question. Howell (1998: 459) suggests it was not necessarily for the reason that the BK is a feminist movement challenging masculine authority structures. It was more likely for the reason that it offered these male recruits the opportunity to 'see themselves as a small elite, as spiritual leaders more analogous to the then exclusively male Christian ministry than to the predominantly female Christian congregations'.

Feminist spirituality movements provide an important outlet for feminine spirituality in present-day Australia. These movements are similar to those in the United States (Eller, 1993) and Germany (Krüll, 1995), and network through, for example, Aboriginal, Wiccan, Neo-Pagan, New Age, Goddess, Christian and Jewish feminist, and political feminist groups, essentially to challenge 'masculinist' images of the religious cosmos (Coco, 2001). Some of these movements exist within established mainstream religion and include the movement for the Ordination of Catholic Women (OCW) and The Grove, started by Roman Catholic Sisters of Mercy. Other exclusively female spirituality groups include Pagan Dianic associations that seek among other things to revalue the divine feminine and adopt the practice of consensual decision-making and shared leadership in women-centred rituals and practice (ibid.).

Commodification

Berger (1967) has spoken about American religion as taking on the ethos and management style of secular institutions under the heading of 'internal secularization' and Nakamaki (2003) has described Japanese NRMs in Brazil as 'empresas' or companies that are organized, managed and function on similar lines to other Japanese companies. Of course, opinion on and attitudes towards the relationship of religion and/or spirituality to business can and does vary from culture to culture, the boundary being, at least notionally, more clearly demarcated in more secularized societies than in others. It is an issue, moreover, that raises the question of the role, understanding and context of gift giving in different cultures.

In the Australian context Ezzy (2001) has written about the 'commodification' of religion in relation to Wicca. Such a process is related to that of 'de-traditionalization'. As this process has gathered momentum during late modernity, one of its principal effects on religion has been to further democratize religious belief and practice, making them much more a matter of individual choice, a choice made on the basis of experimentation.

Spirituality is not entirely, however, a question of pure, unfettered choice on the part of the individual. De-traditionalization has not only involved the de-coupling of religious belief from religious institutions but has also allowed the secular market to move into the space left vacant and to exercise greater control over the form, content and dissemination of religious beliefs and practices. By this process of commodification religious beliefs and practices assume the character of commercial products with a monetary value and through the buying and selling of these items new social bonds are created. As Lyon (2000) suggests, New Age religious consumerism represents the reconstruction of religious identities to facilitate the formation of these new forms of social bonds as the traditional sources of identity, including established religion, disintegrate. Hughes and others (2004) have discussed the declining importance of established religion in identity formation in Australia.

Thus, although the profit motive arguably has never been absent from religion, the context of late modernity in which freedom of choice is celebrated allows it greater opportunity to flourish. Ezzy's (2001) research on a limited number of Wiccan/Neo-Pagan groups in Australia contends that this is what is happening in these cases. Ezzy does not, of course, intend to question the motives of those who become involved in Wicca or to deny findings such as those of Coco (2001) which highlight the positive benefit some women derive from participation in Wiccan/Neo-Pagan groups. His research focuses instead on the Witchcraft websites of three leading Australian Witches. In so doing he seeks to illustrate how an ideology of consumption is disseminated, one which manipulates people's concerns about their spiritual practices for the purpose of advertising and selling products such as books of spells and bottles of lotion. Ezzy writes regarding the websites of the three prominent Witches he examined: 'The main aim of these websites is to encourage people to buy their products' (2001: 34). This change in function and purpose has been made, Ezzy maintains, at the expense of personal self-discovery. It could also be said to run counter to the process of freeing religion and spirituality from what are described by analysts of de-traditionalization as the oppressive control of traditional institutions.

A similar question could be raised about the New Age Movement (NAM) (see Chapter 2), which according to Hanegraaff (1999: 153) has come to rest on essentially secular foundations, and about Jedi religion. According to Possamai (2003: 74) Jediism has over 70,000 adepts in Australia compared with an estimated 390,000 in the United Kingdom. In both cases the majority are in their twenties. Possamai (2003: 78), making use of data from interviews and internet sources that describe the movement's mission and practices, uses the term 'hyper-religion' to define this and similar movements. He means by this term 'a simulacrum of a religion created out of popular culture which provides inspiration for believers and consumers at a metaphorical level'. Although it makes use of the myth created by George Lucas, the author of the film series *Star Wars*, which centres on an epic struggle between the forces of good and evil in which the Force sustains the Jedi warriors fighting for God, Jediism insists that its teachings transcend fiction. One way of understanding it is to see it as making use of popular culture for a religious purpose in a manner similar to other contemporary movements including the Neo-Pagan Church of All Worlds. The latter's teachings are in part based on Robert Heinlein's novel *Strangers in a Strange Land* which centres on the story of a Martian with god-like powers living on earth.

Jediism wants to distance itself from fictional narratives and characters and defines itself in much the same way as any Religion of the True Self or Self-religion (see Chapter 1), or New Age group, as 'a supportive spiritual community that helps individuals worldwide to attain and sustain a one-to-one relationship with the Light of their own true Inner Self and therefore reconnect to their own True Divine Nature to which we refer as Jedi' (http: www.jediism.bigstep. com/html?pid=1). Jediism also claims to have a 5,000-year-old history and to share many beliefs and practices with other religions including Buddhism, Hinduism, Confucianism, Daoism, Gnosticism and Roman Catholicism (Possamai, 2003: 75–6). There are temples, and practices, principally meditation, including white light meditation which every Jedi is encouraged to perform every day to make the connection between the 'outer self' and the 'Spirit/true Jedi within' (www.jediism.bigstep.com/html?pid=1). At the same time it could be argued, in the way Ezzy (2001) has suggested has happened with a number of Wiccan websites, that this 'spiritual path' is in danger of being obscured by the emphasis on Jedi commodities. The latter include a whole range of goods from action figures, their apparel and accessories, to beauty, health, education, computer, electronic, food and wine, and education products.

A similar anxiety is evident among some Buddhist reformers, academics and journalists in, for example, Thailand, who fear the consequences for Buddhist culture of rampant commercialism and secularization, as business, sometimes with the assistance of government, transforms the purpose of meditation or vipassana (see Chapter 11) from a spiritual exercise to an exercise designed purely for the purpose of procuring greater efficiency in the market place.

New Zealand

Although it greatly resembles that of Australia, the religious culture of New Zealand is in several respects unique. Maori 'religion' could be described as the country's traditional religion, although there are problems with both the terms 'traditional' and 'religion'. The term 'traditional' is not used to mean here static, as Maori belief and practice have changed greatly over time due to internal factors and under the influence of contact with Christianity, Hinduism and other religions. Today some 60 per cent of the Maori, who make up 9 per cent of the country's population, identify themselves as Christian and many Maori-Christian churches have been started, as we will see below. Although the situation is changing, the term 'religion' is also problematic, as it is in the case of Aboriginal religion, in that the Maori use of the term, at least historically, differs from the way it is applied by Westerners to Christianity. This difference in understanding apart, Christianity since its arrival in New Zealand in the early nineteenth century has increasingly become part of Maori religious culture. As Tawhai (1991: 96) comments:

> The Maori of Ruatoria will accept that Christianity is an integral part of his fellow Maori's life, but each will have his own brand of religion for historic and other reasons . . . while the Christian God provides Maoridom with its first redeemer, he appears mostly to ignore the needs at the temporal and profane level, leaving this domain to the ancestral gods who continue to cater for those needs.

Notwithstanding the advances made by Christianity – the first Christian missionaries began to preach to the Maori in 1814 – and Western education, traditional rationality persists. Maori ancient explanatory myths – each tribe has its own – continue to influence behaviour and are used as an important source of explanation of everyday events. To quote Tawhai (1991: 98) again:

> The Maori on the street of Ruatoria, nowadays at least, is content that he has the knowledge of the *tohunga* [an expert in various fields of knowledge] . . . to outsiders he is inclined to present a front of learning in

defence of anything that might question the worth of his tribal culture; the treasures transmitted to him by his ancestors.

If one can speak of a typical traditional Maori cosmological structure it would have at its core the belief in the existence of a superhuman realm inhabited by controlling powers and in a physical world where humans dwell. The two realms are not rigidly separated. Among the inhabitants of the superhuman realm are gods (atua), spirits (wairua), ancestors (tipuna) and ghosts (kehu) who can assume a single form or manifest themselves in a variety of different forms. What most concerns humans is their relationship with these powers and their capacity to influence their will in order to ensure that the relationship remains in good order and benefits them. And this depends on knowledge of the myths or ancient explanations (korero tahito) that express the beliefs and values of the community.

From the beginning of Christian missionary activity distinctive types of Maori NRMs began to emerge, the aim of which was the preservation of Maori identity under threat from a plethora of so-called historic Christian churches and sects, including Anglicans, Catholics, Presbyterians, Methodists, Baptists, Quakers, Churches of Christ, Plymouth Brethren, Seventh Day Adventists, and Mormons, among others. By the 1960s many of these older forms of Christianity had started to decline, a decline partly offset by the rise of Neo-Pentecostalism in the 1970s, which began to attract increasing numbers of followers in the twenty to forty age group, an age group which the mainline Christian churches were failing to attract. Also on the increase in recent times is the number of Samoan ethnic Christian churches and the number of Buddhists, Hindus and Muslims, an increase due in every case to immigration. Indian religions and Islam remain small, both of them accounting for less than 1 per cent of the population, and the same applies to the Jewish community which has been present in the country since 1831.

Ellwood's previously mentioned study (1993) maintains that conventional religion in New Zealand is weak. However, to put this conclusion in perspective it needs to be borne in mind that historically Church attendance in New Zealand has never been high. Hill and Zwaga (1989: 66) account for this in part by migration, followed by the high level of geographical mobility, which 'weakened the cohesiveness of Church congregations and reduced the social pressures in favour of attendance'. Hill and Zwaga (1989: 68) further suggest that relatively high levels of religious pluralism and the firmly secular constitution of the country from an early stage of its modern history are other reasons for the large number of purely nominal members of the Christian churches in New Zealand. All of these factors go at least some way to account for the presence of large numbers of alternative and new religions and lend some support to the thesis that new religions tend to thrive where conventional religion is weak (Stark and Bainbridge, 1985). However, while there is much new and alternative religion and spirituality, as will be seen below, its appeal is as yet limited to a small percentage of the population, as in Australia, thus challenging the view that competition makes for a more dynamic religious culture (Stark and Bainbridge, 1985).

A synthesis of the ideas of the Swedish engineer, mystic and occultist Emmanuel Swedenborg (1688–1772) (see Chapter 4), of Anton Mesmer (1733–1815) (see Chapter 5) and of Theosophy, established in New York in 1875 (see Chapter 5), has provided the foundations of much of the alternative spirituality from abroad that began to attract New Zealanders of all ethnic groups from the second half of the nineteenth century. To recapitulate: among the most influential of Swedenborg's ideas were his 'realized eschatology' – he believed that the Second Coming of Christ began in the spiritual realm in 1757 – his ideas on healing which derived from his theory of correspondences between the spiritual and material realms summarized in the adage 'as above so below', his description of the Afterlife in his *Heaven and Hell* (1758), his liberal moral views, and his search for ancient wisdom, all of which have found an echo in New Age and/or Aquarian discourse. The Swedenborgian Church or New Church founded by his disciples in London in 1772 for the purpose of preserving his teachings was introduced to New Zealand in 1865.

Mesmer, popularly associated with 'mesmerism' or hypnotism, believed he had found the key to unlock the capacity of the mind, which, he claimed, was unlimited. Deeply interested in the psycho-somatic character of illness, he was persuaded that the key to healing lay in the transmission by the healer to the patient of a universal energy or vitality through a process of animal magnetism. He also claimed that this animal magnetism could awaken powers that lay dormant in an individual and enable her/him to see past, present and future, develop extrasensory perception and unravel the mysteries of nature.

Swedenborgian and Mesmerian ideas fused over time to form the basis of Spiritualism as it took shape from the 1840s. Through the Victorian Association of Progressive Spiritualists it began to establish itself in both Australia and New Zealand in the 1860s. In New Zealand, where it has been adapted to the local culture, Spiritualism, which was originally greatly disparaged by newspapers such as the *Otago Daily Times*, soon began to attract, as we pointed out above, members from all ethnic groups including the Maori. Spiritualist circles and associations were the norm until churches began to be founded from 1900 in all the major cities beginning in Auckland.

The highly influential esoteric group Theosophy came to New Zealand, and Australia, in the 1880s. The principal agent of its early dissemination in New Zealand was Edward Toronto Sturdy (1860–1957), who founded the first lodge in Wellington in 1888. For some time it clashed over doctrine with the mainstream churches, who dismissed it as a teaching without compassion and love. Several movements influenced by Theosophical ideas, including the Arcane School founded by Elizabeth Bailey (1880–1949) and Anthroposophy, started by Rudolf Steiner (1861–1925) in Germany in 1913 and described as a liberalizing form of Theosophy (Ellwood, 1993: 140), arrived in New Zealand in the first half of the twentieth century.

Countless forms of Spiritualism and of UFO religion established a presence in New Zealand in the twentieth century, including the spiritualist Urantia Movement whose main scriptural text, *The Urantia Book*, contains revelations of the material and spiritual super-universe, the history of the earth, Urantia, and of the life of Jesus and, in particular, of his hidden years. Interest in UFOs dates back to the beginnings of the twentieth century and in the 1950s a number of UFO groups with links to similar groups in Australia and the United States started to spring up. This was partly in response to the controversial visit of the Polish American Ufologist George Adamski (1891–1965), who believed that the beings who drove the UFOs conveyed divine messages to those on earth.

With regard to Occult movements the most historically interesting is the Hermetic Order of the Golden Dawn, which was established in the village of Havelock in Hawke Bay by Dr Robert Felkin of the London group in 1912. The Golden Dawn, started in London by a group of Occultists in 1888, began to teach ideas that echoed those of Swedenborg. These included the notions that the material universe was but a part of the whole of reality, that humans were a microcosm of the universe as a whole, that willpower properly trained could achieve every kind of result whether in the supernatural or natural realm, and that by mentally imagining or visualizing something that one desires one could shape its form in astral light and eventually in physical reality.

Modern witchcraft or Wicca and Neo-Paganism had begun to attract increasing attention in New Zealand by the 1980s, both benefiting from the feminist and environmentalist movements of the time and the interest in Maori religion. By the 1980s the New Age Movement, which, as we have seen, draws on so many of Swedenborg's ideas, also began to attract greater interest.

The variety of new and alternative forms of religion in New Zealand is further evidenced in the presence there of many Gurdjieffian-influenced groups (see Chapter 4), among them the School of Philosophy, which derives from the British NRM the School of Economic Science, and the Emin Foundation, also British. Mystical movements influenced by Sufism or mysticism present in New Zealand include the Indonesian movement Subud (see Chapter 11). Other movements present in New Zealand include the Emissaries of the Divine Light, established by the American Lloyd Arthur Meeker in 1932 and strongly supported by the British aristocrat Lord Martin Cecil, the BK, Rajneeesh, Baha'i movements, the Johannine Daist Community, formerly the Free Primitive Church of Divine Communion, and the Free Daist Communion, founded by the American Franklin Jones whose aliases include Da Free John, Da Love-Ananda and Da Kalki (b.1939). This last-mentioned movement teaches a seven-step approach to Transcendental Consciousness. Also present are Sant Mat movements in which Sikhism,

Hinduism and Islam overlap, modern 'secular' religions such as Scientology (Wilson, 1990) and Japanese new religions, which include Soka Gakkai (Value Creation Society) (see Chapter 12).

Maori new religions

Various forms of Maori NRMs, most of which have been heavily influenced by Christianity, began to emerge in New Zealand in the nineteenth century reaching a peak in the 1920s. Almost all were millenarian including the Pai Marire (good or peaceful), more commonly known as the Hauhau movement founded in the 1860s. This movement was founded by the Maori prophet Te Ua Hua Haumene, a former student of the Wesleyan missionaries. Te Hua adopted the role of *tohunga* or traditional priest and sought to adapt Old Testament prophecies of the Promised Land to the Maori situation. The leader and his followers identified with the Jews and expected God to enable them to repossess their land, which the Pakeha or Whites had stolen. Inspired by the Book of Isaiah and the Book of Revelation, this short-lived millenarian movement won considerable acclaim among the Maoris for its successful assaults on several white (pakeha) targets.

The millenarianism of Hauhau movement appeared to show less interest in restoring the past than, for example, North American Indian movements (see Chapter 5) and this was possibly due to the much greater degree of acculturation and Christianization of the Maoris by the 1860s. As Wilson notes (1973: 251):

> Their patterns of tribal life had been seriously affected by Christianity; traditional agencies of social control had declined, and the dissemination and use in tribal warfare of Western weapons had completely disrupted the power balance of the past.

The Ringatu movement founded by Te Kooti Rikirangi contrasts with the Hauhau movement in that it tended to espouse pacifism rather than militancy. In its pacifist phase the Ringatu reworked as it were Hauhau symbolism and ritual, interpreting the up-raised hand, for example, as a sign of homage to God rather than as a spiritual means of warding off bullets. Also educated in a mission school Te Kooti's teachings consisted of a synthesis of Old and New Testament and Maori beliefs. The leader likened himself to Moses and the Maori, in Rastafarian-like fashion (see Chapter 9), to the lost tribes of Israel. Other movements followed on the Ringatu and, while clinging to the notion of themselves as Israelites, were in turn to reinterpret its traditional symbols and rituals.

Increasingly politicization became a feature of most of the Maori movements of the first half of the twentieth century, including the Ratana Church, which began in practice in 1918 and was formally established by

Tahupotiki Wiremu Ratana in 1925. Many of the conditions necessary for a successful mass movement of the Maori such as the Ratana Church were present in the immediate post-War War I (1914–18) period. Young, mainly Church-educated Maori had begun to return to their villages dissatisfied with their lack of status and the lack of opportunity. As in Africa and India, the level of racial consciousness had grown among the returning servicemen, who were increasingly dissatisfied with Pakeha political and economic power, and the general lack of heathcare facilities and amenities. An estimated one in fifty Maori died during the influenza epidemic of 1918 compared with one in two hundred Pakeha. These developments made it much easier to respond positively to the Tahupotiki Wiremu Ratana's claim that he had been appointed in a vision of the Holy Spirit Ratana to be the mouthpiece of God for the Maori people.

Ratana, like so many prophets a largely self-educated man, who claimed to possess miraculous powers of healing, was by several accounts someone of considerable practical ability. According to a Methodist minister, he was 'the most practical faith healer I ever knew'. At the outset a faith-healing movement, this Church became, relatively rapidly, a major force in the country's politics. Initially, it passed on its teachings by word of mouth in Maori but later wrote them down in English to accommodate the increasing number of younger, Western-educated Maori members who only spoke English. Based to a much greater extent than those Maori movements previously mentioned on the Jewish and Christian traditions, membership reached a peak in the 1930s when the Church was able to claim 20 per cent of the Maori population.

Although much of its teaching affirmed traditional spiritual notions of causality and upheld traditional moral values, the Ratana Church was, nonetheless, a modernizing force in New Zealand society. It gave supernatural legitimacy, so to speak, to political innovations that greatly impacted on Maori traditional society. With four Maori seats in parliament the Ratana Church held the balance of power for the Labour Government for twenty-five years, during which time it supported legislation that improved the social and economic conditions of the Maori. However, the Church's successes on behalf of the Maori have resulted not in an increase but in a fall in Maori membership, which by the early 1980s stood at less than 9 per cent of the Maori population.

We now turn to another indigenous phenomenon much influenced by Western forms of Christianity, the New Religions known as Cargo cults of Melanesia, which as was already mentioned are characterized by their own distinctive form of 'commodity millenarianism'.

Melanesia and commodity millenarianism

This term 'Melanesia' is used here in a limited sense to refer to those islands covered by Papua New Guinea and inhabited by Melanesian peoples for over

4,000 years. There are over 700 local languages and dialects and people traditionally lived – many still do – in small communities separated by dense forests. While the traditional religions continue to be practised they are rarely practised in their 'pure' and 'unadulterated' form, so to speak (Lanternari, 1991). A whole series of movements collectively known as Cargo cults began to emerge from the 1890s. Melanesians used the term 'cargo' for material goods and Europeans applied it to the movements which they called 'madness' cults on account of the shaking and speaking in tongues that occurred when a leader would claim to have been reborn. These 'cultists' were, however, much more than deluded visionaries.

Accounting for the rise of these Cargo cults in this part of the world provides a further opportunity for a comparative discussion of impact–response schemas of religious change. Many of these new movements, like those of North America (Chapter 5), Africa (Chapters 7 and 8) and India (Chapter 10), emerged under the impact of colonial rule and Christian missionary expansion, and share the same concern with the imminent advent of the millennium. These Melanesian movements, nevertheless, developed their own particular version of millenarianism and their own particular, and persuasive, form of situational logic. Wilson (1973: 312) identifies as distinctive features of Melanesian millenarian movements, which he refers to collectively as 'commodity millennialism', 'their profusion, localism and the similarity of their concerns'.

The response of these movements to colonial, white culture was not automatically to reject it but varied depending on the extent to which the society which produced them had been influenced by it. The principal demand of most was for a transformation of the social situation, in the form of economic betterment and improved social status – both proof of ability in the new order of things.

To understand this desire for Cargo and the manner in which it was lived out it is necessary to look in broad outline at the modern history of Melanesia. Through contact with Europeans and, in particular, missionaries, beginning in the 1870s, customary rituals gradually came to be abandoned, and this, with the appeal of modernity, had serious consequences for the moral and social life of Melanesians. Lanternari (1991: 88) believes that the 'forced abandonment' of customary rituals, for which the missionaries were chiefly responsible, and the attraction of modern cultural models led to the 'collapse of old spiritual sanctions and the deterioration of moral standards'. It produced the conditions, in his view, for the upsurge of new forms of millenarianism in the twentieth century. As he explains (1991: 88), 'the uneasiness and the feeling of frustration caused by these factors underlie the spreading of the Cargo cults, which clearly express a deep yearning for the renewal of the traditional way of life.' Economic forces such as the introduction of a cash economy also greatly contributed to the rise of these movements, which were not only traditional in orientation but also strikingly 'new'. They bore a close resemblance to what Burridge (1969: 13) identified as the characteristics of millenarian movements generally, which he wrote: 'involve the adoption of new assumptions, a new redemptive process, a new politico-economic framework, a new mode of measuring the man [sic], a new community, in short: a new man [sic]'.

The coming of the Whites presaged the start of a New Age that would see the return of the heroic ancestors and of all the dead bringing with them everything necessary for a trouble-free life. Various indigenous religious movements were based on the myth that, as a result of some original misdemeanour or sin, their glorious, heroic ancestors had departed from the land of the living (Worsley, 1968). A similar theme is echoed in other millenarian movements in other cultures threatened by colonialism, including that of the Xhosa of South Africa, from among whom the Cattle-Killing movement of 1856–57 emerged (see Peires (1989) and Chapter 8). In this case also, there would be no more labouring in the garden or on European plantations or in mines. There would be no more suffering, disease and death, and even the natural landscape would be changed to make journeying more pleasurable and less hazardous and strenuous. It should be noted, however, that colonialism and missionary activity are not a necessary part of the explanation for the emergence of millenarian movements of this kind. The millenarianism of the Tupi-Guarani, which consisted of the march towards the Land-Without-Evil where likewise there would be no labour and food and fruit would grow of their own accord, possibly predates colonialism (Chapter 9).

A 'situational' logic and pragmatism underpinned the thoughts and actions of Cargo cultists in Melanesia. They asked how it was possible to receive 'cargo' from another land in return for a simple piece of paper and without labour as the Whites did in their midst. This in terms of their local experience was a 'miraculous' event and was, therefore, with recourse to the world of the 'supernatural' broadly understood.

Myths supplied those involved in the Cargo cults with the explanation that the White man's ships, and later American cargo planes that used Papua New Guinea as a staging post during World War II, were filled with cargo made in the Land of the Dead by the spirits of their dead ancestors, from where the Whites had taken it. Moreover, they applied the teachings they had heard from the European missionaries concerning the Apocalypse and the return of the dead at the millennium, when the just would receive rewards for good conduct in this life and for the sufferings they had undergone, to their own situation. They concluded that they would be recompensed for the exploitation they had suffered on the plantations and in the mines, and for the social and other forms of discrimination that they had experienced from White people. Now that their future had been assured, working on the land no longer made sense nor did the hoarding of possessions, including European money. Their 'situational' logic also led them to the conclusion that the

Whites had derived special power from their faith and knowledge, which enabled them to control others, but had not revealed all the details of this to the people.

Of the well over one hundred Cargo cults known, some were more prone to reject colonial, white culture than others, some were more open to Christian influences than others. To qualify what has been said above about the impact of colonialism the emergence of all these movements cannot be explained in terms of significant colonial contact. As Wilson (1973: 315) pointed out, cargo could arise at almost any stage of cultural contact. Moreover, in almost every case large movements appear to have required a 'big man' with sufficient charisma and status to command respect. Also important in the emergence of these movements, as Wilson again underlines (ibid.), was the pre-existence of the cargo idea. Where such a belief existed, a Cargo cult could be touched off by a seemingly very ordinary happening. The importance of European colonialism to the Cargo cult movement consisted in increasing the sense of relative deprivation already widespread in society. Wilson (ibid.) explains, with reference to the Semeira Cargo cult of New Guinea and others in which there was continuity with traditional feast giving and a preoccupation with wealth, that these movements expressed among the indigenous peoples 'the urgency induced by the awareness of an ever-extending cultural gap in the material accoutrements of life, and a growing self-disparagement and sense of inferiority . . ..' Thus, in this case also, the impact–response unit of analysis would seem to be inadequate as the framework of explanation of the rise of these millenarian movements.

The best-known Cargo cult is the 'Vailala Madness' of the Orokolo tribes of the Gulf of Papua, founded by the prophet Evara after World War I. This movement's concern was with the transformation of everyday life. Although preoccupied with the ancestors, the movement was not what is usually referred to as a nativistic movement, that is, one that seeks exclusively the restoration of old rituals and customs. It called upon the assistance of ancestors, as was traditional, but in a new way. They were called upon to destroy traditional rituals and provide new ones that were of greater power. The movement was also anti-European, while at the same time desiring European cargo. The ancestors were implored to bring the commodities only the Whites had previously enjoyed. Evara prophesied the arrival of a cargo ship loaded with rice, meal, tobacco and, revealingly, guns. And, under the influence of spirits and in a state of trance characterized by frantic physical movement – a marked feature of the ritual behaviour not only of the prophet but of the cult as a whole and hence its name – he also predicted that the Whites would be expelled from the island and that their cargo would pass into local ownership.

The number of Cargo cults increased after World War II despite the failure of these and other prophecies to come to pass. For example, it was initially claimed that the ancestors would return from the Land of the Dead by canoe.

This belief was then changed to reflect the changing times to the belief that they would return by ship, and again, with the arrival of American military aircraft during World War II, to the belief that they would make their return by aeroplane. Such changes in belief led to changes in preparation for the return of the ancestors, including the building of docks for the ships and airstrips for the planes to enable them to land. However, eventually with the failure of the millennium to materialize most of the Cargo cults of the nineteenth and first half of the twentieth century became extinct.

There are some striking comparisons and contrasts to be made between Melanesian millenarianism and other forms including Maori and Native American expressions of this belief (Chapter 5). Moreover, in discussing the Melanesian millenarian movements, some of the main limitations of the impact–response schema of analysis have been highlighted, as in the chapters on South Asia, Africa and Latin America. Accounts of religious innovation, the evidence suggests, in the case of Melanesian society in modern times need to give as much consideration to internal as to external factors rather than assume that the forces which shape this kind of change are simply a response to pressures from without.

Conclusions

The religious landscape, thus, of all three societies discussed in this chapter has undergone considerable reconfiguration in modern times. At first the settler character of Australia and New Zealand made for diversity, and from the late 1940s, and particularly from the 1970s, economic migration from Asia and elsewhere brought with it ever greater religious pluralism, particularly in the form of Oriental and Middle Eastern religion, both old and new. Meanwhile, the core ideas of alternative spirituality that arrived in the nineteenth century, including those of Swedenborg, Mesmer and Blavatsky, have remained influential and have shaped much of New Age Thought in Australia and New Zealand.

The religious diversity, thus, of both of these countries is now shaped somewhat less by Christianity, although this remains the dominant religious tradition, and somewhat more by Oriental religions and spiritualities, and especially by Buddhism, Hinduism, Sihkism and Islam, NRMs from Japan and India, contemporary Neo-Pagan, Wiccan, and Female Spirituality groups, esoteric movements such as Urantia and popular myth-fiction-based movements such as Jediism. Although it would be easy to exaggerate its extent, it is possible to discern not only a new religious diversity in terms of content but also a new diversity in relation to cognitive styles and approaches to being religious or spiritual. This is particularly evident with regard to the increasing emphasis placed on coming to know the truth from personal experience at the expense of the way of faith, which is based on revealed doctrines that are transmitted by an external authority to the believer for her/his acceptance.

Although the divide between the two is by no means clear-cut, there would also appear to be a growing involvement in subjective spirituality at the expense of formal religion (see Chapter 1).

In Melanesia, where the old Cargo cults have died Neo-Pentecostalism has begun to thrive. However, the core ideas of 'commodity millennialism' have remained powerfully appealing, if not in the urban then in the rural areas.

References and select bibliography

Berger, Peter (1967) *The Social Reality of Religion*, Harmondsworth: Penguin Books.

Bilimoria, Purushottama (1997) 'The Australian South Asian Diaspora' in John Hinnells (ed.) *A New Handbook of Living Religions*, Oxford: Blackwell, pp. 728–56.

Bouma, Gary (1999) 'From Hegemony to Plurality: Managing Religious Diversity in Modernity and Postmodernity', *Australian Religion Studies Review*, 12(2), 7–27.

Bouma, Gary (2003) 'Globalization, Social Capital and the Challenge to Harmony of Recent Changes in Australia's Religious and Spiritual Demography: 1947–2001', *Australian Religion Studies Review*, 16(2), 55–69.

Bouma, Gary, Smith, Wendy and Vasi, Shiva (2000) 'Japanese Religion in Australia: Mahikari and Zen in a Multicultural Society' in Peter B. Clarke (ed.) *Japanese New Religions: In Global Perspective*, Richmond, Surrey: Curzon Press, pp. 74–112.

Burridge, Kenelm (1969) *New Heaven, New Earth: A Study of Millenarian Activities*, Oxford: Blackwell.

Clarke, Peter B. (1993) 'Why Women are the Priests and Teachers in Bahian Candomble' in Elizabeth Puttick and Peter B. Clarke (eds) *Women as Teachers and Disciples in Traditional and New Religions*, Lampeter: Edwin Mellen Press, pp. 97–115.

Clarke, Peter B. (2000) 'Modern Japanese Millenarian Movements' in Peter B. Clarke (ed.) *Japanese New Religions: In Global Perspective*, Richmond, Surrey: Curzon Press, pp. 129–81.

Coco, Angelo (2001) 'Searching for Reflections: Women's Paths to a Feminist Pagan Spirituality Group', *Australian Religion Studies Review*, 14(1), 19–31.

Eller, Cynthia (1993) *Living in the Lap of the Goddess: The Feminist Spirituality Movement in America*, New York: Crossroad.

Ellwood, Robert (1993) *Islands of the Dawn: The Story of Alternative Spirituality in New Zealand*, Honolulu: University of Hawai'i Press.

Ezzy, Douglas (2001) 'The Commodification of Witchcraft', *Australian Religion Studies Review*, 14(1), 31–45.

Finke, Roger and Stark, Rodney (1988) 'Religious Economies and Sacred Canopies: Religious Mobilization in American Cities, 1906', *American Sociological Review*, 53, 41–9.

Glock, Charles Y. and Stark, Rodney (1965) *Religion and Society in Tension*, Chicago: Rand McNally.

Hanegraaff, Wouter (1999) 'New Age Spiritualities as Secular Religion: A Historian's Perspective', *Social Compass*, 46, 145–60.

Heelas, Paul (1996) *The New Age Movement*, Oxford: Blackwell.

Hill, Michael (1987) 'The Cult of Humanity and the Secret Religion of the Educated Classes', *New Zealand Sociology*, 2(2), 112–27.

Hill, Michael (2001) 'Cult Busters in Canberra? Reflections on Two Recent Government Reports', *Australian Religion Studies Review*, 14(1), 113–22.

Hill, Michael and Zwaga, Wiebe (1989) 'Religion in New Zealand: Change and Comparison' in James Beckford and Thomas Luckmann (eds) *The Changing Face of Religion*, London: Sage, pp. 64–88.

Howell, Judith Day (1998) 'Gender Role Experimentation in New Religious Movements: Clarification of the Brahma Kumaris Case', *Journal for the Scientific Study of Religion*, 37(3), 453–61.

Hughes, Philip J. (1997) *Religion in Australia: Facts and Figures*, Kew, Victoria: Christian Research Association.

Hughes, Philip, Black, Alan, Bellamy, John and Kaldor, Peter (2004) 'Identity and Religion in Contemporary Australia', *Australian Religion Studies Review*, 17(1), 53–69.

Hume, Lynne (1997) *Witchcraft and Paganism in Australia*, Melbourne: Melbourne University Press.

Hume, Lynne (1998) 'Creating Sacred Space: Outer Expressions of Inner Worlds in Modern Wicca', *Journal of Contemporary Religion*, 13(3), 309–21.

Hume, Lynne (2002) *Ancestral Power: The Dreaming, Consciousness and Aboriginal Australians*, Melbourne: Melbourne University Press.

Iannaccone, Lawrence R. (1994) 'Why Strict Churches are Strong', *American Journal of Sociology*, 99(5), 1180–211.

Iannaccone, Lawrence R. (1995) 'Voodoo Economics – Reviewing the Rational Choice Approaches to Religion', *Journal for the Scientific Study of Religion*, 34(1), 76–88.

Kerkhove, Ray (2004) 'Towards a Multi-Faith History of the Sunshine Coast', *Australian Religion Studies Review*, 17(1), 94–122.

Krüll, Marianne (1995) 'Women's Spirituality and Healing in Germany', *Women and Therapy*, 16(2–3), 135–47.

Lanternari, Vittorio (1991) 'Melanesian Religions' in Stewart Sutherland and Peter Clarke (eds) *The Study of Religion: Traditional and New Religion*, London: Routledge, pp. 85–95.

Lyon, D. (2000) *Jesus in Disneyland: Religion in Postmodern Times*, Cambridge: Polity.

Maddock, K. (1991) 'Australian Aboriginal Religion' in Stewart Sutherland and Peter Clarke (eds) *The Study of Religion: Traditional and New Religion*, London: Routledge, pp. 78–84.

Mulcock, Jane (2001) '(Re)-discovering our Indigenous Selves: the Nostalgic Appeal of Native Americans and other Generic Indigenes', *Australian Religion Studies Review*, 14(1), 45–65.

Nakamaki, Hirochika (2003) *Japanese Religions at Home and Abroad*, London: Routledge/Curzon.

Palmer, Susan J. (1993) 'Women's "Cocoon" Work in New Religious Movements: Sexual Experimentation and Feminine Rites of Passage', *Journal for the Scientific Study of Religion*, 32, 343–55.

Palmer, Susan J. (1994) *Moon Sisters, Krishna Mothers, Rajneesh Lovers: Women's Roles in New Religions*, Syracuse, NY: Syracuse University Press.

Pecoti, David (2001) 'Three Aboriginal Responses to New Age Religion: A Textual Interpretation', *Australian Religion Studies Review*, 14(1), 65–82.

Peires, J. B. (1989) *The Dead Will Arise*, Johannesburg: Ravan Press.

Phipps, Peter and Possamai, Adam (2003) 'After September 11th: Religion, Diversity and Social Cohesion under Globalization', *Australian Religion Studies Review*, 16(2), 8–19.

Possamai, Adam (2001) 'Not the New Age: Perennism and Spiritual Knowledges', *Australian Religion Studies Review*, 14(1), 82–97.

Possamai, Adam (2003) 'Alternative Spiritualities, New Religious Movements and Jediism in Australia', *Australian Religion Studies Review*, 16(2), 69–87.

Possamai, Adam and Murray, Lee (2004) 'New Religious Movements and the Fear of Crime', *Journal of Contemporary Religion*, 19(3), 337–53.

Richardson, James T. (1995) 'Media Bias toward New Religious Movements in Australia' (unpublished paper).

Richardson, James (2001) 'New Religions in Australia: Public Menace or Societal Salvation?', *Nova Religio: The Journal of Alternative and Emergent Religions*, 4(2), 258–65.

Spuler, Michelle (2000) 'Characteristics of Buddhism in Australia', *Journal of Contemporary Religion*, 15(1), 29–45.

Spuler, Michelle (2003) *Developments in Australian Buddhism: Facets of the Diamond*, London: Routledge/Curzon.

Stark, Rodney (1996) 'Why Religious Movements Succeed or Fail: A Revised General Model', *Journal of Contemporary Religion*, 11(2), 133–47.

Stark, Rodney and Bainbridge, William Sims (1980) 'Secularization, Revival and Cult Formation', *Annual Review of the Social Sciences of Religion*, 4, 85–119.

Stark, Rodney and Bainbridge, William Sims (1985) *The Future of Religion*, Berkeley: University of California Press.

Stark, Rodney and Finke, Roger (2000) *Acts of Faith: Explaining the Human Side of Religion*, Berkeley: University of California Press.

Tawhai, T. P. (1991) 'Maori Religion' in Stewart Sutherland and Peter B. Clarke (eds) *The Study of Religion: Traditional and New Religion*, London: Routledge, pp. 96–105.

Wallis, Roy (1976) *The Road to Total Freedom: A Sociological Analysis of Scientology*, London: Heinemann.

Wallis, Roy (1986) 'Figuring out Cult Receptivity', *Journal for the Scientific Study of Religion*, 25(4), 494–503.

Wilson, Bryan R. (1973) *Magic and the Millennium*, London: Heinemann.

Wilson, Bryan R. (1979) 'The Return of the Sacred?', *Journal for the Scientific Study of Religion*, 18(3), 268–80.

Wilson, Bryan R. (1990) *The Social Dimensions of Sectarianism*, Oxford: Clarendon Press.

Worsley, Peter (1968) *The Trumpet Shall Sound*, New York: Schocken Books.

Part III

New religions

North Africa and the Middle East, and Africa, south of the Sahara

Chapter 7

North Africa and the Middle East

This chapter focuses on new, but not necessarily sectarian, Islamic movements in North Africa (Egypt) and the Middle East, regions which have been closely linked by Islam since the first century of the Muslim era, that is, from shortly after the hijra or withdrawal of the Prophet Muhammad from Mecca to Yathrib or Medina in 622 CE, the first year of the Muslim calendar. There is also one brief account of an Israeli radical orthodox movement, Gush Emunim, which arose on a wave of patriotism following the Arab–Israeli conflict in 1967.

Although often seen as a response to modernization and globalization, several of the core issues that engage Islamist groups, who are defined essentially by their demand for an Islamic state, have a long history. The contemporary debate over the relationship between Muslim and non-Muslim societies, the use of jihād or holy war against lapsed Muslims, and over martyrdom in the sense of the giving of one's life for the cause of Islam goes back to the first century of Islam. Then the Kharijites – a group of movements that emphasized works over faith and withdrew their support for the Shi'ites or party of Ali, cousin and son-in-law of the Prophet Muhammad, after the battle of Siffin in 657 CE – were in strong disagreement with other Muslims who opposed their use of jihād, particularly against lapsed Muslims.

Likewise, the debate on the relationship of revelation and reason did not begin in the Muslim world with the rise of modern science and the impact of Enlightenment thinking from the West, but can be traced back to earlier times. Also controversial in so-called pre-modern times were the heated debates and divisions which continue today over the role of the Caliphate, and over such principles of legal theory as the relative weight to be given to ijtihād or individual interpretation of the Qur'ān and Sunna, the path followed by the Prophet Muhammad, and ijm'a or the consensus of the community, as formulated and made known by the 'ulama or scholars. Islam and nationalism, and Islam and secularism, have also been frequent topics of controversy in Islamic history.

The adoption of a historical perspective does not, however, imply either that contemporary interpretations and understandings of notions such as jihād or ijtihād are not in their own way distinctive and new developments, or that modernization and Westernization have not widened and complicated the issues that Muslims have had to grapple with for centuries. The historical perspective simply illustrates that following the Sunna or path of the Prophet Muhammad, and even understanding what this consists of in all its detail, has never proved to be either easy or uncontroversial. It also illustrates that such changes that are occurring in North Africa and the Middle East cannot be fully understood and explained if seen solely as responses to Westernization and modernization, or the enlargement and greater cultural diversification of the Umma or Muslim community in modern times.

While modernization has posed problems for all of the historic religions, including Islam, it is important to note, as Gibb pointed out, that internal as well as external factors have given rise to modern Islamic reformism (islāh). In his words: 'The history of Islam in the nineteenth and twentieth centuries is a history of revival and readjustments under the double stimulus of challenge from within and pressing dangers from without' (1978: 113).

Many examples could be cited in support of this interpretation of the modern history of Islamic reform including the example of the militant, puritan Wahhābi movement founded in c.1744 by Muhammad ibn ahl Wahhāb, a member of the House of Suud, which at the time consisted of the Emirs of Dar'īya. This movement was opposed not only to growing secularization – the espousal by Muslim rulers of values often very different from Islamic values and their dependence on Sufis or mystics rather than Muslim jurists for advice – but also to what it perceived as the excessive devotionalism surrounding the Prophet Muhammad, a devotionalism encouraged by the Sufi or mystical orders, some of which were extremely powerful international organizations. Sufis were controversial for other reasons including coffee-drinking and the opening of coffee houses, an innovation introduced in the early sixteenth century by Yemeni Sufis who found that it enlivened their devotional exercises. The practice quickly spread across the Middle East and North Africa to the alarm of some of the 'ulama or scholars who opposed its drinking on the grounds that it not only led to intoxication but also encouraged unedifying gatherings.

It is important to note that contemporary Islamic reform movements are not all of a kind. The most important concern of some is the reform of Islam by peaceful means to enable Muslims to embrace in a positive and constructive way the modern world, while others are determined to throw a 'cordon sanitaire' around Islam and protect it by jihād or holy war, if necessary, from the corrosive influences of modernization which for them is synonymous with Westernization. For the latter an essential part of this defence of Islam is the restoration of authentic Islam, which includes the establishment of an Islamic state, that is, a state in which Shari'a law is recognized as the law of the land. I do not use the term 'fundamentalist' to describe those who hold this position for, as Hassan (1990: 157) points out, this label clearly embodies a negative value judgement regardless of the evidence and evokes an image of all those who seek to establish an Islamic state as irrational and wantonly violent. The previously mentioned Kharijite movement, and in particular the extremist Azāriqa faction, was condemned by both Sunni and Shi'ite movements for its readiness to declare all opponents apostates and, therefore, legitimate targets of jihād of the sword. Moreover, Islamist groups active today do not all espouse militancy, though in recent times there has been a growing tendency among such movements to support the use of force (Zahab and Roy, 2002).

Despite the problems it poses there are those who believe that Islamic society is better equipped than most religions to escape secularization and defend its public influence while undergoing modernization.

Modernization and Islamic exceptionalism

Gellner is among those who have argued the case for Islamic exceptionalism in the face of modernization and Westernization, claiming that these processes do not constitute a serious danger to the public character of Islam. He writes (1981: 5): 'In Islam, and only in Islam, purification/modernization on the one hand, and the re-affirmation of a putative old local identity on the other, can be done in one and the same language and set of symbols.'

Gellner suggests that, unlike what has happened or is happening in non-Muslim societies, in the case of Muslim societies Islam can remain as the core idea of the nation and the language of political discourse during the process of modernization and nation building. The robust tradition of the previously mentioned 'ulama or scholars who interpret the Qur'ān and Hadith (Tradition), which is essentially the source of the Sunna or Way of the Prophet Muhammad, and the Shari'a (Islamic law) can, Gellner insists, ensure this.

This thesis of Islamic exceptionalism begs a number of questions, particularly in an age like the present when many progressive Muslims, Islamists and Jihadi groups are calling for a return to ijtihād, or the right of individual interpretation of the law. The concept of ijtihād, which in its earliest uses was equated with kiyas or analogy (Gibb and Kramers, 1974: 1580), means essentially the application by a competent individual of analogy to the Qur'ān and the Sunna, or the 'Way' of the Prophet Muhammad, as a method of arriving at an opinion on a particular case or rule of law. This is much more common in Shi'a Islam where the Shah is simply the locum tenens, as it were, until the Hidden Imam, who is ruler de iure divino, returns. Ijtihād in principal, and on occasion in practice, as the Iranian case since the 1970s illustrates, gives special muftis, regarded as the mouthpiece or spokesperson of the Hidden Imam in Shi'a Islam, a great deal of control over the decisions and actions of the Shah.

This preference for ijtihād reduces the importance of ijmā', or the principle of consensus of the community, which was traditionally formed from the ijtihād of its individual members and interpreted and expounded by those scholars or 'ulama considered competent enough to do so. However, it came to be widely accepted among Sunni orthodox Muslims that the door to ijtihād was closed in medieval times and it is this that makes the present demand for its return appear radical and for many a source of bid'a or innovation. Those who would exercise ijtihād must be of good character and conduct themselves in conformity with Islamic moral and ethical principles. They must also possess, as was indicated above, competence in a number of disciplines considered essential for a sound understanding of Islamic scripture and tradition, including Arabic, the principles and purposes of Shari'a and hermeneutics. They must also have a good knowledge of the contribution of the jurists (mujtahidin) and be well acquainted with developments in the contemporary world.

Although, as we have seen, for Sunni Muslims the so-called 'door of ijtihād' was officially closed in medieval times, a minority of scholars have continued to claim the right to exercise it, and in the contemporary context the number of those who assume this right has greatly increased. Moreover, the interpretation they give to the scope of ijtihād, which was once confined to interpreting only those points on which no agreement or consensus had been reached, appears to be wider now than in the past, leading some to speak of the 'ijtihād revolution' in modern Islam.

The idea of 'Muslim exceptionalism' tends, thus, to ignore the divergent opinion among Muslims concerning the role of the 'ulama, a divergence, which becomes even clearer in the modern context in debates on the compatibility of Islam and democracy. Abou El Fadl (2004: 36) in an important contribution to this debate warns against placing authority in the hands of the scholars:

> democracy is an appropriate system for Islam because it both expresses the special worth of human beings – the status of viceregency – and at the same time deprives the state of any pretence of divinity by locating ultimate authority in the hands of the people rather than the 'ulama.

And Khan (2004: 64) places even stronger emphasis on ijtihād or the right of individuals in a democracy to explicate the law:

> In an Islamic democracy every individual is a vicegerent of God and therefore has the legitimate authority to act in God's name. Thus every individual has the right to interpret or claim what is law (divine or otherwise).

Views such as these, also aired long before they were taken up again in the nineteenth and twentieth centuries, clearly parallel those of Reformation

Protestantism. They also show that Gellner's position on 'Muslim exceptionalism' not only ignores the diversity of opinion in the Muslim world regarding the role of the 'ulama but also the debate on the nature and character of Islamic society and how it should be governed, a debate that is becoming increasingly complex with globalization and the vast numbers of Muslim migrants from different parts of the world settling permanently in the West.

Islamism, the Muslim Brotherhood and the creation of an Islamic state

Islamist movements, as we will see in the case of the Muslim Brotherhood and Al-Qaeda, reject the consensus of the scholars in favour of ijtihād. Such movements as defined by Roy (1998: 41) place an overriding emphasis on the construction of an Islamic state as a prerequisite for any successful realization of an Islamic society. They are political in that for them Islam is an ideology and their appeal, Roy contends, is largely to 'a modern intelligentsia or to new professional groups and social strata whose upward social mobility is thwarted by a conservative elite, whether traditional or secular' (1998: 54).

Within this broad category of Islamist movement there are two basic types, whose thinking on strategy has increasingly tended to converge in recent times. These are the salafi and the jihadi types, the former demanding a return to strict Islam stripped of local customs and traditions by peaceful rather than militant means, while the latter is committed to militancy as the way to unite all Muslims and restore the practice of true Islam. Jihadists are persuaded that too much attention has been paid to da'wa or mission and not enough to struggle in the form of jihād in defence of and for the restoration of authentic Islam. What they encourage is politico-religious action aimed at the creation of an Islamic state based on the Shari'a. That is a state free of such anti-Islamic Enlightenment ideas as the separation of religion and the state, which gained momentum after the collapse of the Ottoman Caliphate in 1922. However, while anti-secularist and anti-Western, Islamist movements are not anti-modern in every respect. As we will see below, even such a dedicated proponent of an Islamic state and devastating critic of the West as Sayyid Qutb (1906–66) did not, as the impression is sometimes given, reject all of Western culture or Western law.

The following account of the predominantly lay Muslim Brotherhood will look at how this movement was influenced by the Salafi reform movement, at its historical development and the impact of the thoughts of Sayyid Qutb, one of its leading theorists whose writings continue to exercise a powerful influence on Islamist thinking today. Finally, it will examine the Brotherhood's philosophy and in particular its concept of an Islamic state.

The Muslim Brotherhood (Ikhwan al-Muslimin), also frequently referred to as the Muslim Brothers, was founded in Cairo in 1928 by the Egyptian schoolteacher Hassan al-Banna (1906–49) who came from the village of Damanhur situated to the northwest of Alexandria. The movement went on to become the most radical and influential Islamic reform movement of modern times. Although outlawed in Egypt since the early 1950s, its ideas continue to motivate radical Islam the world over.

The ideology of the Brotherhood is best understood if seen as the conclusion pushed to extremes of the reformist notions developed by such important reformers as the founder and inspiration of the Pan-Islamist movement, the Afghan Jamāl al-Dīn (1839–97), his disciple the Egyptian Shaykh Muhammad Abduh (1849–1905) the leader of the Salafi movement, and Rashid Rida (1865–1935), Abduh's devoted Lebanese disciple. Rida translated Muhammad Abduh's commentary on the Qur'ān and became the editor of the widely respected and scholarly journal *Al-Manār* which al-Banna read as a student in Cairo. A Pan-Islamist Rashid Rida was, according to Gibb (1978: 122): 'steadily driven back on fundamentalism, and at length recognized and cultivated a relationship of purpose and thought between the Salafīya and the Wahhābīya'.

But Gibb continues – and this is what has been underlined above as one of the 'new' features of Islamist movements:

> In their final doctrinal position, the Salafiya rejecting the too pronouncedly sectarian mood of the Wahhābis, confess themselves 'Neo-Hanbalites', conservatives claiming the reopening of the 'Gate of Ijtihād' . . . and the right of reinterpretation in matters of theology and law.

It was this line of thinking that provided the doctrinal basis for new movements such as the Muslim Brotherhood, the Association of Muslim Youth and others in the Arab and Muslim world as a whole. However, it was not always accepted uncritically.

The point of departure of the Salafi critique of Islam was the decadence that had overcome Muslim lands by the middle of the nineteenth century. These lands were not only under the control of foreign, non-Muslim rulers but were also divided among themselves, and steeped in popular devotionalism – there are echoes of Wahhābism here – that was believed to be destroying the purity of the Islamic faith. Without any moral and intellectual standards Muslims were said to be groping around in jahiliyya or ignorance, and failing in their obligations to God and to each other.

The cause of this decadence, the reformers argued, was the abandonment by Muslims of true, authentic Islam under the impact of Western influence. The remedy, therefore, had to include managing that influence constructively while returning to the Qur'ān and Sunna or way of the Prophet Muhammad, that is, to the early days of the Muslim community known as the days of the pious ancestors, or al-salaf al sālih. Those who accepted this diagnosis of the plight of Islam became know as Salafis.

Managing Western influence went along with the eradication from Islamic practice of all forms of shirk, or the association of the human with the divine, the elimination of all superstitious practices including the very popular cult of holy men and women, and the disbanding of the Sufi or mystical orders or turuq.

Another major salafi objective that exercised so much influence over al-Banna and the Muslim Brotherhood was the union of Sunni and Shi'ite Muslims. This union also envisaged the resolution of differences between the Muslim law schools (Arabic: maddhahib; singular: madhhab) and the regeneration and spread of the use of Arabic – described as a civilizing language not tied to any particular nation and the liturgical language of Islam – across the world. This reform plan envisaged granting Arabs a special place in the Umma or community of Muslims.

Also an important part of the salafi programme was the reform of the Islamic education system, which would involve opening it up to the modern sciences in order to demonstrate that there was no conflict between Islamic belief and reason. This was part of a strategy designed to defend Islam against Western influence, seen as more or less synonymous with European influence, and against Christian missionaries. Western culture was not to be rejected outright but what was to be avoided was an over hasty and uncritical acceptance of its attitudes, moral and social, and of its ideas and goals. Nor was its dissemination and interpretation to be left to missionaries.

The Salafi movement saw itself as following a middle-way between the strict puritanism of the Wahhābis and the secular approach of the Turks. It thought of itself as Islamic conservatism with an open mind, and of its reform programme as balanced. Its ideas provided the subject matter of lectures and seminars at the major Islamic universities in Cairo and throughout the Middle East and were frequently discussed on radio and in the press. Many among the middle and lower middle classes in Egypt and across the Arab world not only found this conservative Islamic reform programme much more in keeping with their own ideas and ideals than say the puritan brand of reform supported by Wahhābism or the secular approach of Turkey, but were also attracted to the emphasis it placed on praxis, or its joining up of theory and practice. This was also to be an important part of the appeal of the Muslim Brotherhood.

However, while the Brotherhood acknowledged its considerable debt to Salafism it was also critical of what it saw as the narrow scope of its reform programme, which limited itself to religious and moral issues. The Brotherhood, thus, set out to provide a more comprehensive programme of reform, in fact it regarded its own reform programme as the most comprehensive reform programme in the history of Islam.

Whether this was the case or not, the Brotherhood could certainly be considered 'new' in the sense that it was the first highly and efficiently organized, essentially Islamic, urban mass movement in the modern world that sought to address the plight of Muslims (Mitchell, 1969: 321). Moreover, and very unusually, it distinguished itself from other reform movements by evaluating everything including Sufism and/or mysticism in terms of its contribution to social action in pursuit of its goal of uplifting Muslims.

The movement's founder, al-Banna, an ardent mystic, strongly opposed what he described as 'isolated spirituality' and repeatedly stressed the fundamental importance to Islamic reform of 'socially engaged' spirituality. He argued that the purpose of becoming a mystic was to acquire the discipline necessary to address and find solutions to social problems, an argument used by modern Buddhist reformers in Thailand and elsewhere regarding the purpose of enlightenment (see Chapter 11).

On his arrival in Cairo, aged seventeen, to train for the teaching profession at the prestigious Dar ul-Ulum Teacher Training Institute, al-Banna was already a member of the Hasaliyya Society for Charity, a forerunner of the Muslim Brotherhood. He was also already familiar with some of the Islamic classics in philosophy and mysticism. Among his mentors was the renowned Persian philosopher and mystic Ahmed al-Ghazali (1058–1111) 'a man', Gibb (1978: 94) writes 'who stands on a level with Augustine and Luther in religious insight and intellectual vigour'. He is also comparable in stature with the eminent medieval Catholic theologian Thomas Aquinas (1224?/26–1274).

Nothing, however, prepared al-Banna for the disappointment he was to experience on his first encounter with Islam in Cairo. He was deeply shocked and shamed at the serious moral and social decay of the city. He was humiliated by the British occupation of Egypt, which he now experienced more at first hand, and was stunned by the high rate of defection from Islam of Muslim youth of his own age. Much of what was now justified in the name of intellectual freedom, freedom of choice and individual liberty was, al-Banna believed, a pretext for destroying the influence of religion among the masses. While in this state of shock and disappointment, he came to know Rashid Rida, discussed his feelings with him and spent much of his free time browsing in the Salafi bookstore, helping to form the Young Muslim Association – a Salafi association, and a counter to the Young Men's Christian Association – and organizing student protests.

Appointed to his first teaching post at a school in Ismailiyya in Upper Egypt, al-Banna and six companions who were working at the British Camp in the city started the 'Muslim Brothers in the service of Islam and hence the Society of the Muslim Brothers' (Mitchell, 1969: 8). Initially and for some time Hassan al-Banna seems to have wanted to reform Islam through the Brotherhood by peaceful means. By the early 1940s, however, he had established close ties with young army officers including the future President of Egypt, Anwar Sadat. The Brotherhood was also in possession of stockpiles of weapons, which were entrusted to the care of a select group within the Brotherhood known as the secret apparatus. This section of the movement was organized on the basis of cells, each one composed of no more than five members. By 1943 al-Banna was speaking about jihād as a means of self-defence.

From the middle to late 1940s the Brotherhood became involved in anti-British riots, the burning of books in the English language and, allegedly, the dynamiting of buildings, the assassination in 1948 of the Egyptian Prime Minister, al-Nuqrāshi Pasha, and an attempted coup d'état. It was also sending its members to fight against what it regarded as the Israeli occupation of Palestine, a cause that has remained at the heart of Islamist ideology.

Between 1946 and 1948, the peak period for membership, the Brotherhood consisted of 2,000 branches and had increased its following to somewhere between 300,000 and 600,000 active members, and may have had a similar number of sympathizers. It had developed close contacts with royalty, leading politicians and those discontented young army officers who were to become known as the Free Officers and who included in their number the future President Gamel Abdul Nasser, as well as the previously mentioned future President, Anwar Sadat. The Brotherhood had effectively become a state within a state.

The assassination of Prime Minister al-Nuqrāshi Pasha, allegedly by members of the Brotherhood, in 1948 led to the dissolution of the Brotherhood in December 1948 on the grounds that it was in the process of organizing a revolution. It continued to function largely from prison, a recruiting ground and training school second to none. In February 1949 Hassan al-Banna was executed outside the Young Muslim Men's Association in Cairo, an assassination widely thought to have been organized by the Government.

In 1951 the Brotherhood's property was restored and it had entered into close collaboration with the Free Officers. The latter overthrew the Government in July 1952, deposed the King and appeared to be willing to come to some agreement with the Brotherhood, now led by the rather aloof, uncharismatic, uninspiring, former judge, Hassan Ismail al-Hudaybi, on the question of an Islamic state. Further negotiation with the enigmatic Hudaybi was never going to be easy for he rarely let it be known where he actually stood on such important issues as jihād, at one time supporting its use, at another placing the emphasis almost exclusively on the intellectual and spiritual training of members. He was also ambivalent about his political and royal connections, which did little to endear him to the Free Officers.

The Free Officers, under the chairmanship of Nasser, for their part, soon came to the realization that the Islamic agenda of the Brotherhood was much more radical than their own, which was for a modern, socialist society that respected Islamic principles but was not based exclusively on these. The Brotherhood was banned again in 1954 for attempting to overthrow the Government under the cover of religion. When made legal a few months later the movement played a prominent part in the demonstration against the

Anglo-Egyptian agreement of July 1954. This issue seriously divided the Brotherhood, particularly over the question of whether it should use force against the Government or, as its leader appeared to want, rely solely on peaceful means.

An attempt on Nasser's life at a rally in Alexandria in October 1954, said to have been staged by members of the Brotherhood, provided the Government with another opportunity to ban the movement yet again, this time for attempting to cause fitna or civil strife and destroy the country. Thousands of members were subsequently imprisoned, some 500 sentenced to death, six of whom were hanged and who immediately came to be venerated as martyrs.

Not all those believed to have been involved in the assassination attempt and in other violent acts were apprehended. The occupations of those on the Government's wanted list reveal something of the social composition of the Brotherhood at this time. As the list shows the movement received support from all the various socio-economic groups and professions including lawyers, army officers, police officers, civil servants, teachers, doctors, labourers, carpenters, students from both Islamic and secular institutions of higher education, white collar workers in the private sector, engineers, accountants, journalists, mechanics, tailors, doormen, farmers and the unemployed (Mitchell, 1969: 328–9). The urban middle classes were prominent among the activists and more influential than rural members in shaping policy. While many became Islamists mainly for nationalist and economic reasons, for others the Brotherhood filled the spiritual void left by their direct experience of the erosion of the faith under the impact of Western culture.

The influence of Sayyid Qutb (1906–66)

With the assassination of Hassan al-Banna in 1949 the Brotherhood lost its balance, cohesion and direction, although the arrival of Sayyid Qutb, a literary intellectual or adib, was in due course to compensate somewhat for this loss. While working as a civil servant for the Ministry of Education in Cairo, Qutb was sent for further training to the United States (1948–51), where the culture shock he experienced was profound and disturbing, leading him to see in virtually everything, everyone and every institution, including the Christian Church, little but evil. This experience turned his opposition to the excesses of Western culture into a crusade. What Cantwell Smith (1957: 159 n. 203) wrote of progressive Arab thinkers in general certainly applied to Sayyid Qutb: 'Most Westerners have simply no inkling how deep and fierce is the hate, especially of the West, that has gripped the modernizing Arab.'

What disturbed Qutb most about the culture of the United States was what he saw as its 'fanatic racism', the materialism there 'that deadened the spirit', the vulgarity and lewdness which he believed was caused by the emancipation of women and the valuing of individual freedom over one's duties to

God, evils which he claimed could also to be found in and were even promoted by the Christian Church (1965: 119). Like Hassan al-Banna, Sayyid
Qutb was highly critical on the one hand of Western Christianity and more
tolerant on the other of the Eastern rites. Both men believed that Eastern
Christians, like Muslims, were in need of protection from Western missionaries whom they saw as agents of Western cultural and political imperialism
and whose goal, they maintained, was to undermine not only Islam but also
the local Coptic and Orthodox heritage.

Qutb, like al-Banna, stressed the need for Muslims to purify their souls in
order to purify their land in the sense of ridding it of imperialism. He and al-
Banna spoke and wrote as much about spiritual and mental imperialism as
they did about political and military forms. Indeed, according to Qutb, the
former types were the real danger for, unlike political and military
imperialism which inspired opposition, they calmed, dulled and deceived
their victims (Mitchell, 1969: 230). Hence the war to be waged by Islam,
Qutb was convinced, at least prior to his imprisonment in 1954, was a war of
disciplined faith not of arms, and was to be waged not only on Western
missionaries but also on aid agencies, cultural institutions including
UNESCO, foreign academic researchers – in particular social scientists and
Orientalists – and against all the sources by means of which Western ideas
and ways were disseminated, including: 'the pens and tongues of the people's
democracies – radio, television, journalism and Western literature' (Mitchell,
1969: 231). Qutb was also highly critical of the Western model of women's
liberation, a model which he saw as being devoid of honour and dignity. A
woman could become a doctor, or lawyer or politician, providing she was
rigorous about dressing modestly. Qutb seems to have accepted in principle
the mixing of the sexes but to have seen it as impractical on account of the
weak nature of man and woman (Mitchell, 1969: 256 n.27).

During his years in prison (1954–65) where he wrote *Milestones* (1965),
now a classic of Islamism, Qutb began to address his thoughts not just to
Muslims but to humanity as a whole, pleading with it to wake up before it
was destroyed by the moral decadence of its own making. But *Milestones* is
not a purely anti-Western tract for it also speaks of 'the genius of Europe'
which must it insists be preserved. It seeks to propose a third way between
Capitalism and Communism, arguing that neither of these ideologies can
provide human beings with the high ideals necessary for their full development in harmony with their nature. Even Islam, corrupted by alien ideas and
practices, was failing in this task and hence the apocalyptic warning that a
catastrophic end was imminent unless Muslims returned to living by the
Shari'a.

Qutb, like many of his fellow Brothers, believed that the corruption of
Islam had given birth to a new age of jahiliyya or ignorance similar to that
which had existed before God's final revelation to the Prophet Muhammad
in the form of the Qur'ān. Qutb, however, used this term in a wider sense than

its original meaning, applying it to cover all Muslim societies past and present that failed to rule according to the Shari'a, and to all forms of nationalism and political ideologies that failed to base themselves on the Shari'a and to recognize God's absolute sovereignty. This extension of the concept of jahiliyya was yet another 'new' interpretation of traditional Islamic ideas developed by one of the Brotherhood's leading theorists.

A new interpretation was also given to the old concept of hijra or flight, which, as we have seen, refers to the flight of the Prophet Muhammad and his followers from Mecca to Yathrib or Medina in 622 CE, the first year (1 AH) of the Muslim calendar. In Qutb's understanding of it, hijra meant flight from any society, regardless of the epoch, that existed in a state of jahiliyya. As Voll points out (1991: 372), the message Qutb was sending out to committed Muslims by this new meaning given to hijra was that they must stand back from such a society and form a core of activists who would work to turn such a society into a Muslim state.

I want at this point to attempt to provide a brief overview of other key aspects of the Brotherhood's philosophy of Islam, with the caveat that for many of its members the movement was more about action than ideas, action not only to relieve the plight of Muslims in Egypt but action over Palestine. Like many other Muslim movements in the Middle East before and since, the Brotherhood was persuaded that the United States and Britain were involved in a conspiracy with Israel to prevent the establishment of a Palestinian state and thereby undermine Islam in the region.

The Brotherhood's idea of an Islamic state

The Brotherhood's thinking on the content of Shari'a, the nature of an Islamic state and other important issues was never systematically thought through. It gives, thus, the appearance at times of being inconsistent if not self-contradictory.

This notwithstanding, several core ideas informed and inspired its theorist, including the concept of Islam as a universal order (nizam) without any equal, an order that was revealed by God and that was in possession of his truth which covered every aspect of human activity. In the words of Hassan al-Banna: 'Islam is at the same time a system of belief and worship, a fatherland and a nation, a religion, a state, spirituality and action, Qur'ān and sword' (Mitchell, 1969: 29).

The Brotherhood's thinking about the nature of an Islamic society was also based on the idea of a fundamental and unbreakable link between the spiritual and temporal in Islam, although, following the Sufi inclinations of its founder, it stressed the importance of the spiritual over the temporal. This providing of the spiritual in question was not the 'isolated spirituality', which al-Banna dismissed as of no worth, but the 'social spirituality', which he insisted was the most authentic form of Islamic spirituality. Islam was to be a source of activity, a jihād for the improvement of the socio-economic conditions of Muslims and against all forms of materialism, including atheistic materialism.

Through jihād or struggle the Brotherhood believed it would be possible to establish the 'virtuous society'. It would begin with the education of the young and extend this programme to the masses. The education provided by the Brotherhood would focus more on the practical sciences, which, it believed, Islam had neglected, than on the deep theoretical sciences. The approach then was practical rather than intellectual and one, thus, that tended to feed the militant belief in Mahdism, a concept that bears a close resemblance to messianism and which tends to foster the conviction that the truth can be demonstrated by force.

The Brotherhood stressed that to be a true Muslim one must live like a Muslim not only by observing the five pillars of Islam – recitation of the profession of faith, prayer five times a day, fasting, alms giving and the performance of the hajj or pilgrimage to Mecca at least once in a lifetime if possible – but also by displaying one's Muslim identity in the wearing of Muslim dress, by abstaining from non-Muslim foods and beverages, by following the Muslim calendar, by using customary Muslim greetings, by speaking only Arabic and by eschewing all forms of escape from life, including monasticism. Islam was to be lived as a this-worldly religion for it was about committing oneself to the transformation of this world. Being Muslim meant all of these things and it also meant being concerned about public health issues, the physical fitness of the young, and with the struggle against poverty.

The Brotherhood understood Islam to be both religion and state (din wa dawla) and contended that where Egypt's or any Muslim society's political arrangements were concerned these should be derived from Islamic political ideas and institutions, or from ideas and institutions reformed along Islamic lines. The Brotherhood was not concerned with establishing a theocracy, at least in the narrow sense of that term. This much was implied by Hassan al-Banna's successor, the previously mentioned former judge Hassan Ismail Hudaybi, who stated in the 1950s that the existing parliamentary framework in Egypt if reformed would satisfy the political requirements of Islam for a Muslim state (Mitchell, 1969: 235).

The Brotherhood did not rule out the possibility of some secular law in an Islamic state providing that law was not incompatible with the Shari'a, and this was also to be the position of a number of contemporary and later Islamist movements. The Dar'ul Islam movement in Indonesia, for example, opposed that country's 1945 constitution – which, while it recognized God, was officially a secular constitution – and fought to replace it by having created an Islamic state governed by Islamic law. However, it was also prepared to accept modern provisions in the Constitution and Penal Code. Moreover, it anticipated that the Islamic state for which it was fighting would be a republic, that the legislative power would be exercised by an elected parliament, and that the head of state who would be referred to as the Imam would have no power to act independently of parliament. There would also be equality before the law for all citizens and freedom of worship, speech and assembly (Nash, 1991: 721).

The actual contents of the Shari'a were rarely discussed by the Brotherhood in any great detail and this suggests that its demand for Shari'a was not only a theological but also a cultural and social imperative. This demand was not born of nostalgia for the past. It was a statement that contemporary Muslim society had no direction, no sense of itself and of its history and development, of the reason for it existence, without Shari'a.

Hassan al-Banna limited his discussion of the content of Shari'a to declaring that it derived from the 500 verses of the Qur'ān and the authentic Hadith or Traditions concerning the Prophet Muhammad's actions and decisions. It was widely believed among members that very few of those traditions relied upon by Muslim jurists would survive careful historical scrutiny. The Brotherhood also refused to accept the schools of Islamic law (maddhahib) or the opinions of legal experts as part of Shari'a. It was opposed to a state run by a clerical class and argued that since there was no religious class in Islam there could be no theocracy. In practice the Brotherhood was a Qur'ān-only based movement. This meant that it understood itself and all contemporary Muslims to be free to apply the previously mentioned principle of ijtihād and interpret the Qur'ān in a way that was relevant to their own times.

Theorists like Qutb also took what might be described as a non-traditional line on the question of the source of a Muslim leader's authority, maintaining that this comes from God through the people. It is the latter who have the authority to endow their ruler with power on the understanding that he will rule according to Shari'a and, by means of checks and balances and in particular shura or consultation, it would be possible to determine whether this was the case or not.

The Brotherhood's objective was the renewal of Islam, not imitation of the past. A Muslim ruler using ijtihād would be able to adapt Shari'a to the present age and interpret in a liberal sense punishments such as amputation for theft and stoning for adultery. Indeed, the movement saw the debate about amputation as academic since such a punishment could only be enforced in a truly Muslim society where justice and equality reigned and where the needs of every citizen were being met by the Government. In such a society there would, of course, be no reason to steal. As to the penalty of stoning the Brotherhood believed this also to be virtually unenforceable since confession by either one or both of the accused parties or evidence of four witnesses was required. The Shari'a was, thus, flexible and adaptable.

This view of Shari'a may seem to conflict with the Brotherhood's call to Muslims to return to living according to the sources of Islam. In making this call the Brotherhood was not, however, calling for the restoration of the Caliphate as it existed during the Golden Age of Islam, the age of the first four caliphs. Qutb, for example, argued that such a policy would entail the abandonment of most of the gains made by civilization for a life in the desert. As far as it is possible to know their minds, it would seem that Qutb was reflecting the thinking of most of the movement's members, who would not have wanted a return to the past but to live in a modern society that accepted Shari'a law as the source of its law. While, moreover, this kind of society would not be opposed in principle, as we have seen, to all non-Islamic law, it could still be justly called Islamic.

In Mitchell's (1969) opinion there was no call among members for the restoration of the Caliphate in the sense of the Caliphate of the Golden Age or for an Islamic state as such. The Brotherhood, he was persuaded, was not a reactionary movement dedicated to the recreation of a seventh-century political order but one that addressed itself to the modern plight of Muslims brought upon them by their own failures and by outside intervention in the form of colonialism and Westernization.

The Brotherhood continues to be active across North Africa and the Middle East, although in Egypt it is only tolerated by the present Egyptian Government. It also continues to be banned from acting as a political party. Seventeen of its members, nonetheless, sit as Independents in the Egyptian parliament and are noted for their opposition to Mubarak's decision to open up the political system, largely in response to the United States' call for greater democracy in the Middle East. The proposed changes have been opposed by the Brotherhood as cosmetic. Indeed, one of their leading officials was recently arrested (May 22nd 2005) at his home in Cairo, allegedly as part of a clampdown on the movement. At the time, the movement was campaigning ahead of a forthcoming referendum against acceptance of the Government proposals for multi-candidate elections, on the grounds that the new rules for election to parliament would still prevent any serious challenge to the President and the ruling party.

This is an appropriate point at which to turn to a brief discussion of other Islamist movements, some of whose ideas and objectives, but by no means all of them, even the most casual of observers will see, bear a close resemblance to those of the Muslim Brotherhood.

Hizb ut Tahir

Hizb ut Tahir, Islamic Liberation Party, was founded in 1949 by Taqi Uddine al-Nabahani, a former Palestinian qadi or judge who once practised in Palestine. This movement maintains a presence in a number of Middle Eastern and Central Asian countries, including Uzbekistan, and in Europe. It has been especially active in Britain where its mosque at Turnpike Lane, known as the London Muslim Cultural Centre, was in pre-September 11th

2001 days attended mainly by Muslims of South Asian origin, most of whom were between the ages of eighteen and thirty and who share much in common with the members of Maududi's Jama'at-i-Islami (see Chapter 10). Like the latter this movement has placed the emphasis on preaching and social daw'a or mission rather than jihād of the sword. Historically, and in principle, Hizb ut Tahir and Jama'at-i-Islami, unlike Sayyid Qutb, have argued that Muslims must first return to the true faith before any call can be made to jihād. Where there has been, as in Pakistan, involvement in violence it has been directed not against the state, as in the case of the Muslim Brotherhood in Egypt, but against a number of local and international, non-Muslim targets.

Hizb ut Tahir's principal preoccupation has been the creation of an Islamic state under the jurisdiction of the Caliph. In accounting for the decline of Islam and the rise of Western capitalist society to the position of oppressor of the Muslim world, two events, Hizb ut Tahir is convinced, were of crucial importance: the abolition of the Caliphate in 1924 and the Israeli defeat of the Arabs in 1948 (Gillespie, 1995). It interprets the liberation of Palestine as a 'redemptive act'.

The revival, thus, of Islam is dependent upon the restoration of the Caliphate and its moving away from the economic, political and cultural control of the West. This revival, Hizb ut Tahir believes, is the collective duty (fard kifaya) of the Umma or Muslim community. A revolutionary vanguard will lead the way in the endeavour to transform the current way of Muslim thinking about freedom and democracy by exposing Western democracy for the corrupt system that it is. It will also make Muslims aware of how invidious and how alien the Western idea of freedom is to Islam.

Al-Qaeda

Here the purpose is to show briefly how Al-Qaeda fits into the mould of contemporary Islamic radicalism fashioned by the many forces of reform and renewal of Islamic society mentioned above and in what ways it is new. Much has been written about this movement since the destruction of the World Trade Center on September 11th 2001 and the tragic loss of life that ensued. The reason given by Al-Qaeda for the attack on the World Trade Center was that it held the United States responsible not only for the situation in the Middle East involving Israel and Palestine but also for sustaining corrupt Islamic regimes in return for being allowed to maintain a military presence on Muslim soil.

It is widely known that in the 1980s the future leader of Al-Qaeda, the Saudi Arabian millionaire Osama bin Laden (b.1957), with American support, became deeply involved as one of the mujahideen (those who struggle and fight) against the Russian military occupation of Afghanistan. Al-Qaeda was not formally in existence at this stage but later came into being through networking, personal contacts and the shared experiences of jihadists fighting against the Russian occupation of a Muslim land.

Osama bin Laden's intellectual mentor was a Palestinian scholar and jihadist from Jordan, Shaykh Abdullah Azzam (1941–89), who was a leading member of the Palestinian branch of the Muslim Brotherhood. Bin Laden had come to know Azzam while he was a student at the Wahhābi-influenced King Abdul Aziz University in Saudi Arabia where the former taught for a number of years. He became acquainted with Azzam again when he travelled to Afghanistan in 1980, where he not only acted as Azzam's paymaster and recruiting sergeant but also took part directly in combat. For example, bin Laden was part of the resistance to the Russian attack on the Masada camp of mainly Arab fighters at Khost in 1987. This attack was effectively the beginning of Al-Qaeda as a movement in the sense that several of those who engaged the Russians at Khost were later to work as Al-Qaeda operatives in Saudi Arabia, Chechnya, and Bosnia.

By the end of the Russian occupation Osama bin Laden's network of real and potential allies ready to perform jihād was considerable. He offered to assist the Saudi Government to repel the attack on Kuwait by Saddam Hussein in 1991 and when this offer was rejected and American assistance accepted he became disillusioned with his country and extremely hostile to the United States. He then entered into an alliance with Hassan Al-Turabi in the Sudan who was of the view that the collapse of the Saddam Hussein regime in Iraq would provide the opportunity for the creation of Islamic states across the region.

The philosophy was one of integration through conflict. Any resistance should be destroyed until all those who were united in the common aim of creating Islamic states were in control. This would eventually result in unity and harmony in the Muslim world, the end of Western domination and the resolution of the Palestinian-Israeli conflict.

After six years in the Sudan (1990–96) bin Laden relocated to Afghanistan and joined forces with the Taliban. He also, and this was of fundamental importance to the development of Al-Qaeda, formed an alliance with the Egyptian medical doctor and jihadist Ayman al-Zawahiri (b.1951). The latter came from a middle-class professional but not well off – they did not own a car for example – Cairo family (Al-Seta, 2002). Many radical Muslims have come from similar backgrounds, that is, professional, often academic but relatively deprived compared with the political class.

On graduating from Cairo medical school in 1974 Ayman al-Zawahiri, took a higher degree and while in Pakistan a doctorate in medicine, which he completed in 1978. As one of the well-known radicals in Cairo whose writings were widely read by Islamists, al-Zawahiri's presence in the city during the coup in which President Sadat was assassinated in 1981 inevitably led to suspicion of his involvement and to his arrest. He was imprisoned on the grounds that he had been the one-time leader of a jihadi cell which like many others was associated with the Gama'a al-Islamiyya (Islamic societies), which acted as, among other things, a front for the banned Muslim Brotherhood. Zawahiri's cell was charged with engaging in the revolutionary practice of *takfir*, that is the identification and declaration of a regime as infidel. While in prison he was cruelly tortured but this clearly did little to lessen his revolutionary zeal for later in his Confessions, as reported by Al-Zayyat (2004), he seemingly stated categorically that his objective was to topple the Government.

Ayman al-Zawahiri, who had also fought against the Russians in Afghanistan, like Osama bin Laden, came to see in the Taliban regime the best hope for the creation of an Islamic society. But the Taliban's understanding of the scope of the Islamic revolution was narrower than that of both al-Zawahiri and bin Laden. Although it allowed foreign jihadi camps to train on Afghani soil, the ultimate objective of the Taliban was the implementation of the Shari'a in Afghanistan and nothing beyond. On the other hand, the vision and aims of al-Zawahiri and bin Laden had come to resemble increasingly those of the leaders of the Iranian revolution, which were more international and expansionist.

In 1998 Osama bin Laden's Al-Qaeda and Ayman al-Zawahiri's movement, Egyptian Islamic Jihād, came together to form the International Islamic Front for Jihād on Jews and Crusaders. Their fatwa or declaration of jihād identified their principal enemies and grievances. It referred to the United States' seven-year occupation – the presence of American troops on Saudi and Kuwaiti soil since the Gulf War in 1991 – of the 'holiest territories of Arabia', America's continued aggression against the Iraqi people, and that country's support for the 'petty' state of the Jews (Lewis, 2003: xxiii–xxiv). Attacks followed on American Embassies in Africa and on American naval vessels in Yemeni waters. The Taliban ruler of Afghanistan, Mullah Omar, a close ally of Osama bin Laden and Ayman al-Zawahiri who funded many of his regime's projects, did eventually agree to internationalize the Islamic struggle and this resulted in the invasion and overthrown of his regime by America and her allies in 2001.

While the Taliban regime was destroyed by the 'Crusaders', the term used by Al-Qaeda to refer to the powers that brought down that regime, Osama bin-Laden and Ayman al-Zawahiri claim victory against the United States and other Western countries, and against corrupt Islamic regimes including Saudi Arabia. Their victory consists, they boast, of having instilled a greater awareness among all Muslims of the need to renew Islam and restore its prestige.

The 1998 fatwa was a new departure. It changed what had come to be widely understood and accepted as the purposes of jihād of the sword: self-defence and the reform of Islam. It shifted the focus of militant Islam from what is termed 'the near' to 'the far' enemy, that is, from Muslim countries run by what are perceived to be a corrupt elite to governments that support them and that create the conditions which foster the oppression and subjugation of Muslims who under Shari'a would prosper.

Although the motives and objectives differ, the craving for orthodoxy is also a feature of several new Jewish movements including the previously mentioned Gush Emunim movement.

Gush Emunim (Block of the Faithful)

This movement has been inextricably linked with the growth of Israeli settlements in the occupied territories since its beginnings in the late 1960s and early 1970s. It is not only opposed to the return of these territories but also to the secularism of Israeli society. What initially inspired this movement was the settlement after the 1967 Arab–Israeli conflict, which saw Israeli take over the Temple Mount once again, and other holy sites of the Promised Land.

Gush Emunim only really developed a structure and organization after the 'concessions' made by Israel after the 1973 Arab–Israeli conflict. This policy of concessions on the part of Israel alarmed a percentage of young Orthodox Jews who espoused Zionist values and symbols. Eschewing militancy, the movement adopted the strategy of civil disobedience in the areas where Jewish settlements had been built.

During the late 1970s, when the links between Gush Emunim and the Israeli establishment were tightened, the movement witnessed rapid expansion. Apart from a few brief periods following on such political developments as the Sinai agreement (1981), it became difficult to distinguish between Gush Emunim's and the establishment's views on the settlements in the 1980s. In the 1990s with the agreement known as the Oslo Accords (1993–5) relations between the movement and the Government cooled.

In the view of Gush Emunim political issues have a profound religious significance, and everything to do with the nation of Israel has a Jewish significance that is not always evident (Aran, 1999). It sees itself as the outrider of the enlightened whose role is to provide a vision of Israel as sacred space and to ensure that Israel's sovereignty is extended over all Israel, by which is meant the territories returned to Palestine, which it regards as part of biblical Judea and Samaria. Territorial sanctity is a core religious belief. When all is eventually revealed of the divine plan for Israel everyone including Arabs will join together in harmony to rebuild the temple.

The religious inspiration behind this ultra-orthodox, millenarian movement are the teachings of former Chief Rabbi, Kook (d.1935), who was already active building the Israeli State prior to its foundation in 1948. Kook believed that it was a precondition of the salvation of all that the Holy Land be first inhabited once again by the Jews. Such a conviction, also held by Gush Emunim, makes of the politics of the settlements a matter of religious faith, and a fundamental tenet of Orthodox Judaism.

Although in practice Gush Emunim occupies relatively few settlements, its influence on government and on public opinion has always been much greater than its numerical size warranted, at least until recent times when its support has waned considerably.

Conclusions

Thus, throughout the modern period both internal and external factors have acted as catalysts of reform in North Africa and the Middle East. Here the focus has been mainly on contemporary Islamic reform movements. Although there has been and continues to be much interaction and mutual influencing of each other, no homogeneous, uniform, united radical Islamist front has yet emerged. The Muslim Brotherhood has come closest to achieving this. Moreover, the orientation and strategy of Islamist movements tend to change. In Wahhābi times the enemy was popular Islam and in colonial times what were perceived to be decadent Muslim rulers and the foreign oppressor. In more recent times it continues to be corrupt Islamic regimes, and in particular those that are protected by and collaborate with what is perceived to be the exemplary centre of Western power and decadence and the main support of Israel against the Palestinians, the United States.

The emergence, however, in modern times of so many Islamist movements that recruit mainly among the young and their recourse to ijtihād suggest that there is a strong fear among sections at least of the Muslim population that Islam's 'robust tradition' of 'ulama or scholars who interpret the Qur'ān and Sunna or way of the Prophet Muhammad will not be able to protect their religion from the forces of secularization.

References and select bibliography

Abou El Fadl, Khaled (2004) 'Islam and the Challenge of Democracy' in Khaled Abou El Fadl (ed.) *Islam and the Challenge of Democracy*, Oxford: Oxford University Press, pp. 3–49.

Al-Seta, Montessori (2002) *The Road to Al-Qaeda: The Story of Bin Laden's Right Hand Man*, London: Pluto Press.

Aran, Gideon (1999) 'Jewish-Zionist Fundamentalism' in Martin E. Marty and R. Scott Appleby (eds) *Fundamentalisms Observed*, Chicago: University of Chicago Press.

Gellner, Ernst (1981) 'Flux and Reflux in the Faith of Men' in E. Gellner (ed.) *Muslim Society*, Cambridge: Cambridge University Press, pp. 1–85.

Gibb, H. A. R. (1978) *Islam*, Oxford: Oxford University Press.

Gibb, H. A. R. and Kramers, J. H. (1974) *Shorter Encyclopaedia of Islam*, Leiden: E. J. Brill.

Gillespie, Thomas (1995) 'Hizb-ut-Tahir: A Growing Phenomenon amongst Britain's Young Muslims or a Diminishing Force with a Political Agenda, Which Will Never Be Implemented?' MA Dissertation, Dept of Theology and Religious Studies, King's College, University of London.

Hassan, Riffat (1990) 'The Burgeoning of Islamic Fundamentalism: Toward an

Understanding of the Phenomenon' in Norman Cohn (ed.) *The Fundamentalist Phenomenon*, Grand Rapids, MI: Eerdmans, pp. 151–71.

Khan, M. A. Muqtedar (2004) 'The Primacy of Political Philosophy' in Khaled Abou El Fadl (ed.) *Islam and the Challenge of Democracy*, Oxford: Oxford University Press, pp. 63–9.

Lewis, Bernard (2003) *The Crisis of Islam*, London: Phoenix Press.

Mitchell, Richard P. (1969) *The Society of the Muslim Brothers*, Oxford: Oxford University Press.

Nash, Manning (1991) 'Islamic Resurgence in Malaysia and Indonesia' in Martin E. Marty and R. Scott Appleby (eds) *Fundamentalisms Observed*, Chicago: University of Chicago Press, pp. 691–739.

Qutb, Sayyid (1965) *Milestones*, Cedar Rapids, IA: Unity Publishing.

Roy, Olivier (1998) 'The Divergent Ways of Fundamentalism and Islamism among Muslim Migrants' in Peter B. Clarke (ed.) *New Trends and Developments in the World of Islam*, London: Luzac, pp. 41–58.

Smith, Wilfred Cantwell (1957) *Islam in Modern History*, Princeton, NJ: Princeton University Press.

Voll, John O. (1991) 'Fundamentalism in the Sunni Arab World: Egypt and the Sudan' in Martin E. Marty and R. Scott Appleby (eds) *Fundamentalisms Observed*, Chicago: University of Chicago Press, pp. 345–403.

Zahab, Mariam Abou and Roy, Olivier (2002) *Islamist Networks*, London: Hurst.

Chapter 8

Africa, south of the Sahara

While established or standard religion is usually seen as conservative in its attitude to change, new religion is thought of as radical in this regard. However, in certain contexts, as in modern Africa during the colonial era, it was the new religions that attempted, albeit not indiscriminately, to preserve 'cultural capital', a term that includes religious culture, while the so-called historic or mission churches, and mainstream Islam, attempted to transform the local religious landscape. The adoption of the role of defenders of cultural capital accounts in great measure, as Stark's (1996) theory of religious success and failure would expect it to do, for the success of NRMs in Africa – in the form of African Independent Churches (AICs) – of new Islamic movements such as the Murid Brotherhood of Senegal, and of Neo-Traditional movements such as the Mungiki (or Muingiki) movement in Kenya.

Here the focus is principally on new forms of religion in Africa, south of the Sahara – North Africa is treated separately (see Chapter 7) – where one encounters a variety of versions, Christian and Islamic in particular, of Prosperity Theology and Weber's *Protestant Ethic* thesis (1992). Most attention is given to AICs, more contemporary forms of Christianity including the African Charismatic movement, new movements that derive from Islam or that claim to be Islamic, Neo-Traditional movements, and finally African-Caribbean, African-Brazilian, Brazilian Neo-Pentecostal and Oriental forms of new religion that began to enter Africa from the 1960s. The discussion, albeit brief, of new forms of Islamic and Oriental religions will offset the tendency to concentrate almost exclusively on the rise and impact of Christian forms of new religion in Africa.

Colonialism and religious innovation

Colonized by European powers in the nineteenth and twentieth centuries, the African situation resembles that of other parts of the world including Asia and Latin America. Colonialism and its consequences, including the disruption of local culture and the undermining of individual and collective identity, can be seen to constitute some of the main underlying reasons for the rise of NRMs of all kinds – Christian, Muslim and Neo-Traditionalist, particularly from the first half of the twentieth century when it was at its height. Since independence the failure of the political and military leadership, due to both internal and external factors, provides part of the explanation for the turning of the educated in ever-increasing numbers to more conservative forms of religion whether these be Christian, Muslim or Neo-Traditional.

Religious change in modern Africa was not simply a response to colonialism, neo-colonialism and the failures of post-independence governments. It is best understood if seen as an interactive process that has sought to discover and then construct the most viable, and culturally and spiritually meaningful, form of religion in new and rapidly changing cultural, social, political and economic circumstances.

This emphasis on religious change as an interactive process not only does justice to the evidence but also avoids the rather simplistic explanation of it in terms of impact–response theory, as a reaction to the impact of colonialism and the mainstream mission churches or of Islamic expansion on local culture and values, or as purely a defence of personal and communal 'authenticity' and identity undermined by these external forces. Africa, never static, was changing in the sense of modernizing prior to the intrusions on the part of colonialism and mission Christianity. What, therefore, was new was not modernization per se but the takeover and control of this process by outside forces which then directed it in their interests.

While it is dangerous to generalize, it can, nevertheless, be said that many of Africa's new religions, including the AICs, have been part of the process of rationalizing and streamlining the outcome of the encounter between colonialism and society, more specifically between mission Christianity and Traditional Religion. And seen from this angle they furnish classic examples of how globalizing religious and cultural forces become domesticated and reshaped, and their vitality and creative capacity channelled along different pathways through their meeting with the local. In turn, many of the modern African religious movements discussed below – Christian, Muslim and Traditional – have been transformed from local regional concerns into international movements, having established themselves across Europe, the Americas and elsewhere, and impacting mostly but not exclusively on the religious and cultural activities and outlook of the African diaspora community in particular.

Neo-Traditional movements, which as was previously mentioned have likewise featured as part of the changing religious life of Africa in recent times, also display an increasingly international if not global dimension. Usually thought of as dependent on traditional mythology and rituals, a number have re-invented themselves, doubtless with a view to their growing global relevance. These movements have incorporated into their cosmology beliefs and practices from a wide variety of sources, including Oriental religions. As the sources of religious innovation in modern Africa have become increasingly diverse, this has been reflected not only in the neo-traditional religions but in African NRMs generally, and this development calls for a revision of Turner's (1991) typology of modern African movements.

AICs in West Africa (c.1890 to the present)

While the specific reasons for the emergence of modern AICs vary from period to period and region to region, the general ones remain constant across time and space. These include the demand for the implementation by the mainstream or mission churches of the principle of self-governing churches, and the opposite side of the same coin, the rejection of the assumption, whether explicit or implicit, that Africans were incapable of self-rule. The concern for cultural preservation, not in an arbitrary sense as we have already pointed out, was also crucial to the establishment of these churches. This concern is reflected in, among other things, the demand that the style and form of worship and its symbolic expression be adapted to African culture. In some cases this kind of demand was part of a nationalist agenda.

The pursuit of independence in church affairs began to take hold from the late 1880s. This is not surprising as it was the point in time when many of the historic or mission churches, as they are known, began in practice to abandon their goal of establishing self-governing, self-supporting African churches. In the 1890s this new attitude came to the fore in the removal from his post and his replacement by the Anglican church of the Nigerian bishop of the Niger Delta, Samuel Ajayi Crowther (1857–90). As the historian of Nigerian Christianity Ajayi (1966), among others, remarked the investigation and subsequent dismissal by the London-based Church Missionary Society of Crowther had the psychological effect of putting on trial the capacity of a whole nation to govern itself, and found it wanting.

Prior to Crowther's dismissal in 1888, a new wing of the American Baptist Missionary Society emerged in the form of the African Baptist Church, which temporarily split off from the American Baptist Missionary Society over, among other things, the question of leadership. Also important in bringing about this split was the issue of African identity, which the Nigerian Christian elite in Lagos and elsewhere in West Africa felt was being destroyed by the culture and ritual of this particular society, and of mission Christianity as a whole. Dissatisfaction emerged over the imposition of European names at baptism, the wearing of European dress, the use of European musical instruments and English at worship, and the veneration of white-only representations of Christ. These same criticisms were also made later by Black Americans, including Ali Drew who helped found the Nation of Islam (see Chapter 5) and Rastafarians (see Chapter 9), among other diaspora Africans.

Also rejected was the imposition of what were subjectively interpreted as immutable moral laws but in practice were perceived as 'foreign social arrangements', and these included such practices as monogamy. Africa, it was argued, was polygamous for entirely worthy social, cultural and economic reasons which in no way violated God's moral law. One of the Nigerian founder members of the African Baptist Church, Mojola Agbebi (baptized David Vincent), expressed many of these objections and the anxieties over cultural and personal identity and African self-esteem to which they gave rise when he spoke out against Christianity as preoccupied with inessentials and, as practised in Africa, as 'foreign':

> Hymn books, harmonium, dedications, pew constructions, surpliced choir, the white man's names, the white man's dress, are so many non-essentials, so many props and crutches affecting the religious manhood of the Christian Africans.
>
> (Clarke, 1986: 160)

As in South Africa and the Democratic Republic of the Congo, doctrine as such was rarely an issue for the West African AICs. The principal concerns were the denial of the local capacity for leadership and the disregard for the expressive and symbolic dimensions of worship and of certain social conventions, which, it was believed, had served societies well. It was not being suggested by Agbebi and others of the same mind that everything African was good and wholesome and everything foreign negative and destructive. Like their Zionist and Ethiopian counterparts, many West African AICs and prophets, including William Wade Harris (see below), rejected certain aspects of local culture, while attaching great significance to other dimensions of it, such as the use of the local language in worship, dreams and visions as guides to action, traditional ways of healing, of expressing belief and commitment and of ensuring that morality and social norms were upheld. Thus, in many West African AICs such practices as dancing and clapping and ecstatic behaviour were permitted, as were more restricted forms of polygamy.

The importance attached to the issues of African identity, culture and social customs notwithstanding, the question of leadership was never far below the surface. It came to the fore in the aftermath of the Crowther episode in the formation in 1891 by ex-members of the London-based Church Missionary Society (CMS) of the United Native African Church in Lagos, Nigeria. Pointing to the reasons for the establishment of this church, the founders stated they had resolved that 'a purely native African Church be founded for the evangelization and amelioration of our race, *to be governed by Africans*' [my italics] (Clarke, 1986: 161).

Other splits from the mission or historic churches were to occur down the years and in all cases foreign leadership, which was seen to smack of paternalism, was the crucial issue, followed by the importance of adaptation or inculturation.

The AIC movement in West Africa, and Africa as a whole, owes much to inspirational charismatic figures, such as the Liberian prophet William Wade Harris. The latter, like Isaiah Shembe (see below) displayed the awesome power of charisma by establishing a virtually unbreakable relationship between himself as leader and his followers, based on faith in his claims to supernatural gifts. A former Methodist, and then a lay preacher in the Episcopal Church of Liberia, Harris (c.1860–1929) revolutionized the religious life of parts of southern Ghana and right across the southern Ivory Coast.

Imprisoned for what was termed a treasonable offence – the lowering of the Liberian flag and the hoisting in its stead the British Union Jack in 1909 – Harris claimed to have received a vision of the Angel Gabriel in which he was commanded to preach to all those who had not as yet heard the word of God. On release from prison and clothed in a long white robe, black scarf, and small white hat, Harris began his mission in Liberia but enjoyed little success and moved in 1913 into the southern region of the Ivory Coast, which at the time was under French colonial rule. From there he crossed into the southwestern part of southern Ghana. Claiming, as charismatic leaders tend to, that he was above all laws made by humans, Harris proved an almost instant success. According to one official report compiled in 1915 by a French colonial civil servant:

> The hypnotic effect of the 'Prophet' [Harris] was extremely effective in the administrative regions of Assinie, Bassam, the Lagoons, Lahou and in other parts of the Indenie and N'Zi-Comoe administrative regions, involving the conversion of about 100,000 people.
>
> (Clarke, 1986: 181)

Harris's success can partly be accounted for by his this-worldly interpretation of Christianity, and in particular of Christian baptism as the new and most effective remedy for evil, moral and social, and by his preaching of what today would be referred to as the gospel of prosperity. In his preaching he upheld the traditional world view that evil spirits could cause misfortune and even death, and while he denounced the use of traditional religious practices and images thought to protect people from their negative effects, he remained strongly convinced of their existence, and insisted with his listeners that baptism was the best defence against them.

Harris's mission was also helped by his acceptance into the Christian church as full members all those who, regardless of whether they were polygamous or not, agreed to renounce the traditional religion. This was in contrast to the Christian mission churches that insisted on monogamy for full participation. As a consequence of this bar on polygamous marriages Christianity became known in the early years of its mission in Africa as the Church of children. Harris also told his listeners of the material benefits that could be derived from becoming a Christian, including the ownership of a two-storey house – a potent symbol of status and prestige – and of education, the key to economic and social advancement.

Another major reason for the success of Harris's message was the strong element of continuity it contained with the past. Though a charismatic figure, there was little that was completely new to his listeners about his manner, style of dress, delivery, or in a good deal of what he had to say. In many ways he resembled traditional prophets, the most notable difference being his claim to be the spokesperson for the one, true God. Nor did his conversion strategy lead to social dislocation in the form of the break up of families and communities. Moreover, while he challenged the power and authority of the traditional priests, chiefs and elders, he at the same time offered them an opportunity to wield that authority and power even more effectively by becoming his followers. And while he attempted to destroy some of the external trappings of traditional religion, he accepted much of the existing social structure, and, indeed, defended it in his preaching by retaining many of the traditional beliefs themselves and the social and moral norms which they supported, interpreting them, however, from a Christian perspective.

Harris's teaching, thus, did not make for a clean break with the past nor did it lead to intolerable amounts of social disruption. Indeed, he gave support to the indigenous social structure at a time when it was being shaken by the imposition of colonial rule, euphemistically referred to as the process of pacification. Moreover, as group conversion to the Harris movement was the norm it did not involve a major break intellectually, psychologically, socially, or morally from family and friends. Liturgically, furthermore, there were close parallels with traditional forms of worshipping, including the use of gourds and rattles and the performance of dances to the indigenous spirits, while adding to their songs the name God.

Harris was rarely overtly political or anti-colonial in his preaching. However, his conversion campaign happened to coincide with the outbreak of World War I, which involved West Africans as soldiers and carriers in campaigns in West Africa itself, East Africa and Europe. In this situation, the French, who were still 'pacifying' the southern Ivory Coast, felt that the prophet Harris was too big a risk to be allowed to wander round preaching and increasing his following to hundreds of thousands who might be inspired by him to oppose their presence in the country. For this reason the colonial authorities took the decision to expel him, to the satisfaction of Catholic and Protestant missions who both, though they did not realize it at the time, had benefited greatly from Harris's conversion campaigns. Nor did they seem to be aware that Harris would frequently encourage his listeners to become members of their churches.

After his expulsion from the Ivory Coast, Harris continued as itinerant preacher in Liberia until his death in 1929. Today there are over twenty Harris Churches in the Ivory Coast, one of which has an estimated membership of 100,000. The Ghanaian Grace Thannie, known as Madam Harris, who accompanied the prophet on his mission in the southern Ivory Coast, established in Ghana the Church of William Wade Harris and His Twelve Apostles, better known simply as the Church of the Twelve Apostles, a Spiritist church in which great emphasis was placed on healing through the Holy Spirit and blessed water.

The Musamo Christo Disco Church, another Ghanaian Spiritist church, and largely made up of people of Fante origin, was founded in the 1920s by the former Methodist, Joseph William Egyanka Appiah, and is now an international church with branches in many of the world's major cities and towns, including London. Appiah who underwent three baptisms, which gave him the power to heal sickness and conquer evil, also believed that the Holy Spirit had descended upon him and called him to be a great king (Akaboa) and his companion Abena Baawa (alias Hannah Barnes) to be the queen (Akatitibi) of his people. Though dismissed by the Methodists as a sorcerer, Appiah in fact was a strong critic of traditional customs and religious practices. His message, often apocalyptic in tone and content, was mostly derived from the Old Testament, as it was in the case of Pastor Shadare, the inspiration behind the Nigerian Aladura (praying) churches.

The first of the Aladura churches to emerge in Nigeria at the end of World War I was the Precious Stone-Faith Tabernacle movement. Dreams and visions played a crucial role in this development. The previously mentioned Nigerian Anglican pastor Joseph Shadare, from St Saviours Church, Ijebu Ode, 45 miles north of Lagos, was to claim that in a divinely inspired dream he learnt that much of the world was being ravaged by an influenza epidemic and that with a young teacher, Sophia Adefobe Odunlami, he was to found a church to combat that epidemic. Odunlami, who had recovered from influenza, had also received a personal revelation from the Holy Spirit and was told to meet Shadare and help him deliver a prophecy. Together they formed a prayer association to combat the epidemic. Shadare's son explained to this writer that 'as a woman Sophia Odunlami was a special sign from God for it was unusual to have women prophets' (Clarke, 1986: 167).

What Shadare and Odunlami essentially proclaimed was healing through prayer and blessed water only, and this message lies at the heart of the Aladura movement. Prayer was understood among the Yoruba as much more than a simple request or petition. Such words as the names for God were believed to contain their own intrinsic power and prayer itself was believed to contain within itself its own fulfilment (Clarke, 1986: 167). Early Yoruba Christians, known as Onigbagbo, believed moreover that through their faith in Jesus they possessed what they described as 'word power', an indispensable element of healing.

The Precious Stone-Faith Tabernacle Society, and the Aladura churches that it inspired, were not introducing a radically new idea when they preached about the miraculous healing power of prayer and blessed water. Traditionally, recourse was had to incantations and rituals for the cure and prevention of sickness. A babalawo or diviner might, for example, recommend that certain invocations be chanted and rituals be performed in the case of a difficult pregnancy. The Aladura message did not, therefore, conflict with the traditional understanding of illness and disease but rather reaffirmed it from a different perspective. What it did oppose was the undermining by the spread of Western scientific ideas traditional notions of the cause of sickness and how it should be treated. For the Aladura illness was part of the problem of evil in the world and had, therefore, a crucially important spiritual dimension that needed always to be addressed, however spectacular the medical advances made.

The Aladura movement advanced rapidly in western Nigeria and beyond, and this owed much to local prophets, including Joseph Babalola, a mechanic and steam-roller driver, Daniel Orekoya, Moses Orimolade Tunolase and Christianah Abiodun Emmanuel, also known as Captain Abiodun Emmanuel, who were hailed by followers as 'clear proof of the Gospel's power' (Clarke, 1986: 171). Some of these prophets preached more than healing through prayer, blessed water and fasting. They also spoke out against price increases and taxation. One of them, Prophet Oshitelu, a former Anglican and founder of the Church of the Lord, Aladura, was branded by the colonial regime as a subversive on account of the 'dangerous prophecies' he made, which predicted among other things bloodshed and riots in the wake of government taxation. Prophet Oshitelu tended to use religious language to express his discontent and opposition to colonial rule, which he interpreted as the white oppression of blacks.

Generally, the Aladura response, like the Zionist response, to the mission churches was not to reject them on doctrinal grounds. The Cherubim and Seraphim movement – a group of indigenous Aladura churches founded by the previously mentioned itinerant preacher from Ikare in the eastern sector of Yorubaland, Moses Orinmolade Tunolase, and Christianah Abiodun Emmanuel – retained much from Anglicanism. This church gave considerable emphasis to belief in angels and attached great importance to prophecy, visions, and dreams, and to other signs of the visible presence of the Holy Spirit, and insisted that prayer, faith in God and Jesus and consecrated water, oil and traditional soap were the most effective means of healing. It also taught that witchcraft was at the root of most sickness, disease and disharmony. On the other hand, it affirmed the central teachings of Christianity and retained the Anglican Book of Common Prayer, Sunday as the day of worship, and many of the sacraments.

The differences with mission church Christianity were most obvious in matters of worship, where the Aladura movement encouraged the practice of hand clapping, stamping on the ground – a way of obtaining spiritual power, prosperity and peace – drumming, and demonstrations of the efficacy of sacred words through such exclamations as Hallelujah, Hosannah, and Iye (life), shouted three or seven times depending on the occasion. Pilgrimages to traditional sacred places such as mountain tops were introduced. Simple, praying uniforms – usually a long white dress – with colourful waistbands were worn and this created a sense of equality and togetherness. Sacred space was also understood differently in the two cultures and the ways of preserving it were not identical. The Aladura used a number of rituals – some of them familiar to Muslims – to protect the sacredness of the house of prayer as the church was called. The wearing of shoes was forbidden, and menstruating women banned from entry. There was also a ban on the use of alcohol, the eating of pork and the use of charms, and bathing was compulsory after sexual intercourse before entering the house of prayer.

Somewhat different in its teachings and liturgy from other West African NRMs is the Brotherhood of the Cross and Star, also known as the Christ Universal School of Practical Christianity. This movement began in Calabar, Nigeria, in the 1950s (Mbon, 1986). Founded by the trader and itinerant preacher Olumba Olumba Obu (b.1918), the movement's teachings consist of a strong belief in the presence of the 'living dead' at all meetings and ceremonies, in the widespread influence of sorcery and in the sanctity of the earth, all traditional beliefs. On the other hand, it rejects polygyny, secret societies and divination, all traditional institutions.

Obu's Brotherhood places the emphasis on the creation of communities and/or brotherhoods that bond through love rather than on purification and cleansing. Reincarnation is an important belief, perhaps as a result of Oriental influence. Adam, the first man, is described as the 'first divine incarnation' followed by six others before God came into 'mortal life' through Obu to judge the living and the dead. Followers who appear to believe that Obu is divine have spread his teachings across Nigeria, establishing bethels or chapels wherever they went. Missionaries, students and immigrants have also taken the movement to Europe and the United States.

Thus, most of the AICs of West Africa offered a compelling critique of the cultural, moral and social assumptions underlying mission Christianity, questioning whether they were biblically based or derived from the Western value system. They also sought to provide a more relevant version of the Christian message, expressed in such a way as to encourage active participation. Their concern was also, as we have seen, to assume the leadership of the churches, in order to promote an African understanding of divine revelation, refusing to accept that they were ordained by God to be passive recipients of the message of salvation. As one independent church leader expressed it 'to have done so would have been tantamount to race suicide' (Clarke, 1986: 158).

These churches cannot, therefore, be meaningfully described as reactionary or anti-modern. They accepted the need for change and challenged the traditional order on many issues without, however, welcoming the modern indiscriminately or rejecting the latter in its essentials.

AICs of South, Central and East Africa (from c.1890)

The AICs that began to emerge in southern Africa in the 1880s have come to be known as Ethiopian and/or Zionist churches. The term 'Ethiopian' describes a desire for freedom, which included the demand for equality, and self-rule for Africans in church life. It is also a descriptive term for Africa as a chosen land. The word appears to have been used for the first time to designate a church started in Losotho by Mangena Makone, a former Wesleyan minister. One of the largest and most influential of the Zionist churches, amaNazaretha (Nazareth and/or Nazerite Baptist Church) was founded in Zululand, South Africa, in 1913, by Mdlimawafa Mloyisa Isaiah Shembe (1867–1935). Sundkler describes the founder of this sabbatarian church as an 'unusually quiet, withdrawn and soft spoken Zionist prophet' (1970: 164).

A former farm-hand with no formal education, Shembe became a well-known member of the Methodist and later the African Native Baptist Church, which had seceded from the White Baptist Church. He began to speak to fellow church members of his privileged access to God's mind through dreams and visions, in which he was commanded to leave his four wives and children and to renounce the use of Western medicine. One of Shembe's first innovations was to baptize converts in the sea, by triune emersion, a practice derived from the liturgy of the Zion Church in Illinois and adapted to the local situation. It was later adopted by many churches in South Africa and widely regarded as a means of healing. Healing is here understood in a holistic sense, covering all aspects of one's well-being, physical, spiritual, psychological, moral and social. Among other practices introduced by Shembe were the removal of shoes in worship, the wearing of long hair – a sign of resistance – abstention from pork, night communion with the washing of the feet, and the seventh day Sabbath.

Baptism became the main ritual of the amaNazaretha church and the sacred wooden drum – not used in mission churches, which regarded it as a separatist symbol – became its main ritual instrument. The import of the hymn was also radically changed. In this and other Zionist churches, and in the AIC setting generally, it changed from being primarily a statement in verse about certain religious facts into a sacred rhythm expressed chiefly through the medium of sacred dance that paralleled Zulu dances. Following a Zulu pattern, dances were also introduced as public expressions of faith and identity at the January Feast of the Tabernacles and the July festival of the amaNazaretha church itself. These festivals were held in God's earthly residences, the holy mountains in Durban of Inhlangakazi and Ekuphakameni.

This Zionist church, and modern African religions generally, have often been less concerned with the orthodoxy of belief than with its practical relevance to Africa. Their concern has been to deliver healing and purification, including the 'purification' of their traditional moral and religious structures in the light of their own understanding of the Old and New

Testament. Like the above-mentioned Aladura churches, the AICs of South Africa could be as critical of traditional spiritual and cultural values and practices as they were of Western values and practices. This is evident from the prohibitions they introduced, including the ban on the eating of pork, on the eating of the meat of an animal that had not been slaughtered, on the drinking of the blood of animals, and on the use of alcohol and tobacco, all practices acceptable to traditionalists.

Parallels to the amaNazaretha can be found across Africa, including the Democratic Republic of the Congo, where evidence exists of an eighteenth-century AIC, the Antonian movement of KimpaVita (Dona Beatrice). A more recent AIC from the Democratic Republic of the Congo is the Kimbanguist Church, founded in 1921 by the prophet Simon Kimbangu (c.1887–1951) and known as the Église de Jesus Christ sur la Terre par Le Prophète Simon Kimbangu (henceforth EJCSK). This is the largest AIC in Africa.

Like other African prophets of the period, Kimbangu preached against the use of traditional rituals to combat evil. In contrast to other prophets and church leaders, Kimbangu also emphasized the importance of monogamy, and spoke of the duty on all to obey the Government. Like the amaNazaretha and the Aladura churches of West Africa the EJCSK introduced the use of blessed water for healing, purification and protection. It has also become, like other AICs, a major enterprise with schools, hospitals, brick-building factories and various other large companies.

The Belgian Colonial Government feared the growth of this kind of movement, as the French Government feared the influence on large numbers of people of prophet Harris, and, despite Kimbangu's protestations of loyalty, it had him court-martialled without any defence on charges that included sedition and hostility to whites. He was found guilty, sentenced to 120 lashes and then to death. The latter sentence was commuted to life in solitary confinement, in Lumumbashi, 2,000 kilometres from his home in the village of Nkamba in the western region of what was then known as the Belgian Congo and is presently the Democratic Republic of the Congo.

Throughout the colonial era Kimbangu's followers were persecuted and/or deported, and by this means and through forced migration caused by war and poverty the movement began to internationalize. A clandestine movement also began operating underground until 1959 when EJCSK, six months before independence in 1960, received official recognition. By this time considerable fragmentation had occurred and Kimbangu had little time and opportunity to reunite his Church before his death in 1951. His remains were re-interred in his home village of Nkamba, which was given the name of Nkamba-Jerusalem and which has become an important place of pilgrimage.

East Africa has seen the emergence of several new religions in recent times, some of which have completely lost their way and ended in violence, the most notable being the Lord's Resistance Army and the Movement for the Restoration of the Ten Commandments of God (Melton and Bromley, 2002).

The first of these two movements, the Lord's Resistance Army (LRA), started in Acholi in northern Uganda in the 1980s when self-proclaimed prophets announced as their mission the overthrow of the National Resistance Army (NRA), which at the time was under the command of Yoweri Museveni who later became President of Uganda (Behrend, 1999). Among the prophets of resistance was Alice Auma from Gulu in Acholi, who claimed to be possessed by a previously unknown Christian spirit named Lakwena, meaning 'messenger' or 'apostle' in Acholi. In pre-colonial and pre-Christian times possession by *jok* (spirit) of humans, animals and material objects could endow them with the power to heal or make the land fertile and turn an immoral, decadent society into a moral and upright one. Such possession could also result in harm in the form of moral, social and natural catastrophes. In Alice Lakwena's case – she came to be called after the name of her possessing spirit – she declared that her possession had endowed her with the powers to heal society.

This kind of mission made a fit with the Christian notion of spirits, which had begun to be spread in the region from the early years of the twentieth century. According to this understanding, spirits were thought to heal and purify from witchcraft without harming the one who was responsible for bringing it about, thus breaking the cycle of retaliatory bewitching. This came to be contrasted with the traditional spirits or *joki* (plural of jok) who were believed not only to heal and release from witchcraft but also to kill the one who had perpetrated the affliction.

It was this new, Christian understanding that, under Lakwena's guidance, Alice tried to advance by working as a healer and diviner. She soon resorted, however, to the traditional interpretation and in August 1986 she organized the 'Holy Spirit Mobile Forces' (HSMF), a movement that was joined by many regular soldiers for the purpose of waging war on the Government, witches and 'impure' soldiers. Initial successes against the NRA were attributed by Alice Lakwena to 'Holy Spirit Tactics' – a method of warfare that combined modern techniques with magical practices – and led to further support from among the Acholi population at large for her armed resistance.

In 1987 Lakwena's army of around 10,000 soldiers, who in theory were under the command of spirits, reached within 30 miles of the Ugandan capital, Kampala, before being defeated by government forces. While many of the rebel soldiers were killed, Lakwena escaped to nearby Kenya where she continues to reside.

The spirit Lakwena then took possession of Alice's father Severino Lukoya, who for a short time led the various remaining HSMF forces – these were never fully united into one movement – until the one time soldier in another of Acholi's rebel groups, Joseph Kony, took over. Kony was also from Gulu and claims to be a cousin of Alice. Sometime after Kony took control from Severino he renamed the movement the Lord's Resistance Army (LRA).

Although he has sought to distance himself from Alice, Kony has retained many of the rites and ritual techniques that she devised, including the same rite of initiation for army recruits. He likewise has endorsed the Holy Spirit Safety Precautions, a set of behavioural rules drawn up by Alice, and has used, as she did, the Holy Spirit Tactics and fought as vehemently as her against witchcraft and pagan spirit mediums or *ajwakas*.

However, there are marked differences between Kony and Lakwena, which the former has used to highlight the discontinuity between his movement and that led by Alice. For example, he claims to have been possessed not by Lakwena but by the spirit Juma Oris who replaced Lakwena as chairman and commander of his army. Another of his spirits is Silli Sillindi (St Cecilia) from the Sudan who leads the Mary Company, which consists of the women soldiers of the movement and acts as commander of operations. Kony has even established an international network of spirits that goes well beyond Africa to China, Korea and the United States, and though their names are new the functions they perform are very often the same as those undertaken by Alice's spirits.

Where Kony seems to have made a cleaner break with Alice is in the area of army discipline and recruitment. Under him abduction of children for initiation into the army is seemingly commonplace, as is drug use by soldiers and the practices of torture, rape and pillage. Thus, a movement that began with the aim of healing and unifying society and of reconstituting the moral order has turned into one of random violence and killing.

The Movement for the Restoration of the Ten Commandments, a millenarian movement, appears to have started in Rwanda in the 1970s with reports by school children of visions of the Virgin Mary in their playing fields. Credonia Mwerinde, who claimed that she had been in contact with the Virgin Mary since 1984, brought the fledgling movement from Rwanda to Uganda. Mwerinde, one of the principal members of a newly formed cult of the Virgin Mary which came into existence in the late 1980s, accompanied by some of her peer group, approached Joseph Kibwetere requesting him to be the leader of the new movement. Kibwetere, a father of sixteen, and in local terms a wealthy Catholic teacher, from Kabumba in southeastern Uganda, accepted the role. Mwerinde, who received continuous guidance from the Virgin Mary, along with a group known as the twelve apostles, retained considerable influence over teachings, organization and practice. Kibwetere's farm became the movement's headquarters until it moved to Kanunga in 1992, the year he was excommunicated from the Catholic Church. Kibwetere, however, continued to receive support from Catholics, including a former Catholic priest, Dominic Kataribo.

Teachings were set out in the document entitled 'A Timely Message from Heaven: The End of the Present Times', which contained the revelations received by Kibwetere, Mwerinde and other apostles. While the movement's principal goal was the creation of a world based on the Ten Commandments, much emphasis was placed on the renunciation of material possessions, which were to be handed over to the leadership, abstinence from sexual relations and the importance of silence. Sign language was the main means of everyday communication between the members. All of this was rationalized by reference to visions that told of the imminent end of the world (1999 was the date given for this). Usually when such a prediction is not fulfilled devotees react in different ways. If free to do so, some move on quietly and by forgetting the whole episode attempt to put together again their fragmented lives. Others accept the explanation that the End did not come about not because the prediction was wrong but on account of their own lack of faith, and redouble their efforts and commitment so that on the next occasion when it is prophesied that it will occur they will not be responsible for its not happening.

In the case of the Movement for the Restoration of the Ten Commandments when the prediction of the End failed to come to pass strong differences surfaced between the members, some deciding to leave but not before their possessions were returned to them. Some investigators are convinced that these members were put to death before the fire on March 17th 2000 in which others also tragically died. Others reportedly committed suicide or were eliminated later. Kibwetere and Mwerinde both escaped death, along with an unspecified number of members, leaving the precise number of those who died unknown. Mayer (2001) estimated the number of dead to be about 780.

Africa's new Charismatic and Evangelical movements

In the 1970s a new wave of Charismatic Christianity that started from within the existing churches began to sweep across Africa. Essentially composed of young, educated high school and university students, this movement emphasized baptism in the Holy Spirit, the ready availability for Christians of the gifts and fruits of the Spirit, and speaking in tongues (*glossolalia*). Among the attractions of this ecstatic, optimistic religion is the contrast it makes with the despair generated by politics, which, despite the pledges, seems to be incapable of radically tackling such serious concerns as corruption in public life, managing efficiently and effectively public resources, and guaranteeing safety and basic medical facilities.

In Kenya and Tanzania this movement took shape in and was spread through associations such as the Fellowship of Christian Unions (FOCUS) in the mid-1970s. Owing to tighter control over students in Ethiopia and Uganda, it was the 1980s before Charismatic Renewal came to occupy centre stage of Christian life among the young. This was also the case in Zambia in central Africa, most of French-speaking Africa, and Zimbabwe and South Africa.

Although distinctive, the Charismatic Renewal movement shares in common with the AICs the insistence on the need for Christianity to become embedded in African culture. Charismatic Renewal, however, is more engaged with issues of growing importance, such as gender equality, the use of modern technology, and modern medicine. Although it eschews direct political action, it is not a world-indifferent movement, nor is it an apolitical movement, as demonstrated by the response of Charismatics and Evangelicals in the election of the 'born again' President Chiluba in Zambia in 1991.

Neo-Pentecostalism from abroad runs parallel to, and sometimes overlaps with, the Charismatic Renewal movement in Africa (Gifford, 2004). It involves missionaries from many parts of the world not associated historically with Christian missionary activity in Africa, including Korea and Brazil. The objective is to present Africa with the real, authentic conversion to Christianity, as opposed to that incomplete and harmful form brought by the historic churches. Moreover, in contrast to the more ecumenical and conciliatory spirit of the historic churches to other non-Christian religions, the Evangelical and Charismatic religions, paradoxically, denounce on the one hand all forms of belief and practice that diverge from their own and, on the other hand, reinforce the traditional worldview by insisting on the power and hold of the devil and evil spirits over those involved in so-called false religion and superstition.

The Brazilian Igreja Universal do Reino de Deus (Universal Church of the Kingdom of God) (see Chapter 9) is but one of the new Pentecostal churches to enter Africa since the 1970s and is growing rapidly not only in Lusophone or Portuguese-speaking Africa but also in Anglophone and Francophone Africa, including Nigeria and the Ivory Coast. Quick to adapt and employ local ministers and ready to use the local language, this church insists on the reality of the spiritual world and on its direct influence on success and failure. As is the case with many other new churches of its kind, the Universal Church gives priority in its practice to the rite of exorcism of evil spirits, which are said to block progress to the kingdom of God. This psychologically uncomfortable theology is balanced by the prosperity doctrine, not unfamiliar to African traditional religion, which promises that turning to Jesus can lead from poverty and sickness to wealth and well-being.

Neo-traditional religions

Revitalization movements grounded in the indigenous religious tradition are not infrequent in Africa among people who are persuaded that Westernization and modernization have brought them little but suffering and cultural degradation. While some of these movements have a local or regional vision of revitalization of indigenous culture, that of others is pan-African.

In the 1930s a movement of Nigerian (Yoruba) Christians formed the neo-traditional church of the Ijo Orunmila to ensure that core elements of their religious culture were not destroyed. Again in Nigeria, in the 1960s the Arousa movement composed mainly of Bini beliefs and practices merged with the neo-traditional National Church of Nigeria, to form Godianism, which focused on belief in a single God of Africa as understood in ancient Egyptian sources.

The Mungiki, or Muingiki, is another revitalization movement to have emerged in recent times, also in East Africa. Like a number of other movements in Uganda and elsewhere, not all of them religious, Mungiki was started by two schoolboys Ndura Waruinge, grandson of a Mau Mau warrior, General Waruinge, with whose spirit he often communicates, and Maina Njenga, the recipient of a vision from the God Ngai, who called him to lead his people out of bondage to Western ideologies and ways of living. The movement began as the Tent of the Living God movement and has appealed in the main to impoverished youth and young men and women, who lacking the resources to enter secondary education, are clearly inspired by the Mau Mau struggle for their land, freedom and indigenous culture.

Following the practice of the Mau Mau, whom they aspire to imitate not only in their thinking but also in their lifestyle, the Mungiki wear dreadlocks and undergo initiation by means of which they are purified or cleansed of the impure, contaminating influences of the West. The genitals are cut and an oath is taken that binds them to secrecy. In their prayers they ask the God Ngai, who dwells on Mount Kenya, for mercy. The Mungiki disciplinary code shows its rejection of Western values, including the use of tobacco and alcohol, and the movement will often employ extremely harsh methods to enforce this code. In what it forbids the Mungiki movement resembles Evangelical Christianity. Although hostile to the type of Christianity brought by the missionaries, the Mungiki are not opposed to Christianity in principle or to Islam or to other religions.

Mungiki claims to have a following of one and a half million, a claim that would appear to be greatly exaggerated. A majority of its members are young and deprived, lacking as they do the necessary resources for a secondary education.

New Islam-related movements

Millenarianism or, to use the equivalent Islamic term 'Mahdism', and a version of Prosperity Theology and of Weber's Protestant Ethic idea, figures prominently in a number of New Islamic movements, including the previously mentioned Murid tariqa (brotherhood) (O'Brien, 1971) founded in Senegal in the late nineteenth century by the Wolof Muslim cleric Ahmadu Bamba (1850/1–1927). Bamba combined Sufism or mysticism with an unrelenting commitment to hard and continuous agricultural work. The outcome is the Murid order, a thriving entrepreneurial movement with considerable assets and political influence in Senegal, the Gambia, elsewhere in Francophone West Africa, and a trading diaspora that extends to Europe and the United States.

Bamba, who acquired a reputation as a miracle worker like Kimbangu in the Congo, was judged to be a potential threat to French authority, and hence the decision to send him into exile on occasion and at other times to have him imprisoned or placed under house arrest. This reaction only served to increase his appeal and support, especially among the more deprived sectors of Wolof society, who treasured the memory of his miracles and wrote songs and poetry based upon popular accounts of their content.

Bamba never preached violent resistance to French colonial rule. On occasions such as that following his house arrest, which ended in 1927, he actually dissuaded his followers from engaging in jihād in the form of holy war against the French. He promised them instead that paradise could be attained by those who were willing to dedicate themselves to work in the form of unrelenting agricultural labour, and prayer. This was a message the Government welcomed and one that contributed to a noticeable improvement in groundnut production, on which the economy of Senegal as a whole was dependent.

By the time of Senegal's independence in 1960 the Murid movement had established itself as an important institution in Senegalese society and its influence was such that the new Government could not easily ignore its opinions. Two million strong in a population of some eight million the Murid movement continues to be led by descendants of Ahmadu Bamba and, although one of its members is President of the country, it has come to resemble a state within a state with its 'capital' and main mosque at Touba, a large city and a place of Murid pilgrimage. For some time now Murid members have no longer concentrated solely on farming but have diversified their activities, turning to commerce, trade, road transport and education among other occupations, and, under their leader or Khalifa General exercise a powerful influence over national politics.

Mahdism, which we have mentioned is the Islamic version of millenarianism that believes in the advent of the Mahdi or god-guided who will ensure the triumph of authentic Islam, has been a strong feature of several other new African Muslim movements. Among these is the exclusive Bamidele movement founded in Ibadan, Nigeria in the 1930s by a former Christian, Abdul Salami Bamidele. It is also the main belief of the Mahdiyya movement, which began in the early 1940s in Ijebu-Ode, southwestern Nigeria, under the leadership of the charismatic Muslim teacher Al-Hajj Jumat Imam, who, perhaps uniquely, endeavoured to develop a theology that would integrate Muslims, Christians and Traditionalists (Clarke, 1995). Pacifism is a distinguishing feature not only of the Murids but of these movements also.

Mahdism has, however, contributed to outbreaks of violence, the worst case being that of the Maitatsine movement which originated in the northern Cameroon and spread to northern Nigeria in the 1980s (Clarke, 1987). The movement ended in catastrophe in the 1980s when an estimated 6,000 people lost their lives in riots in Kano city. This was a movement of the 'lonely' poor, the displaced and marginalized – the street vendors, water carriers and so on – who had received no benefits whatsoever from the oil boom of the 1960s and 1970s and who were without any protection against dire poverty.

Women often play a leading role both as founders and as supporters of religious change in Africa, as we saw in the case of the Cherubim and Seraphim church in Nigeria. Their intention is not necessarily to radically change the position of women in society although as in the case of the Zar movement they can be sometimes seen as embryonic forms of feminist movements (Lewis, 1971).

The Zar movement is composed in the main of women and those of low social and economic status. It resembles the West African Islamic Bori-cult, which appeals to women whose husbands convert to Islam. The Zar has its largest followings among women in Ethiopia, Somalia, Djibouti and Sudan, North Africa and the Gulf States. Although followers are mostly Muslim, some Christians are also involved in Zar whose basic assumption is that various categories of spirits – some Muslim, some former colonial administrators including General Gordon, some European Christians, some spirits of the River Nile – can invade and possess individuals.

Those whom the spirits enter manifest this presence through an illness, which can only be cured by their being placated. This is done by others, usually husbands, complying with the requests made by the possessing spirits for relatively expensive items in the form of perfumes and delicacies, and by having dances performed in their honour. This kind of possession complicates customary male–female relations. Where, for example, a spirit or *jinn* enters a woman the latter is usually thought of as the spiritual wife of the former, creating a measure of psychological conflict with her 'real' husband.

The usual response is to treat the 'illness' and this can be done in a number of different ways, including through the performance of elaborate rituals known in Somalia as 'beating the zar'. Sessions are presided over by female shamanic leaders, known by different names, such as *shaikha* in Somalia and *alaqa* in Christian Ethiopia. Exorcism is also used as a form of treatment. In this rite, either a Christian or Muslim cleric uses the power of their holy scriptures to expel the spirit in question. The one possessed will usually enter trance during the performance of these therapeutic rites.

Lewis (1971), as we have mentioned, interprets the possession of women in this way as an embryonic form of female protest against their inferior status in relation to men. It can also be a means of attaining higher status and authority, as it provides the opportunity for those possessed to become cult leaders, a position that gives considerable influence over others. The content of the Zar movement is forever changing as it incorporates new spirits and addresses new concerns thrown up by rapid social change.

Unlike the Zar in every respect and resembling more the new evangelical and fundamentalist Christian movements are the Islamic reform and missionary-minded movements, composed in the main of committed, fervent young educated Muslims – mainly high school and university students – guided by Muslim scholars often of considerable standing in society. Such movements began to emerge across Africa in the 1970s and were dedicated to the advancement of a more orthodox, more assertive Islam. One such was the Bid'a Yan Izala of northern Nigeria, whose members were inspired by, among others, the uncompromising stand taken by the Muslim jurist and judge or *qadi*, Al-Hajj Gumi.

The rise of a more assertive style of Evangelical and Charismatic Christianity that actively proselytized in Muslim areas contributed to this development, as did outside support, intellectual and financial, for a more radical Islam from North African and Middle Eastern countries. The writings of such Muslim reformers as the Egyptian teacher and scholar Al-Imam Hassan al-Banna (1906–49), founder of the Ikhwan or Muslim Brotherhood in Cairo (see Chapter 7) have also been influential. Al-Banna's advocacy of the creation of an Islamic state in Egypt and his active opposition to the proclamation of the State of Israel in 1948 have proved to be particularly attractive to young, educated Muslims. Sayyid Qutb (1906–66) (see Chapter 7), a leading member of the Ikhwan, was also widely read, especially his *Ma'alim fi al-tariq* (or *Milestones*), as were the writings of the Muslim reformer Abul Ala Maududi (1903–79), founder of the Jama'at-i-Islami (see Chapter 10), which addressed head on the thorny and vexed question of the relationship between Islam and Western culture, by stressing that Islam was a complete and independent way of life.

Thus, various Muslim associations – the mirror image of Evangelical, Neo-Pentecostal and Charismatic Renewal movements – influenced by Muslim revivalism in the wider world, began to embark on daw'a or mission, ignoring as did their Christian counterparts, the 'traditional' boundaries between Christians and Muslims. This new, more assertive Islam was facilitated by the politics of integration and attempts at nation building that made the old colonial notions of Christian, Muslim and Pagan areas untenable. In the new context of Nation States, underpinned by their secular constitutions, all religions had an equal right to exist in any part of the country and, thus, no longer felt obliged to respect the old boundaries that had been put in place under colonial rule to avoid inter-religious strife.

The political effects of these developments became manifest with the search for constitutions more appropriate to the African context. Such an exercise opened up for Muslims who believed their faith and traditions had been marginalized by the Western, 'Christian' bias of existing 'secular' constitutions – the term secular is anathema to many Muslims – the opportunity to demand the constitutional rights that they believed had been denied them for so long. Thus, began in earnest the demand in Nigeria, during the drafting of the constitution for the Second Republic in the late 1970s, for Shari'a law and for a Federal Shari'a court.

Several Muslim missionary movements from outside Africa have become well established on the continent and among these is the Ahmadiyya movement (see Chapter 10), founded in what is today Pakistan by Ghulam Ahmad and which is particularly strong in West Africa. A modernizing movement, the Ahmadiyya, regarded as heretical by mainstream Islam for its refusal to accept the Prophet Muhammad as the last of the Prophets, promotes a balanced school curriculum of Islamic Western subjects, and accepts Western dress, strictly forbidden by many other more conservative Muslim reformers, and conducts marriage ceremonies in a Western, Christian style. The objective of such adaptations as these is to persuade young, educated Muslims that they can be modern and advanced without becoming Christians.

NRMs of Asian origin

As was previously mentioned, a variety of NRMs of Asian origin have established themselves mainly in West, East and South Africa, in recent times, among them Neo-Hindu movements, such as the Sathya Sai Baba, Brahma Kumaris (BK), and the International Society for Krishna Consciousness (ISKCON), more widely known as Hare Krishna. These movements add to the strength of Hinduism, which has long been part of the religious culture of both East and South Africa. The Baha'i religion of Iranian origin can be found in many African countries, both north and south of the Sahara, and even in the Sahara itself in the overwhelmingly Muslim, self-proclaimed Sahara Democratic Republic, which is located in the westernmost segment of the desert to the south of Morocco.

Although there is evidence of Buddhism, mainly in the form of Indian Buddhists but also some Chinese Buddhists, in South Africa in the early part of the twentieth century, a Buddhist *sangha* (community) did not emerge until the 1970s. In 1979 a Buddhist Retreat Centre and a Buddhist Institute were opened in Natal, and from that point on various Buddhist traditions – Zen, Theravada, Mahayana, and Pure Land – started to open centres in all the main towns of South Africa.

Since the 1970s modern forms of mainly lay Buddhism of Japanese origin have been making an even greater impact than these older traditions on African culture and spirituality. These new movements include Soka Gakkai (Value Creation Society), present in Nigeria and South Africa, among other places.

Ritually Shinto and philosophically Buddhist Japanese NRMs are also widely spread across Africa and include Tenrikyo (Religion of Heavenly Wisdom), which has been active in the Congo since the early 1960s, and more recently (1992) Sekai Kyusei Kyo (Church of World Messianity and henceforth SKK). This last-mentioned movement entered Africa via Brazil and began to disseminate its message of divine healing (*johrei*) in Lusophone

Africa – Angola and Mozambique – before moving into South Africa and the Democratic Republic of the Congo. This movement has plans to send African-Brazilian missionaries to open centres in Nigeria.

Often seen as differing greatly from each other, there are, nonetheless, clear parallels between Japanese and African NRMs at the level of belief and ritual. These religions also tend to serve similar purposes. For example, the previously mentioned Japanese movement SKK not only emphasizes the importance of dreams and visions as guides to action, and the fundamental importance of pacifying the ancestors as do many AICs, but also offers both a spiritual explanation of sickness and faith-healing as the sole remedy. Moreover, SKK, like the Neo-Traditionalist movements, serves for several of its Brazilian missionaries of African descent, either as a vehicle for the discovery of their African roots which Catholic Christianity in Brazil is perceived to have destroyed, or as a way of making reparation for the wrongs committed by their ancestors who sold their kin into slavery. This is the principal motivation in the case of several African-Brazilian SKK mission-aries in Angola (author's research interviews, Luanda, February 2001). Another and the last parallel to be mentioned here is that of reincarnation, a belief found, for example, in the Yoruba religions of southwestern Nigeria and the Republic of Benin and most of the Japanese NRMs.

Conclusions

While by no means all foreign missionaries were hostile to indigenous beliefs, rituals and customs, the rapid rate at which the AICs and prophet-healing movements grew suggests that overall there was a widely felt need for a more balanced, more empathetic response to traditional society than that offered by the historic or mission churches, some of which appeared to give priority over everything else to the uprooting of customs, beliefs and rituals. Although colonialism undoubtedly hastened the process already underway of de-coupling traditional beliefs from the traditional, political, economic and moral structures to which they lent plausibility for so long and which served to give them much of their meaning, these beliefs and rituals continued to provide some kind of meaningful explanation of good and evil, success and failure and sickness and death, and preserved some measure of social harmony and security. It was widely understood locally that their complete elimination could lead to total breakdown and anomie.

Seen from the perspective of African society, change had to be a gradual process, something missionaries sometimes failed to understand. The AICs adopted a more cautious approach not solely for the purpose of protecting tradition in itself but also for the reason that what they were being offered as essential Christianity by the missionaries was no more than a sacralization of the Western style of being a Christian rather than the transmission of its fundamentals.

The response, thus, of the African Independent Church (AIC) movement was not based on an uncritical attitude toward traditional society or on a complete rejection of modernization but was grounded in a more realistic understanding of the negative consequences of a root and branch approach to African culture, and cosmology. The Neo-Traditional NRMs that we have discussed have been and continue to be more thoroughgoing in their commitment to the preservation of the traditional religious and cultural heritage of Africa.

Once again in Africa as elsewhere we can see the increasing convergence of different religions, a convergence that sometimes leads to tension and conflict while at the same time providing new sources of spirituality and new ritual practices from which new religions are born. The new developments and movements discussed here offer interesting examples of what globalization theorists such as Robertson (1992) refer to as the process of 'glocalization', of the dynamics of inter-cultural and inter-religious exchange.

References and select bibliography

Ajayi, Jacob Festus Ade (1966) *Christian Missions in Nigeria, 1841–91: The Making of a New Elite*, London: Longmans.

Behrend, Heike (1999) 'Power to Heal, Power to Kill: Spirit Possession and War in Northern Uganda' in Heike Behrend and Ute Luig (eds) *Spirit Possession: Modernity and Power in Africa*, Oxford: James Curry, pp. 20–34.

Clarke, Peter B. (1986) *West Africa and Christianity*, London: Edward Arnold.

Clarke, Peter B. (1987) 'The Maitatsine Movement in Northern Nigeria in Historical and Current Perspective' in Rosalind Hackett (ed.) *New Religious Movements in Nigeria*, New York: Edwin Mellen Press, pp. 93–117.

Clarke, Peter B. (1995) *Mahdism in West Africa*, London: Luzac Oriental.

Gifford, Paul (2004) *Ghana's New Christianity: Pentecostalism in a Globalizing African Economy*, London: Hurst.

Lewis, I. M. (1971) *Ecstatic Religion*, Harmondsworth: Penguin.

Mayer, Jean-François (2001) 'Field Notes: The Movement for the Restoration of the Ten Commandments of God', *Nova Religio: The Journal of Alternative and Emergent Religions*, 5(1), 203–10.

Mbon, Friday (1986) 'The Social Impact of Nigeria's New Religious Movements' in James A. Beckford (ed.) *New Religious Movements and Rapid Social Change*, London: Sage, pp. 177–97.

Melton, J. Gordon and Bromley, David G. (2002) 'Lessons from the Past, Perspectives for the Future' in David G. Bromley and J. Gordon Melton (eds) *Cults, Religion and Violence*, Cambridge: Cambridge University Press, pp. 229–45.

O'Brien, D. B. C. (1971) *The Mourides of Senegal*, Oxford: Oxford University Press.

Olupona, Jacob K. and Nyang, Sulayman S. (eds) (1993) *Religious Plurality in Africa*, Berlin: Mouton De Gruyter.

Peel, John D. Y. (1968) *Aladura: A Religious Movement among the Yoruba*, Oxford: Oxford University Press.

Robertson, Roland (1992) *Globalization: Social Theory and Global Culture*, London: Sage.

Stark, Rodney (1996) 'Why Religious Movements Succeed or Fail: A Revised General Model', *Journal of Contemporary Religion*, 11(2), 133–47.

Sundkler, Bengt G. M. (1970) *Bantu Prophets in South Africa*, Oxford: Oxford University Press.

Turner, Harold W. (1967) *History of an Independent Church: The Church of the Lord* (2 vols), Oxford: Clarendon Press.

Turner, Harold W. (1991) 'Africa' in Stewart Sutherland and Peter B. Clarke (eds) *The Study of Religion: Traditional and New Religion*, London: Routledge, pp. 187–94.

Weber, Max (1992) *The Protestant Ethic and the Spirit of Capitalism* (trans. Talcott Parsons, with an Introduction by Anthony Giddens), London: Routledge (first published 1930 by Allen & Unwin).

Wilson, Bryan R. (1973) *Magic and the Millennium: A Sociological Study of Religious Movements of Protest among Tribal and Third World Peoples*, London: Heinemann.

Zahan, Dominique (1979) *The Religion, Spirituality and Thought of Traditional Africa* (trans. Kate Ezra Martin and Lawrence M. Martin), Chicago: University of Chicago Press.

Part IV

NRMs in South and Central America and the Caribbean

Chapter 9

South and Central America and the Caribbean

Religious change and diversification are occurring at a such a rapid pace across South (also known as Latin) and Central America and the Caribbean as to signal the beginnings of a reconfiguration of the religious landscape in the so-called New World. The change and diversification though not confined to the urban metropolises is most noticeable there and two of its most distinctive features are the rise of Evangelical Christianity, particularly in the form of Neo-Pentecostalism, and the declining monopoly of Catholicism. Regarding the latter development, the 2000 census in Brazil not only confirms the decline but also shows that the pace of it is accelerating (Pierucci, 2004). During the period 1991–2000 Catholicism decreased by 9.4 per cent to 73.9 per cent of the population while during the same period Evangelical Christianity rose by 6.6 per cent, a rise due principally to the growth in Neo-Pentecostalism (Pierucci, 2004: 18–22). In 1980, Brazil, with the exception of Rondonia where Evangelicals accounted for just over 17 per cent of the population and the far South of the country where Lutheranism was relatively well established, was overwhelmingly Catholic. Twenty-five years later researchers are writing about the end of traditional Brazil where they suggest both the old Catholicism – although there has been a Catholic Charismatic Revival with little social outreach in recent times – and the old Protestantism are on the wane and Neo-Evangelicalism is on the rise. This analysis also fits other countries in South and Central America, in particular.

However, while the rise of Neo-Pentecostalism has undoubtedly been the most significant religious development during the past forty years, it should not be allowed to obscure other new developments. Relatively recent innovations include the emergence of pan-regional and even global forms of African-Brazilian and African-Caribbean religions, and the continuing appeal of the Spiritism of the nineteenth-century French educationalist, Allan Kardec (see below), all across the region. Other new features include the transformation of Japanese New Religious Movements (NRMs) from ethnic to global movements and the rise of Amerindian-Catholic and Amerindian-Spiritist movements.

The resurgence of Neo-Pentecostalism in South and Central America and the Caribbean, and parts of Africa and Asia, has caused theorists of secularization to rethink their position and speak not of the decline of religion but of the desecularization of the modern world (Berger, 1999). The Neo-Pentecostal advance has all the appearance of a new religious reformation, which if it continues could prove to be as significant in terms of its consequences for Christianity worldwide as the Reformation, which occurred in Europe in the sixteenth century. In Mexico the total number of Pentecostals outnumbers that of all other minority religions taken together, including Mormonism, and the various Protestant denominations. In Guatemala the number of Protestants, a majority of whom belong to Pentecostalist Churches, increased sevenfold between 1960 and 1985 (Stoll, 1990: 8), while the movement began to grow vigorously in Brazil in the 1970s, Venezuela in the 1980s and Bolivia in the 1990s.

The phenomenal rise of Neo-Pentecostalism, as Martin (1990) has shown, is not to be interpreted as part of a United States strategy to extend its hegemony over South and Central America. To understand its success it is necessary to examine local conditions, local history and politics, local people's expectations of the established churches and how these have so often been disappointed. One of the main attractions of Neo-Pentecostalism when compared with Catholicism is its lack of involvement with the old political order.

The political influence of the new Pentecostalism in South and Central America and the Caribbean has varied. Overall it has been mostly indirect. In Argentina the continuing hold of Peronism – a political philosophy which insists on the principle of the people as the source of political power, and constitutes a culture of everyday life in which citizens recognize who they are – has limited Pentecostalism's political influence, despite its having been rapidly 'nationalisée' (Saraco, 1989).

Any clear evidence of Pentecostalism as an effective political force is also largely absent in Haiti. As Corten (2001: 246) points out, its major functions in that country have been to enable individuals to assume control, albeit symbolic, over their lives and to inspire them with the self-confidence needed to erect a frontier between themselves and the universe of malign forces which they continue to take extremely seriously. It also provides a rampart against the political language of dehumanization, which turns the crushing misery adepts experience into something banal. In Brazil, where over 13 per cent of the voters are Protestant and where there are a considerable number of Pentecostal politicians, attempts to use this religious affiliation to gain political advantage or support have proved unsuccessful.

I will confine the rest of my comments on the Neo-Pentecostal upsurge in South and Central America and the Caribbean to Brazil. Three periods of Pentecostal growth can be identified in Brazil, beginning with the early period that began with the arrival of European missionaries, followed closely by American evangelists of the Assemblies of God in the first decade of the twentieth century.

The first church of the early period was the Christian Congregation (Congregação Cristã) founded by an Italian immigrant to Chicago, Luigi Franciscon. The Christian Congregation and early Pentecostalism in Brazil in general, was strongly anti-Catholic and stressed the imminence of the Second Coming of Jesus and speaking in tongues (glossolalia). Initially entirely Italian, the Christian Congregation in Brazil today has a mixed membership of around two and a half million. The second period ran from c.1950–c.1970, the period of intensive urbanization and modernization, which saw the arrival of new denominations from outside Brazil, including the American International Church of the Four Square Gospel. It was during this period that the emphasis began to be placed on the use of modern means of communication. There was also a shift in emphasis from glossolalia to healing. Among the local Pentecostal churches that emerged in this period were Brazil for Christ (Brasil Para Cristo) and God is Love (Deus e Amor).

In the 1970s, a third phase known as Neo-Pentecostalism began. This phase has been characterized mainly by its stress on the necessity to engage in spiritual warfare against the Devil and evil spirits using the rite of exorcism as the principal weapon, and by its insistence on the necessity of true conversion to Jesus as a condition of improved spiritual, and material, well-being. Its theology is essentially the same as that of Prosperity Theology, which attributes poverty and sickness to spiritual causes.

Neo-Pentecostal churches

The most successful of the Neo-Pentecostal churches is the Universal Church of the Kingdom of God (Igreja Universal do Reino de Deus or IURD), founded in Rio de Janeiro in 1977 by Edgir Macedo (Oliva, 1997), who came from a large and extremely poor family in northeast Brazil.

IURD is largely an urban phenomenon and one of the crucial factors in explaining its success is the spiritual and social role it performs for the destitute legions of small farmers from the dry, parched sertão or interior of northeast Brazil who have moved into the shanty towns within the vast urban agglomerations of cities such as São Paulo in search of a livelihood. Oliva's research on IURD's success, influenced by Girard's theory of the psychological, sociological, political and religious processes of redemption, concludes that it is 'a product of the badly disguised violence of our urban life' (1997: 22).

Movements such as IURD have been strongly opposed not only to Catholicism but also to African- and Asian-derived religions, which they condemn as evil, and they ritually exorcise all those who have participated therein. Although the competition for members is driving even the more intolerant churches like IURD into forms of reflexive syncretism it would never have tolerated even a decade ago. In one of its attempts to compete with the Catholic Church, it has introduced a rival pilgrimage to the shrine of

Nossa Senhora de Aparecida, Our Lady of Aparecida, in the state of Minas Gerais, the most important, popular religious pilgrimage in Brazil. IURD has extended its mission well beyond Brazil to Africa, and not only to the Lusophone territories such as Angola and Mozambique, but also to Anglophone and Francophone Africa, and to North America, Europe and Japan.

Neo-Pentecostalism challenges Catholic hegemony in ways that cannot easily be countered. For example, in terms of leadership and ministry many of these small-scale churches can provide training for the ministry within a matter of weeks while Catholicism requires years, and they can enlist both women and men and endow them with full responsibility in both spiritual and temporal matters concerning the church. The rapid growth of Neo-Pentecostalism has, nevertheless, triggered a Catholic revival led by charismatic priests. The latter have attempted to invert IURD's and Neo-Pentecostal cosmology by stressing Catholicism as vocation as opposed to Catholicism as a tradition into which one is born, and by their emphasis on the positive potential of all experience rather than attributing the material and emotional difficulties that affect people to fallen spirits (Clarke, 1999a).

Becoming Pentecostalist is often presented as turning away from a life ruled by habits of the heart to a more sober, joyless, dull, serious, rational, routine-bound lifestyle. On the contrary. It is by no means as joyless as is sometimes imagined. While enabling people to develop the seemingly more relevant and fitting responses to the change from close-knit, community-centred societies to the more self-reliant, individualistic, rational, bureaucratic world that increasingly marks South and Central American and Caribbean society, Pentecostalism is not a stark alternative to joyful Catholic culture but another version of the festive community (Brandão, 1986; 1994). Pentecostalism, as it forms its members in the new aptitudes, attitudes and virtues, at the same time involves them in a new community, an involvement which, Brandao (1986: 143) insists, is an involvement in a new 'festive' community, and the feast is always one that is powerfully affective in character.

Neo-Pentecostalism and Liberation Theology both fished in the same pool and while the latter sought to develop among the deprived a more critical evaluation of their condition its cause was not helped by the strength of the conservative forces within the Catholic Church or by its lack of a purely spiritual dimension. Liberation Theology was, as Martin describes it, 'a religion *for* the poor [my italics]', an earnest, intellectual form of religion, while Pentecostalism was perceived as a 'religion *of* the poor [my italics]' (1990: 290). Moreover, while Liberation Theology was bound by traditional ecclesiastical structures and politics, Neo-Pentecostalism benefited from the freedom and flexibility enjoyed by early Methodism in eighteenth-century England. It was and continues to be more mobile and flexible than 'embedded' Catholicism, with, as we have seen, much shorter training periods for evangelists. Neo-Pentecostalism is not, however, a quick fix or soft option but offers millions the possibility of a more orderly, responsible and self-disciplined lifestyle, along with what are widely understood moral and spiritual explanations and remedies for the extremely adverse material and moral conditions of society.

Surveying the South American and Central American situation as a whole, Martin (1990) accounts for the massive transfer of religious allegiance, the 'walk out' from Catholicism to Neo-Pentecostalism, in terms of the widespread perception that the former is inextricably linked to the old, failed political and economic order which is responsible for the corruption and material deprivation that exists everywhere. More specific reasons include the fragmentation of communities that once conferred identity on their members consequent on modernization, and the resultant demand for a different kind of cognitive map and moral and ethical code for living in a more open-ended, less predictable world in which thrift and self-discipline are seen as the key to success.

Spiritism, based on the writings and teachings of the French educator Hippolyte Leon Denizard Rivail (1804–69), better known by his alias Alain Kardec, and distinguished from Spiritualism chiefly by its acceptance of reincarnation (Hess, 1991), has influenced almost every aspect and form of religion in South and Central America and the Caribbean. It is also an important source of medical and social service for the urban poor.

Spiritist and esoteric NRMs in Brazil and Argentina

Kardecian Spiritism has an estimated six million adepts in Brazil alone where it has become an essential element of Umbanda, an African-Brazilian tradition (see below), and has provided founders of new religions with one of their principal sources of doctrine and ritual. Along with Amerindian Shamanism, Spiritism has also greatly influenced Brazilian New Age spirituality.

Kardecism believes in the possibility of communication between humans and disincarnated spirits, in the idea of many worlds, each one a step on the path to progress, with the earth being the third step on this path, and in the oneness of the supernatural and natural orders. While believing in its own version of the law of karma or cause and effect, and while stressing the importance of self-effort, Kardecism is also convinced of the ability of the recently departed disincarnated spirits to assist the living, and in that of the spirits of light of the seventh dimension to do likewise. Mediums in trance are believed to be able to communicate with these spirits and to receive messages from them for those who attend their sessions. Versions of all of these teachings are commonplace regardless of religious allegiance, thus facilitating large-scale involvement with Spiritism.

Kardec's ideas were widely promoted in Brazil in the second half of the nineteenth century through the activities and writings of, among others, the medium Adolfo Bezzera Menezes de Calvacanti (Bastide, 1967) and, for much of the twentieth century, by Francisco Cândido Xavier, alias Chico Xavier, particularly through his 'psychographed' treatise *Nosso Lar* (Our Home) (1944). Menezes' explanation of the spiritual roots of sickness has proved extremely popular, and in particular that aspect of his theory that claims that in cases of mental illness where there is no sign of cerebral lesion the cause is spiritual (1897–1939). The basis of *Nosso Lar*'s continuing appeal is to be found in its millenarianism. The name of the volume itself is that of the, as yet incomplete, celestial colony founded by the Portuguese in the sixteenth century which is believed to be situated directly above Rio de Janeiro and reserved for Brazilians (Hess, 1991: 31).

Bastide (1967), when writing of Spiritist 'scientific' thought in Brazil, misleadingly implies that Spiritism is an upper-class pursuit. He speaks of the upper classes as plantation owners, industrialists, doctors, engineers, civil servants and teachers. In the opinion of others (Brandão, 1986; Hess, 1991) Spiritist thought is not confined to one particular class or associated with one particular system of ideas but occupies a mediating position between different religious systems of thought and practice.

Spiritist-Catholic NRMs in Brazil include the Blue Butterflies (Borbeletas Azuis) founded by Roldao Mangueira (alias Padre Cicero), a former cotton merchant, in December 1961 in the city of Campina Grande in the interior of the northern state of Paraiba in Brazil. This movement was heavily involved in the healing ministry, an activity for which it was strongly criticized by the ecclesiastical and political authorities. Also criticized was its preoccupation with the coming apocalypse, which was to begin, it predicted, in May 1980 with a deluge that would last for 120 days.

The deluge, it was believed, would constitute divine proof and justification for the movement's healing activities, which it carried on in its Confraternity, the House of the Charity of Jesus. Claiming to act as medium for well-known local personalities such as Padre Cicero Romao, for popular Catholic saints, and for the Infant Jesus, Mangueira was credited with countless cures by local people, a response that greatly concerned the local Catholic bishops who obviously saw the movement as a potential rival and who, accordingly, dismissed its claims as the 'fruit of religious ignorance' (Novaes and Romalho, 1990: 39).

Other new Spiritist-Catholic NRMs with a strong millenarian emphasis include the Legião da Boa Vontade (the Legion of Good Will or LBV), founded in Rio de Janeiro in January 1950 by Alziro Zarur (1914–79) for the alleged purpose of promoting universal solidarity. The Spiritist Zarur contended that since Kardec had been unable to finish his mission it fell to him to complete it. From this he drew the conclusion that Legião da Boa Vontade was the fourth revelation of God to mankind. Frequently criticized by the media and the wider public for profit-making and financial irregularities, the movement on the death of Zarur in 1979, and the installation of

Paiva Netto as leader, separated its religious activities from other activities including its charitable and publishing outlets. Criticism notwithstanding, this socially engaged, millenarian movement, for which the Book of Apocalypse is the most important of its scriptures, has attracted widespread support by its successful use of the media, its widely read publications and charitable enterprises.

The Legião attempts to reflect the ethnic diversity and the growing religious pluralism of Brazil. To promote these objectives, LBV has built in the Brazilian capital, Brasilia, a large ecumenical Temple of Good Will – with a pure crystal tower to symbolize the unification of nations, cultures and races – and a World Parliament of Ecumenical Fraternity as a way of facilitating contact with cosmic forces.

Argentina is home to the largest Spiritist organization in the world in the form of the Escuela Cientifica Basilio. This movement was founded by the French Spiritist Henry Jacob (1829–1913), and brought to Argentina by his pupil Blanche Aubreton de Lambert (1867–1920) during the First World War. In Argentina the latter began channelling, with a certain Eugenio Portal (1867–1927), Jacob's father Eusebio, one of whose instructions was that they should restore primitive Christianity, which the Christian church is accused of having abandoned in the fourth century. Its most serious deviation was its having started to believe in Jesus as the Son of God, a belief not held by the early Christian church. It was to fulfil this restorative mission the Escuela Cientifica Basilio was opened in 1917. This school like so many others in South America also derives its essential teachings from the Spiritism of Allan Kardec, and has spread beyond Argentina to Paraguay, Uruguay, Brazil and other South American countries and to North America and Europe.

A more recent Spiritist movement of Argentinian origin is the New Acropolis movement founded in 1957, also in Buenos Aires, by Jorge Angel Livraga Rizzi (1886–1951). This politically conservative movement describes itself as a school of classical philosophy. New Acropolis teachings are based on such diverse sources as the Greek philosophy of Plato (428/27–347 BC), the Theosophical ideas developed by Madame Blavatsky (1831–91) (see Chapter 5) and those of René Guenon (1886–1951) on the theme of the philosophia perennis. One of this movement's main beliefs is in the advent of the Age of Aquarius, which, it warns, will give rise to great pain and suffering at the outset. Like the Escuela Cientifica Basilio the New Acropolis has also become an international movement with a presence in some fifty countries.

Spiritist movements, some of which are heavily influenced by Amerindian beliefs, are to be found in the Caribbean, including the Mesa Branca in Puerto Rico. This island also gave birth in 1940 to the millenarian, Pentecostal-style Mita religion, whose main temple holds around 5,000 worshippers. This movement has also built a school, a clinic, retreat centres for fully committed devotees and several large businesses in San Juan and has spread to the Dominican Republic, Haiti, Mexico, Colombia and Venezuela (Hurbon, 1991).

While there are Spiritists in South America who oppose the fusion of their beliefs with those of other traditions, Spiritism has, nonetheless, been integrated with other streams of spirituality, including African spirituality, as we shall see. But before moving on to African-derived religions of the New World, I want first of all to discuss Amerindian-Catholic spirituality.

Amerindian-Catholic spirituality and New Religions

There are numerous movements across the Amazon region of South America that derive their beliefs and practices from Amerindian-Catholic sources, and others that juxtapose Amerindian, African, Catholic and Shinto sources. Below we will look at examples of Amerindian-Catholic-derived religions from Brazil, including the Brotherhood of the Holy Cross and the Santo Daime movement, which in recent times has spread to other parts of South America and beyond. These and similar movements are characterized by their millenarianism, a feature of Tupi-Guarani spirituality, and one which would appear to predate colonialism.

Studies of the Tupi-Guarani search for the Land-Without-Evil suggest that this pursuit of paradise on earth began before Portuguese and Spanish colonial intervention and was more than likely activated by an internal power struggle between the spiritual and political leadership. Harsh environmental conditions caused by infrequent rain and poor irrigation may also have done as much as anything else to motivate the Tupi-Guarani to embark on their long and arduous journey (Clastres, 1995).

The Tupi-Guarani description of the Land-Without-Evil suggests in this case that the environment was an important factor in stimulating belief in the imminent advent of heaven on earth. When it came, it would be, they imagined, a privileged, indestructible place in which the earth would be capable of providing all that was needed for living well, a place filled with fields of fruit near a beautiful river where all they would have to do would be to dance (Clastres, 1995: 23). Tupi-Guarani and Amerindian thinking generally on religion, like much Traditional religion, sees it not as a theological idea that places an external creative deity or groups of deities on one side and humans on the other, but as a present and active force that produces tangible effects, a perspective shared by those who engage in New Age and contemporary forms of spirituality.

The teachings of the Brotherhood of the Holy Cross, founded in 1972 by Brother Joseph of the Cross among the Indian Tikuna and their neighbours of European descent in the Brazilian Amazon region (Oro, 1989), consist of Amerindian Shamanism and Catholicism. As Oro's study of this Brotherhood stresses, its aims were not the restoration of the traditional Amerindian order undermined by modernization, nor the total transformation of the world, but the inversion of their actual, present social situation, not only in terms of material betterment but also in terms of social integration. What the

Amerindian followers sought was not full but limited entry to the wider world in which their European contacts lived.

The pursuit of a deeper understanding of oneself and of explanations for the conditions of deprivation, in which so many millions are obliged to exist despite every effort to overcome them, are central concerns of Amerindian Shamanism and of African-Brazilian-derived religions. In the latter, uncontrollable exhilaration is often expressed in becoming one's ancestor during trance, this being a form of rebirth, both psychologically and symbolically, into pre-slave conditions. It was this type of preoccupation that also inspired the Santo Daime movement founded by Raimundo Irineu Serra (1892–1971) in the state of Acre in Brazil in the 1920s.

Raimundo, himself from Maranhão, was one of the migrants involved in rubber extraction in Acre who, when the production of latex declined, fell into poverty. At first he started a collective to try to alleviate the material and social distress that followed from unemployment and then in the early 1930s founded with his closest collaborators a religious body which was called the Centre of Christian Illumination, Universal Light and Alto Santo or Holy Elevation. Using his knowledge of Tambor da Minas Spiritualism and Amerindian Shamanism, Raimundo developed appropriate rituals for the taking of *ayuhasca*, meaning in Quechua 'vine of the soul'. This drink, taken by the rubber tappers, was obtained from the *jacupe* plant and the leaf known as *chacrona*. A hallucinogenic substance believed to have the power both to clarify what was obscure or hidden and to cure, Raimundo turned the content of the spiritual experiences he enjoyed while under its influence into the movement's doctrines.

Hallucinogenic potions are used to serve different purposes in different religious settings and these can be interestingly compared and contrasted with each other and with secular usage. As Wilson (1973) has pointed out, the use of drugs by religious movements is often a sign of introversionism, a means of withdrawal from the wider society at the behest of God or some supernatural power, as in the case of the North American Indians who turned to Peyotism in the second half of the nineteenth century (see Chapter 5). Santo Daime's use of the hallucinogen which it calls *daime* resembles the peyote case but differs from others, including the use of similar substances by those in the counter-cultural movement in the United States and Europe in the 1960s and 1970s. While the latter sought freedom from the limitations imposed by the mainstream culture, from all the perceived outmoded illusions and regulations that inhibited self-expression, and so on, for the Santo Daime community it was the spirit that was anxious for freedom, that sought to reconcile itself with its lost origins, with its essence from which it felt alienated (Soares, 1990).

This craving for unity and wholeness notwithstanding, the Santo Daime movement began to fragment on Raimundo's death in 1971. A new group emerged under the leadership of Sebastião Mota de Melo (1920–90) and it was this group that started to spread the movement to various parts of Brazil and beyond. By the late 1980s a branch had been opened in Boston and in 1996 the first European meeting was held in Gerona, Spain and was attended by members from twenty-nine European countries. There are also members in Argentina, Uruguay and further afield in Japan. Over time the social composition of the movement has changed, a change triggered in part by the interest in its ideas and rituals shown by New Agers of middle-class background.

African-derived religions: Brazil

Although in more recent times they have come to form part of a pan-regional, and indeed global pantheon, with which Africans everywhere increasingly identify, the African-derived religions of South and Central America have, historically, varied from each other in terms of their structure, beliefs, rituals and to some degree, their response to the wider society. I will, therefore, focus first of all on Candomblé and Umbanda in Brazil and in a separate section on Santeria and Voodoo in the Caribbean.

'Candomblé', a term which appears to have initially referred to a dance and then a musical instrument, came to be applied to the ceremonies performed by African and former African slaves and their descendants in Brazil, especially in the northeast of Brazil in the states of Bahia, Pernambuco and Maranhão. It is also practised in São Paulo and as far south as Porto Alegre in the state of Rio Grande do Sul, and in other South American countries including Argentina and Uruguay. More recently the religion has spread to North America and Europe.

The most historic casa (house) of African-Brazilian religion in existence today is probably the Casa das Minas in São Luiz de Maranhão, founded in the first half of the nineteenth century and identified by its use of rituals derived mainly from the Jeje culture of Dahomey (now the Republic of Benin) in West Africa. Later, around the middle of the nineteenth century, some of Brazil's foremost African-Brazilian centres, including the Casa Branca (White House) and the Casa do Gantois, were founded in the city of Salvador, capital of the state of Bahia, in northeast Brazil, which has come to be widely regarded as the spiritual home of the religion.

The practice of African-Brazilian religion predates these formal beginnings. African slaves from Central Africa (the Congo), from West Central Africa (mainly Angola), from a large area of West Africa and from East Central Africa (mainly Mozambique), most of whom were baptized Catholics either before they were shipped as slaves to Brazil or on arrival there, continued from the outset to perform their rituals while labouring on the sugar and tobacco plantations or working in the urban centres of the New World. From the second half of the nineteenth century the rituals and cosmology of the Yoruba people from the previously mentioned West

African Republic of Benin and southwestern Nigeria came to exercise the greatest influence on the development of Candomblé in Bahia, which, outside of Africa itself, has preserved in its most complete and authentic form the worship of Yoruba divinities or orishas (Yoruba: orisa pronounced orisha and Portuguese: orixa also pronounced orisha).

Candomblé traditions are distinguished from each other not only according to the African tradition with which they are most closely associated historically, but also on the basis of the so-called 'nations' (Portuguese: nacoẽs) into which slaves were grouped. These nations were in practice ethnically mixed. Other ways of distinguishing one tradition from another include the type of drums used in a terreiro and the way they are played, for example with or without drumsticks, and the language, dance and music of the ceremonies. Thus, there is Candomblé Nago or Yoruba Candomblé, Candomblé Jeje which, as we have seen, refers to a type of Dahomean (Republic of Benin) Candomblé, Angolan and Congolese Candomblé, and what is known as Candomblé-de-Caboclo, an essentially Amerindian-based Candomblé in which the mediums are possessed by Amerindian spirits known popularly as caboclos. African-Brazilian practitioners of Candomblé, referred to as candomblistas, also reverence these Amerindian spirits or caboclos as the spirits of the original owners of the land to which their own ancestors were sent as slaves.

Candomblé also developed close links with Catholicism and to a greater or lesser extent, depending on the terreiro and its traditions, with the Spiritism of Alain Kardec, which, as we have seen, has a widespread presence in Brazil, Argentina and most of South America. Each Candomblé centre has an ancestral house usually situated away from the main place of worship. Candomblé centres have traditionally acknowledged correspondences between African gods and Catholic saints. While there is much debate as to why this was so, the practice may have begun as a kind of smokescreen behind which slaves carried on the 'illegal' worship of their own gods. It is also possible that it served two very different but complementary ends by protecting both the African and the Brazilian Catholic identity of the slaves and their descendants. A small number of casas or terreiros are dedicated exclusively to the veneration of ancestors (Yoruba: egun) as an independent cult and these are strongly opposed to any form of mixing of African and non-African traditions.

As in most other forms of African-derived religion in South and Central America and the Caribbean, the correspondences made between African gods and Catholic saints often surprise and include the pairing of the violent and virile Yoruba god of thunder Shango (Portuguese: Xango) with the quiet, studious, pensive, balding, elderly St Jerome. The head of the Yoruba pantheon, Oshala (Portuguese: Oxala) is paired with Christ and Yemanja, the mother of several orishas and goddess of the sea, corresponds with Our Lady of the Immaculate Conception.

Changed circumstances in the New World made for a change in emphasis regarding the functions of the orishas who came to be regarded much more as personal deities than, as was traditionally the case in Africa, associated either with a city or a 'nation'. In Africa Shango, for example, is associated with Oyo, Yemanja with the Egba nation, and Oshala-Obatala with Ife. Orishas travelled with their followers and in this way devotion to them spread. Where, however, a person lived alone or with his immediate family, the orisha would take on the characteristics of a personal divinity.

The result of the break up of the family unit through slavery meant that each individual member of a terreiro, known as a filha (daughter) or filho (son) de santo (saint or god/goddess), became personally responsible for fulfilling all the demands imposed by her/his orisha. A priestess (mae de santo) or a priest (pae de santo), mother or father of the saint and/or divinity, and spiritual head of the terreiro, has responsibility for initiating into the cult those called to become a filha or filho de santo.

At the core of Candomblé religion is the mystical power (Yoruba: ase; Portuguese: axe) of the orishas, which the latter transmit to their descendants during possession. Not all devotees are of African descent and for those who are not possession cannot easily be explained by recourse to traditional theological ideas. Non-Africans can, however, claim to have certain personality traits and affinities of temperament in common with a particular orisha, which would facilitate their being possessed, the main purpose of Candomblé.

Candomblé is also, Verger suggests (1993), a psychology in the sense that the orishas come to be seen as archetypes of personality who manifest in their behaviour the fulfilment of an individual's latent tendencies and the resolution of unresolved personal conflicts that arise from the 'unnatural' rules which are designed to promote socially accepted behaviour. In this situation initiation and possession become the means of self-liberation, enabling people to express their innermost tendencies, which would otherwise be repressed. Today, Candomblé's psychological role is recognized by so-called orthodox psychology, which refers patients suffering from certain types of psychological illnesses – described as 'illnesses of the gods'– to well-recognized and respected priestesses and priests for treatment.

The previously mentioned Yemanja, goddess of the sea, archetype, for example, is wilful, rigorous, strong, protective, proud and, at times, impetuous and arrogant, and puts her friendships to the test. She bears grudges for a long time, and, if she does forgive, she never forgets. She is maternal and responsible, enjoys luxury, beautiful blue cloth and expensive jewels and tends to live beyond her means.

The purposes of Candomblé cannot be limited to its psychological role. It is also about preserving African identity, culture and tradition. Without Candomblé and similar belief systems African culture in the New World would most likely have ceased to exist, and with it innumerable plants and herbs and their healing properties which come under the dominion of the god Ossaim. African legends, dance and music, aesthetics, leisure activities, sculpture, art, and cuisine, which it has helped preserve, would also have been lost.

Umbanda, a more Europeanized version of African-Brazilian religion than Candomblé, reflecting the more ethnically European character of the south of Brazil, started in São Paulo in the 1920s, a time of ever-increasing urbanization and industrialization. A doctrinally and ethnically inclusive movement, Umbanda drew upon teachings and practices from African-Brazilian religions, Kardecist Spiritism, Amerindian religion and Catholicism, bringing together in this way three of the major ethnic groups that make up the population of Brazil: African, Amerindian and European.

As in Candomblé, a centre is headed by a pai or mae de santo (father or mother of the saint) who is assisted by filhas and filhos de santos (sons and daughters of the saint). The father or mother of the saint has a spiritual parallel known as the guia-chefe or chief guide of the centre and together with this guide the former prepares the sons and daughters of the saints for initiation and trains them to serve as ritual assistants and mediums.

The eclectic character of Umbanda and the virtual autonomy of local groups mean that there can be considerable variation in belief and practice from one Umbanda centre to another. There is, however, a federation to which each centre is affiliated and which takes care of the material side of the various centres. The federation consists of a president, vice president and secretaries and treasurers. The father or mother of the saint – ritual leader of the centre – has little or no influence in theory over the federation for the reason that the spiritual and material side of Umbanda should not be mixed. In practice there is mixing and where a ritual leader is weak the federation assumes control over his territory as well as its own.

Umbanda made rapid strides in São Paulo, the industrial hub of Brazil, in the 1950s, and continued to do so until the 1990s. More recently there appears to have been a decline in the number of those involved. Many who do attend Umbanda centres do so on an irregular basis and learn little about the teachings and rituals. While ritual leaders have considerable authority over the sons and daughters of the saint they have little control over the clients who attend sessions, the majority of whom are 'accidental' visitors, so to speak, coming and going at will.

The Umbanda cosmos has three tiers, the astral, the earth and the underworld. The African gods or orishas inhabit the first tier, along with Caboclos or Amerindian spirits and the Pretos Velhos or Old Blacks, who are considered to be the founders of Umbanda. The spirits of this sphere are referred to as spirits of the light or right, are considered good and are linked to the 'white' magic of Umbanda. The earth is inhabited by human incarnations who are at the lower stages of spiritual evolution, and the underworld by evil and ignorant spirits such as the trickster god, Eshu, and the Pomba Giras, his female counterparts. The spirits of the underworld are known as spirits of the shadows and are associated with the left, are considered immoral or amoral and are associated with evil and 'black' magic (quimbanda). Because these spirits are more human-like, humans can more easily make use of them to resolve the material problems of everyday life. Their presence at sessions, therefore, is considered indispensable, as the majority of clients' problems arise from material circumstances rather than being caused by spiritual agencies.

The orisha occasionally visit the earth to help human incarnations but are not as active or as important as they are in Candomblé. When Eshu and his counterparts visit the earth it is to create problems for people. They rarely possess their mediums and when they do they remain mute. In Umbanda it is the spirits of the dead who function as consulting spirits that are the main focus of the sessions.

Umbanda offers its clients solutions to their material and spiritual problems, and mainly the former. Its teaching on the spiritual evolution of human beings also offers an explanation for human weakness and failure. In this way it functions, like Candomblé, as a form of personal psychology.

African-derived religions: the Caribbean

Although, as will be evident, there is much overlap on fundamentals between the African-derived religions of the Caribbean and say those of Brazil, there are also differences, as there are even within the same country. Candomblé, for example, is more of a congregational religion than certain other African-derived religions including Cuban Santeria.

Santeria is one of the two most culturally, politically and spiritually significant of the African-derived religions of the Caribbean, Voodoo which has its roots in Haiti, being the other. Both of these religions have become internationalized in recent times, as have Candomblé and Umbanda, through economic migration, exile, particularly to the United States, and through the return 'home' of increasing numbers of later generations of African-Americans and African-Caribbeans in search of their roots.

As in the case of the African-derived movements of Brazil, the spiritual content of these movements includes the worship of the West African Yoruba divinities known as orisha (Yoruba: orisa; Spanish: oricha); Roman Catholic practices; and that previously mentioned form of Spiritism devised by Allan Kardec which began to attract many in the Caribbean and South America during the nineteenth century.

I will first consider briefly the history of Santeria before moving to that of Voodoo. As with several other of the African-derived religions of the Caribbean and South America, Santeria is a Yoruba religion in origin, which has developed its own distinctive religious and social traditions. The Yoruba were among those enslaved Africans brought to Cuba from the early days of the transatlantic slave trade. Until the 1840s they constituted only a small portion of that traffic and then for more than thirty years their number totalled one-third of all the Africans enslaved and brought to Cuba, where Catholicism was the official religion.

A main goal of the Catholic Church in Cuba as in Brazil was to rescue the enslaved African population from what it saw as the harm caused to their spiritual well-being by their attachment to their traditional 'superstitions'. What transpired was not the total change from Traditional religion to Catholicism expected but as in Brazil and elsewhere in South America a juxtaposing of the two religions. This did not constitute a haphazard mixing of religious traditions, as is often suggested, nor was it hybridity, for adepts of African-Cuban religions such as Santeria were fully aware that the meaning and purpose of ritual in both traditions were different and did not confuse the two. Moreover, this positive relationship to other religions in the case of Santeria, and African religions generally, derives from their unitary view of the supernatural order. This is not a divided order, although there can be several channels of access to it.

The Catholic Church's vision was different and, supported by the colonial government, convinced that santeros (adepts of Santeria) were mixing their Catholicism with African 'superstition' would, from time to time, engage in a campaign of persecution against Santeria, thus driving it underground. The present Cuban Government has Marxist fashion, dismissed Santeria as anti-modern and a hindrance to progress and modernization. However, in recent years it has become more tolerant, as has the Catholic Church which since the Second Vatican Council (1962–65) has encouraged dialogue with all faiths. Moreover, as in Brazil, the Catholic Church has gradually come to accept that by banning practitioners from participating in Catholic ceremonies it would severely reduce the numbers attending church, as the most frequent churchgoers were santeros, and in the case of Brazil, adepts of the African-Brazilian religions.

Santeria has developed a close relationship also with the Spiritism (Espiritismo) of Alain Kardec, whose writings began to reach Cuba in the 1850s, and which between 1870 and 1880 became popular throughout the French and Spanish Caribbean, as they did in South and Central America. The links between the two traditions became so close that Cuban Santeria priests came to regard it as an important part of their training to learn the tenets and practices of Espiritismo. This close relationship and the influence on it of Catholicism and Spiritism notwithstanding, Santeria has remained essentially Yoruba in terms of its cosmology, rituals and orientation to the world.

As to its orientation toward the world, Santeria, like many African and African-derived religions, does not divide the world into distinct realms. The spiritual and natural orders exist within the world that we experience. Thus, Santeria has as its main concern the ritual control of the spiritual and natural forces that impinge on everyday life, on relationships and on all that a person does.

There exist in Santeria as, for example, in Candomblé and Umbanda, the notion of a Supreme Being, known by different Yoruba names including Olodumare, Olorun, and Olofi, or by the Spanish name Dios (God). Under the sovereignty of the Supreme Being and serving as Her/His ministers are lesser gods referred to, as we have already mentioned, in Santeria as orichas or santos. These divinities were assigned different functions including populating and making the earth habitable and fit for harmonious living. As in Candomblé, each oricha and/or santo corresponds to a Catholic saint.

From the outset, it is believed human beings were granted ritual knowledge that would enable them to tap into the powers of the lesser gods and thereby live in harmony with the Supreme Being. Through the performance of ritual they would establish the appropriate degree of equilibrium between themselves and their natural environment and between their outer, so to speak, and inner, selves. It is this philosophy that underpins the importance attached to possession and trance by the gods, the core ritual act of Santeria, as it is of Voodoo, Candomblé and Umbanda.

On the occasion of the festival of a god, santeros will assemble and in Yoruba chants accompanied by drums will call upon the gods to descend and mount their devotees. Outside of these collective ceremonies the daily practice is to make offerings to the gods in the home. In addition to training future devotees, Santeria priests and priestesses provide counselling and healing to devotees and the general public.

Santeria has spread outside of Cuba, mainly in modern times through Cuban exiles who left the country in 1959, and also through immigration. In the United States Santeria has established a presence not only in various Southern states and African-American communities but also among the White and Asian populations (McGuire and Scrymgeour, 1998). Moreover, it has made its way back from the United States to parts of the Caribbean including Puerto Rico and the Dominican Republic. It has also been brought by Cubans to Central America (Mexico), and South America (Venezuela) and Spain and from there to other European countries.

At present Santeria is undergoing a resurgence in Cuba after being denigrated for so long as an obstacle to true religion on the one hand and social, economic and scientific progress on the other. Greater openness and tolerance on the part of the Government and the involvement of economic migrants of African origin who see it as their mission to ensure the survival of African culture have contributed to this resurgence. The ease with which diaspora santeros can communicate with each other via the Internet has also assisted this revival.

In the same way as the practice of Santeria continues to be closely associated with Cuba despite its international outreach, Voodoo is associated with the Caribbean island of Haiti. Voodoo itself is a term used by Europeans, usually in a negative sense, to describe the religion of the Fon of the Republic of Benin in West Africa (formerly Dahomey), who venerate a varied pantheon of spiritual beings called Vodun. These spiritual entities manifest in their adepts in trance-possession, as in Santeria, Candomblé and Umbanda.

After a successful rebellion against French rule in 1791 and the establishment of the first ever Black Republic in 1804, the emancipated African captives of Haiti, most of whom were Roman Catholics by baptism, were left free to practice Voodoo, which consisted of Fon and Catholic beliefs and rituals, the rituals of Taino shamans that had survived in the hills despite Catholic opposition, and the Free Masonic rituals of the French colonialists.

As in Santeria and Candomblé, every Fon lwa (divinity) was made to correspond to a Catholic saint, often adopting the same iconography, prayers and feast days. The Masonic ritual elements selected included such symbols as the All-Seeing Eye and the elaborate Masonic handshakes.

Voodoo has never declared itself to be ritually or doctrinally complete and continues to develop by selecting new ideas and practices from other traditions. The converse also holds. People from other spiritual paths, including New Agers, look to Voodoo for ideas and inspiration. For example, there are New Age seekers for whom the Voodoo Iwa are manifestations of the same universal pantheon to be found in other esoteric traditions. Neo-Paganism in the West has also derived spiritual ideas from Voodoo. In the opinion of the French ethnographer and Voodoo specialist Alfred Metraux, Voodoo is 'The paganism of the West: Many of us go to Haiti in search of our classical heritage, and find in Voodoo the charm of fairy tales. Without compelling us to give up our habits and ties with the present, it take us into a magic realm' (citation from: Cosentino, 1995: 53).

Others link Voodoo with quantum physics, claiming that both demonstrate that reality has both a visible and an invisible side, an insight said to be evident in Zombie rituals. For others, the whole Voodoo system is, like Candomblé, a sophisticated form of social psychology.

As in the case of Santeria, Voodoo has been taken by immigrants to various parts of the world and in particular to the United States, and in the process some of its rituals and ceremonies have undergone a process of adaptation (Brown, 1991). Moreover, this once largely ethnic-based religion is becoming increasingly multi-ethnic in terms of its social composition as it expands further north into the North American cities such as New York where Caucasians have also become involved.

A similar change in ethnic composition is evident in the Rastafarian movement. This movement began in the 1920s during the time of the Great Depression and was inspired by the Jamaican Marcus Garvey's Back to Africa movement in the United States and his call for 'Africa for the Africans'. The fledgling movement was uplifted and energized by the occasion of the accession of Ras Tafari (Ras meaning Prince, and Tafari, Creator) to the imperial throne of Ethiopia in 1935. Haile Selassie was seen as the fulfilment of Psalm 68, which was interpreted to mean that God, Jah, had singled out the Black Race for special attention. Its thinking was greatly influenced by the tradition of resistance to foreign dominance found in such indigenous movements as Myalism, one of whose purposes was the counteracting of the 'sorcery of the slave masters', by the resistance to cultural imperialism offered by the African-Christian religions. Among the latter was the Native Baptist movement. Rastafarianism was also influenced by notions already long current in Caribbean society, particularly the notion of Ethiopianism, an idea that conflates Ethiopia, meaning black, with the entire continent of Africa and fills the imagination with dreams of freedom and liberation.

'Ethiopia, Thou Land of Our Fathers', was the title that Garvey gave to the anthem of his Universal Negro Improvement Association (UNIA). The mission of the UNIA was to inform the world about Africa's great civilization and undermine such assumptions of cultural imperialism as the Hamitic hypothesis, a hypothesis used by the ruling minority to underpin and legitimize apartheid in South Africa. The hypothesis assumed that anything of excellence, refinement and of great beauty found in Africa had to be the creation of the White Race. All the different elements of biblical messianism and Ethiopianism were joined together by Garvey's movement, whose mission it was to rebuild Africa destroyed by slavery and colonialism, a mission foretold, it was believed, by the psalmist in the words 'Princes shall come out of Egypt; Ethiopia shall soon stretch out her hands to God' (Psalm 68: 31).

Using the Bible as a historical text that contained the true history of the Black Race as opposed to that disseminated by colonialists, early Rastafarians identified themselves as one of the twelve tribes of ancient Israel and some came to have faith in Haile Selassie as the Messiah who would redeem them from white oppression (Babylon) and return them to their homeland, Africa. While some have returned to Ethiopia to live in the black paradise of Shashemane, this return is now widely interpreted in a psychological sense to refer to a journey of self-discovery leading to an authentic understanding of oneself as an African entrusted with a mission to protect African culture and the African way of life, by 'living naturally' (Clarke, 1986).

Although it assumes responsibility for the African race as a whole, Rastafarianism can be also aptly described as a 'Self religion' (Heelas, 1991). Everything about the movement from its rituals – taking the chalice, another expression for the ganja weed – its language: the use of I and I for We – to its songs and music and its theology in the broadest sense of the term is meant to facilitate the discovery of the God within, Jah, who constitutes one's inner, divine Self. This not only empowers the individual – in part of the Caribbean, for example in Dominica, Rastafarians are known as 'Dreads', meaning the power that lies within every individual – but will also enable Africans to purify their minds and their whole personality of the stains of inferiority and self-doubt left by colonialism and slavery.

The music and fame of Bob Marley and the Wailers in particular brought the movement to the attention of the world in the 1970s. Rastafarian communities emerged in Bahia, Brazil, and in other parts of South America, North America, Australia and New Zealand, where they have influenced the Maoris in particular. White people have also been attracted to the movement and this has made for a change in its philosophy. Initially, fearing exclusion some whites would claim to have been African in a previous existence, but as their numbers increased the 'check on the colour of the skin' was dropped, leaving only the 'check on the spirit', implying that what was required in a 'brother' or 'sister' was the African spirit. Not only has there been a change in the social composition and ethnic background of the membership worldwide but there has also been an improvement in the socio-economic circumstances of a substantial number of followers in the Caribbean.

Two aspects in particular of Rastafarianism have come in for sustained and widespread criticism and those are its patriarchal structure and the related issue of gender inequality. Obiagele Lake (1998) has provided one of the more serious academic critiques of the position of women in the movement, showing how they are marginalized and objectified, a position which would appear to be the very antithesis of what the movement aims to achieve for men. Lake believes that the Rastafarian movement cannot be considered to be, in this respect at least, a force for positive social change in the Caribbean or elsewhere, since it simply lends legitimacy to the traditional patriarchal structures that ensure the subordination of women. On the same topics, Austin-Broos (1987) compares and contrasts the male-centred attitudes of the Rastafarian movement with those of the Pentecostal churches in Jamaica.

Other critics from among the growing intellectual wing of the movement range much wider, taking as their unit of analysis the whole social and religious character and aims of Rastafarianism. While most would agree that Rastafarianism has been concerned with the restructuring of African-Caribbean and African diaspora identity from an African perspective, there are those who are concerned to see the movement function less as a religion preoccupied with legends and myths surrounding Marcus Garvey and that regards the Bible as the source of infallible truth rather than simply as an interesting book. They would also like to see the belief in Haile Selassie as Creator and Messiah dropped and for him to be regarded instead as a symbol of divine–human unity.

What is being suggested by these last-mentioned critics is that Rastafarianism be developed as a social theory that provides an agenda for social, political and economic action that would lead to true self-understanding for all human beings and to solidarity among all peoples (Semaj, 1985). Others, following the widely respected historian Walter Rodney, also want to rid the movement of its quietist, pacifist, escapist image by emphasizing the role it has played in Jamaica, the Caribbean and beyond both as a resistance movement and as an instrument of social and cultural change (Campbell, 1987). Although the movement will, doubtless, be taken in these directions by some, being a global concern with no central authority, it seems destined to acquire a multiplicity of identities.

There is a tendency to focus exclusively on African-derived religions when discussing the NRMs of the Caribbean. However, NRMs in this part of the world are much more diverse than the literature suggests. As Hurbon (1986) points out, much less attention has been given to movements of Hindu-Caribbean, Japanese-Caribbean, and Amerindian-Carib types. Healing is an important reason for the appeal of these movements. One example of a new healing religion is the Hindu-derived movement of Guadeloupe. Worship centres on the south Indian vegetarian goddess of smallpox, Mariamman, known locally as Maliemin, whose temple is guarded by the Hindu demigod Maldevilan, and is frequented in large numbers by the African population of the island (Hurbon, 1986).

Japanese NRMs as the route to African roots

Japanese NRMs constitute the majority of the non-indigenous NRMs in South and Central America. Most of the more than thirty Japanese NRMs in Brazil are Buddhist in content and Shinto in ritual. There are also a number of Shinto movements, two of the largest being the Nambei Daijingu (the Great Sanctuary of South America) and the Shinto Ikyo Daijinmeigu (the Great Shinto Sanctuary of Brazil), both of which are dependent upon the 'Ise Jingu', the imperial Shinto shrine at Ise, Japan, where the cult of Amaterasu Omikami, the Great Goddess of the Sun, is said to have started. Shinto-based groups that date back to the 1920s and 1930s are also to be found in Belem and elsewhere in the Amazon region of Brazil. These groups tend to be highly inclusive in terms of their content and have fused core Shinto beliefs and practices with African, Catholic and Amerindian beliefs and rituals to provide a form of ecstatic religion known as batuque.

Brazil acts as the South American centre for several of the larger of these movements, which have branches in Peru, Argentina, Chile, Paraguay and several other countries of South America. Membership size is extremely difficult to calculate exactly but it is generally thought that Seicho no Ie (House of Growth) and Sekai Kyusei Kyo (the Church of World Messianity) each have several hundred thousand adepts. Others with a relatively large following include Soka Gakkai (Value Creation Society) and Perfect Liberty Kyodan, with between 50,000 and 100,000 members each in South America as a whole. Mahikari has an estimated 20,000 adepts in South America.

Japanese movements have made little headway to date in Mexico and Central America in general. The early Japanese immigrants to Mexico who began arriving there in the late nineteenth century appear to have shown more interest in religion than the early Japanese settlers in Brazil (Okubo, 1991). Many of them followed the largest of the traditional Japanese Pure Land Buddhist traditions founded by the monk Shinran (1173–1262). The new Japanese religions active in Mexico include Tenri kyo (Heavenly Wisdom), Seicho no Ie and the Buddhist movement Reiyukai, a development derived from the Nichiren school founded by the monk Nichiren (1222–82). Like other Japanese NRMs the veneration of the ancestors is at the centre of Reiyukai worship. Soka Gakkai, also of the Nichiren Buddhist school, is the largest of the Japanese movements in Mexico, with an estimated 5,000 members (Okubo, 1991). This movement drew its first converts from among the Japanese settlers in the late 1960s and later attracted converts from among the Catholic population of Mexico City and Guadalajara.

Soka Gakkai's attempt to attract members beyond the Japanese-Mexican community has entailed adapting its Japanese observances and rituals to Mexican and Catholic custom and practice. The Japanese *obon* festival of the dead, for example, which takes place in August in Japan, has been changed by Soka Gakkai to coincide with the Catholic practice in Mexico of observing days of respect and prayers for the dead on November 2nd and 3rd. Moreover, it is left to members of the movement to decide if they are going to have a Catholic or Buddhist form of wedding or funeral (Okubo, 1991: 201).

Overall, there has been a decline in the membership of Japanese NRMs in South and Central America since the mid-1980s. This has not, however, deterred new movements from entering, the latest of these being Kofuko no Kagaku (Institute for Research in Human Happiness) which began its activities in Brazil in the early 1990s and now has an estimated 2,000 members. With a few exceptions that include Tenrikyo, Reiyukai and Risshokoseikai, the membership of Japanese NRMs is now mostly composed of Brazilians of non-Japanese descent, a remarkable change compared with forty years ago when well over 90 per cent of adepts were either Japanese immigrants or descendants of Japanese (Clarke, 2000).

It has been suggested that successful Japanese NRMs like Seicho no Ie (House of Growth) owe much of their appeal to the ambiguity surrounding their identity (Carpenter and Roof, 1995), leaving it an open question as to whether they are religions or philosophies. This, it is implied, makes it easier for members of other faiths to join without abandoning their traditional faith and without, therefore, expending too much of their cultural capital. Buddhism's appeal in the West might be accounted for in a similar way.

Another undoubted reason for the success of some of these movements since the 1960s is the remarkable speed at which they turned from being ethnic Japanese movements to movements in which the vast majority of the members were Brazilians from all ethnic backgrounds (Clarke, 1999b). The new members, mostly Catholics if only nominally so in many cases, explained how by turning to movements such as Seicho no Ie they began to acquire an in-depth knowledge about Christianity for the first time. Others, African-Brazilian members, recalled in interviews with the author how as missionaries of Sekai Kyusei Kyo to Angola, Mozambique and South Africa they discovered their African roots for the first time. They speak in the way a born-again Christian speaks of her/his return to Jesus, about the profoundly meaningful experience of returning to Africa by means of Japanese spirituality (author's interviews with Sekai Kyusei Kyo African-Brazilian missionaries, Angola, January 2002).

Other Asian NRMs

New movements from East Asia (see Chapter 13), including the Unification Church and/or the Moonies, the Chinese movement Falun Gong, and the Taiwanese movement Tzu Chi or the Buddhist Compassion and Relief Association, are all active in South America, principally among Korean, Chinese and Taiwanese communities. NRMs from the Asian subcontinent – the Hare Krishna, Rajneesh and the Sai Baba movement being the best known of these – are also present in South America and the Caribbean but, lacking a comparable cultural, social, ethnic and economic base, have not enjoyed anything like the same success as the Japanese movements.

The writings of the late founder of the Rajneesh movement, the Bhagwan (God) Shree Rajneesh, later known as Osho, continue to be widely available in bookstores throughout South America and in particular in Brazil and Argentina, as are the works of the late founder of Scientology, L. Ron Hubbard. Moreover, New Age writings and those of Gurdjieff have found their way onto the shelves of all bookshops throughout South America, while the Gurdjieffian Enneagram (see Chapter 4) is widely used by counsellors and retreat masters. It is not unusual to find even in the shanty towns Enneagram groups, yoga meditation groups, bio-dance groups, classes in massage techniques of various kinds including the Japanese Shiatsu method, and courses in alternative medicine.

The situation of the New Age Movement in South America, a phenomenon that, as we saw in Chapter 2, defies easy classification, is similar in many respects to elsewhere. Historically it was strikingly different in that it was much more closely connected with political radicalism and radical psychoanalysis. More recently there has been greater emphasis on the mystical, a development borne out by the great interest shown in the writings of Paulo Coelho, which has superseded that once enjoyed by the writings of Paulo Freire, Herbert Marcuse and Erich Fromm. Ecological discourse has also been a much more prominent theme, as is the interest in Amerindian beliefs and rituals. This last-mentioned interest would appear to be more important elsewhere in South America where Amerindian spiritual and religious influence is much stronger than in Brazil.

Conclusions

NRMs, among which are included the Neo-Pentecostal churches discussed above, have exerted considerable influence on the religious culture of South America, an influence not gone unnoticed as we have seen by the Catholic Church. NRMs in revealing the existence of a widespread interest in mysticism and spiritual healing have led to a reassessment by the Catholic hierarchy of its church's methods of evangelization. The 29th General Assembly of the National Conference of Brazilian Bishops meeting in Indaiatuba in April 1991 in an effort to prevent the steady flow of Catholics to alternative spirituality groups and new religions decided to focus on the themes of mysticism and the ministry of healing, old Catholic themes, they insisted, that had wrongly been consigned to the margins of the ministry (Brandão, 1994: 25–6).

This notwithstanding, the phenomenal rise of Neo-Pentecostalism, undoubtedly the main innovation in South American and Caribbean religion in modern times, continues unabated. It is now one of the region's principal religious exports, as IURD and other Neo-Pentecostalist churches take it to all parts of the world including Africa and Japan. Simultaneously, countless movements, many of them once largely ethnic-based, strongly millenarian and composed of Amerindian, Christian, Buddhist (mainly Japanese) and Spiritist beliefs and practices, have taken on the character of worldwide movements. No movement, finally, has remained untouched by the convergence of so many forms of spirituality in one place. Even shrine-based Shinto has assimilated and been assimilated by local Amerindian, Catholic and African-Brazilian religion to provide a unique form of spiritual belief and practice.

References and select bibliography

Austin-Broos, Diane J. (1987) 'Pentecostals and Rastafarians: Cultural, Political and Gender Relations of Two Religious Movements', *Social and Economic Studies*, 36(4), 1–39.

Barrett, Leonard E. (1988) *The Rastafarians: Sounds of Cultural Dissonance.* 2nd rev edn, Boston: Beacon Press.

Bastide, Roger (1967) 'Le Spiritisme au Bresil', *Archives de Sociologie des Religions*, 24, 3–16.

Bastide, Roger (1978) *The African Religions of Brazil*, Baltimore, MD: Johns Hopkins University Press.

Berger, Peter L. (ed.) (1999) *The Desecularization of the Modern World*, Grand Rapids, MI: Eerdmans.

Brandão, Carlos Rodrigues (1986) *Os Deuses do Povo: Um Estudo sobre a Religião Popular*, São Paulo: Editora Brasiliense.

Brandão, Carlos Rodrigues (1994) 'A Crise Das Instituições Traditionais Produtores De Sentido' in M. Moreira and R. Zicman (eds) *Misticismo E Novas Religiõs*, Petropolis: Editora Vozes, pp. 23–42.

Brandon, George (1993) *Santeria from Africa to the New World: The Dead Sell Memories*, Bloomington: Indiana University Press.

Brown, Karen (1991) *Mama Lola: A Vodou Priestess in Brooklyn*, Berkeley: University of California Press.

Campbell, Horace (1987) *Rasta and Resistance: From Marcus Garvey to Walter Rodney*, Trenton, NJ: African World.

Carpenter, Robert T. and Roof, Wade Clark (1995) 'The Transplanting of Seicho no Ie from Japan to Brasil: Moving Beyond the Ethnic Enclave', *Journal of Contemporary Religion*, 10(1), 41–54.

Clarke, Peter B. (1986) *Black Paradise: The Rastafarian Movement*, Wellingborough, UK: Aquarian Press.

Clarke, Peter B. (1998) 'Accounting for Anti-Syncretist Trends in Catholic-Candomblé Relations' in Peter B. Clarke (ed.) *New Trends and Developments in African Religions*, Westport, CT: Greenwood Press, pp. 17–44.

Clarke, Peter B. (1999a) 'Pop Star Priests and the Catholic Response to the "Explosion" of Evangelical Protestantism in Brazil: The Beginning of the End of the "Walkout"?', *Journal of Contemporary Religion*, 14(2), 203–16.

Clarke, Peter B. (1999b) 'Japanese New Religions in Brazil: From "Ethnic" to "Universal" Religions' in Bryan R. Wilson and Jamie Cresswell (eds) *New Religious Movements: Challenge and Response*, London: Routledge, pp. 197–211.

Clarke, Peter B. (2000) 'Modern Japanese Millenarian Movements: Their Changing Perception of Japan's Global Mission with Special Reference to the Church of World Messianity in Brazil' in Peter B. Clarke (ed.) *Japanese New Religions: In Global Perspective*, Richmond, Surrey: Curzon Press, pp. 129–81.

Clastres, Hélène (1995) *The Land-Without-Evil: Tupi-Guarani Prophetism* (trans. Jacqueline Grenez Bovender), Urbana: University of Illinois Press.

Corten, André (2001) 'Haïti: le pentcôtisme face à la déshumanisation' in André Corten and André Mary (eds) *Imaginaires politiques et pentcôtismes*, Paris: Karthala, pp. 233–52.

Cosentino, D. (1995) *The Sacred Arts of Haitian Vodou*, Los Angeles: Fowler Museum.

Edmonds, Barrington Ennis (2003) *Rastafari: From Outcasts to Culture Bearers*, Oxford: Oxford University Press.

Hall, J. H. (1981) 'The Apocalyse at Jonestown' in T. Robbins and D. Anthony (eds) *In Gods We Trust: The New Patterns of Religious Pluralism in America*, New Brunswick, NJ: Transaction Books.

Hall, J. H. (1987) *Gone from the Promised Land: Jonestown in American Cultural History*, New Brunswick, NJ: Transaction Books.

Heelas, Paul (1991) 'Western Europe: Self-Religions' in Stewart Sutherland and Peter B. Clarke (eds) *The Study of Religion: Traditional and New Religion*, London: Routledge, pp. 167–73.

Hess, David J. (1991) *Spirits and Scientists: Ideology, Spiritism and Brazilian Culture*, University Park: University of Pennsylvania Press.

Hurbon, Laënnec (1986) 'New Religious Movements in the Caribbean' in James Beckford (ed.) *New Religious Movements and Rapid Social Change*, Thousand Oaks, CA: Sage.

Hurbon, Laënnec (1991) 'Mahikari in the Caribbean', *Japanese Journal of Religious Studies*, 18(2/3), 242–65.

Lake, Obiagele (1998) 'Religion, Patriarchy and the Status of Rastafarian Women' in Peter B. Clarke (ed.) *New Trends and Developments in African Religions*, Westport, CT: Greenwood Press, pp. 141–58.

Martin, David (1990) *Tongues of Fire: The Explosion of Protestantism in South America*, Oxford: Blackwell.

McGuire, Brian and Scrymgeour, Duncan (1998) 'Santeria and Curandeirismo in Los Angeles' in Peter B. Clarke (ed.) *New Trends and Developments in African Religions*, Westport, CT: Greenwood Press, pp. 211–23.

Murphy, Joseph (1993) *Santeria: African Spirits in America*, Boston: Beacon.

Novaes, Regina and Ramalho, Jose (1990) 'Borboletas Azuis: Mediunidade, Catolicismo e a Espera da Nova Mensagem' in Leilah Landim (ed.) *Sinais Dos Tempos: Diversidade Religiosa no Brasil*, Rio de Janeiro: ISER, pp. 27–36.

Okubo, M. (1991) 'The Acceptance of Nichiren Shoshu Soka Gakkai in Mexico', *Japanese Journal of Religious Studies*, 18(2/3), 189–211.

Oliva, Margarida (1997) *O Diabo no 'Reino de Deus'*, São Paulo: Musa Editora.

Oro, Ari Pedro (1989) *Na Amazonia um Messias de Indios e Brancos: Tracos Para Um Antropologia Do Messianismo*, Petropolis: Editora Vozes.

Pierucci, Antonio Flavio (2004) '"Bye, bye, Brasil" – O Declinio das Religiõs Traditionais no Censo 2000', *USP – Estudos Avancados 52, Dossie Religiões no Brasil*, 18(52), 17–46.

Saraco, Norberto (1989) 'Argentine Pentecostalism, its History and Theology', PhD Thesis, University of Birmingham.

Semaj, Leahcim (1985) 'Rastafari: From Religion to Social Theory', *Caribbean Quarterly*, Kingston: University of the West Indies, pp. 22–31.

Soares, Luiz Eduardo (1990) 'A Doutrina do Santo Daime' in Leilah Landim (ed.) *Sinais Dos Tempos. Diversidade Religiosa no Brasil*, Rio de Janeiro: ISER, pp. 253–64.

Stoll, David (1990) *Is South America Turning Protestant? The Politics of Evangelical Growth*, Berkeley: University of California Press.

Usarski, Frank (ed.) (2000) *O Budismo no Brasil*, São Paulo: Editora Larosae.

Verger, Pierre Fatumbi (1993) 'The Orishás of Bahia' in Carybé (ed.) *Os Deuses Africanos no Candomblé da Bahia* [African Gods in the Candombé of Bahia], Salvador, Bahia: Bigraf, pp. 235–61.

Wilson, Bryan R. (1973) *Magic and the Millennium*, St Albans: Paladin.

Worsley, Peter (1970) *The Trumpet Shall Sound*, St Albans: Paladin.

Xavier, Francisco Cândido (Chico) (1944) *Nosso Lar Pelo Espirito de Andre Luiz*, Rio de Janeiro: Federacao Espirita Brasileira.

Part V

New religions of South, Southeast and East Asia

Chapter 10

South Asia (India, Pakistan and Sri Lanka)

In modern times considerable numbers of new Buddhist, Hindu, Muslim and Sikh religions have emerged in South Asia – this label is used here in a restricted sense and covers India, Pakistan, and Sri Lanka – and are characterized by their emphasis on engaged and/or applied religion and spirituality. It is this form of religion and/or spirituality, they are convinced, more so than modern technology, that can provide the most effective means of transforming the world.

In South Asia, as elsewhere (see for example the chapters on Southeast Asia, East Asia, Africa, and Australia, New Zealand and Melanesia (Papua New Guinea)), the emergence of NRMs is often accounted for solely in terms of an external impact (colonial accompanied by Christian missionary)–local response schema. While the great importance of external influences cannot be denied in certain cases, to emphasize that impetus alone is as was pointed out in other chapters to misunderstand the dynamics of religious change in which external forces are often no more than catalysts that hasten a process already under way. Although, as we have seen, he was referring to the Muslim world, Gibb's analysis of the forces of change there is of wider application and supports this argument. In accounting for modern Islamic revivalist movements, he is careful to emphasize the importance of both internal and external causes (1978: 113).

Likewise in Southeast Asia, external factors alone cannot provide an adequate explanation for the religious changes that occurred during the period under review here (c.1820 to the present). Reform, renewal and innovation were in the air anyway and the principal effect of the challenge from without was to hasten their denouement and help shape their content. With hindsight many of the changes seem to be little more than minor efforts at reform and renewal. On the other hand, to those who witnessed them the changes appeared radical, even revolutionary.

The first public performance of *seva* or service in 1899 in Bengal is a case in point. Followers of the Bengali mystic Sri Ramakrishna, considered a full *avatara* of God, were in complete shock at this performance, whose radical, innovative character was in no way diminished by the explanation given by

Swami Vivekananda (1863–1902), who introduced it, that the concept of *seva* or service to humanity was deeply rooted in Indian tradition. Those who witnessed this 'so novel' and 'controversial' event are said to have 'woke[n] up to see a sight that took their breath away!' (Beckerlegge, 2004: 47). Previously, the concerns of sannyasins or world renouncers had been with purely spiritual matters. (Beckerlegge, 2004: 47).

Its innovatory character is also evidenced in the fact that later movements who made *seva* an integral part of their mission, including the Rastriya Swayamsevak Sangh, were regarded by local Hindus as new expressions of Hinduism. Vivekananda was also largely responsible for another significant innovation, the development of the practice of Raja Yoga, which forms the core element of 'Modern Yoga' (De Michaelis, 2003). 'Protestant Buddhism' (Gombrich and Obeyesekere, 1988) in Sri Lanka with its emphasis on and practice of the 'selfless gift of labour' must have seemed equally radical to those who witnessed it in action for the first time.

Although the term 'new' in this chapter, as in several others including those already mentioned above, needs to be understood more in a sociological and ritual sense than in a doctrinal sense, the intellectual or doctrinal dimension, which is becoming increasingly important, cannot be completely ignored.

The above are but two examples from a vast number of religious innovations in South Asia. While, as Sen (2003: 5) points out, it is difficult to identify common elements, the reforms overall tended to take the form of structural adjustments rather than structural reorganizations, and in most cases those who initiated them had received some degree of Western education. The reforms were a response to important existential, moral and social questions, including the definition of the self under new social, economic and political circumstances, and in the Indian context included such gender issues as widow marriages and although not, at least initially, female infanticide. They were also a response to the call for a more engaged Hinduism and the abandonment of what was denounced as the 'selfish' path of self-realization, a shift in the purpose and orientation of religion evident in much of Asia.

Many of the religious reforms encapsulated in the Buddhist, Neo-Hindu, Muslim and Sikh derived NRMs of South Asia also emerged by way of a response to the perceived corruption and decline of mainstream religion on the one hand and to the impact of Western colonialism and Christian missionary penetration on the other. Some, including the Ahmadiyya movement, developed complex strategies that combined Islamic and Western systems of education, and introduced the Christian form of marriage rites, Western style of dress, and modern means of communication, to counter this penetration. Others reacted to the same processes by searching for a common core to all religions and the promotion of a global spirituality, making use of the most advanced technology for purposes of communication, organization and the dissemination of information. The Rajasthan-based Brahma Kumaris movement (Daughters of Brahma), which strongly counsels celibacy for all, has built one of the largest and most efficient solar energy systems in the world. Installed at its main conference centre near Mount Abu in Rajasthan, this highly efficient and cost-effective system can provide cooked meals for 30,000 guests at one sitting in a matter of minutes.

Neo-Hindu movements

The historical context for this discussion of the New and/or Neo-Hindu NRMs is the so-called modern period of the subcontinent's history, which can be roughly divided where India and Pakistan are concerned into a pre-independence or colonial period (c.1800–1947) and an independence period from 1947 to the present. Sri Lanka regained its independence in 1970, making in this case for a rather arbitrary division into a pre-1970 and a post-1970 period.

The term 'Neo-Hinduism', in circulation in India at least since the 1890s, and used increasingly in the West from the 1950s, purports to describe the distinctive philosophies of those reforming, modernizing Hindu thinkers and organizations that inspired what is referred to as an Indian renaissance. Historians, concerned as they are with the particular, will always be inclined to regard as problematic the use of general labels such as renaissance, as in this case. There are those who not only question the conventional dates – c.1830–c.1947 – given for that renaissance but even its very existence. While granting that such a movement did occur other historians want to limit the force and scope of its social and religious impact to the period c.1870–1947. Here the term is kept for many of the same reasons outlined in Chapter 1 for using the term 'new religion', and for specific reasons such as the priority these Neo-Hindu movements give to social reform and missionary activity.

Thus, here not only is the earlier date chosen as a rough beginning of the Neo-Hindu renaissance but, since there is much evidence that its impact is still being felt, the period is extended to the present. One important reason for the choice of the earlier date is that it allows for the inclusion as part of the Neo-Hindu movement the ideas and reform programmes of such forceful and influential thinkers as the founder of the Brahmo Samaj movement, Raja Rammohun Roy (c.1772–1833).

Other prominent contributors to the Neo-Hindu renewal movement include the previously mentioned Swami Vivekananda (1863–1902), at one time a member of the protestant-like, puritanical, anti-image worshipping, and deistic Brahmo Samaj movement. The first Hindu to teach in the West and founder of the Ramakrishna Mission in 1897, Swami Vivekananda, who rejected Advaita Vedanta or non-dualism, is also credited with raising Hinduism to the status of a world religion. He was further a pioneer of Raja Yoga, a form of yoga that constituted a departure from classical Indian forms and whose content, techniques and purposes were greatly influenced by

Western-derived notions of 'harmonial relaxation' or 'salvation through relaxation' developed by Annie Payson Call and Edmund Jacobson and strongly advocated by William James with whom Vivekananda was personally acquainted (Singleton, 2005).

Vivekenanda, who was persuaded that all the various branches of Hinduism were essentially wholesome, influenced Mohandas Karamchand Gandhi (1869–1948) in the formulation of three of his main ideas: *satyagraha*, adherence to truth which he combined with *ahimsa*, non-violence, and *sarvodaya*, universal uplift or the welfare of all. The ideas of Sri Aurobindo Ghose (1872–1950) were also a catalyst for change, particularly in regard to the beginnings of the New Age Movement in South Asia where they led to the founding of the now international New Age community Auroville, near Pondicherry.

Neo-Hinduism was not an intellectually integrated movement. The above-mentioned thinkers and others who were influenced by their ideas, held different views on the meaning of Hindu reform, and adopted different strategies for achieving their objectives, which were not always acceptable to the wider society. Vivekananda, for example, was criticized for his attempt to reform Hinduism along Christian lines, no doubt an oversimplification. The interaction between Hinduism and missionary Christianity in India resulted in a degree of restructuring and remodelling, symbolic and otherwise, by both sides. Differences existed also over the relationship between religious and social reform, some stressing that religious and spiritual reform should precede social reform while others wanted both to be undertaken simultaneously. Others, like Vivekananda, while convinced of the importance of socially engaged religion, insisted that the real purpose of religion was spiritual and not the provision of this-worldly social benefits.

Views among reformers on Hindu identity and on what being Hindu meant varied. The non-proselytizing Neo-Hindu movements that stressed the importance of social reform regarded Hinduism as the religion of the people of Indian descent only, while those that viewed their mission as global, not surprisingly, included all nationalities as potentially Hindu.

Both kinds of movement not only raised fundamental questions about the nature and purpose of Hinduism as a religious tradition, and the related issues of religious and/or spiritual identity, but also started a debate on the role and position of women in religion, on the requirements for becoming a brahmin, and on the meaning and manner of being a world renouncer. Also from these movements came much talk about world transformation and renewal, and a vast range of detailed predictions about the impending apocalypse and the terrestrial paradise that would follow on from it.

Differences notwithstanding, Neo-Hindus broadly shared a number of views and attitudes on substantive issues, including a critical attitude toward the worship of images – something also found in a number of new Buddhist movements including Santi Asoke (Chapter 11) and Won Buddhism

(Chapter 13) – and a keen interest in the relationship between religion and nationalism. Other common elements included a belief in the importance of reinterpreting religious concepts such as karma and *dharma*, in the Bhagavad Gita as the most important scriptural source, and a commitment to philanthropy, and to applied spirituality and/or engaged religion.

The religious and social reform objectives of the previously mentioned Brahmo Samaj movement, founded in 1828 by Raja Rammohun Roy, a member of a Bengali Brahmin family, set much of the agenda for future socially engaged Hindu movements. His successor, Lala Lajpat Rai (1865–1928), continued with this commitment to socially engaged religion. He even went so far as to dismiss the Brahmanical emphasis on self-realization as 'escapist' and 'mere selfishness', and called for active engagements in social service (Sen, 2003: 14).

The Brahmo Samaj came to epitomize what Basham (1971: 247) identified as the main features of Neo-Hinduism, a 'deep sense of social purpose and a tendency to what may be called puritanism'.

Among its principal aims were the purification of Hinduism of its innumerable 'meaningless accretions' – Roy insisted that true Hinduism was theistic and strongly opposed the use of images – and the implementation of fundamental social reforms. Kopf (1978: 334) maintains this movement was of great significance in the shaping of social awareness among sections of the Indian elite in the second half of the nineteenth century:

> It introduced among the upper classes of Bengal and elsewhere an ethos of heroic self-sacrifice, a sense of justice, a sense of compassion for the underprivileged, a sense of devotion to nation, a sense of accomplishment in creative synthesis, a sense of individual responsibility and freedom.

These, as will be seen below, are also among the main features of Protestant Buddhism in Sri Lanka (Gombrich and Obeyesekere, 1988).

The Brahmo Samaj, sometimes referred to as the 'first church of Hinduism', in a similar vein to the then advancing Christian missionaries, sought to found a spiritual religion on a genuine Hindu foundation. For this project Roy drew upon Christian organizational forms, ethical ideas and practices.

It is sometimes difficult to image how many and varied were the intellectual and spiritual currents to which founders of Neo-Hindu were exposed. In the case of Rammohun Roy he was not only a follower of Chaitanya but also a student at Patna, a Muslim College, an experience which may have influenced his thinking about idolatry. Roy also studied Christianity and Greek and Hebrew. In 1820 he wrote the *Principles of Jesus* in which he claimed, as did Muslims, that his message had been distorted by his followers. Christ, he insisted, was a theist like himself but his disciples had not understood this.

Roy introduced congregational services modelled on Christian lines to which there were four parts: chanting of selected passages from the Upanishads in Sanskrit attended only by the elite, translated passages in Bengali for the rest, a sermon in Bengali, and the singing of theistic hymns in Sanskrit and Bengali. This was seen as pure Hindu worship, the object of which was the Eternal Unsearchable and Immutable Being. The deistic theology with which he underpinned this worship made a fit with the rationalism that formed the basis of the Brahmo Samaj ideology.

The Brahmo Samaj movement not only condemned what it saw as idolatry in the form of polytheism and the veneration of images but also campaigned tirelessly to outlaw such abuses as the burning of widows. In this case also, the previously mentioned emphasis on orthopraxy as opposed to orthodoxy in Hindu and Buddhist contexts notwithstanding, the Brahmo Samaj's effectiveness in bringing about reform was severely reduced by internal doctrinal division, particularly in the 1870s and 1880s. For example, the question of the nature of God as immanent, a view promoted by Debendra Nath Tagore, father of the poet, or transcendent, Roy's position, seriously divided the movement. And in 1881 the reformer Keshab Chandra Sen broke away and founded the New Dispensation with the purpose of building a more eclectic church that made use of the scriptures of the major religions of the world.

More radical than either the Brahmo Samaj or the New Dispensation, and less tolerant of Christianity and Islam, was the Arya Samaj movement. Once again reform begins with the reform of Hinduism as if this was indispensable to the reform of society, showing how closely religion, society and culture were linked in people's minds. Founded by Dayanand Sarasvati (1824–83) from Gujarat this movement took a root and branch approach to Hindu reform. Committed to demythologizing on an even grander scale than Roy, Sarasvati claimed that the experience of a spiritual crisis had endowed him with the insight to see that Hinduism in its entirety was corrupt and that the Vedas alone were the authentic sources of pure religion. He, thus, dismissed as false many commonly accepted beliefs and interpreted scriptural accounts of age-old practices as merely symbolic.

Polytheism and image-worship were condemned as idolatrous, the names of the divinities to whom the Vedic hymns were addressed were reduced to alternative titles for the Supreme Being, and all references to animal sacrifices were interpreted as merely figurative. As to social reforms, the caste system was explained away as yet another false accretion that obscured the authentic religion of the Vedas. Other radical social teachings advocated the prohibition of child-marriages and the acceptance of remarriage for widows.

This strong emphasis on and commitment to social reform contrasted with the approach of influential and well-known spiritual leaders such as the 'non-dualist' Romana Maharshi (1879–1950) who followed what might be described as the 'conversionist' path (Wilson, 1970) of *jnana yoga*, insisting that self-improvement in a spiritual sense was the key to the improvement of society as a whole. This desire to purify Hinduism and the resistance to Christian missionary and Islamic influence in late nineteenth-century India were also part of the project of the Theosophical Society, founded in New York in 1875 (see Chapter 5).

As we have seen, the Ramakrishna Math and Mission was established in 1897 in Calcutta under the leadership of the previously mentioned Swami Vivekananda (1862–1902), an opponent of Advaita Vedantism (non-dualism) of the School of Shankara. Vivekananda sought to continue on the mission of the Bengali mystic and devotee of the goddess Kali, Ramakrishna (1836–86), who was himself regarded by his followers as a full manifestation or *avatara* of God. Ramakrishna would admonish his followers, including Vivekananda, for losing themselves in *samadhi* (a meditative condition of total absorption) rather than attending to the needs of society. As was previously noted, it is extremely difficult now to imagine how major a change took place in the movement under the leadership of Vivekandana when it decided to give priority to *seva* or the cause of service to others over personal spiritual progress.

The Ramakrishna Math and Mission also became renowned for, among other things, its empathetic approach to other religions. Determined to acquire as objective an understanding as possible of the major religions, Ramakrishna read the scriptures of Buddhism, Christianity, Islam and Zoroastrianism, and practiced their principal spiritual disciplines, to arrive at the conclusion that all religions were one in the sense that all led back to the same truth. Vivekananda continued on this inclusive tendency, and it is an approach that has informed the philosophy of several other Neo-Hindu movements, including the Sathya Sai Baba movement. Parallels to this kind of inclusivity can be found almost everywhere in Asia, including Vietnam in the case of the Cao Dai movement (see Chapter 11) and in Japan in the case of the Ananai-kyo new religion (Religion of 'Three' and 'Five'), a name which implies that the goal or intention of this religion is to create a synthesis of the world's major religions.

Religious tolerance and concern for the social welfare of those in need were, thus, two of the most prominent themes in the teaching of Vivekananda. Swami Vivekananda, inspired by the interest in his teachings at the World Parliament of Religions in Chicago (1893) began establishing the mission outside of India in the late 1890s. These events provided the impulse for the setting up of a number of Vedanta Societies in the United States. A further lecture tour of Britain in the same year also led to the opening of centres in that country. Engagement with society was a constant theme in Vivekananda's talks which stressed that the purpose of the Ramakrishna Society in India was not only the teaching of Vedanta, but, just as important, the relief of suffering.

As was previously mentioned, not all Neo-Hindu movements have viewed the reform of Hinduism in the same way. Vivekananda's Ramakrishna Mission was much more gradualist and far less inclined to take a root and branch approach to such reform than, for example, the Brahmo Samaj and Arya Samaj movements. While the former accepted that some forms of Hinduism had been corrupted, it was persuaded, nonetheless, that all forms were essentially valid. Also, like Theosophy, it insisted that Hinduism itself was the most pure and the most ancient of the world's religions and that India, although lagging behind the West technologically and materially, had greater depths of spiritual reserves, and was, therefore, ultimately more powerful. Such ideas – along with the rejection of the caste system, the demand for equality for women and the development of national awareness – were to become a powerful force in twentieth-century India.

Among those Indians greatly inspired and influenced by Vivekananda was the previously mentioned Western-educated Bengali political activist, reformer and spiritual leader Sri Aurobindo Ghose (1872–1950), who claimed to have heard the former's voice and to have received instructions from him while in prison in 1904 for his political activities. Another was the previously mentioned Mahatma Gandhi who appropriately practised *karma yoga* in pursuit of social reform. As we have seen, Aurobindo's ideas were later to greatly influence the development of the NAM in India by inspiring Mira Richard (1878–1973), whom he met in 1910 and who became known to its members as Mother, to create the New Age planetary village of Auroville, ten miles from Pondicherry in south India in 1968. The main purpose of this community is to provide a model of planetary consciousness, which consists in placing the needs of humanity above those of any individual, tribe or nation. To emphasize its role as a model of the human community, Auroville has been placed in the 'ownership' of humanity as a whole and the only requirement placed on members is that they serve the 'Divine Consciousness'.

The Swadhyaya (the discovery of self movement) started by Pandurang Shastri Athavale (1920–2003), though a much less structured movement than anything so far discussed, has been one of the more intellectually creative and socially radical of the Neo-Hindu movements. This movement's principal ideas encapsulate the core notions of the NAM (see Chapter 2) and those of the Religions of the Real or True Self or Self-religions (see Chapter 1). Athavale, who was born into a wealthy Brahmin family and attended a traditional Sanskrit school, taught what he regarded as a universally valid truth: that the discovery of the *Real Self* would lead individuals to find a god within who would enable them to develop constructive and mutually beneficial relationships with others. This, Athavale's guiding principle, is the one which, perhaps more than any other, lies behind much of the new, socially concerned spirituality found in the Neo-Hindu movement.

Athavale was also greatly concerned, in the manner of the reformist branch of the Neo-Hindu movement, to make practical use of his knowledge of the

Bhagavad Gita, and to improve the condition of the poor, rejecting the ideologies and methods of both Capitalism and Socialism on the grounds that both systems undermined in their own different ways human dignity. Athavale's movement has provided assistance to millions of the materially deprived, especially in the areas in and around Mumbai (Bombay), through its social action programmes which include the sponsoring of housing and agricultural projects

The Sathya Sai Baba movement, perhaps the largest NRM in contemporary India with a membership estimated at between two and three million, like the Ramakrishna Mission also advocates inclusivism. Led by a highly charismatic personality and controversial thaumaturge – Sai Baba's miraculous feats have given rise to heated controversy between scientists in India among others – this movement, with more than 1,000 temples and associations and affiliated with the All-India Sai Samaj, teaches the validity of all religions. This teaching is applied in practice by the inclusion of readings and hymns from the main world religions in its ceremonies. Some observers are convinced that it is not the truth of all religions that is being proclaimed by this movement but the very opposite: that the essence of religious truth is to be found only in Hinduism (Sharma, 1986: 230).

Whether it describes accurately the purpose of the Sai Baba movement, there can be little doubt that that aim is at the core of the ideology of the Vishnu Hindu Parishad (World Hindu Council) (see Chapter 4), an offshoot of the Rastriya Swayamsevak Sangh (National Volunteer Organization – RSS). Founded in 1925 the RSS developed an ideology in which Indian identity became synonymous with Hindu culture, and claimed it was necessary for other cultures to be assimilated into this culture or endorse its central or key elements. Part of this movement's strategy, not unlike that of other movements (see the Ahmadiyya movement below), was to adopt from those it opposed – mainly Muslims and Christians – methods and tactics they used with in converting Hindus (Jaffrolet, 1996).

Despite the ambiguity surrounding its aims, or perhaps on account of it, the Sai Baba movement has become one of the most international of India's NRMs in terms of its social composition and presence in so many countries. After 1918, more people with a Western education – administrators, lawyers, business people, and others from the Brahmin, Kayastra and Bania communities – replaced peasants as the majority of the devotees and with this change in its social composition came the widening of the movement's influence and the creation of more centres in southern India. In a relatively short space of time the Sathya Sai Baba movement had become a pan-Indian and an international movement, attracting large numbers of followers among the Hindu diaspora communities, particularly second and third generations who have tended to find in it a bridge between the Indian cultural background of their parents and grandparents and that into which they were born and educated. Large numbers of followers are also to be found in South American countries, including Chile and Argentina.

The Sathya Sai Baba movement has not only helped to turn Hinduism into a more international religion but also, notwithstanding its emphasis on the miraculous, into a modernizing force, particularly with regard to such issues as the status and position of women, which it has tended to enhance, education, and in the positive evaluation it has made of modern scientific medicine, and technology. The movement has constructed an ultra-modern hospital – one of many social welfare projects – in the town of Puttaparthi, close to Bangalore, where its headquarters are located. These modern emphases apart, there is also, as with other Neo-Hindu movements, an insistence on the primacy of spirituality, which is considered essential to balance material and technological progress, and something which India is called to bring to the rest of the world, and in particular, to what it describes as the materialist Western world.

Differing in style, content, ethos, and structure from the Sathya Sai Baba movement is the Brahma Kumaris (BK) movement, also a truly global Neo-Hindu movement with over 3,000 centres around the world with a Hindu message for humanity. Members are known as Brahma Kumaris and Brahma Kumars, the pure daughters and pure sons of Brahma, respectively. The movement was given the name Brahma Kumaris Spiritual University in 1937, emphasizing its fundamental purpose of spreading spiritual knowledge throughout the world with a view to constructing paradise on earth.

Dualism is an essential feature of BK teaching, as is the imminent advent of the millennium, which will be preceded by catastrophe unless there is a radical change of understanding of the nature of the self, leading to a radical change in lifestyle, particularly in the matter of sexual relations. Each individual, the movement teaches, is a soul under the Supreme Soul, and what matters is not one's body, gender or race but one's soul, and hence the recitation several times daily of the principal mantra: 'I am a soul, my body is a garment'. The purpose of life, upon which the mantra focuses the mind, is to develop soul consciousness which body consciousness, particularly that kind promoted by sexual acts, obstructs.

Although founded by a man, Dada Lekhraj (1876–1969), who since his death at least appears to have been deified, the BK provides one of the few examples anywhere of an NRM in which there exists a high level of gender equality. But it is this movement's distinctive approach among Neo-Hindu movements to the revision of Hinduism and to the imminent arrival of the millennium that merits special attention here. In a manner similar to Raja Rammohun Roy, Dada Lekhraj, once a well-known diamond merchant from Hyderabad, became well versed in sacred literature including the *Bhagavad Gita* and the principal Sikh sacred text the *Guru Granth Sahib*. His studies convinced him that the truths of the former had been grossly distorted and hence the necessity of his mission to preach the true meaning of this sacred treatise. Even more radical was his teaching on the millennium.

This teaching developed out of the founder's interpretation of the visions he had received in 1936. One of these was a traumatic double vision involving on the one hand Shiva as a point of incandescent light, which he referred to as the Supreme Soul. In another, Lekhraj saw cities being totally destroyed by guided missiles, which he later interpreted as a forewarning of a nuclear holocaust. Through these visions Lekhraj came to believe that the Supreme Being or Soul had descended upon him to entrust him with a new message of profound significance and importance for humanity. After the first vision he was heard by a relative proclaiming: 'I am the Form of Bliss, Shiva, Shiva; I am the Self of Knowledge, Siva, Siva; I am the Self of Light, Shiva, Shiva; I am the Self of Knowledge, the Self of Bliss, the Self of Light' (Whaling, 1995: 4).

According to Lekhraj, who believed he had been gifted with divine knowledge of the unfolding of its history, now in the final period of the age of *Kali Yuga*, the world had already entered a critical point and was headed for a catastrophe. The atom and hydrogen bombs, made for the destruction of the planet, were proof of this for they would proliferate 'until every population centre is in range of such incinerators'. Though a final world war could not be prevented there was hope, since through that war, he explained 'the present evil world order would be obliterated instantly and mercifully' and a Golden Age on earth, restricted to the righteous, would follow. The righteous were those who had previously so transformed themselves that they had come to acquire 'the power to live in utter harmony'. During the ensuing cycle of 2,500 years 'no quarrel will erupt on earth, no accident or illness will befall a single person [and] . . . as much sorrow as there is in the world today so much happiness and more will be present there' (Chander, 1983: 235–6).

Predictions such as this of the inevitability of a catastrophe preceding the Golden Age unfailingly contained a silver lining in the form of an escape through the practice of Raja Yoga, a method of yoga developed as we have seen, by Vivekananda, and the living of a celibate life. These were the means by which Armageddon could be averted. According to one informant, a teacher by profession,

> By the turn of the twenty-first century a Golden Age of peace, purity and love will have been established through the divine work initiated by Brahma Baba, our founder, who is the vehicle of Shiva (God) and the one who transforms and recreates souls in the image of God.
>
> (Chander, 1983: 236)

In this anxiously awaited earthly paradise, environmental pollution caused by spiritual and moral weaknesses, the BK is confident, will have been eradicated and the beauty of nature restored. For, it insists, we are immortal, a truth we have lost sight of, and endowed with the limitless capacity to achieve all that is necessary for the creation of paradise on earth, a paradise very similar in form and content to the traditional Hindu version. A paragraph on the devastating effects of the failure of human beings to realize immortality found in the biography of the movement's founder summarizes the project of much alternative contemporary spirituality in India and worldwide:

> Man's desperation arises from what is perceived as the human situation: we are mortal it is thought; we shall die; we live in an uncaring universe of chance. With such a world view it is little wonder that human beings have opted to get the most out of life through material acquisition and sensual pleasure. The fear of death is fertile soil in which the poison plant of greed may thrive. The ultimate thing we hunger for is love. But since we have taken ourselves for material beings, we have mistaken sex lust for love, thus exploiting each other and devaluing ourselves still further. In this desperate condition we have despoiled our home, our earth. Yet this whole chain of events was based on a single mistake. *We are not mortal, after all.* We are souls, non-material units of consciousness and our bodies are simply temporary earthenware costumes. We fell through the trap door of history with the fall from self consciousness and now we have reached rock bottom. Two choices lie before us: either we clean up our act and become pure once more or we drown in a maelstrom of destruction. [my italics]
>
> (Chander, 1983: 262–3)

This version of millenarianism, which in certain respects echoes that of the Franciscan Spirituals of Medieval Europe, is about empowerment and clearly offers hope for this world through a return to a life of purity. The importance of celibacy to self- and world-transformation cannot be underestimated. Although there is no vow as such of celibacy, individuals are given 'advice' about the disadvantages of sex, which is presented as the most serious impediment to reaching the highest levels of spirituality and enlightenment. Guided by this advice and persuaded of its truth, some members, including a number of married people, have in fact taken the vow of celibacy. Sexual love fosters, it is taught, possessiveness and jealousy. Moreover, directing love towards one person demands a partner that lives up to expectations, one that is perfect, and when this does not happen the result is anger. By way of contrast, spiritual love knows no possessiveness and no anger, and frees one to accomplish much more, gives more physical energy, more concentration and better quality of thought, and a better sense of well-being. Through the practice of Raja Yoga as interpreted by Brahma Baba union with the Supreme Soul can be attained, turning individuals into channels of light, love and power.

The BK mission to spread Hinduism worldwide has been particularly evident since the movement's headquarters were moved back to India from Karachi in 1950 and located at Mount Abu in Rajasthan. Soon after, an intensive campaign of evangelizing began with the provision of courses and seminars in spirituality to those interested, and by mounting exhibitions across India. It was at this time that women were placed in charge of local centres where meditation was open to all who wished to participate. All were encouraged to overcome body consciousness through a form of inner-worldly asceticism that included abstinence from selfish pursuits, from material gain, and from sexual pleasure in order to live in 'soul consciousness', a state that consists, as previously noted, of realizing that one is a soul, that all the material and physical attributes of a person are of secondary importance, and in treating oneself and others accordingly.

Unlike many other charismatic-based movements, including the Hare Krishna movement, the Brahma Kumaris movement survived intact the death of its founder, and even began to expand more rapidly. While the majority of its followers are to be found in India, the BK movement has attracted large numbers of devotees and sympathizers elsewhere, beginning in the United Kingdom, where it opened its London centre in the early 1970s. From there the movement spread to the rest of Britain, into Europe and worldwide, initiating numerous projects relating to global co-operation, peace, justice and inter-faith dialogue, and developing courses that relate its spirituality to every aspect of modern life from the home to the workplace.

Since Lekhraj's death the movement has been headed by women with the assistance and counsel of senior and influential male members known as Brothers, some of whom were close associates or sons of associates of the founder. From the perspective of the membership at large Lekhraj lives on today through his early and closest female disciples. In the early morning discourses prior to meditation, and at other gatherings, at Mount Abu in Rajasthan, the present overall head of the movement, Dadi Prakaskmani, one of his first followers, recalls constantly the life and activities of Brahma Baba as she remembers them. This endows her with charisma and lends enormous credibility and legitimacy to her teaching in which Brahma Baba is elevated to the status of a partner of the God Shiva, the Supreme Soul, and an object of *bhakti* or devotion in his own right, making him as essential now to the spiritual life of the movement as he was during his life. Moreover, his guidance and teachings continue to be transmitted in the form of *merlis* through the mediumship of another of his early disciples, Sister Gulzar, who is in charge of the New Delhi centre.

Reasons for the disastrous condition into which the world has fallen vary among Neo-Hindu movements, as do remedies. The Hare Krishna movement, in which *bhakti* (devotion) to Krishna is paramount, is also a missionary movement intent on disseminating its version of Hinduism worldwide. Devotees have a duty to spread the idea of the path to Krishna Consciousness to everyone through *bhakti*, the distribution of literature, chanting and dancing in the streets and through teaching and preaching based on the Bhagavad Gita, the Upanishads, and the Bhagavada Purana. The movement's founder, A. C. Bhaktivedanta Swami Prabhupada (1896–1977), a former graduate in English, Economics and Philosophy of the University of Calcutta, who had close contacts with evangelical Christian movements in India, brought his teachings West to New York in 1965, but made no claim to be presenting a new version of Hinduism. He insisted rather that he was only the latest in an unbroken line of spiritual teachers stretching back to the fifteenth-century Bengali Brahmin, Chaitanya Mahaprahbu, a teacher of Vaishnavism.

As Vaishnavas, worshippers of the God Vishnu, the Hare Krishna, guided by the teachings of the Bhagavad Gita, advocate devotional surrender to Krishna whom they recognize as the highest personality of the Godhead. By means of devotion to Krishna the devotee attains Krishna Consciousness – defined as the revival of the original consciousness of the living being and the conscious awareness that one is related to the living God – and hence the formal name of the movement, the International Society for Krishna Consciousness or ISKCON.

This movement like the BK movement is also deeply pessimistic at one level about the present age, which it describes as one of decline due to the difficulty of recognizing truth, which it attributes to karma. The most serious and debilitating of contemporary evil is ignorance, a view widely shared among NRMs of Oriental origin, and others like Scientology, some of whose teachings parallel those of the Oriental spiritual traditions. Blind to reality, ISKCON insists, most people are caught up in *maya* or unreality, defined as the illusory world where the pursuit of material pleasures dominates thinking and motivates activity. Real pleasure is spiritual and comes through that purification which takes place through surrender to Krishna. It is not only a question, as the previously mentioned Vedanta or Mayavada philosophy of Shankara teaches, of merging with Brahman. The Hare Krishna accept that while this will ensure eternity, surrender to Krishna, believed to be the Supreme Personality, the Absolute Truth, the Lord, not only guarantees eternity but also includes the pleasure of Brahman realization.

The interplay of monism and dualism is an important feature of Hare Krishna philosophy. On the one hand, the entire cosmos is contained in Krishna who, though entirely spiritual and above all laws and limitations, manifests in the material world in every age and often assumes different forms. The most important of these forms for the Hare Krishna movement is his appearance with his consort Radna as Chaitanya. On the other hand, individuals have a material body which is the result of the desire for material things and is produced along with all other cosmic manifestations – shadows reflecting the spiritual world but without real substance – by Krishna's lower energy called *maya shakti*.

In reply to those who question the logic of both of these positions and other aspects of its philosophy the Hare Krishna movement's response is to stress that they become comprehensible and intelligible as they are experienced and lived, a response that tends to encourage a literal acceptance of the scriptures.

It also tends to strengthen the importance and authority of the spiritual guide or guru who alone can reveal the deeper meaning of scripture. This was the role that Swami Prabhupada came to fulfil, becoming the ultimate authority on Krishna Consciousness, and devotees responded by giving him the reverence, respect and attention due to Krishna.

The devotional path is complex and a number of rules must be followed including abstinence from meat, fish and eggs. Gambling, illicit sex, drugs and intoxicants are all prohibited. Celibacy is an ideal not a requirement, and sex is permissible only in marriage and its purpose is procreation. Eventually the intense desire for mystical union with a loved one – visualized in meditation as the amorous sport carried on by Krishna with the milkmaids and to be understood spiritually – supersedes all else. This focus on the immense desire for pleasure of the Supreme Lord is explained as the most appropriate path to an understanding of his transcendental loving service. Authentic sexual urges are spiritual and in a state of low-level Krishna Consciousness these are expressed through the material body, and as such are unworthy of our concern and interest. The objective or goal where sexual desire is concerned is spiritual sex, which becomes available in the transcendental realm or Supreme Abode of Vrindaban.

By the time of Swami Prabhupada's death in 1978 the Hare Krishna movement had spread across the world, but had failed to ensure a successful transfer of authority. Disputes began and rival factions emerged as this charismatic leader was succeeded by eleven young gurus, whose claim to be self-realized souls was not taken seriously, and a Governing Body Commission (GBC) of non-gurus. Nowhere has the movement attracted large numbers of devotees as the Hare Krishna movement per se. Where the following is large outside India it generally consists of a majority of diaspora Hindus, a development which in itself has given rise to changes in the movement in the West, which has made it necessary to broaden the interpretation of the role, purpose and legitimate uses of its temple (Zaidman, 1997).

Though they have many supporters and admirers among people of all nationalities controversy has surrounded Neo-Hindu movements for different reasons. The Hare Krishna movement has been the object of criticism for its supposedly medieval attitude to women, the Brahma Kumaris movement for disuniting families by insisting on celibacy, and the Sai Baba movement for charlatanism and Hindu nationalism. The most controversial and the most radical of all the Neo-Hindu movements has been the Rajneesh movement founded by the former philosophy professor, the Bhagwan Shree Rajneesh (1931–90), later known as Osho. After attracting a following in India, mainly of Western disciples who were there to become world renouncers (sannyasins), Rajneesh established an ashram at Poona in 1974. A second phase of this experiment in communal living was began with the establishment of Rajneeshpuram in Oregon in the early 1981, an experiment that ended in failure.

This complex and multi-faceted movement is best understood if seen as an experiment in creating a synthesis of Western ideas of gender and Oriental spirituality using a traditional form of Bhakti Yoga as its main vehicle. The movement derived many of its most challenging and controversial ideas from 'alternative' sources such as the Human Potential Movement (HPM), from such thinkers as Wilhelm Reich on sexual repression (Puttick, 1997), and from the enigmatic master George Ivanovitch Gurdjieff (see Chapter 4), founder of the Institute for the Harmonious Development of Man at Fontainebleu near Paris in 1923. Both Gurdjieff and Rajneesh adopted a style of teaching similar to that of the Sufi master, whose use of paradox to counter the tendency to rationalize spiritual experience often leaves disciples thoroughly confused. Rajneesh also innovated in the area of spiritual techniques, creating his own version of dynamic meditation.

The enigmatic Rajneesh intended to shock the outside world. However, while his communes were liberal, some would say excessively so, in matters regarding sexual relations, it has been suggested (Puttick, 1994) that the ultimate objective of Rajneesh was not to flout convention and defiantly encourage promiscuity but to lead his disciples to a state of being beyond sex.

The Rajneesh movement, like the BK movement, has also been seen as an experiment in gender equality. However, the founder's insistence that women provided a better model than men of the fundamental importance of surrender to a guru raises questions about this interpretation of the movement's aims. Athough it has to be said, Rajneesh's view of woman as the model of surrender did not appear to offend even the more feminist-inclined female members of the movement.

These female devotees, some of them former members of radical feminist groups, had come to regard political feminism as too one-dimensional. They had tired of being driven by the sole pursuit of achieving equality on all fronts with men, wanting also to develop a sense of themselves as women and 'to just do female things' (Puttick 1993: 68) without having to compete on every issue with men. This process of 'refeminization' was balanced out by a process of 'male feminization', and this was part of a radical agenda by means of which men were encouraged to get in touch with their feminine side, and attain the highest levels of discipleship by acquiring feminine virtues. As to their opinion of Rajneesh, female disciples were inclined to see him not as a patriarchal figure concerned with strengthening his own male ego and personal power, but rather as in 'some sense androgynous', or as 'beyond gender' (Puttick, 1993: 67).

On gender, Rajneesh was certainly ambivalent. He could be both highly progressive and highly traditional in his views, and this ambivalence is reflected in what has been referred to as his 'celebration of femininity' (Puttick, 1993: 68). In this mode he insisted that feminine virtues were indispensable to Bhakti Yoga and emphasized love, trust, devotion and intuition in particular. Since, he argued, these virtues were more *natural* to women than to men it was easier for women disciples to attain the highest levels of spiritual development through Bhakti Yoga. This traditional outlook did not prevent the Rajneesh movement, even in the context of the 1970s when feminism was highly vocal, from becoming one of the most sought after NRMs among Western women, most of whom were well-qualified professionals.

As was previously mentioned, Rajneesh began the construction of a very much larger ashram, the Rajneeshpuram commune, in Oregon, USA, in 1981. This commune was to end in disaster as it came up against Oregon's strict land-use regulations and planning requirements and responded by threatening the use of violence to overcome what it saw as a hostile world attempting to undermine its essential work. Accusations of stockpiling weapons, embezzlement, fraud and other serious crimes ended with the deportation of the leader to India in 1986, and it was then that Poona stage 2 began. On the death of Osho in 1990, many followers moved away and the movement as a whole, and the commune now far less controversial, continues to attract considerable numbers of would be sannyasins.

Like many of the movements discussed above, the Rajneesh movement developed its own particular, if not unique, version of millenarianism. Sannyasins were convinced that their religion was the religion of the future, as predicted by Nostradamus and by Native American prophecies. This again was met with a great deal of concern, if not alarm, particularly in Germany where the movement had its largest European following. The German ACM (Anti-Cult Movement) claimed Rajneesh's intention was to create a community composed of new, superior people and compared his experiment in communal living with the Nazi project for the creation of a flawless, perfect Aryan race (interviews, Germany, 1984). This kind of response, however exaggerated, was not totally surprising considering that the movement appeared to take immense delight in publicly ridiculing all existing mainstream religion and most of mainstream culture.

Also seen as a cause for alarm was the deification of a leader who was to the wider public a symbol of all that was morally wrong with the world. Accounts began to circulate from the time of the Poona stage 1 period of the Bhagwan's unusual but highly appropriate spiritual origins. These recalled that his last birth was 700 years ago and that he had taught seekers of many faiths from many lands in his school for mystics. Also highlighted was his enlightenment at the age of twenty-one while, appropriately, under a tree, like the Buddha. However, unlike Sai Baba and Swami Prabhupada, and other founders of the Neo-Hindu movements mentioned, Rajneesh did not seek to legitimate his authority through a connection with a guru lineage. Instead he proclaimed himself to be the sole source of his spiritual knowledge and the sole authority for his teachings.

This proclamation of divinity was reflected in the change he made in his title from *acharya* or teacher to Bhagwan or God. Osho, the name he adopted after Rajneeshpuram, is a much less pretentious title, being the Japanese term for a Zen priest. The change of name to Bhagwan was met with a hostile response from many in India for whom a Bhagwan, unlike the founder of the Rajneesh movement, was an ascetic who had renounced material possessions and the ways of the world. By contrast, Rajneesh gave the appearance of enjoying material wealth, although sources close to him, including his personal assistant who knew him intimately, report that, apart from a well-stocked library – he was an avid reader – Rajneesh's private life was unostentatious and basic in terms of comforts (Pers.com 1: 05/03/ 99).

Since the founder's death the movement has undergone considerable change and has lost the image it once had in the public mind of an outrageous, iconoclastic, antinomian, even anarchist, group, substituting for this that of an intellectually and spiritually tolerant and inclusive organization. Networking and publishing are its two principal means of making known its philosophy of self-transcendence. According to one source it sold 500,000 books in thirty-five languages internationally in 2003, and 750,000 books and 250,000 audio discourses in India in eleven languages (Pers.com 2: 20/02/04).

Although the interpretations of reform differed as did some of their priorities, Neo-Hindu movements of the nineteenth and first half of the twentieth century reflect a deep preoccupation with issues of cultural identity and material and social divisions. Also evident is a preoccupation in some movements with the creation of a more homogenized religious tradition, and in others in turning Hinduism into a religion of the book, like Christianity. In the second half of the twentieth century the outlook shifted as more movements became missionary oriented and emphatically millenarian as they sought to spread their teachings to all regardless of nationality, to save the earth from catastrophe and to build a new world.

Islamic new movements in India and Pakistan

The Islamic movements discussed here arose in almost identical circumstances to the Neo-Hindu movements and with a few exceptions, one being the Ahmadiyya movement, they are considered orthodox. While some have remained local movements others have become international spreading across the world chiefly through immigration, the pilgrimage to Mecca and missionary activity.

All of these movements have been influenced to a greater or lesser degree, either directly or indirectly, by internal reform movements such as the eighteenth-century fundamentalist anti-Sufi Wahhābi movement and the nineteenth-century scripturalist Salafi movement, and by their offshoots, and by the impact of Western civilization. While much of the focus of these reform movements has been on eliminating superstition and error, a number of newer Muslim movements, inspired by among others, Sayyid Amir Ali, author of *The Spirit of Islam* which presents the teachings of Islam in terms of contemporary social ideals, have promoted the cause of 'Engaged Islam', a cause also advanced by adherents of a very different ideology and perception of Islam, the Muslim Brothers or Ikhwan (see Chapter 7).

Faced with the challenge from without which posed fundamental questions about the relative vitality of Islam in relation to Christianity in particular, Muslims in Pakistan and India in ways similar to Hindus and Buddhists had broadly three options, one of which was to affirm modernity by giving it Islamic foundations. This would take the form of demonstrating that Islam had nothing to fear from the 'new' philosophy, technology and science by pointing to the Golden Age of Islamic Civilization, and to the intellectual feats of Islamic Spain and other historical examples. This strategy would enable Muslims to demonstrate Islam's primacy as the first modernizing religion by showing the unparalleled contribution it had made to the development of modern science and philosophy. The intention behind this response was also to show that there was no conflict between Islam and science, between Islam and the acquisition of knowledge whatever its origins.

Another response was to discount the proclaimed benefits of modern civilization by seeking to revive and show that Islamic learning was sufficient in itself to meet all human needs. The madrasah or Islamic school was the key to the success of this strategy of protecting Islam from the corrosive influences of Westernization. Of course, it was not only Western influences that were seen as corrosive but all non-Islamic influences, which included popular forms of Sufism, and Hindu, Buddhist and Sikh influences. Some chose the first option, some the second and some a third, which consisted in continuing on with indifference to the religious and political issues posed by the dual challenge from internal reform movements and from the West. These three kinds of responses are reflected in the content and strategies of the new Islamic movements considered below.

We begin with the Deobandi movement whose goal has been to return Islam to the monotheism of the early years of its history. This goal combined with its opposition to popular forms of meditational Sufism are two of the most recognizable features of modern Islam. The movement was founded in the 1860s by two Delhi 'ūlama or Muslim teachers, Muhammad Qasim Nanautwi (1833–77) and Rashid Ahmed Gangohi (1829–1905), in the small town of Deoband in Uttar Pradesh. This preference of two Delhi teachers for this small rural town or qasbah was based largely on the need they felt for a better environment for preserving Muslim culture than the more British, Western-influenced world of Delhi. Learning was to be the core activity of a new type of madrasah or Muslim school, new in the sense of being separated from the mosque. Its publication of an annual report and of scholarly Islamic texts in Urdu was also an innovation.

Though the Deobandi movement represents the more puritanical tendency in modern Indian Islam by prioritizing learning in the Qur'ān, Shari'a (Holy

Law) and Hadith (Tradition), it did not until recently share the same extremist views on Sufism as the Wahhābi, largely because its own roots are in the elite traditions of a number of Sufi orders. Moreover, it has not only continued to pursue the practice of initiating members into these orders, but has also developed what might be termed a refined form of Sufism or mysticism based on an individual spiritual discipline learned from a Shaykh or guide. This is contrasted with the more exuberant, less rational Sufism of meditation, with its popular shrine-based cults where holy men or pirs mediate on behalf of devotees for divine favours and guidance. The latter type of Sufism is practised by among others the Barelwi movement, which also originated in the second half of the nineteenth century in Uttar Pradesh. The success of the popular Sufism of the Barelwi, founded by Shaykh Ahmad Reza Khan (1856–1921), and of similar movements whose constituents are to be found mainly among the less well off in the rural areas, is one of the main reasons why the more urban-based radical movements such as the Deobandi and Alh-i-Hadith believe reform to be necessary.

Barelwi teaching on the person of the prophet Muhammad also distinguishes the movement from the Deobandi, and from other nineteenth-century 'new' Islamic reform movements. It implies, for example, that the Prophet is part of God's light (Nur-i-Muhammadi) and, therefore, above the status of a human being. Given his superhuman status and his special knowledge of and insights into the unknown (ilm ul-ghaib), the Prophet Muhammad is believed to be in a unique position as an intermediary between God and his creatures. Thus, there is intense personal devotion to the Prophet, and also to saintly mystics, to pirs or holy men believed, as we have seen, to have special intercessory powers, and great importance is attached to the celebration of festivals. Given the world view that these devotional activities entail, it is not entirely surprising that the Barelwis were among the most outraged of those Muslims who campaigned for a ban to be placed on Salman Rushdie's *The Satanic Verses* in 1988.

In some respects the conflict between the Barelwi type of Islam and that of the Deobandi and Alh-i-Hadith is a conflict between a popular religion that attends to everyday needs and a scholarly religion, respectively. The former is practical religion concerned with explaining disease and sickness and offering cures, of predicting what is going to happen in the here and now of everyday life and how it is to be managed, the latter intellectual and academic, a religion of scholars that is concerned with rule-observance, order, sobriety, learning and 'aversion to the excessive use of the audio-visual aids of religion' (Metcalf, 1982: 11). Deobandi and Alh-i-Hadith Islam is an essentially scripture-based Islam of the middle classes and has exercised a considerable impact on modern Islam in South Asia and abroad.

By the late 1960s, the Deobandi had opened more than 9,000 schools or madrasahs and its University at Dar ul Uloum in Deoband is regarded as the finest Islamic university in the world after the university of Al Azhar in Egypt

(Robinson, 1988: 17). The core curriculum of the university is to train scholars in Islamic religion and culture, which means, as we have seen, the teaching of a pure, austere, scholastic version of Islam in the tradition of the Hanafi jurists, which allows no room for unorthodox, or Hindu or Western influence, and allows for only 'a restrained Sufi practice in which there is no hint even of intercession' (Robinson, 1988: 4).

The previously mentioned Alh-i-Hadith, founded by Sayyid Nazir (d.1902) who came from a family of judges (qadis) who practised at the Mughal court, is also part of the intellectual Islamic reform tradition that began to develop in the mid-nineteenth century in India. Most of its recruits came initially from the higher echelons of society and together they forged a cohesive, exclusive, reform movement with a strong apocalyptic strain, a response no doubt to British rule, which it interpreted as a sign that the End was nigh. The Alh-i-Hadith looked to Muslim teachers as a class to undertake the task of restoring Islam to its authentic condition (Metcalf, 1982: 278–9, in Clarke, 1998: 62). Extremely confident in their position as scholars of Islam, members refused to accept the legitimacy of the four orthodox schools of Islamic law and campaigned for the use of ijtihād, a method of arriving at an opinion in matters of law through individual scholarly exertion.

It was over this question of the law schools and related matters that the Alh-i-Hadith clashed with the Deobandi, who banned them from using their mosques, a ban which the distinctive beard and attire of the former ensured could be easily enforced. The acquisition of its own mosques, schools, journals and the holding of its annual pan-India conference have made the Alh-i-Hadith more readily identifiable as a separate movement. With separation it was able to continue unimpeded with its total opposition to Sufi or mystical Islam, to the four schools of law, and to such widely accepted traditional practices as Eid and funeral prayers. All of this sets it apart and ensures that it retains its image of an elitist and exclusive reform movement.

The Alh-i-Hadith also teaches, like a number of other Muslim reform movements, a policy of separation of Muslims from non-Muslim society. Moreover, recent research (Zahab and Roy, 2002) suggests that it has become more open, as has the Deobandi movement, to the militant jihadi approach to reform.

The Aligarth 'movement' provides an example of a more tolerant response to the external dimension of dual challenge arising from the external impact in the form of colonialism, the Christian missionary enterprise, and the perceived need for internal reform and even radical change. While the Alh-i-Hadith and similar movements were defending Islam from the corrosive influences of popular Sufi Islam and Western thought, others including Sayyid Ahmad Khan (1817–98) were attempting to show that Islam and modern science were perfectly compatible and, indeed, that the true justification of Islam lay not only in its conformity with Nature but also with the laws of science. To develop and disseminate these ideas Khan founded

Aligarth College in 1875 where the study of religion and science were integrated. Opposition was strong and took the form of accusing Khan of teaching pure materialism.

Khan's rationalizing approach to Islam also included a reassessment of Islamic social teachings and it was this aspect of his reform that held out the biggest attraction for intellectuals in particular, some of whom were determined to have what they saw as the evils of slavery and unregulated polygamy and divorce outlawed. Sayyid Amir Ali, the previously mentioned author of *The Spirit of Islam*, took this concern with social teaching further and argued that such obligatory duties as fasting and almsgiving could be defended on rational grounds of social benefit. Divorce by repudiation, slavery, polygamy and other social evils were, he argued, contrary to the teachings of the Qur'ān, and, thus, dismissed by him as the innovations of incompetent, ignorant jurists.

A different reaction to Sayyid Ahmad Khan's modernizing and rationalizing programme came in the form of the Ahmadiyya movement founded by Mirza Ghulam Ahmad, of Qadian in Kashmir, who claimed to be the Promised Messiah of the Christians who looked forward to the Second Coming of Jesus, the Mahdi or God-guided one of Islam, a reincarnation of Prophet Muhammad and an avatar of Krishna. He also claimed to be the recipient of a new revelation to reinterpret Islam for the requirements of a New Age. Ghulam Ahmad's claim to be a prophet put him outside the Sunni fold, which holds that there can be no further prophets or no new revelation after the Prophet Muhammad, the last and final prophet. Ahmadis would see this as a misinterpretation of their position since for them the prophet is an avatar, an understanding of his status that does not conflict with Muhammad being the seal of the prophets. His orthodoxy is also questioned over his claim that the era of jihād, in the sense of holy war, had come to an end.

The Ahmadiyya began with a mission to halt the conversion of Muslims to Christianity by means of modernizing the Islamic curriculum. This entailed the introduction of Western subjects alongside the Islamic sciences. The movement was also concerned to 'improve', by modernizing, the image of Muslims, and to this end permitted the adoption of many aspects of Western culture. Thus, the introduction also of Western dress, and marriage and naming ceremonies modelled on those held in Christian churches, were all encouraged to give Islam a modern look and pre-empt thereby conversion to Christianity. The movement split in 1914 into Qadian and Lahore sections. The latter, no longer accepting the claim to prophethood of the founder, took the name the Society for the Propagation of Islam. Both are emphatically missionary in orientation and heavily engaged in this work not only in south India but also in Africa, Europe and the United States.

A twentieth-century reform movement with a very different outlook on the West from that provided by Sayyid Ahmad Khan and Sayyid Amir Ali, and adopting a very different strategy than the Ahmadiyya movement, but sharing much in common with the more exclusive, intellectually conservative movements already referred to, is the Jama'at-i-Islami founded by Abdul Ala Maududi (1903–79). A knowledge of the political context in which the Jama'at emerged is essential to understanding its objectives. It was founded in 1941, the year in which Maududi moved to what was to become Pakistan, as the Indian independence movement became ever more determined to insist on self-governance immediately World War II was over. During this period Maududi began to reflect seriously on the issue of the encounter between Islam and other cultures and on the effects of Indian nationalism on Muslim identity.

While the political leadership of the independence movement was engaged in arguing the merits of one or other political ideology and democratic system, the polity which Maududi sought to create was a 'theo-democracy' in which the state is merely God's khalifah (vice-regent) on earth, and the citizens of the state participants in this vice-regency with the state. He distinguished Islamic democracy from Western democracy, pointing out that while the latter was based on the concept of popular sovereignty, the former rested on the principle that sovereignty is vested in God with the people as His representatives.

Maududi developed a strategy for the transformation of society in accordance with these ideas, the core of which consisted of the creation of small, informed, dedicated and disciplined groups that would work to achieve social and political leadership. His plans went far beyond India/Pakistan involving, as they did, the establishment of an international network of 'born again' Muslims dedicated to the observance of Shari'a or Islamic law, and to daw'a or mission. It is worth noting here that, as in the case of the Muslim Brotherhood or Ikhwan in Egypt (see Chapter 7) and generally in Islamist groups across the world, daw'a was given a new meaning. It was not only to be concerned with doctrinal and ritual purity but was also to be 'engaged' daw'a in the sense of concerning itself with the improvement of the social conditions of Muslims.

Maududi also sought to promote Islam as a complete way of life with its own culture, its own political and economic, philosophical, theological and educational system, all of which were to be considered as superior to anything that Western or any other civilization could offer. Like other Islamist movements, this movement has also become more radicalized and militant since the invasions of Afghanistan (2001) and Iraq (2003).

Tablighi Jama'at, in Robinson's (1988: 17) view one of the two great Islamic movements generated in South Asia, presents a different face of Islamic reform from those outlined above. Tablighi, founded by Muhamad Ilyas (1885–1944), acts, according to Nielsen (1992: 133), as the 'active pietism of the Deobandi movement' the former providing the missionaries, the latter the mosques. Its purpose is to wage war on ignorance among Muslims, many of whom, it claims, have little knowledge of even the fundamentals of their faith, and are often steeped in non-Islamic customs and traditions. Tablighi preaches against shirk, or mixing, and stresses the fundamental importance of teaching tawhid (literally making one or asserting oneness) the oneness of God. It is a classic example of an Islamic reform movement that aims primarily at improving the knowledge and practice of the Muslim community.

Though recent events, including the invasions of Afghanistan (2001) and Iraq (2003), have hardened most Islamic reform movements and disposed some of the membership or branches to consider a more militant approach, Tablighi by intent is both quietist and apolitical. Historically, it has emphasized that the setting of a good example in social behaviour combined with individual piety are the key to restoring Islamic society and winning others to Islam. Use has been made of the pilgrimage to Mecca, workers who migrate to the West, and the network of South Asian merchants in Europe, Africa and Southeast Asia, to spread information about its reform programme. Tablighi also employs methods of evangelism devised by the Deobandi, one of which is the teaching of the fundamental importance not only of making but also of understanding the meaning of the proclamation or confession of faith 'There is no God but God and Muhammad is the prophet of God'. Another teaching stresses the essential importance of personal prayer to the missionary, another the correct behaviour toward Muslims and another the willingness to take part in preaching and teaching within the community.

By the early 1970s the movement had not only long since spread throughout the subcontinent but also to over thirty countries beyond, and by the beginning of the 1990s it was engaged in preaching daw'a missions (Urdu: gush, Arabic: khuruj) in over ninety countries (King, 1998: 76). Although it follows a different school of Muslim law, Tablighi relations with communities of North African, Moroccan and Algerian, Muslims are particularly well developed (King, 1998: 77) providing further evidence of its capacity to transcend not only linguistic boundaries but also different schools of thought within the Umma or World Muslim community. An idea of the cosmopolitan character of this movement can be gleaned from the international make up of the student body studying at the Tablighi seminary in Dewsbury, England, which although it can vary from year to year may at any one time consist of Burmese, Zambian, South Indian, Moroccan and South African Muslims.

The Islamic new movements of Pakistan and India, thus, have offered different responses to the dual challenge from within and without. Some have attempted to show that there is in principle no incompatibility between Islam and modernization, indeed that historically Islam has been at the forefront of cultural, technological and scientific change. The major concern of other movements has been with safeguarding Islam as a religion and a culture, some insisting on the all sufficiency of daw'a or mission, while others have advocated both daw'a and jihād, although the divide between the first and the second approaches has become increasingly blurred in recent times due to events in Afghanistan, Iraq, and the Middle East generally. We will now turn to a brief overview of the response of Sikhism and Sikh-derived movements to the dual challenge from within and without.

New Sikh-related movements

A fifteenth-century movement started by Guru Nanak (1469–1539) near Lahore in present-day Pakistan and distinguished principally by its doctrine of guru worship, Sikhism's response to both internal challenges and Western missionary influence and modernization has differed from that of both Hindus and Muslims. This difference can be attributed in part to the considerable difficulties Sikhism has encountered in attempting to separate itself from the Muslim and, in particular, the Hindu environment in which it emerged, while at the same time protecting itself from Christian missionary activity. Some scholars (Cole, 1997: 336) would argue that it has never fully succeeded in this.

In the nineteenth century several new Sikh movements arose, including the influential Singh Sahba (Sikh Society), in response to both Christian and Hindu missionary activity among young Sikhs of the Punjab. The Singh Sahba was founded in 1873 in Amritsar to counter Christian missionary influence and the activities of the Brahmo Samaj movement, which were thought to be undermining Sikh self-esteem. The Singh Sabha reply was to construct Khalsa colleges to promote wider access to and higher levels of education. One outcome was the 1909 Anand Marriage Act, which gave legal recognition to the Sikh wedding ceremony thereby furthering the cause of a separate Sikh identity, culture and religion. The Gurdwaras Act of 1925 saw the Sikhs regain control of their places of worship and assembly, which had passed into Hindu control in the mid-nineteenth century. The threat to Sikh identity persists in the minds of some and is reinforced by the Hindu nationalist movement, the Vishnu Hindu Parishad, which refers to Sikhs as 'Keshadhari Hindus', really Hindus (Cole, 1997: 328). The response from Sikhs is to call for the creation of their own state of Kalistan in the historical and geographical Punjab.

Other nineteenth-century Sikh reform movements include the Namdhari (meaning the one who has adopted God in her/his life) movement founded in 1857 by Ram Singh (1816–85). This movement differs from mainstream Sikhism in ways similar to those in which the Ahmadiyya movement differs from mainstream Islam. It acknowledges a lineage of human gurus after Gobind Singh, the founder of Khalsa and regarded by a majority of Sikhs as the last of the lineage of human gurus. Its three main rules of life are: meditation on the name of God; earning a living through honest work; and sharing with the poor. Ram Singh was a reformer who campaigned for women's rights and opposed infanticide practices on females, the selling of girls into slavery and the dowry system. He also campaigned against the slaughtering of cows, sought to promote higher standards of literacy and pursued a policy of non-co-operation with British rule in India, which resulted in his being exiled to Burma.

The Radhasoami movement, which itself disowns the designation religion but is often referred to as a Sikh religion, is difficult to categorize as either Sikh or Hindu. It is probably best described as a synthesis of both. The movement emerged in the nineteenth century under the leadership of Shiv Dayal Singh (Soami Ji Maharaj, 1818–78), who formed a satsang in Agra and developed his own unique interpretation of the *Sant Mat* or Way of the Saints movement, an important historical current within Hinduism. Singh taught a version of yoga of light and sound (*shabd yoga*) that leads to harmony with the luminous and deep-sounding current that issues from God's creative essence. The concept of the Absolute is of a being without qualities. Unlike Sikhism, the movement has no holy book. In terms of lifestyle it is vegetarian and insists on chastity, while being strongly opposed to homosexuality.

Several groups claimed to represent the teachings of the Dayal Singh school after his death. The group led by Jaimal Singh (1839–1903), which established its satsang on the River Beas in the Punjab, became known as the Radha Soami Satsang Beas and it was under this name that the movement began to spread its message abroad to Europe and the United States from the early years of the twentieth century. Kirpal Singh (1893–1974), founder of the Ruhani Satsang based in California, became the most widely respected guru of this tradition in the West. Further splits followed his death leading to the formation of the Sawan Kirpal Ruhani Mission or Science of Spirituality movement under the leadership of Rajinder Singh (b.1946), grandson of Kirpal Singh. This is the most widely practised form of Radhasoami spirituality in Europe with an estimated 300,000 followers.

Despite the splintering the Radhasoami movement has had considerable influence on a number of NRMs in North America and Asia. The number of practitioners – possibly a more appropriate term than member, although there is an initiation rite – belonging to the various branches worldwide is estimated at somewhere between two and a half million and three million.

The emergence of New Buddhist groups has also been a phenomenon of modern Indian history, some of which are more a response to the internal situation than to external influences.

New Buddhist movements

Ambedkar Buddhism is by far the largest and most influential of the new Buddhist movements in India in modern times. A movement of some six million people, most belonging to Untouchable castes, Ambedkar Buddhism was started in 1956 in the state of Maharashtra by Dr B. R. Ambedkar (1891–1956), known as Babasaheb, the son of an Untouchable Mahar couple. Helped by several reform-minded Indian princes, including the Maharaja of Kolhapur, and other Hindu caste reformers, Ambedkar became the first Untouchable to study abroad, obtaining a doctorate in Economics from Columbia University in New York. He then went on to acquire a doctorate in Science from the University of London and qualified for the bar at Gray's Inn. The aim of all of this education was to help abolish the caste restrictions, which affected all aspects of life including access to temples and the right to water, by using the Gandhian non-violent direct action technique or *satyagraha*.

By 1935 Ambedkar had secured a system of reservations for Untouchables and/or Scheduled Castes, that is, castes eligible for benefits, and in 1936 he founded the Scheduled Castes Federation in an attempt to undermine Brahmin power, which he believed gave support and legitimacy to the caste system. However, this future Law Minister in Prime Minister Nehru's first cabinet, having failed in his attempt to gain access for himself and his supporters to the Kala Ram Temple in Nasik in 1935, set out on the path to Buddhism. Untouchables in the past had turned to both Christianity and Islam, in search of a life free from prejudice and discrimination but for Ambedkar, among the great attractions of Buddhism, were its Indian origins, its emphasis on compassion, equality and non-violence.

Ambedkar took his vows as a Buddhist on a field at Nagpur with half a million others in October 1956, one of the largest mass conversion ceremonies ever recorded. An estimated six million others, the vast majority from across the Marathi-speaking areas, followed. Ambedkar followers, not unlike the Protestant Buddhists of Sri Lanka (Gombrich and Obeyesekere, 1988) and the Neo-Evangelicals of Latin America (Martin, 1990), became noted for their thrift – including the cutting back on the purchase of luxury items for special occasions and on wedding expenses – and the search for excellence through more and better education.

Always conscious of his role as a teacher, Ambedkar described himself as a Neo-Buddhist. He was highly critical of interpretations of karma that attributed being born an Untouchable to wrong deeds in a past life, and also strongly disapproved, as do leading Thai-Buddhist reformers (see Chapter 11), of the emphasis that was widely placed on merit making. Instead he promoted the concept of 'Engaged Buddhism' (see Chapters 1, 5 and 11). In a way similar to Vivekananda in relation to genuine Hindu spirituality, he insisted that while Buddhist teachings were meant for individual self-improvement they provided the fundamentals of a social gospel – a non-violent social gospel and, therefore, preferable to Communism – for the building of a new, harmonious, integrated world. Whether these aspirations and the deeds they inspired have enabled the Ambedkar Buddhists to succeed in breaking the mould of caste in India – most are former members of the Mahar and Jatav castes – remains an unanswered question. Some are of the opinion that the result has been the creation of a new caste. This notwithstanding, their numbers continue to grow, as does the international impact of their interpretation of Buddhist teaching as a social gospel.

The chapter now turns to developments in Buddhism in Sri Lanka and in particular Protestant Buddhism (Gombrich and Obeyesekere, 1988), also known as Buddhist-modernism, to which there are parallels in Neo-Hinduism and Neo-Buddhism in India, and which emerged once again in response to the double stimulus of challenges from within and without.

Sri Lanka's 'Protestant Buddhism'

Formerly Ceylon, Sri Lanka is a predominantly Buddhist country with substantial minorities of Hindus and Muslims. Buddhism in Sri Lanka, where the Theravada tradition is the most widely followed – though Mahayana influence is growing owing mainly to the growing presence of Japanese New Religions – dates back before the Christian era. Moreover, it was in Sri Lanka that the Buddhist canon was written down in the Pali language.

What has been referred to with reference to Sri Lankan Buddhism as both Buddhist-modernism and Protestant Buddhism (Gombrich and Obeyesekere, 1988) began to take shape in the second half of the nineteenth century under British rule. The two main stimuli were British rule and missionary activity.

The British took control of Ceylon, as it was then known, in 1815, agreeing at the time to protect the interests of Buddhism. The competition from Christian missionaries, who gained a virtual monopoly of Western education in the country, gave rise to a Buddhist counter-movement, using similar techniques as the Christian missionaries, that met Christian criticisms of their religion head on in public debates and became involved in a pamphlet war in which each side disseminated their objections to the other. Similar pamphlet wars occurred elsewhere during colonial rule, including between Muslims and Christians in Africa.

The public debates and the pamphleteering led to a revitalization of Buddhism among the more affluent, Western-educated middle classes of Colombo and other urban centres, who resorted to Western notions in their attempts to offer a modern interpretation and description of their religion. They would insist that the Buddha was merely human, that Buddhism was a rational philosophy not a religion and posed no doctrinal obstacles to the advancement of modern science and technology. New associations such as Buddhist Youth Associations, and new kinds of Buddhist colleges, such as Narlanda College, with a partially Westernized curriculum were started by this elite. Other features of this new Buddhism were its lay emphasis, its discouragement of ritual and its application to all aspects of ordinary life. Many of these characteristics, and the last three in particular, it shared with Protestant missionary movements and for this reason Gombrich and Obeyesekere (1988) prefer to label the movement 'Protestant Buddhism' rather than Buddhist-modernism. This term was first used by Obeyesekere in

1970 (Gombrich and Obeyesekere, 1988: 6) in preference to Buddhist-modernism which, he maintains, is more concerned with Buddhism's relationship to politics than religion. Gombrich and Obeyesekere (1988: 216) describe Protestant Buddhism in this way:

> The hallmark of Protestant Buddhism, then, is its view that the layman should permeate his life with his religion; that he should strive to make Buddhism permeate his whole society, and that he can and should try to reach *nirvana*. As a corollary, the lay Buddhist is critical of the traditional norms of the monastic role; he may not be positively anti-clerical but his respect, if any, is for the particular monk, not for the yellow robe as such.

This kind of Buddhism is Protestant, then, in its devaluation of the role of the monk, and in its strong emphasis on the responsibility of each individual for her/his 'salvation' or enlightenment, the arena for achieving which is not a monastery but the everyday world which, rather than being divided off from, should be infused with Buddhism. Gombrich and Obeyeseke (1988) point to Anagarika Dharmapala (1864–1933) as the quintessential Protestant Buddhist. From a wealthy business family and educated in Christian schools, Dharmapala was later to be initiated into the Theosophical Society (see Chapter 5), a movement that exercised considerable influence over modern Buddhism in Sri Lanka.

Initiated in Madras (now Chennai), Dharmapala became the manager of the Buddhist Theosophical Society in Sri Lanka. Later he was to seek to purge Buddhism of all traces of Theosophical influence, and to display contempt for Hindus and Muslims alike. Widely travelled – he visited Japan, the United States where he represented Buddhism at the Parliament of World Religions in Chicago in 1893, and many other countries – Dharmapala founded the Maha Bodhi Society in 1891, today a worldwide movement with particular responsibility for Buddhist missionaries in the West. Despite its enthusiasm for modernity Protestant Buddhism opposed colonial rule and Dharmapala, who might be described as a Buddhist nationalist, was exiled to India for his campaign against British imperialism.

The mission of Protestant Buddhism, thus, was to fashion Buddhists who had internalized the teachings and ethical precepts of their religion, and believed in the fundamental equality of all believers and the practical relevance of religion to every aspect of life.

If Dharmapala personifies Protestant Buddhism, the *Sarvodaya* (Sanskrit: welfare of all) movement founded by A. T. Ariyaratna provides, Gombrich and Obeyesekere (1988) suggest, the clearest expression in the form of an organized movement, of Protestant Buddhism, and in particular of its ethical and social philosophy of compassion and kindness – empathy leading to selfless labour. Concerned with the alleviation of poverty and the ills attendant upon it the movement produced a model of development based on Buddhist ethics and doctrines. Two of its key elements were agricultural collectives and altruism. It was proposed that communities should farm as a unit on a communal, village farm, and offer their labour selflessly – the Buddhist term for this would be *dana* or giving – through the medium of communal work groups known as *kayiya* for the betterment of the poor. As Gombrich and Obeyesekere (1988: 245) comment with regard to Ariyaratna's Buddhist philosophy of selfless labour:

> It was a profound vision of involvement in the world, expressed in Buddhist terms . . .. Undoubtedly this is the major and truly significant innovation of Ariyaratna and the high point of Protestant Buddhism – to inculcate in the laity a sense of Buddhist work for the welfare of others by the donation of selfless labour.

While the *Sarvodaya* movement inspired the creation of other similar groups, Protestant Buddhism generally was a small movement with its influence limited to a few urban centres until the 1940s. It began to develop from that point in time into a phenomenon of national and international importance, as the notion of socially engaged Buddhism became increasingly attractive in Asia and beyond.

In recent times Sri Lankan Buddhism has also been influenced by new, strongly millenarian Japanese lay Buddhist-Shinto movements that promote natural healing and organic agriculture and stress the importance of compassion and social engagement. An estimated 600 Buddhist monks have recently introduced into their temples the practice of *jorei*, a Japanese Mahayana/Shinto method of healing brought to the country by missionaries of Sekai Kyusei Kyo (Church of World Messianity). When asked to account for this 'innovation', Sri Lankan Buddhist monks explained that as it belonged to the realm of practice *jorei* was perfectly acceptable as it did not affect in any way the 'purity' of Buddhist teaching, (author's interviews, Sri Lanka, January 2001). A similar response was given by Thai monks regarding the compatibility or otherwise of New Age ideas and practices with Buddhism in Thailand. Such practices did not contradict the teachings and were, therefore, legitimate (author's interviews, Thailand, April 2000).

Conclusions

The innovations and new developments outlined above provide a perspective from which religious change itself can be understood and also of how such change reflects the social and cultural changes occurring throughout society under the impact of both internal and external stimuli. Some of the new developments and innovations reveal the anxiety of being trapped by both kinds of change. Others are primarily concerned to show that religion and spirituality are of fundamental importance to progress and modernization. Other responses indicate a determination to stand by the real, authentic version of the faith they adhere to and to seek to construct on its foundations an alternative new order that is neither secular and Capitalist nor atheistic and materialist. Others seek to show a fit between the fundamentals of their faith and modern science and technology. Evident in many of the new Hindu, Buddhist, Muslim and Sikh movements is a concern to domesticate Western influences, including Western science and technology, and above all Western education, on account of its inextricable links with the Christian missionary movement.

Millenarian dreams are also present in every form of South Asian new religion, and indeed in almost every NRM regardless of its religious and cultural origins, and offer an insight into people's hopes and aspirations. Millenarian belief is also a recruitment technique and an ideology of change, change that often directly challenges the old, taken-for-granted religious truths, and acts as a catalyst by stimulating a process of reflection on the meaning and purpose of religion and spirituality.

This rethinking in the South Asian context as in others resulted in the emergence of new forms of applied spirituality and socially engaged religion, which have spread, as we have shown in several chapters, beyond South Asia, carried by migrants and missionaries, to much of the rest of Asia, Africa, the Caribbean, Europe and North and South America.

References and select bibliography

The interviews noted in the text were carried out by the author between 1999 and 2004 as part of a larger research project on religious change.

Ali, Sayyid Amir (1964) *The Spirit of Islam*, London: Methuen.

Basham, A. L. (1971) *The Wonder That Was India*, London: Fontana.

Beckerlegge, Gwilym (2004) 'Iconographic Representations of Renunciation and Activism in the Ramakrishna Math and Mission and the Rastriya Swayamsavak Sangh', *Journal of Contemporary Religion*, 19(1), 47–56.

Chander, Jagdish (1983) *Adi Dev: The First Man*, Mount Abu: Prajapita Brahma Kumaris World Spiritual University.

Clarke, Peter B. (1998) 'Islam in Western Europe: Present State and Future Trends' in Peter B. Clarke (ed.) *New Trends and Developments in the World of Islam*, London: Luzac, pp. 3–41.

Cole, Owen W. (1997) 'Sikhism' in John Hinnells (ed.) *A New Handbook of Living Religions*, Oxford: Blackwell, pp. 310–39.

De Michaelis, Elizabeth (2004) *A History of Modern Yoga: Patañjali and Western Esotericism*, London: Cassell Continuum.

Gellner, Ernst (1992) *Postmodernism, Reason and Religion*, London: Routledge.

Gibb, H. A. R. (1978) *Islam*, Oxford: Oxford University Press.

Gombrich, Richard and Obeyesekere, Gananath (1988) *Buddhism Transformed: Religious Change in Sri Lanka*, Princeton, NJ: Princeton University Press.

Jaffrolet, Christophe (1996) *The Hindu Nationalist Movement*, New York: Columbia University Press.

King, John (1998) 'Tablighi Jama'at and the Deobandi Mosques in Britain' in Peter B. Clarke (ed.) *New Trends and Developments in the World of Islam*, London: Luzac, pp. 75–92.

Kopf, D. (1978) *The Brahmo Samaj and the Shaping of the Modern Indian Mind*, Princeton, NJ: Princeton University Press.

Martin, David (1990) *Tongues of Fire*, Oxford: Blackwell.

Metcalf, B. (1982) *Islamic Revival in British India (1860–1900)*, Princeton, NJ: Princeton University Press.

Nielsen, Jorgen (1992) *Muslims in Western Europe*, Edinburgh: Edinburgh University Press.

Puttick, Elizabeth (1993) 'Devotees and Patriarchs: Women Sannyassins in the Rajneesh Movement' in Elizabeth Puttick and Peter B. Clarke (eds) *Women as Teachers and Disciples in Traditional and New Religions*, Lampeter, UK: Edwin Mellen Press, pp. 63–76.

Puttick, Elizabeth (1994) 'Gender, Discipleship and Charismatic Authority in the Rajneesh Movement', unpublished PhD Thesis, King's College, University of London.

Puttick, Elizabeth (1997) *Women in New Religions: In Search of Community, Spirituality and Spiritual Power*, Basingstoke: Macmillan.

Robinson, Francis (1988) 'Varieties of South Asian Islam', Research Paper No. 8, Centre for Research in Ethnic Relations, University of Warwick.

Sen, Amiya, P. (ed.) (2003) *Social and Religious Reform: The Hindus of British India*, Oxford: Oxford University Press.

Sharma, Arvind (1986) 'New Hindu Religious Movements in India', in James Beckford (ed.) *New Religious Movements and Rapid Social Change*, London: Sage, pp. 220–39.

Singleton, Mark (2005) 'Salvation through Relaxation: Proprioceptive Therapy and its Relationship to Yoga', *Journal of Contemporary Religion* (forthcoming).

Whaling, Frank (1995) 'The Brahma Kumaris', *Journal of Contemporary Religion*, 10(1), 3–29.

Wilson, Bryan R. (1970) *Religious Sects*, London: Weidenfeld & Nicolson.

Zahab Mariam Abou and Roy, Olivier (2002) *Islamist Networks*, London: Hurst.

Zaidman, Nurit (1997) 'When the Deities are Asleep: Processes of Change in an American Hare Krishna Temple', *Journal of Contemporary Religion*, 12(3), 335–52.

Personal communications

1 Robin Puttick, March 5th, 1999.
2 Elizabeth Puttick, February 20th, 2004.

Chapter 11

Southeast Asia (Thailand, Vietnam and Indonesia)

Any overview of Southeast Asian society – a term used here to cover for the most part Thailand, Vietnam and Indonesia – whatever the aspect being considered, needs to keep in mind Stockwell's (1999: 1) observation that so marked is its diversity that 'even the recent history of each country, indeed of each community, possesses its own periodization, and invites examination as a more or less autonomous entity'. Any generalizations made here need, thus, to be read with that observation in mind.

Regarding the religious diversity of Southeast Asia, this consists mainly of Buddhism, which is widely practised in Thailand, Burma (Myanmar), Laos and Cambodia and Vietnam, a variety of Hindu traditions in all of these countries, Confucianism, Catholicism and Daoism in Vietnam, and all of the major world religions in Indonesia, the largest of these, numerically, being Islam.

While contemporary reform and revivalist religious movements can appear to be defensive responses to external forces undermining local culture and morals, one of their aims is to restore to their religion its universal features. The pursuit of this goal often drives the demand for religious reform and renewal in Southeast Asia. Many of the revivalist movements are engaged in a struggle to free mainstream religion from what they perceive as its spiritually unhealthy relationship with local culture, which disguises their universal character. In order to project itself as a world religion and contribute to the formation of global society reformers such as the Thai monk Buddhadasa (1906–92), a stringent critic of popular Buddhism, which he believed was rooted in ignorance, maintain that it is of fundamental importance for Buddhism not only to extract itself from the grip of local culture but also to offer an alternative to Capitalism. Many modern Christian and Muslim movements pursue this goal in relation to Islam and Christianity, respectively.

In Thailand and across the region of Southeast Asia where mainstream Buddhism is the majority religion two main developments can be identified, one a spiritual revival that seeks to restore 'authentic' Buddhism and use it as an instrument for transforming people's lives both spiritually and materially in the modern world, and the other increasing rationalization and internal secularization. We will consider both of these trends as they have unfolded in Thailand in the modern period before turning to the questions of new developments in Thai Buddhism and Thai New Religions. The focus then shifts to Vietnam where Engaged Buddhism emerged as an important dimension of the country's religious life in the 1960s. A number of Vietnamese New Religions, including Caodaism, will also be examined before turning to new developments in Indonesian Islam and the rise of New Religions there including Subud.

Thailand's reformed Buddhism

The modern reform of Buddhism in Thailand, regarded as the 'inherent state religion' or *sasana pracham chat*, and the religion of over 90 per cent of the country's *c*.68 million inhabitants, began in the mid-nineteenth century with the creation of the Thammayut monastic *nikaya* or fraternity by the royal monk Mongkut, later King Rama IV (1851–68). This reform included the restoration of the Forest Monk tradition. Mongkut's reforms were also strikingly similar to those occurring in the West today. Keyes (cited in Swearer 1991: 654) sees the reformed Buddhism of Mongkut and of Vajiranana (his half-brother) as representing 'a move away from seeing the world in cosmological terms to seeing it psychologically and . . . from practice centred on communal rituals to practices centred on self-cultivation'.

Forest monks who generally decry the institutionalized form of monasticism, particularly as lived by the urban monks, follow strictly the *vanavasi* ideal, the core of which is concentration on *vipassana* or meditation, mendicancy, the use of rags for robes, and of urine for healing, and live a peripatetic existence in the forest. As in the Indian sannyasin or renouncer tradition, there is a turning away from society. Informants among the forest monks of northeast Thailand can be highly critical of urban monastic life and dismissive of the urban monks who live what they describe as 'useless lives' and who are 'only interested in money' (author's interviews, January 10th 2004). Forest monks maintain that a true monk should not only be preoccupied with his own spiritual progress but has a duty to engage with the spiritual and social concerns of the community.

Thus, forest monks serve their communities as teachers, healers, advisers and counsellors. They also either initiate or become involved in environmental projects and protest movements against, for example, deforestation, an activity that has led to confrontations with the Royal Forestry Department and even the military, as in the case of Phra Prachak Kutachitto. This monk who fought to save the Dong Yai Forest in the northeast province of Buri Ram, and who was later suspected of corruption, fought relentlessly against the Government's forced relocation programmes and eucalyptus schemes that he believed were detrimental to Dong Yai.

The dilemma for monks who take to the forest is that they come to be regarded as especially pure in the sense of authentic, committed and incorrupt, and, consequently, tend to attract large numbers of people from the urban areas who believe that merit making, *tum bun*, with these monks as recipients of their gifts is highly efficacious. Several Thai forest monks have become well known and highly respected for their learning and piety both in Thailand and abroad, including Phra Ajaan Man Phuurithato (1870–1949) and his disciple Ajaan Chan (1924–93). The latter's monasteries in Northeast Thailand, Wat Hong Pah Pong and Wat Pah Nanachat, an international monastery attract people from all over the world who are interested in being ordained as Buddhist monks. Ajaan Chan also founded the British Forest Sangha, branches of which have been established in California, Switzerland, Italy, New Zealand and Australia (see Chapter 4).

Though close to people and often involved in their struggles, forest monks can be extremely doctrinaire and critical of traditional rituals and beliefs, a case in point being the previously mentioned and highly influential Buddhist teacher Buddhadasa Bikkhu (1906–92), founder of the Suan Mokkh community, a forest monastery established in 1932 in the southern province of Surat Thani. One of the founder's dictums – if a rite is not Buddhist let it fall into disuse (Gabaude, 1990: 215) – reveals his passionate concern to purify Buddhism of all non-Buddhist practices, especially the veneration of spirits, widespread practices such as *sadokroh*, a rite by which a bad destiny is replaced by a more favourable one, and every form of merit making for a better next life. Buddhadasa, who was greatly influenced by Zen, also broke with conventional wisdom by insisting, as do some of the founders of the Japanese NRMs (see Chapter 12), on the possibility for everyone, including lay people, of attaining enlightenment in this life, thus rejecting interpretations of this goal as an extremely vague and distant possibility (Gabaude, 1990: 212).

Again, in a manner similar to that of modern Buddhist reformers – and Hindu and Muslim reformers – in India, Sri Lanka and East Asia (see Chapters 10, 12 and 13), Buddhadasa believed that by uncovering the core truths of Buddhism he would also reveal its universal character. He sought, thus, to strip away what he saw as the myths that obfuscated its essence. In this he alarmed the Thai Buddhist hierarchy and many ordinary Buddhists also. Particularly traumatic for the elders of the Sangha was his assertion that the words and content of the Pali canon were not necessarily those of the Buddha. By demythologizing the canon, Buddhadasa believed he was laying bare Buddhism's foundations in those 'natural truths' that were the spiritual and intellectual property of all regardless of race, nationality or creed. In line with this attempt to display this universal character of Buddhism, he made use of the concept of *sunyata* or voidness to explain the fundamentals of modernity including the modern revolution in communications and how human beings should respond to both the contents and effects of that revolution (Thipaythasana and Progosh, 2000).

Not only was Buddhadasa's teaching or *sasana* doctrinally radical in the Thai context, it was also perceived as socially radical in that same context, especially in the way it attacked the widespread understanding of *kum* (karma), which people used to make sense of inequalities of all kinds. As in the Protestant Buddhism of Sri Lanka (Gombrich and Obeyesekere, 1988) he placed the emphasis on each individual's moral responsibility for their own condition.

The response to Buddhadasa's radical if unsystematic reinterpretation in the Thai context of Buddhism has been either extremely positive or totally negative. There are those who greatly appreciate what they see as his attempt to present Buddhism in a new, but authentic, light, as a culture of awakening from 'greed (capitalism) and ignorance (conservatism, traditionalism)'. His great achievements are seen as having been his teachings on the identity of Nature and *Dhamma*, his creation of a middle way between the vocation of books (*gantha-dhura*) and/or dedication to the intellectual and/or textual dimension of Buddhism and the vocation of meditation (*vipasana-dhura*). Others speak of the balance he achieved between the attention he gave to wisdom or knowledge (*panna*) and the importance of the observance of the rule (*vinaya*).

Buddhadasa's focus on the practical concerns of Buddhism, such as economic and social inequalities and corruption among the religious and civil leadership, also constitutes part of his appeal, although what has been construed as, if not approval of, then a failure to denounce political dictatorship, created serious problems for his liberal supporters. Also much appreciated by his admirers was his belief, previously mentioned, in the possibility of enlightenment in this life. For some (McCargo, 1999: 219), this understanding of *satori* or enlightenment in the here and now forms part of his endeavour to create a more democratic foundation for the doctrine of karma.

Anyone who described the way in which Thai Buddhists venerated the Lord Buddha, the Dhamma and the Sangha as 'mindless' and an 'obstacle to spiritual liberation' was inevitably going to meet with strong opposition. Negative, even hostile, responses came from, among others, Phra Bodhirak or Photirak (b.1950), the founder of the utopian Santi Asoke reform movement, characterized by what Gabaude (1997: 167) describes as a form of 'inquisitorial asceticism'. The moral attack launched by Bodhirak on the Sangha in Thailand was as severe as any of the attacks made by the most radical of Protestant churches against Catholicism during the Reformation in Europe in the sixteenth century. Bodhirak was equally critical of Buddhadasa and his disciples. His principal objection was to what he viewed as Buddhadasa's intellectual approach to reform, to the emphasis he placed on intellect or wisdom (*panna*) at the expense of morality (*sila*). This, Bodhirak believed, would destroy rather than revive true Buddhism.

However, as we have just mentioned, Bodhirak's primary target was the Sangha, which he claimed engaged in various activities that had nothing to do with Buddhism: the making of amulets, the use of lustral water, the veneration of statues – this is also prohibited by Korean Won Buddhism (see Chapter 13) – and the use of money. Also heavily criticized was the Sangha's subservience to the rich, which was necessitated by its acceptance of expensive gifts.

In 1975 Bodhirak committed, in the view of the Thai political and religious establishment, two major errors, the first of which consisted of declaring himself independent of the Association of the Ancients, thus placing himself outside the three legally recognized Buddhist religious groups or orders in the country, the Thai, Chinese and Vietnamese orders. Then, without himself being one of the 'Ancients' for a period of ten years, he began to ordain monks, an act of defiance which, in Gabaude's words, constituted an 'unpardonable crime for a Buddhist religious' (1997: 167). This notwithstanding, people continued to come forward for ordination and among his followers there were a number of other influential lay people with high ranking positions in the army.

For Bodhirak, life lived according to the rule, *vinaya*, as laid down and practised by Buddha Gotama, which entailed the renunciation of the use of money, of meat eating, smoking, amulet making, and the veneration of icons of the Buddha, among other things, was the only sure means to save Buddhism from total decline. Ironically, he was defrocked – but not until 1992 – for violating the monastic precepts. Some would argue that the real motive for his dismissal, which he never accepted, was his close association with the now defunct, radical political party the 'Force of the Dharma' (Thai: *Phalang Tham*).

Though also anti-establishment, an 'asceticism of witness' (Gabaude, 1997) rather than one of 'inquisition' has been the main feature of other, modern Buddhist reform movements in Thailand, including the Sekhiyatham movement started in 1989 by the scholar-monk Sulak Sivaraksa. Though twice charged with lese-majesty for attempting to undermine the State but never actually prosecuted, Sivaraksa spends less time on directly criticizing the Sangha as an institution than, for example, Bodhirak. He does, however, appear to doubt the Sangha's ability or even desire to reform itself, and whether the State is seriously interested in such reform. It is against this background that the Sekiyatham movement attempts to provide a form of engaged asceticism that not only contributes to the reform of Buddhism but also provides citizens with a model of how to protect the environment and enable society to retain its essential identity under the impact of Westernization.

Although he describes himself as a 'Buddhist with a small b' and one who is open to the values of other faiths and cultures, Sivaraksa stresses the fundamental necessity of providing an alternative to Western education, which he describes as a system that is preoccupied with property, money, power and the ability to consume. What Sivaraksa, and reformers like him, are seeking to promote is learning for life, which involves learning about what separates people from one another and blinds them to their natural 'inter-relatedness', and their interconnectedness with all sentient beings. The principles of this kind of education – promoted in seminars and workshops on 'Humans and Their Learning' – will, it is envisaged, advance the cause of 'Engaged Buddhism' by making for greater awareness of social inequalities and of the need for social solidarity with those affected by venture Capitalism. This Sivaraksa attacks for its profit-only mentality, which, he believes, militates against the interests of the underprivileged. This philosophy lies behind his involvement in such campaigns as the attempt to prevent the construction of the Pak Moon Dam on the Mekong River, the Yadana gas pipeline, and the Thai-Malaysian gas pipeline schemes.

Increasing numbers of professionals – teachers, journalists, and doctors, among others – are attracted to this kind of 'Engaged Buddhism', which questions the narrow criteria used by politicians and economists to define development and implement development strategies. Locally, it provides a focal point for discontent with the way development is managed politically and at the same time creates sympathy and support for such groups as the World Social Forum anti-globalization movement whose main targets are the economic policies of big business and the United States.

On the other hand, there is also a growing concern that the real goals of Buddhism, and of religion generally, may be forgotten by an overemphasis on their social and psychological functions. The reaction to the Thai Government's decision in principle to introduce *vipassana* or meditation as a element of the personnel development programme for civil servants, a decision influenced by numerous 'scientific' studies which suggest that meditation improves work performance, is a case in point. Some critics are asking whether or not this will serve to illustrate the true meaning and purpose of Buddhist meditation, which, it is believed, is to free people from mental suffering by enabling them to understand that there is no 'me' to cling to and that 'we are interconnected'. Or will it further the goals of the mainstream economy, which 'spur[s] greed and consumption while intensifying the exploitation of nature as well as the weak and the poor . . . the opposite of Buddhism' (*Bangkok Post*, January 22nd 2004)? The Buddhist 'principle of interconnectedness', as it is called, is being championed as the way to counter the 'materialistic approach to meditation' taken by governments, companies and founders of new religions, and global Capitalism's negative economic and social effects on the poor. From this perspective the introduction of religious techniques into the workplace by governments and companies does not signify a religious revival but rather a hastening of the process, already advancing steadily, of secularization.

'Managerial' Buddhism is but another example of this process of the 'internal secularization of religion', of the impact on both its form and content of modern consumerist, secular attitudes and management styles. A striking illustration of this development is the controversial, but rich and influential, Wat Dhammakaya temple, founded in 1969 on a 1,000-acre estate in Pathum Thani province just north of Bangkok. In contrast with Suan Mokkh, this temple is both a symbol and a product of advanced consumerism. The attributes of a typical, modern corporation are in evidence. Even the great importance attached to cleanliness, order and a quiet atmosphere are in keeping with the ethos of such an organization. This is not fortuitous for this monastery in which senior monks act as managers and are accountable to a management board chaired by the abbot, a kind of Chief Executive Officer, has intentionally modelled itself on Thai International Airways. A controversial movement, mainly on account of the enormous wealth it has allegedly accumulated and the materialist, secular image it conveys, the Wat Dhammakaya, as McCargo (1999) points out, provides a 'managerial' alternative to orthodox Thai Buddhism, and at the same time a more autonomous form of Buddhism less influenced and controlled by the state. It often appeals directly over the Government to Thailand's wealthy elite, and increasingly, by placing greater stress on education and scholarship, to the better educated.

Although there are numerous NRMs present and active in the country from other parts of Asia, including Japan and China, there are relatively few indigenous Thai NRMs. There are also numerous cults that originated outside Thailand, one of the most popular being that of the bodhisattva of compassion, a male figure in Thailand, who is known by the Chinese name Guanyin (Sansrkit: Avalokiteshvara). Flourishing indigenous cults include that of the earth goddess Nang Thoranee. According to a widely known legend in Thailand, Nang Thoranee saved the Buddha when on the brink of his enlightenment, from attempts by Mara to hold him back, by wringing her long, flowing hair – upon which the Buddha had poured water when performing his rituals – to produce a mighty torrent that drove the devil and his army from the land. Also widespread is the cult of the Luong Phor, literally 'uncle' but implying 'venerable', monk. Sometimes called *arahat*, one whose mind is free of desire for and clinging to sensuous objects and of the accompanying sorrow and pain, and who is possessed of extraordinary powers, such monks are to be found in every region and in every district.

Among the few Thai NRMs that have acquired an international following is the Healing Dao movement founded by Mantak Chia (b.1944). Chia began opening centres in Thailand in 1974 – he established his national and international headquarters in Chiang Mai – to teach previously unknown aspects of esoteric knowledge, based upon his own version of the principles of the *Quanzhen Dao* school (Complete Reality School), for the purpose of expanding consciousness, improving health and for, if not immortality, then greater longevity. Other Thai NRMs include the Hindu-Buddhist movement started in 1978 by Luang Phor Bunleua Surirat in Nongkai, northeast Thailand. This yogi-shaman put together a philosophy derived from Hindu and Buddhist sources and created a mythological garden of Hindu and

Buddhist icons which has attracted a large following in northeast Thailand and Laos. The main altar of the principal temple, known as the Indian temple (*Wat Kaek*), contains portraits of several well-known founders of Indian NRMs, including Sathya Sai Baba (see Chapter 10).

Among NRMs from elsewhere in Asia that are active in Thailand are the Brahma Kumaris (BM) movement (see Chapter 10), the Vietnamese Cao Dai movement (see below), the Chinese *Falun Gong* movement (see Chapter 13), and a number of Japanese NRMs, the most successful of which is *Sekai Kyusei Kyo* or Church of World Messianity with an estimated 300,000 members. The size of membership alone does not indicate the impact this movement is having on Thai society. What is just as significant in this regard is the popularity of its courses in organic farming, which have been taken by hundreds of thousands of Thai farmers, and the numerous agricultural and environmental projects that the movement has initiated in co-operation with the Thai army. By contrast, Western movements such as Scientology appear to have made relatively little impact outside the large urban centres.

Though they may appear disconnected and different in content and aims, the changes and innovations in Thai religious culture can be considered to be part of what Taylor (1990) points out is 'an individualistic revolution'.

Vietnam: Engaged Buddhism

The focus in this part of the chapter is on Engaged Buddhism, the new Cao Dai Church and the Hoa Hao movement, referred to as a church manqué (Jumper, 1966).

Inclusiveness is a marked feature of the religious history of Vietnam, where, according to Jumper and Normand (1964: 418), the principal religion, Mahayana Buddhism, is 'eclectic, pragmatic, and strongly tinged with Confucianism and Daoism'. Moreover, most of the population, though nominally Buddhist, 'practice varying combinations of ancestor reverence, animism, Buddhism, Confucianism and Daoism' and for them 'religion is an individual and family matter, requiring little formal organization' (ibid.). Popular religion, which consists in the main of the cult of the spirits of the ancestors and of the communal spirits – both are believed to be very active in daily life – as well as of the spirits that populate the forests and countryside, also contains elements of Catholicism. But popular religion can vary greatly from region to region and even within the same region, a characteristic that has led to its being described as a 'geographical fact' (Keyes, 1977: 197).

Hindu influence in Vietnam dates back almost a thousand years and there is also a small Muslim presence, a variety of forms of Spiritism, including that developed by the nineteenth-century French medium Alain Kardec, of Spiritualism, of Chinese systems of divination and Japanese New Religions.

Historically, Chinese influence has always been strong and even after independence the Vietnamese continued to look to China for cultural inspiration. The mandarins and emperors of traditional Vietnam under the Nguyen in the first half of the nineteenth century 'saw themselves as Chinese players on a Chinese historical stage' (Woodside, 1971: 235). With French colonization in the nineteenth century, Catholicism, present in the country since the sixteenth century, began to assume greater influence. The overall cultural and psychological effect of French colonial rule on Vietnam was in Mus's words to throw the 'nation off balance' (McAlister and Mus, 1970: 38), and after repeated recourse to Confucianism to restore the equilibrium, it was eventually Buddhism that came up with the answer to the colonial crisis, but not until the 1930s.

Some of the Neo-Buddhist movements that emerged in the nineteenth century were essentially nationalist movements, while the American/ Vietnam War (1963–75) acted as a catalyst for those of the post-1960 era. This does not surprise given the long history of Buddhist nationalism in Vietnam, although not all of the Neo-Buddhist movements that emerged during the struggle with the United States gave unqualified support to the armed conflict.

Neo-Buddhist movements cannot be fully explained in terms of a response to colonialism or the American/Vietnam War. Internal factors were also at work, as in South Asia and in Thailand.

Although the majority of the country's more than 80 million inhabitants are Buddhist, few Vietnamese practised their religion with any regularity until a revival got under way in the 1930s. Moreover, until recently, Buddhism and Daoism, were considered to be an extension of popular religion rather than separate independent, distinctive traditions. For only a few, including the Khmer minority, had Buddhism, for hundreds of years, provided the dominant world view. Most people had a low opinion of monks and their status (Keyes, 1977: 198). The English envoy Crawfurd, in his report on his trip to Southeast Asia in 1820–21, described ministers of religion as the meanest orders and little respected (1967: 499). Many were 'full-time specialists' in the magical arts. A majority of practitioners were elderly women, and only a very few had more than a smattering of knowledge of Buddhist doctrines. On the other hand the bodhisattva of compassion, Guanyin, was widely venerated and the guidance, prayers, blessings and protection of *arahats* greatly prized (ibid.).

In the 1930s organizations such as the Cochin China Buddhist Study Society, the Amnan Buddhist Study Society and the Vietnamese Buddhist Study Society were founded in an attempt to rescue Buddhism from its parlous state and to use it to resolve the cultural crisis of colonialism, something which Confucianism as was mentioned above appeared incapable of accomplishing. This endeavour was actually supported by the colonial administration. The motives were not purely altruistic for, as Thich Nhat Hanh points out, the reasons included the colonial Government's desire to place its own people in these institutions and thereby control them, and to focus people's attention on religious observance and to gain their gratitude (Nhat Hanh, 1967: 41). Thich Nhat Hanh refers to other more religiously motivated influences on the revitalization process in Vietnam from China, and from Cambodia and Thailand. External influences notwithstanding, the effect was that by the outbreak of World War II when the country came under Japanese occupation Buddhism was in a position for the first time in modern times to provide many Vietnamese with an acceptable solution to the cultural crisis generated by colonialism. The purpose of this new Buddhism was to enable practitioners to become truly aware of themselves and of the situation they were in, for, according to Thich Nhat Hanh, what was lacking was 'awareness of what we were [and] of what our situation really was' (Nhat Hanh, 1974: 147).

Other Buddhist reform movements emerged and headed in a different direction, and among these was the previously mentioned Hoa Hao movement. The defining moment, however, for modern Vietnamese Buddhism came in the early years of the American/Vietnam War (1963–75).

The American/Vietnam War and Engaged Buddhism

The year 1963 saw the persecution and jailing of monks by the Ngo Dinh Diem regime, and the self-immolation by fire in protest against this American persecution and against the Vietnam War by several monks, including Thich Quang Doc. Two of the most important consequences to follow this persecution and protest were: the full-scale intervention of the United States in Vietnam and the establishment of the umbrella organization the Unified Buddhist Church of Vietnam (UBC) and/or the United or Unified Buddhist Congregation (UBC), the most significant of the recent developments in Vietnamese Buddhism. The original aims of this movement were threefold: to end the suppression of Buddhist activities by the Catholic authorities in South Vietnam, who were supported by the Americans; the creation from a disparate group of Buddhist and ethnic groups, an integrated Buddhist response to the War; and the promotion of Engaged Buddhism, a concern also of many monks in Thailand and elsewhere, as we have seen.

Despite internal differences over the role of Buddhism in politics, the UBC became for a short time, under leaders that included Thich Tri Quang, Thich Quang Do and the previously mentioned Thich Nhat Hanh, the strongest voice in Vietnamese politics. In 1966 monks in their thousands were arrested and imprisoned and the UBC driven underground, from where it continued its engagement with society through relief work among those worst affected by the War.

After the fall of Saigon in 1975 the new, independent, socialist Government was unprepared to tolerate such an effective and independent-minded institution as the UBC and, consequently, severely limited its activities. In 1981 the UBC was banned and replaced by a more manageable and compliant Buddhist Church of Vietnam which Buddhist groups were encouraged to join. The UBC continued in its struggle, without official recognition, for religious freedom and a more open society under the new socialist regime and this campaign reached the attention of many outside Vietnam as house arrests and the imprisonment of monks became more frequent in the 1980s. These reached a turning point, in terms of international publicity, with the house arrest and imprisonment of the UBC leader, the Nobel Prize winner Thich Quang Do, in 1992.

The global interest in Engaged Buddhism owes much to Thich Nhat Hanh's initiatives in Vietnam and abroad, particularly in the United States and Europe. One of the founders in 1964 of the Van Hanh University in Saigon and the School for Social Service, which did much to promote Engaged Buddhism during the American/Vietnam War, Thich Nhat Hanh also started in 1965 a new branch of the Lam-Te movement, the Order of Interbeing (Tiep Hien Order). The purpose of this order, composed of monks and lay people, was also to further the cause of Engaged Buddhism. Prior to going into exile in 1966 he played a prominent role as strategist and spokesperson for the Struggle Movement, which sought to make known the Buddhist perspective on peace in Vietnam without supporting either North or South. He has ordained over 100 monks into the Lam-Te order since its foundation.

Throughout his period in exile Thich Nhat Hanh has supported the peaceful approach to the resolution of conflict, and had a profound influence in this respect over the leaders of the Civil Rights movement in the United States in their opposition to the American/Vietnam War. He was eventually to establish the Église Bouddhique Unifiée (United Buddhist Church) in France, which has a large following both among Vietnamese abroad and North American and European converts to Buddhism. While people do convert to Buddhism, Thich Nhat Hanh does not himself seek to proselytize, but rather encourages inquirers to take Mindfulness Training courses in an ecumenical spirit, as guides for mindful living while remaining committed to their own faith. This ecumenical spirit, long embedded in Vietnamese culture, is also manifest in Vietnam's largest NRM, the Cao Dai movement. A comparison between this movement and the Hoa Hao movement provides an insight into the diversity in terms of content, structure, social composition and aims of Vietnamese new religions.

The Cao Dai and Hoa Hao movements

Both the Cao Dai and Hoa Hao movements are millenarian, both are conservative and both have acquired a reputation for political pragmatism (Rambo, 1982: 429). Beyond this they are very different in terms of social composition, doctrine, ritual and structure. The Cao Dai movement is mainly middle class and has developed an elaborate hierarchical system headed by the equivalent of a 'pope' and a complex system of doctrine and practice, derived from the various religious traditions present in Vietnam, for the purpose of creating a global religion. By contrast, the Hoa Hao movement initially took the form of a puritanical, peasant-based religion of poor tenant farmers or smallhold peasants and is mainly confined to the western Mekong Delta, with no pagodas – their construction was prohibited – and few communal ritual activities.

Although it differs in these and other respects from the Hoa Hao movement, the Cao Dai movement, which claims to represent the third and final manifestation of God in the Orient, shares several features in common with other Asian NRMs, particularly in relation to its stated aims. It seeks to move away from the position of understanding and interpreting religions from the perspective of a specific region, religion and culture and, instead, to promote an understanding of all religions as essentially one. This new perspective is demanded, it maintains, not only by Cao Dai (literally high tower), or God, but also by globalization, which makes all distinctions of religion and race irrelevant. The concept of universal brotherhood is a fundamental idea and the movement's symbol for God is an eye – 'the master of the heart' – surrounded by clouds. An octagonal palace (*Bat Quai Dai*) is the abode of the Supreme Being, with whom the executive branch of the movement communicates through a body of mediums.

Cao Dai officially dates from 1926 but in fact it was a continuation of what a number of Spiritist movements were already practising. According to the movement's own account of its origins, various employees in the colonial administration involved in Spiritism and the use of opium were responsible for starting the religion, among them a certain Mr Lee van Trung, an official in the Colonial Council of Cochinchina. Trung was called upon by the spirit of an allegedly famous Chinese scholar under the T'ang to join others who were already worshipping Cao Dai. Later Trung and fellow Spiritists were ordered by Cao Dai to meet with Ngo Van Chieu, at one time an official in the French colonial administration in Vietnam. It was at this gathering that Cao Dai allegedly revealed to Ngo Van Chieu his intention to create the new religion of Cao Daism. Members worship Cao Dai, translated by the movement as God the Father, the Creator of the Universe, and the Father of Mankind and of all religions, and the Mother Goddess. The movement also defines itself as the God-Way (*Dai-Dao*), and insists that God is its founder, and Ngo Van Chieu simply his medium, and in this it believes itself to be unique. At first followers came in the main from smallhold rubber growers and other sectors of the middle class. Growth was rapid. By 1945 there were an estimated half a million members and by 1955 this had risen to one and half million. Then came repression under President Diem in 1955 and growth slowed down markedly.

Organizationally, the Cao Dai church is divided into an executive and a legislative branch, with the head of the former, the *Giao Tong*, under whom there are numerous dignitaries, exercising overall responsibility for the administration of the religion, and the head of the latter, the *Ho Phap*, acting as protector of the movement's laws. The main temple, known as the Holy See, is located at Nui Ba Den in Tay Ninh province, some 100 kilometres northwest of Ho Chi Min city, formerly Saigon. This temple is meant to show the fusion of the principal characteristics of Buddhist, Catholic and Islamic architecture – 'horizontality', 'verticality' and 'sphericity' [sic], respectively (Rambo, 1982: 431). The composition of its pantheon of superior spirits and deities gives a further idea of the eclectic and inclusive character of Cao Dai. It contains the Buddha, Lao Tzu, Confucius, Jesus, Joan of Arc, Victor Hugo, Sun Yat-sen, regarded by followers as the father of modern China, and Binh Kheim, Vietnam's Nostradamus.

The Cao Dai movement describes its basic tenets as being rooted in Asian and Western religions and philosophies, and like Japanese NRMs including Sekai Kyusei Kyo (Church of World Messianity) it seeks to bring together East and West (Clarke, 2000) in order to save both from catastrophe, a sentiment no doubt reinforced by the experience of World War II. A core belief is that those who live according to the divine precepts as revealed through their founder escape from what is described as the tragic cycle of birth and rebirth and become one with Cao Dai. The principal ceremonials and ritual practices are the adoration of God, the veneration of superior spirits, the veneration of ancestors and prayer four times a day. Vegetarianism is also practiced.

This movement, which has a highly developed social apparatus, is another example in Asia of engaged religion. In stating as its main purpose the unification of all religions, Cao Daism appears to mean in practice Buddhism, Confucianism, Daoism and Christianity, the latter in its French Catholic form. The Sai Baba movement (see Chapter 10) has set itself a similar goal, as did Theosophy (see Chapters 5 and 6) and several Japanese NRMs including the previously mentioned Ananai-kyo (the Religion of the 'three' and 'five'), a basically Shinto-spiritualist movement founded in 1949 that seeks to synthesize what it counted as the major world religions: Confucianism, Daoism, Buddhism, Islam, Christianity, Baha'i, the World Red Swastika Society of China and the Spiritualist tradition in Japan (Kitagawa, 1990: 316).

In a manner reminiscent of how other religions justify theologically the reason for their existence (see Chapter 1 and *passim*) Cao Dai accounts for its own in terms of the doctrine that every age requires a new messenger of God to reveal fully once again the essence of his teaching, which have been obscured by previous ages. According to this line of reasoning divine truth, therefore, does not alter but is obfuscated by desire, greed, self-interest and ignorance. This analysis of the plight of the human condition and of the reasons why God calls new prophets and/or messengers common in Asia and Africa is gaining ground worldwide.

The Cao Dai movement not only offers a lengthy critique of the ways in which the older religions – Christianity, Confucianism, Islam, Hinduism and Daoism, for example – have deviated from the essence of God's teachings, but also an explicit critique of the 'civilizing mission' of the white race, which believing itself to be especially privileged in matters of knowledge and truth, both human and divine, came to regard other peoples as heathen and ignorant and for this reason justified their repression. Fiercely nationalist at times during French rule, the Cao Dai, supported by the Japanese who trained and armed its first militia units, sided with the Viet-Minh independence movement until 1947, when it decided to adopt a neutral stance, and from this point on it became a spent political force.

While the movement claims to have once had as many as six million members in Vietnam, others put the figure at around two million when at its peak. There are reportedly thousands of members in other parts of Asia, including Australia, Japan, Cambodia and Thailand, and several thousand in the United States and Europe, and wherever Vietnamese have settled in significant numbers outside Vietnam.

To return to the Hoa Hao movement, which was briefly compared and contrasted above with the Cao Dai Church. Founded by a twenty-year-old visionary, Huyen Phu So, in Hoa Hao village in 1939, who allegedly prophesied the coming of the Japanese and the defeat of the French, the movement appealed greatly to sharecroppers and small farmers from, as we have seen, the western Mekong Delta region. Again growth at the beginning was rapid, membership allegedly reaching 100,000 by 1940 and several hundred thousand by 1945. By the mid-1970s officials were claiming a membership of three million, no doubt an overestimate of around two million. But a majority of the provinces of An Giang and Chau Doc were involved in the movement.

Like the Cao Dai Church, the Hoa Hao, which had assumed the position of a state within a state, with its own bureaucracy, system of taxation and its own militia, frequently engaged in military action. It deployed its troops against the Communist Viet Minh, who assassinated its prophet in 1947, and against all other comers, including the French, the Vietnamese Nationalist Government and the Cao Dai. During the American/Vietnam War this movement acted as a self-defence force, protecting its territories from Viet Minh control. Meanwhile, it had changed, at least organizationally, from a religious sect to a church with a central administrative headquarters at Tay An Pagoda and administrative committees in districts, villages and hamlets, with prayer towers everywhere for calling members to worship. Serious internal power struggles among aging leaders led to splintering and by the mid-1970s there were at least three sizeable factions. At the same time the movement virtually lost all of its political and military influence. More appealing, especially to students in the late 1970s were peace movements, including that started by the 'coconut monk', Kien Hoa, who had a sanctuary dedicated to peace built on an island near Ben Tre.

Religious change in Indonesia both resembles and differs from that in the rest of Southeast Asia, including Malaysia and Singapore. Its recent history has seen the emergence of new forms of old religion, resurgent Sufism, Islamic mysticism, and the rise of new religions, including Subud.

Indonesia

Indonesia has the largest Muslim population in the world but is not an Islamic state in the constitutional sense of the term, as Kratz (1990: 119) points out. What in fact the country has tried to do is to steer a path between the disestablishment of religion and the founding of an Islamic state. The predominance of Islam notwithstanding, religion is characterized by its variety, a variety that exists both within each religion and between them, and derives in great measure from the high degree of organizational autonomy and cultural integrity that many communities have managed to retain. As Howell (1982: 499) comments:

> In areas free of foreign religious influences or only slightly touched by them, religious beliefs and customs are as varied as the ethnic groups (the number of distinct languages has been estimated at 250 (Geertz, 1967: 24) which is an indicator of the number of ethnic groups). Indeed, *traditions may even vary extensively from settlement to settlement* as they are intimately related to the customary law (*adat*) of the community [my italics].

As was mentioned above, religion in Indonesia is also characterized by new forms of Buddhism, Hinduism, Islam, Christianity and Confucianism, most of which have been developed over the past half century.

Buddhism and Hinduism have a long history in Indonesia. The ninth-century Buddhist monument of Borobudur and its eleventh-century Hindu counterpart, both forming the temple complex of Prambanan, indicate something of the strength of these religions in central Java prior to the emergence of Islam as the main religion. The emergence of such movements as the fourteenth-century Sivva-Buddha cult of Java also suggests that these two religions presented themselves jointly (Kratz, 1990: 124), not unlike the relationship between Shinto and Buddhism in Japan prior to the Meiji restoration in 1868 and the onset of modernization. Though there is little incontestable evidence regarding its early history in the archipelago, scholars relying mainly on the eyewitness account by Marco Polo who visited Sumatra in 1292 are inclined to date Islam's arrival to the late thirteenth century (Van Nieuwenhuijze, 1974: 145) while others, relying more on archaeological and eppigraphical evidence, place it sometime between the late eleventh/early twelfth and the late thirteenth century (Kratz, 1990: 125 ff).

While Buddhism faded, Hinduism was later to become the main religion of Bali. Unlike Buddhism, Hinduism and Islam, which were largely coastal and urban phenomena and more inclusive in relation to local culture,

Christianity, which arrived in the early sixteenth century, concentrated its intensive missionary activity on areas largely unaffected by these other religions. The twentieth century was a time of rapid growth for Christianity, aided by the breakdown of local cultures and belief systems under the impact of the cash economy and Western education, the main passport to advancement in the new order. The Indonesian Chinese communities were particularly interested in this and large numbers converted to Christianity. Reactions from some of the other religions to Christian 'success' took the form of attempting to restrict evangelism by the churches, an attempt that the Government decided to oppose. Another reaction was to disseminate literature critical of Christianity, and yet another, was to adopt Christian approaches to education and missionary activity as in South Asia (see Chapter 10).

The construction of 'theistic' Buddhism, Confucianism and Hinduism

While the beginnings of the first wave of Buddhism over one thousand years ago, and possibly more, are associated with South Asia, the new Buddhism of the twentieth century is a development associated with the Western-educated, upwardly mobile Chinese and Javanese elite, many of whom have experienced considerable racial discrimination in the field of employment and other important areas of social life. Societies such as the Three Religions Association founded in 1934 were important in this revival as was the ethnically mixed Netherlands Indies Theosophical Society, which founded the Java Buddhist Association in 1929. These two organizations jointly organized the celebration of Buddhist festivals at Borobudur and founded multi-ethnic lay Buddhist associations including Perbudi, established in 1958. This organization soon fragmented and left undone its role as national co-ordinator of lay Buddhists and link with the Government.

The number of Buddhist monks and lay members increased slowly from the 1950s – initially most of the monks were ethnic Chinese from the Mahayana Buddhist school but had been trained by Theravada monks from Sri Lanka and Thailand – and by 1965 Buddhism had been recognized by the Government as one of the six religions deserving of protection and support under the Constitution.

Such recognition for a religion widely understood to be without a belief in a Supreme Being caused considerable controversy. The decision, however, by many of the ethnic Chinese members to return to their Mahayana tradition, which was considered more theistic than the Theravada tradition of Buddhism, took some of the sting out of the controversy for it enabled Buddhists to define themselves as theists. Thus, by the 1960s the High Council (*Maha Sangha*) of Indonesian Buddhists had begun to make announcements to this effect, stating that the Buddha God was the *Adi Buddha*, an Indian

Mahayana concept underpinned and legitimated 'with an ancient Javanese lineage' (Howell, 1978: 268).

In recent years Indonesian Buddhists, who number just over two million, 50 per cent of whom are ethnic Chinese, have concentrated their attention on the production and dissemination of literature and the establishment of associations to promote cohesion and unity. In addition to their success in attracting new members, one of the effects of this new Buddhism has been to facilitate closer contact between the Chinese and other ethnic groups in Indonesia.

Confucianism has also undergone redefinition in recent times in Indonesia. Again, under Chinese initiative, several associations were set up to disseminate its teachings in the 1950s including the idea, already mooted in colonial times that belief in *T'ien* or heaven – traditionally understood as an impersonal, cosmological force – was equivalent to the belief in God held by Christians and Muslims. Moreover, *T'ien* was endowed with divine qualities and attributes, and Confucius and other luminaries were described as His prophets. The Four Books and Five Classics were defined as 'sacred texts' by this Neo-Confucianian movement, and a set of rituals was drawn therefrom. All of this enabled Neo-Confucianism – a distinctly ethnic Chinese movement at the time – also to gain recognition as one of the six state-assisted and protected religions in 1965.

The circumstances in which the new Hinduism – which started as a new version of Balinese Hinduism before creating links with the wider Hindu community – arose were those of increased Christian missionary activity, more frequent intervention in every aspect of life by the colonial administration and the widening influence of Western learning. The inspiration behind this revival came from Bali intellectuals (*golongan baru*) in the early years of the twentieth century, who set about attempting to rationalize their religion in order to make it more relevant to the modern world. They were also concerned – and this was a striking innovation – to make its teachings accessible to all Balinese people, who would then be empowered to adapt it to their personal and community situation. As will be seen, Muslim reformers pursued a similar strategy.

Numerous organizations, whose purpose was not only the reform of Hinduism through these means but also the preservation of Hindu culture generally, began to emerge, and all of these eventually formed a single representative body, the Balinese Hindu Council, the *Parisada Hindu Dharma*, in 1959. This Council, like the Buddhist Council mentioned above, took the radically innovative steps in the Indonesian context of formulating and disseminating the idea of the Balinese One Almighty God, *Sang Hyang Widi*, of standardizing ritual practice and of democratizing the priesthood (Howell, 1982: 513). Closer contacts with Hinduism beyond Bali were also developed by the Council in the 1960s and the term 'Hindu religion' or 'Hinduism (*Agama Hindu*)' came to replace Bali Hinduism (*Agama Hindu Bali*). It was this change, similar to the changes in the notion of the Absolute made by Buddhist and Confucians noted above, that made it possible for Hinduism to become a recognized religion under the Presidential Decision and to qualify for official government sponsorship in 1965.

Evidence of the success of this revival can be seen in Java, where though still a very small minority of the total population, increasing numbers of people have started to practice Hinduism and where several new Hindu temples and seminaries for the training of religious teachers (*guru agama*) have been constructed.

Varieties of Islam

Before turning to new forms of Islam in Indonesia, something further needs to be said by way of background about its history and character. Until the nineteenth century Indonesian Islam's major current was Sufism or mysticism, and this was characterized, as was Islam as a whole, by its tolerance of diversity. From the nineteenth century increased contacts with orthodox reformers from the Near and Middle East, which colonialism tried to discourage, resulted in greater insistence on orthodox practice and the implementation of *Shari'a* or Islamic sacred law. Modernization and Westernization have also tended to undermine the acceptance of diversity and the emphasis on tolerance in favour of rigidity and intolerance, particularly in the coastal regions and among those with international connections.

Of all of the external influences, the impact of colonialism in Indonesia was perhaps the most decisive in shaping Indonesian Islam's present form and content. The Dutch attitude to Islam varied. The Dutch East India Company (VOC), which arrived in 1596, was mostly hostile and professed its support for Christianity. The Dutch Government adopted a policy of neutrality in 1803 but throughout its long period of influence on, and rule over, the archipelago its strategy was pragmatic, changeable, and inconsistent. By the early years of the twentieth century radical Muslim ideas from the Middle East and South Asia (see Chapters 7 and 10) were now becoming increasingly popular and led to the establishment of new Muslim schools (madrasahs) that trained students in the fundamentals of Islam. These institutions opposed mysticism, as did their counterparts elsewhere in the Muslim world, on the grounds that it violated the most important teaching of Islam, the Oneness of God (*tawhid*). Also like their counterparts elsewhere in the Muslim world including the Alh-i-Hadith in India (see Chapter 10), they challenged the authority of the schools of Islamic law and advocated ijtihād (Chapter 7), which involved a return to the Qur'ān and Hadith (Tradition) for direction on how to live in accordance with God's Law.

Reforms notwithstanding, a diversity of forms of Islam has persisted. For example, those referred to as *prijayi*, though they may be conservative or liberal Muslims in other respects, continue to emphasize the importance to their self-understanding and their identity of the cult of the ancestors, and generally, the animistic dimension of their religious life. Others, the *abangan*, insist on their Buddhist and Hindu pre-Islamic past and regard the Islam they practise, an Islam heavily influenced by these religions and by indigenous religious culture, as *Agama Jawa* or Javanese religion (Geertz, 1960). For this category, Islam is a local religion and this accounts for its custom to perform the hajj or pilgrimage to shrines of Muslim saints in northern Java rather than going to Mecca. Obviously, time spent away and the costs of travel were part of the reason for this development.

A third category is the Islam of the *santri* or 'orthodox' Muslims. The *santri* spend their lives in devotion in the *pesantren*, place of the *santri*. Somewhat eclipsed by the madrasahs or Muslim schools previously mentioned for most of the twentieth century these mainly rural-based *pesantren*, whose prestige greatly depends on the quality of leadership provided by its leader or *kiai* (Arabic: *alim*, teacher) who is required to display learning and spiritual leadership, have been regaining some of their influence in recent times (Kratz, 1990: 137), as has Sufism or mystical Islam.

Islam gained ground as the nationalist struggle intensified, a struggle to which Islam made an important contribution. With the Japanese occupation of the country from 1942–45 Islam found itself in the unusual position of being supported by a government. According to Howell (1982: 520–1):

> The Japanese, at least initially, promoted the strengthening of Muslim leadership. Thus most notably they sponsored the formation of an organization, the Masjumi, that united Indonesian Muslims both conservatives and modernists in a single, national-level organization.

Japanese support for Islam should not be exaggerated, for during the occupation they, like the Dutch colonial authorities, preferred to work though the traditional ruling families who had little sympathy for Islam, and the secularists. During the drafting of a Constitution for Independence in 1945, Muslim reformers and secularists were to clash over the question of whether Indonesia should be an Islamic or a secular state, secular in the sense of separating out state from religious matters. The eventual outcome involved the secularists accepting belief in God as one of five fundamental principles (*Panca Sila*) of national life. The 1945 Constitution did not contain any reference to Islamic law or Shari'a as the law of the state, nor did it include any statement that Muslims were obliged to follow their faith or that the President of the Republic should be a Muslim. This left everything unresolved, and indeed the question of the character of the state – secular or Islamic – has been a major bone of contention between Muslim reformers in Indonesia and elsewhere in the Muslim world during the past fifty years. Meanwhile there has been a revival of Sufism and a rise in various forms of neo-modernist Islam.

Resurgent Sufism and modernist and neo-modernist Islam

The revival of Sufi orders under the leadership of shaykhs schooled in Islamic colleges and well read in Western literature has come as a surprise to those who in the 1960s believed Sufism was dying for lack of interest among ordinary people and intellectuals alike (Geertz, 1960: 182–4). It was thought that Indonesian modernizers, who had long tried to eradicate mysticism on the grounds that it was non-Islamic, would deal it the final fatal blow by the end of the twentieth century. But the new Sufism of the 1970s was different; it was not only a popular movement but also a movement that demanded reform by insisting that a strongly developed inner life based on Islamic teachings, not just the outward performance of ritual obligations, was indispensable to being Muslim. One of its spokespersons argued that, for example, outward displays of conventional piety could mask the corruption plaguing the country (Howell, 1998: 279). This was clearly a radical line of argument that could be used to critique every aspect of political and social life and one also frequently encountered in the ideology of militant Islamic reform movements (see Chapter 7).

The reasons for the rise of the new Sufi groups throughout Indonesia were not only doctrinal but also existential and social. This was a socially aware form of Sufism that attempted to establish health and education centres wherever resources and personnel permitted. It offered institutional support and guidance to those most affected, both poor and wealthy, by the radical changes, political and economic, of the 1960s and after. It was also new in terms of its social composition. A religion of the elderly in the rural areas, the new Sufism attracted the young, the professional classes and many more women (Howell, 1998).

A new form of modernism, neo-modernism, also began to attract students in recent times. Neo-modernism is not a reaction to the rise of Sufism. It is more a reaction to the exclusive outlook of modernists, who reject not only mysticism but also everything else with the exception of their own 'realist' view of Islam. Kratz (1990: 143) describes them in these words:

> 'modernists' will accuse 'traditionalists' of rigid dogmatism, blind obedience to established teachers, the *kiai* and *ulema*, of insufficient intellectual inspiration and of escapist unrealism in the face of worldly (Western) challenges.

The strategy of modernizers of this kind has been to 'conscienticize' the masses by taking Islam out of the mosques, madrasahs (urban-based Muslim schools) and *pesantren*, and hand it directly to the people in all its purity as revealed in the Qur'ān.

Neo-modernism (Howell, 1998: 279) on the other hand rejects fundamentalism, and while committed to promoting authentic, orthodox Islam, and to eliminating corruption and moral laxity, has also sought to promote 'progressive' causes, including gender equality and monogamy. Students in general have been attracted by this neo-modernizing Islam, finding in it a more satisfactory way of responding to the impact of modernization and Westernization on Muslim culture, for them the most important question of the times. At a question and answer session after a lecture which this writer gave on 'Religion and Development' at Gadjah Mada University in Yogyakarta in the early 1990s the main issue that emerged and that was discussed at greater length than any other was that of the potential effects for good and evil on Islam of modernization and Westernization.

However, since the invasions of Afghanistan and Iraq by the United States and her allies in 2001 and 2003, respectively, a more exclusive, puritanical Islamic radicalism is offsetting the impact of neo-modernism among the student population and the youth generally. This development has seen a rise in the number of students joining Islamic, rather than university-based, organizations and associations, whose discourse is characterized by its anti-Communism – what is interpreted as left-wing literature is burnt – and an emphasis on the importance of reforming the moral situation of the nation. The external enemy is the United States, while bin Laden is recognized as a hero.

Indonesian religion remains far from homogeneous and its best known NRM, SUBUD, exhibits much of the diversity of religion and spirituality in the country, and reveals the status assigned to new movements. It is to a brief discussion of this movement that I now turn.

SUBUD

Though it was founded in the 1920s by Bapak (father) – Muhammad Subuh (Dawn) Hardiwidjojo (b.1901) – who came from the village of Kendungjati in Central Java, it was not until February 1947 that the movement took shape as an organization using the name SUBUD (henceforth written Subud). This acronym derives from the Sanskrit 'Susila Budhi Dharma', meaning surrender to the will of God.

Subud has never been recognized as a religion in Indonesia. Though a distinction was made between faiths, mystical groups and religions and though the range of what constituted 'genuine' religion recognized and supported by government was extended in 1965 by the Presidential Decision on religion to include Buddhism, Confucianism and Hinduism, it still remained the case that to be given public, legal recognition as a religion it was necessary to fulfil a number of criteria, all of which any new movement would find it difficult, if not impossible, to meet. As Howell (1982: 536) points out 'The "religions", in short, are required to approximate the form of orthodox Islam and Christianity more closely than the "faiths" and mystical groups are required to do'. One requirement is a long history and another 'revelations based upon humanity in past ages' (Howell, 1982: 536). Inevitably, then, Subud has remained an essentially Javanese Sufi or mystical movement based on the spiritual practice known as *latihan kijiwaan*.

Some of the reasons why Subud came into being can be gleaned from a brief survey of the founder's early life. He was clearly anxious to make headway in a colonial situation that made progress for all but a few of the elite families difficult. Bapak was not himself poor and his family traditionally enjoyed considerable status, his father worked on the railways. He was deeply involved in Sufi Islam, but as Javanese Sufis have historically tended to do, the focus was not on the externals of the Islamic faith but on the cultivation of 'inner' spiritual life. The formal obligations of Islam were considered to be of secondary importance and it is this tendency found in certain Sufi communities that creates great tension, mention of which has been made above, with orthodox or Sunni Islam. Nor did Bapak's family consider it necessary to make the pilgrimage to Mecca. In other words it bore a close resemblance to that grouping of Muslims whom Geertz placed in the *abangan* (see above) category.

From the age of seventeen Bapak frequented *kebatinan*, the courses on Javanese Islamic spirituality and mysticism given by *kiai* (teachers) to small groups (sometimes called interiority groups). He also learnt techniques for acquiring invulnerability, including the martial art *pencak silat*, and became well versed in the spiritual regimes of the Sufi orders, including those of the Naqshabandi Order, with a view to acquiring ultimate knowledge. He believed that his search had been rewarded in 1925 when a divine source of revelation confirmed his conviction that through the previously mentioned 'spiritual practice', the *latihan*, operating as an 'inner guide', one would develop an attitude of surrender to the Divine, and that the involuntary physical movements that resulted from this practice were indispensable means of self-cleansing and self-empowerment. Some years later in 1933, during an out-of-the-body experience in which he communed with Moses, Jesus Christ and the Prophet Muhammad, Bapak also had his mission to spread the knowledge and practice of the *latihan* worldwide confirmed.

He formed his own student groups or *kabatinan* in the 1930s and these began to thrive after the liberation of the Indies from Dutch and Japanese occupation and the declaration of Indonesian Independence in 1945. Yogyakarta, to where Bapak Subuh moved in 1946, became the main centre of growth. Like other similar mystical or kebatinan groups, Subud sought recognition as a religion, but due to opposition from strict Muslim and Christian groups, this was refused to 'new religions' (*agama baru*) by, as was previously noted, a Presidential Decision in 1965 which recognized as religions only six world religions. Subud decided consequently not to identify itself as a religion and advised members to continue to belong to one of the recognized religious traditions.

As its growth in Indonesia began to decline with economic setbacks from the 1960s, the movement made plans to attract an international membership. A leading exponent of the movement in the West was the physicist John Bennett (Sullivan, 1998: 302) who introduced the *latihan* to his Gurdjieff circle (see Chapter 4). The founder himself visited numerous Gurdjieff groups in the 1950s and by the 1980s the movement had established its European headquarters in Windsor, in the UK, and had opened branches in sixty countries, all of them responsible to the World Subud Association in Jakarta. Officials known as 'helpers' are the principal missionaries and spiritual guides and by 2003 they had established Subud groups all around the world.

Conclusions

In Southeast Asia, as in South Asia, it would be difficult to exaggerate the significance and impact of some of the 'new' interpretations given to old, established truths whose meaning everyone was convinced they had grasped, of the changes in people's understanding of the meaning of religious concepts, and of the purpose of religious rituals and symbols. Increasingly widespread, for example, is the 'new' understanding of enlightenment which growing numbers of Buddhist teachers and practitioners contend should be seen as a means to an end and not, as has been widely taught, an end in itself. If pursued as an end in itself, enlightenment, it is thought, becomes as a mere plaything, its real purpose being to change the world. This way of thinking is common where Engaged Buddhism has taken or is beginning to take hold, for example, in Thailand, Cambodia and Vietnam where increasingly the demand is for a more practical, this-worldly, but uncommercialized spirituality.

As for the rise of NRMs in Thailand, there are a number of attractive explanations including the interpretation that sees them as a reaction to the parlous state of the orthodox Sangha, a view that was given support above, which has come to be widely regarded as ill-informed, secular and without commitment to the real cause of Buddhism. In the absence of a committed Sangha many Thais have become seekers, and the same can be said mutatis mutandis of the Vietnamese. Some of Thailand's New Religions can also be viewed from the perspective of fundamentalisms of an Islamic and Christian kind. They can be compared to the rise of *dakwah* or Islamic movements in Malaysia and Indonesia, for example, and to evangelical Christianity in Singapore, Korea and elsewhere in Asia that critically appropriate elements of modernity alongside transformed traditional elements. Such NRMs create an innovative blend of religion and culture that is designed to preserve Thai Buddhist identity against that represented by the Sangha and what is perceived as a morally compromised secular society (Swearer, 1991). Other NRMs, as we have seen, facilitate such compromise.

Thai NRMs no more than Vietnamese or Indonesian or the NRMs of any other country cannot be correlated simplistically with country-specific patterns of religious, social and economic change but are part of a global phenomenon. The concern for a relevant spirituality, noted in relation to so many NRMs across Asia and the rest of the world, is strongly present in the modern reform-oriented Sufism of Indonesia. Also evident in Indonesian Islam and everywhere across the region is the growing objectification of religious knowledge and the consequent loss of control by the traditional elites or specialists over religious discourse. Simultaneously, competing interest groups have emerged led by their own teachers and guides, giving rise to even greater ambiguity and ambivalence regarding the homogeneity and unitary character of Islam.

Noticeable in Indonesia among Buddhists and Hindus in particular is their concern to display their monotheistic credentials, a concern generated in part by the demands of the country's Constitution. Also noticeable across the region is the increasing popularity of Zen and Mahayana Buddhism generally, a development due possibly to the interest in enlightenment now and with the search for compassion in a world of increasing risk and insecurity. While obvious comparisons can be made with Neo-Hinduism and Protestant Buddhism (see Chapter 10), these must not, however, be overdrawn, for despite the overlaps the cultural and political conditions in which religion operates and the perceptions of its role and function differ markedly from South to Southeast Asia.

References and select bibliography

The interviews noted in the text are from the author's fieldwork on popular Buddhism in Thailand between 2000 and 2004.

Clarke, Peter B. (2000) 'Modern Japanese Millenarian Movements' in Peter B. Clarke (ed.) *Japanese New Religions: In Global Perspective*, Richmond, Surrey: Curzon Press, pp. 129–82.

Crawfurd, John (1967) *Journal of an Embassy to the Courts of Siam and Cochin China*, Kuala Lumpur: Oxford University Press.

Gabaude, Louis (1990) 'Thai Society and Buddhadasa: Structural Difficulties' in Sulak Sivaraksa (ed.) *Radical Conservatism: Buddhism in the Contemporary World*, Bangkok: Thai Inter-Religious Commission for Development – International Network of Engaged Buddhists, pp. 211–29.

Gabaude, Louis (1997) 'Le Renouveau Buddhiste en Thaïlande est-il possible? Le case de l'ascétisme social' in Catherine Clémentin-Ojha (ed.) *Renouveaux Religieux en Asie*, Paris: École francaise d'Extrême-Orient, pp. 155–75.

Geertz, Clifford (1960) *The Religion of Java*, New York: Free Press of Glencoe.

Geertz, Hildred (1967) 'Indonesian Cultures and Communities' in R. T. McVey (ed.) *Indonesia*, New Haven, CT: HRAF Press, pp. 24–96.

Gombrich, Richard and Obeyesekere, Gananath (1988) *Buddhism Transformed: Religious Change in Sri Lanka*, Princeton, NJ: Princeton University Press.

Howell, Julia D. (1978) 'Modernising Religious Reform and the Far Eastern Religions in Twentieth Century Indonesia' in S. Udin (ed.) *Spectrum, Essays Presented to Sutan Takdir Alisjahbana on his Seventieth Birthday*, Jakarta: Dian Rakyat.

Howell, Julia D. (1982) 'Indonesia: Searching for Consensus' in Carlo Caldarola (ed.) *Religions and Societies: Asia and the Middle East*, Amsterdam: Mouton, pp. 497–548.

Howell, Julia D. and Nelson, P. L. (1998) 'Indonesian Sufism: Signs of Resurgence' in Peter B. Clarke (ed.) *New Trends and Developments in the World of Islam*, London: Luzac, pp. 277–98.

Jumper, Roy (1966) 'The Cao Dai of Tay Ninh: The Politics of a Political Religious Sect in South Vietnam' in B. G. Gokhale (ed.) *Asian Studies*, Bombay: Popular Prakashan, pp. 142–54.

Jumper, Ray and Normand, M. Weiner (1964) 'Vietnam' in G. McTurnan Kahin (ed.) *Governments and Politics of Southeast Asia*, Ithaca, NY: Cornell University Press.

Keyes, Charles F. (1977) *The Golden Peninsula*, New York: Macmillan.

Kitagawa, Joseph (1990) *Religion in Japanese History*, New York: Columbia University Press.

Kratz, E. U. (1990) 'Islam in Indonesia' in Peter B. Clarke (ed.) *Islam*, London: Routledge, pp. 119–49.

McAlister Jr, John T. and Mus, Paul (1970) *The Vietnamese and their Revolution*, New York: Harper & Row.

McCargo, Duncan (1999) 'The Politics of Buddhism in Southeast Asia' in Jeff Haynes (ed.) *Religion, Globalization and Political Culture in the Third World*, London: Macmillan, pp. 213–39.

Nasser, Hossein (1987) *Traditional Islam in the Modern World*, London: Kegan Paul.

Nhat Hanh, Thich (1967) *Vietnam: Lotus in a Sea of Fire*, New York: Hill & Wang.

Nhat Hanh, Thich (1974) *Zen Keys*, NewYork: Doubleday, Anchor.

Rambo, Terry A. (1982) 'Vietnam: Searching for Integration' in Carlo Caldarola (ed.) *Religions and Societies. Asia and the Middle East*, Amsterdam: Mouton, pp. 407–44.

Stockwell, A. J. (1999) 'Southeast Asia in War and Peace: The End of European Colonial Empires' in Nicholas Tarling (ed.) *The Cambridge History of Southeast Asia*, Cambridge: Cambridge University Press, pp. 1–58.

Sullivan, Matthew Barry (1998) 'Subud: An Experience' in Peter B. Clarke (ed.) *New Trends and Developments in the World of Islam*, London: Luzac, pp. 299–310.

Swearer, Dan (1991) 'Fundamentalistic Movements in Theravada Buddhism' in Martin E. Marty and R. Scott Appleby (eds) *Fundamentalisms Observed*, Chicago: University of Chicago Press, pp. 628–91.

Taylor, R. L. (1990) 'New Buddhist Movements in Thailand: An "Individualistic Revolution", Reform and Political Dissonance', *Journal of Southeast Asian Studies*, 21(1), 140–3.

Thipaythasana, Machee Pairor and Progosh, David (2000) *The Natural Truths of Buddhism*, Surat Thani: Buddhadasa Foundation.

Van Nieuwenhuijze, C. A. O. (1974) 'Indonesia' in Joseph Schacht (ed.) *The Legacy of Islam*, Oxford: Oxford University Press, pp. 144–55.

Woodside, Alexander (1971) *Vietnam and the Chinese Model*, Cambridge, MA: Harvard University Press.

Chapter 12

East Asia (1)

Japanese NRMs

Japan is often described as a non-religious society and this is how most Japanese would define themselves, especially when asked by non-Japanese, partly for the reason that they wish to indicate that they do not practise a religion in the Western sense. Many visit temples but few actually 'belong' to a religion in the sense of attending on a regular basis the public worship of either of its two main religions, Shinto and Buddhism. These are not, of course, congregational religions in the strict sense of the term. In the past more than today households represented by the household head belonged to the local Buddhist temple, but individual members had no obligation to attend or practise on anything like a regular basis.

Although not religious in the sense of belonging to a congregational religion, most Japanese confess to being spiritual in the sense of holding and attaching importance to spiritual beliefs. Thus, although they do visit temples to pray on important occasions, to petition for things they desire, and to make expiation for wrongs committed, and make pilgrimages to sacred places, the majority of Japanese, like Chinese, fall into the category of being spiritual but unchurched. As Shimazono (2004: 275) comments on the involvement in 'unchurched' spirituality in Japan:

> Established Buddhist sects have long been declining . . . [and] an increasing number of people are now involved in an individualistic spiritual quest utilizing media and various networks outside organized religions . . . the goal of these individualistic seekers is quite different from that of organized religions, so they would rather use the term 'spirituality' than 'religion' to designate their common interest.

Shimazono goes on to say (2004: 276) that the central concern of the new spirituality is 'the transformation of consciousness by using various techniques and bodywork'. In Chapter 1 we have already touched upon the question of whether this new spirituality can also be described as subjective, in the same sense as this term is used in Europe and the United States. As was seen in Chapter 1, in Japan the self would seem to be understood in a more relational, contingent sense, rather than in the sense of the existence of a given, irreducible 'I'. If this is the case, then it will make for a different understanding of the sense given to the term 'subjective spirituality' in Japan than, say, in Europe or North America.

With regard to New Religious Movements (NRMs), these have flourished in Japan throughout the period under review here and many have become global religions in their own right. Among the issues considered in this chapter in relation to these NRMs and the new holistic spirituality are problems associated with the term 'new', theories of the rise of new forms of religion – including new forms of Christianity – and the question of new religions and violence (see also Chapter 3), this last-mentioned issue being discussed with special reference to Aum Shinrikyo and the violence it perpetrated by launching a sarin gas attack on the Tokyo underground station on March 20th 1995.

Consideration is also given to the development and specific features of 'Engaged Buddhism' Japanese style, to the distinctive kinds of millenarianism created by the Japanese NRMs, to the dynamics of religious change in Japan, and to the expansion overseas of the Japanese NRMs. Also addressed are the dynamics of religious adaptation. It would seem to be the case that while Buddhist- and Shinto-Buddhist-related Japanese NRMs can successfully adapt to other religious cultures, Christian-related Japanese NRMs have been unsuccessful in their attempt to adapt to Japanese society.

New religion

This is an appropriate point to make some brief comments on terminology and chronology before discussing the goals and the other aspects of Japan's NRMs mentioned in the opening paragraphs above. The terms 'shinko shukyo' (newly arising religion) and 'shin shukyo' (new religion) came into use among journalists and scholars in the 1950s, and since the 1960s the latter term has been the more widely used of the two. There is also a third label in use and that is the controversial term 'new, new-religions' (shin shinshukyo), which is intended to indicate a more recent stage in the development of the 'new' religions. This term is applied in particular to those movements such as Mahikari (True Light), Agonshu (Agama Sutra Sect) and Kofuku no Kagaku (Institute for Research in Human Happiness) that rapidly increased their membership in the 1970s and 1980s and made maximum use of modern technology and modern means of communication, while other, older movements such as Soka Gakkai (Value Creation Society) had already begun to peak. Although the differences between new and new, new religions are not primarily over ideology (Reader, 1988) the latter place, nontheless, a greater emphasis on traditional spiritual explanations of life accompanied by a strong belief in miracles, and attach greater importance to the appeasement of ancestors and to tradition in general (Blacker, 1994).

As to chronology, four suggestions have been made, the first of which looks to the beginning of the nineteenth century as the starting point. Those who take this position point to the rise and popular appeal at this time of new religions based on mountain worship such as Fuji-Ko. The second proposed starting date is the middle years of the nineteenth century when Kurozumikyo, the Teachings of Kurozumi (Hardacre, 1986), Tenrikyo (Teaching of Heavenly Truth), and Konkokyo (Teaching of the Golden Light) began to attract followers. The principal reason for this choice as starting point is that all three of these movements were to have a great influence on later Japanese new religious movements.

For similar reasons others look to the late nineteenth century as the beginning of the NRM phenomenon, stressing the importance of the ideology and rituals of the new Shinto movement Omoto (Great Origin), which was started in 1892, on the development of future new religions in the twentieth century, including Seicho no Ie (House of Growth) and Sekai Kyusei Kyo (Church of World Messianity). The fourth position suggests the beginning of the post-Second World War era when many new movements such as Soka Gakkai, although founded in the 1920s and 1930s, began to flourish with the introduction of the principles of religious freedom and the separation of 'Church' and State. While there are problems with all four starting points, there is a great deal of support among students of Japanese NRMs for position two mentioned above (Inoue, 1991: 4ff.) and that is the one adopted here.

Japanese NRMs and the religious past

Clearly discernible in a number of Japanese NRMs are elements of so-called Japanese folk religion or shamanism, which shares much in common with Shinto. The latter, although widely thought of as the religion of the Japanese from time immemorial, is a term formed from Chinese characters meaning the 'way' and 'god', a development that suggests that it was influenced by Daoism. Japanese folk religion consists of beliefs and practices concerned with fertility, hunting and rice rituals, among other ritual activities, that remain unsystematized and uncoordinated, while Shinto is a more developed system of these beliefs and practices and this development came about as a response to the arrival of Buddhism, Confucianism, and to a lesser extent Taoism, from China. In time an elaborate theory of Shinto-Buddhist syncretism, known as *honji suijaku* (the prime entity and its manifestations), was constructed, according to which Shinto kami or gods came to be regarded as secondary manifestations of certain buddhas or bodhisattvas, compassionate beings who postpone the opportunity of enlightenment to help others. Various sects, including Ryobu Shinto and Sanno Shinto, emerged in the Kamakura period (1185–1333) to give expression to this idea. However, Shinto scholars were later to invert this theory and claim that the buddhas and bodhisattvas were merely manifestations of the kami, who constituted the primary spiritual entities or principles of order in the universe.

The Meiji emperors (1868–1912) separated out Shinto from Buddhism and turned it into a state or national religion, a link that was disconnected after the Second World War when Japan's new constitution declared the country to be a secular state. In contemporary Japan there exist four types of Shinto: Imperial, Shrine, Sect and Folk Shinto. The basic philosophy and rituals of Shinto have greatly influenced, as will be seen, many of the Japanese NRMs.

The Mahayana tradition of Buddhism arrived in Japan during the first half of the sixth century from China through Korea. Initially it was the religion of the court and was for some time considered a Chinese religion, as was the case in Korea and Vietnam (see Chapter 13). Like Taoism and Confucianism in Japan, Buddhism was to undergo a process of domestication. Confucianism and 'Neo-Confucianism' – the latter term refers to the revival of Confucianism in China during the Sung dynasty (960–1297) – were, at various times, to exert considerable influence on the government, the education system and the ethical and moral life of Japan. According to Earhart, Neo-Confucianism 'defined the major rationale for the Tokugawa Government in achieving the unification of Japan, thereby creating the foundations on which modern Japan rests' (1982: 132).

Essentially, Confucianism provided Japan with a rational and secular philosophy that served the goal of internal unification and a basis for forging a united front in dealing with the outside world.

Christianity, brought by Catholic missionaries in the sixteenth century, reached its high point during what is referred to as the Christian century c.1549–1649. It was driven underground for most of the Tokugawa period (1603–1867), and severely persecuted, especially after the Catholic uprising in Kyushu known as the Shimbara revolt of 1637–38. Christianity has always been perceived as a foreign religion despite attempts to create a synthesis of Japanese culture and Christianity, including that by the Christian Uchimura (1861–1930) (see below). Although historically a weakness, the 'foreign' character of Christianity has become part of its appeal in recent times, as in contemporary China where the young are increasingly attracted to Western culture.

All of the above-mentioned strands, referred to collectively as Japanese religion, have undergone considerable change at regular intervals, sometimes initiated from above, by governments, or powerful interest groups, or scholars, and sometimes from below, by ordinary people discontented with government and religious leaders in equal measure. Over the centuries a synthesis of Shinto-Buddhism emerged which was more than the sum of the parts of either tradition and therefore new. This new synthesis has been occasionally fractured by developments such as Restoration Shinto during the seventeenth to the nineteenth century, whose advocates included the scholars Kamo Mabuchi (1697–1769), Motoori Norinaga (1730–1801) and

Hiratsu Atsutane (1776–1834). The aim of this movement was to purify Shinto of all foreign accretions, which included Buddhist influences. The modernizing Meiji dynasty (1867–1912) attempted, rather unsuccessfully, to replace Buddhism as the effective state religion with a Shinto State Church to ensure the unity of church and state. Internal opposition, outside, mainly Western, influence, and a revival of Buddhism obliged the Meiji Government to accept a non-religious form of Shinto, known as Shrine Shinto, which was disestablished after Second World War.

Aspects of Shinto cosmology that have influenced NRMs in Japan include its view of the human and the spirit world as interdependent. In Shinto thought the whole of the universe is Divine Spirit, which implies that there can be no separation between the divine and human spheres. Heaven, the original source of power and ancestral fountain of all that exists, is immaterialized Divine Spirit; earth is materialized Divine Spirit. Divine Spirit moves forward into self-creative human life and not backwards into immateriality. Shinto is concerned with *musubi* (literally producing) or the power immanent in Nature, also meaning self-growth, the impetus of self-effort, self-developing and self-creative energy. The purpose of Shinto devotion is to assist participants to concentrate on their own spiritual divinity and their responsibility for enabling Divine Spirit to progress to complete materialization. The notion that everything that exists is divine or kami underlies the Shinto principal of symbiosis, according to which there can be no separation of substance between the divine and human or one sphere of the universe and another.

Death is evil and traditionally Shinto offers little by way of rituals to cope with it. Believing that Divine Spirit is immortal, Shinto locates the source of evil in a spirit world, believes in the spiritual roots of sickness and misfortune, and understands salvation as the realization of the harmonious development of this world. Much of this thinking is present in the content of, among other NRMs, Omoto (Great origin) Sekai Kyusei Kyo (Church of World Messianity) and Sūkyō Mahikari (True Light Supra-Religious Organization).

Buddhism's intellectual contribution to the Japanese NRMs is not only clearly evident in lay Buddhist movements such as Soka Gakkai, but also in movements that are based on Shinto cosmology and ritual such as Perfect Liberty Kyodan, founded in 1957. This is not surprising given the history of Buddhism in Japan, which, as we have seen, from its beginnings there in the first half of the sixth century becomes, with occasional periods of stagnation and decline, ever more diverse and complex at every level from doctrine to ritual. Mahayana Buddhism in Japan – and this is important for an under-standing of Japanese NRMs that derive their ethos and worldview from this form of Buddhism generally – offers an affirmative response to society in contrast to the world-denying philosophy of so-called 'original Buddhism' which preaches the pursuit of inner, personal enlightenment as an end in itself, a pursuit which many contemporary reformers reject claiming that enlightenment is a means to an end – the end being social transformation – rather than an end in itself (see Chapter 11).

The Nichiren school of Buddhism has perhaps exercised more influence than any other on Japanese NRMs. This school was founded by Nikko (1246–1333), disciple of the outspoken, militant and messianic monk Nichiren Daishonin (1222–1288) who was the son of a fisherman from southeastern Japan. The strife-ridden and war-ravaged situation of Japan in the thirteenth century provided ideal conditions for apocalypticism and for messianic figures like Nichiren to flourish. Although Nichiren probably derived much of his teaching and practice from the long-standing esoteric tradition of Japanese Buddhism, his apocalyptic, millenarian message, in which he claimed to be the one sent by the Buddha to spread the word that the then present age was the third and final age of mappo, of degeneration, can only be understood in the context of the precarious situation in the Japan of his day.

Nichiren argued for the creation of a Buddhist state as an important part of his strategy for saving Japan from disaster, and under Tokugawa rulers (1603–1868) Nichiren Buddhism was treated as if it was the state religion and used by them to forge and sustain national unity, thereby replacing Shinto as the most powerful and influential religious force in the country. In this period Buddhism, already bound to the family through the rituals of ancestor worship which many had come to see as its primary function, came to exercise even greater influence over the lives of individual citizens and every family through the introduction of the *danka seido*. This was a system which linked every household to a temple, and which was only repealed in 1871 under the Meiji (1868–1912). For its part the Meiji Government not only sought to give priority to Shinto in the task of mobilizing the nation under the authority of the imperial house but also for a time sought to suppress Buddhism.

Although probably more eclectic and far less fundamentalist and exclusive in his views than is usually thought, the modern Nichiren shu school of Buddhism followed by Soka Gakkai (Value Creation Society) has often insisted that it is being faithful to Nichiren Daishonin's teaching by stressing that only the Lotus Sutra can save this world to the exclusion of all other paths. The latter include those of the Pure Land or Jodoshu schools, which teach that the recitation of the short phrase 'I put my faith in Amida Buddha' is all that is needed for salvation.

Goals of the New Religions

Japanese NRMs are often said to pursue the basic goals of Japanese religion, which consist of the attainment of personal well-being, the purification of the souls of the departed and the veneration of the ancestors. Kitagawa (1990: 305), who believes that the establishment of the principle of religious freedom was in large measure responsible for the emergence since the Second World

War of so many Japanese NRMs, attributes their popularity to faith-healing and utopianism (1990: 315) and claims that 'these new religions present nothing new as far as their content is concerned' (1990: 333). Specifically, with regard to the new millenarian movement Ananai-kyo (Religion of Three and Five) founded in 1949 to synthesize, as we have seen in Chapter 11, the teachings of the major religions of the world and which claims that the will of the kami or gods can be discovered by studying the movement of the heavenly bodies, Kitagawa comments: 'One might say . . . that Ananai-kyo is essentially a form of the simple spiritualism common to the Japanese folk religious tradition' (1990: 317).

Earhart (1989: 11) sees Japanese NRMs as 'developing out of the general background of Japanese religion . . . the unified religious world view of the Japanese people', and stresses that there is no substantial break or discontinuity between new and old religion in Japan. Most Japanese NRMs, he believes, like Gedatsu-kai founded by Okano Eizo in 1928, are: 'a reformulation of the unified world view of Japanese religion that enables members to go back to the heart of their tradition while at the same time going forward into the future' (ibid.: xiv).

Generally, Japanese NRMs see themselves as belonging to an old tradition and at the same time revealing for the first time eternal truths or the full and/ or correct interpretation of eternal truths that are part of that tradition. Thus, the tradition is thought to be faulty at its foundations and this provides an opening for an extremely radical view of the past. Agonshu, as we saw in Chapter 1, claims to be new or original as a result of its founder, Kiriyama Seiyu, having discovered the Agama sutras, which he claims are the earliest of the Buddhist sutras and previously unknown. Able to discern the hidden, inner meaning of these texts, Kiriyama went on to claim that he had uncovered a direct and rapid road to Buddhahood for the living and, just as importantly, for the dead. His teachings stress that the pacification of the spirits of the dead and the need to ensure that they attain enlightenment (jobutsu) is essential to the peace, prosperity and well-being of the living (Reader, 1991: 211).

For its part, Shinnyo'en simultaneously emphasizes the Shugendo and Shingon roots of its founder, Shinjo Ito, and, at the same time, points to the latter's 'discovery' of the Mahaparinivana sutra, said to contain the last teachings of the Buddha, and the essence of all he had previously been searching for and all he had so far learned. Out of the old, thus, comes something completely new; by basing their teachings on ancient texts and traditions these two movements claim uniqueness.

NRMs need not therefore be considered new, in the sense of providing entirely new systems of belief and practice, but can be considered new from the way they have restructured and reinterpreted Japanese cosmology and religion to provide for the first time an authentic version of the same. For example, Yamashita (1998) credits the founder of Tenrikyo, Miki Nakayama

(1798–1887), with providing in the Ofudesaki – revelations made to her by God the Parent – a new version of the myth of human creation:

> The Koki (myth of human creation) in the Ofudesaki is highly original because the idea of equality (therein) stood in sharp contrast to the reality of contemporary society in which the concept of karma was used to justify unequal treatment of people.
>
> (Yamashita, 1998: 132)

Examples of how traditional religious ideas and practices have been made *new* by leaders of Japan's new movements abound. Ooms (1993) interprets the use made of *kamigakari* (possession), by the founders of several Japanese NRMs, including Deguchi Nao (1836–1918) the founder of Omoto, in this way. Seeing these founders as essentially mediums and faith-healers, Ooms observes that they extended the related functions of possession and faith-healing to cover wider issues than was traditional:

> Unlike traditional mediums who articulated and structured the experience of their patients in terms of *prevailing models of reality* the founders of new religions made their patients' experiences meaningful in terms of the *new vision of reality* which they were constructing. A successful cure could result, therefore, in the dissociation of the individual from the *established socio-cultural system* . . .. The founders thus *expanded the function of faith healing far beyond the provision of immediate benefits.* They used it as a highly effective means of proselytization, for it enabled them to communicate a *new view* of the world by making it meaningful with regard to an individual's unique experience [my italics].
>
> (Ooms 1993: 17)

Hardacre (1990) also recognizes the ingenuity of Deguchi Nao and highlights this in her discussion of her interpretation and application of the Buddhist notion of the Transformed Male (henjonanshi) and Transformed Female (henjonyoshi). Nao claimed to have been changed by the command of the deity Ushitora no Konjin into a transformed male, or a female in a male body. Her co-founder, Onisaburo Deguchi (1871–1948), underwent a parallel change to become a transformed female in a male body. Hardacre, commenting on the 'originality' of the founder's interpretation of henjonanshi and henjonyoshi, which, she points out, has no antecedents in traditional Buddhist terminology, writes:

> Nao invented a neologism having the same pronunciation but written with different characters than the Buddhist term, and she interpreted the basic idea to mean a symbolic change of gender rather than a change of sex.
>
> (Hardacre 1990: 51)

More generally, Japanese NRMs have made a difference to the religious life of Japan by the emphasis in their teaching on monotheism – the most likely influences in this case being Jesuit Christian literature secretly imported from China and the tradition of the Kakure-Kirishitan or Hidden Christians (Kamstra, 1994) – and more recently on pacifism (Kisala, 1999). They have also created new kinds of religious institutions, developed new ritual techniques, and new ideas and sources of revelation. The stress they have placed on healing and on right thinking as the way to change the world, and the energy they have put into recruitment and expansion overseas among non-Japanese, are also new features.

Accounting for the rise and decline of Japanese NRMs

The reason most often given for the rise of Japan's NRMs is that they are a response to rapid, unprecedented, levels of social change (McFarland, 1967), an explanation discussed in general terms in a previous chapter (see Chapter 1). This kind of explanation fits more with the Meiji era (1868–1912) than with other periods of modern Japanese history.

The basis of McFarland's thesis is that Japan, a largely agricultural country characterized by high levels of interdependence and co-operation, both of which were necessitated by the demands of irrigation for rice production among other activities, and by social conformity, was transformed into an industrial society over a short period of time. Moreover, during the last fifty years of the relatively stable and authoritarian Tokugawa era (1603–1868) the conditions of the peasantry were particularly difficult, and this era saw the rise of among other new religions the previously mentioned new religions Kurozumikyo (1814), Tenrikyo (1838) and Konkokyo (1845), commonly known as the Peasant Sects. What made these conditions a breeding ground for the rise of millenarian movements such as Tenrikyo was the absence of any official channel through which redress could be sought. A similar condition gave rise to the messianic movements of Medieval Europe (Cohn, 1970). Recourse to official religion was not an option, as its standing in the mind of the majority was extremely low.

The new religions such as Tenrikyo not only offered healing but also new possibilities of 'corporateness' and a means of escape from *nayami* or the troubles of daily life. After first appealing to the peasant classes these movements and those that followed began to attract the new working class of the large cities, many of whom found in them beliefs and rituals and forms of association that enabled them to adapt to the new urban way of life.

The harsh conditions of modernization under the Meiji (1868–1912), the new taxes on land, the rapidly expanding money-based system of exchange, and the new criteria of success and failure all contributed to the emergence of the most intensely millenarian movement in the modern history of Japan, the previously mentioned Omoto (Great Origin) (1892), which used every possible symbolic and ritual means to oppose the new order.

A nationalist movement prior to the Second World War, Omoto since then has been strongly opposed not only to Japanese military expansion but to all forms of national expansion. It strives to promote a World Parliament, a World Language, Esperanto, and the unity of all religions. This movement further seeks to apply the Shinto principle of symbiosis to every aspect of life, for it claims that every sphere of life is sacred, and that every individual can interact positively with every other.

The 1920s and 1930s, which saw the rise of movements such as Soka Gakkai, Seicho no Ie and Sekai Kyusei Kyo, were also years of social and economic turmoil in Japan as elsewhere. To many who had left the rural areas for the towns it appeared that history was in reverse and had begun to undermine all their hopes and aspirations. Founders of new religions, themselves often from the same social and educational background as most of their followers, experienced considerable hardship and were looking for explanation and relief. Some like the founder of Sekai Kyusei Kyo had been members of Omoto, and were also searching for solutions to life's difficulties in non-Japanese religious circles, including, for example, the Salvation Army and the Jehovah's Witnesses in Tokyo. From these experiences and encounters they created new versions and explanations of old healing rituals, systems of education that focused on the importance of internal, subjective understanding and development that could provide a bulwark against the harsh and unpredictable effects of social and economic life, and a philosophy that looked to the integration of Eastern and Western civilizations.

The post-Second World War social, economic and cultural context was in stark contrast to the pre-war era. During the period 1945–c.1970, a period of reconstruction followed by economic success, new religions refined and adapted their teachings to life in the new, frantically busy, impersonal urban world preoccupied with rebuilding and modernizing and which was in danger of destroying traditional family and other values. As Inoue (2000: 16) points out, the Japanese NRMs of the post-Second World War period are particularly noticeable for, among other things, their ability to attract converts in the urban areas. They sought like Perfect Liberty Kyodan founded in 1957 to teach the 'Art of Living' in the modern world, provided community, healing in the wide sense of the term, and a refined, somewhat updated but essentially conservative model of family life.

Change since the 1970s, including the increasing Westernization that has come in the wake of economic success, has tended to make both this model, and the rituals and philosophies that underpinned it, obsolete. This, combined with the serious dilemma facing all new religions of sustaining the motivation, enthusiasm and commitment of the second and later generations of members who were born into the religion, has resulted in decline in Japan. Some of the new, new religions (shin shin shukyo) are still attracting large numbers but much of their appeal can be attributed to their pretensions to be authentic, genuine forms of Buddhism, and to their provision of personal rather than corporate forms of spirituality, which allows religious consumers to dictate how much time, energy and involvement they will give to the organization. This shift is not simply due to cultural and economic changes but is also a response to the negative image of new forms of corporate religion created by Aum Shinrikyo (see below).

Other difficulties have resulted from the ending of corporate culture's guarantees of such benefits as life-long employment. This has made for a change in attitudes to total involvement and wholehearted commitment to large organizations, including NRMs. The preference is for personal space to select those spiritual techniques that are seen as directly relevant to personal life, without the obligations and duties of attendance, voluntary activity and giving, which come with membership of a large, controlling, faceless religious body, and this tends to favour more individualistic type associations.

The previously mentioned problem of a motivation of the second and third generations is widespread and serious. This was singled out as a major difficulty in interviews with evangelists and officials of Perfect Liberty Kyodan, Risshokoseikai and Sekai Kyusei Kyo and other Japanese NRMs. A young Japanese-Brazilian minister of Sekai Kyusei Kyo, who arrived in Japan to care for the Japanese-Brazilian members of the movement who have emigrated there for work, spoke of the surprise and even shock at the lack of enthusiasm and inactivity among the second and third generation Japanese members whom he had encountered. (Interviews by the author, 2001.)

Engaged spirituality

Although in recent times Japanese NRMs have begun to display a concern with more purely subjective spiritual activity, many have continued to promote applied, engaged spirituality, an orientation that is given legitimacy by appeal to the Lotus Sutra. While this sutra, the core text of a majority of the new Buddhist movements of Japan, does not offer a set of instructions for changing the world, it does teach the idea that everyone is a bodhisattva and, therefore, a future Buddha or Maitreya. From this the idea emerges of the Sangha or Buddhist community as unbounded. Thus, everywhere becomes the Buddha-land and everyone a potential bodhisattva or compassionate one for everyone else.

This principle has been given practical expression through the engagement of Japanese Buddhist lay movements in a vast range of world-transforming activities, including peace initiatives (Kisala, 1999) whose goals are the elimination of nuclear weapons and all weapons of war and violence. Elaborating on the Lotus Sutra, which identifies two basic bodhisattva practices or means – transforming individuals and purifying Buddha-lands –

Japanese lay Buddhist movements insist that self-transformation must include growth in compassion, a prerequisite which involves engagement in positive action aimed at transforming society as a whole (Lortie, 2004).

It is not only the Lotus Sutra-based new movements that encourage engaged spirituality for the betterment of the world as a whole. New movements that derived their orientation to the world more from Shinto than Buddhism also insist on the necessity of world transformation through self-transformation. Self-transformation leading to total happiness, the goal of human existence, they insist, can only be achieved in this world and is linked to constant improvement by human effort in the condition of this world. This understanding is at the root of the millenarian activities of many Shinto-Buddhist-derived Japanese religions that engage in a wide range of activities aimed at transforming the world (Clarke, 2000).

Although most of Japan's NRMs are Shinto or Buddhist or Shinto-Buddhist in form and content, there are also a number of new Christian movements that, apart from Mullin's (1998) ground-breaking study, are rarely mentioned in studies of NRMs. These Christian NRMs offer valuable insights into the dynamics of the Japanese religious world. Moreover, they make clear that Christianity, and the same can be said of Buddhism, Islam and indeed any religion, does not spread as an organic entity but is taken up in bits and pieces, as it were, by particular cultures and domesticated over time.

Japan's Christian NRMs

The majority of Japan's Christian-related New Religions arose as attempts to indigenize Christianity and remain small. They were often breakaway movements from the mission churches in Japan that contended that truth was to be found not only in the Christian religion but also in the religions of Asia. This is a feature of many modern African movements (see Chapter 8). Orthodoxy they argued could not be determined according to Western Christian criteria and Church Councils. Moreover, just as many of the Buddhist-related Japanese NRMs such as Agonshu attempt to discover the original, authentic sources of Buddhism by returning to its origins, these movements likewise sought and/or seek to discover the true meaning and intent of Christianity by examining the Bible, free of Western interpretations, often reaching the conclusion that there existed no single normative form of Christianity in the first century.

Some of the variation found in new indigenous movements can in part be attributed to the different emphases given to the biblical sources by these movements. The founders, moreover, were influenced to a greater or lesser degree not only by the various local religions but also by different kinds of foreign theological ideas and methods of church organization, including Christian Science, Pentecostalism, and Unitarianism, among others.

For example, the founder of the early nineteenth-century Nonchurch movement, Uchimura Kanzo (1861–1930), was strongly influenced by Buddhism and Confucianism from within Japan and Puritanism and Quaker pacifism from the northeast of the United States. His principal aim was to graft Christianity onto Bushidō (literally 'the Way of the Warrior': Samurai). His Christianity, and therefore the Christianity most suited to Japan, unlike the Western denominational model that he had belonged to when in the United States, would be non-denominational and organized along the lines of a school (juku). It would be based on the model of the teacher/disciple relationship and would stress the ethical values associated most of all with Confucianism – loyalty, duty and filial piety. Services would not be held in churches but in lecture theatres, halls and homes and would be based on the format of seminars and prayer. Critics of Uchimura claim that his Nonchurch movement retained much of the Puritan ethos and organization that he had known in the United States. Moreover, his emphasis on the Bushidō tradition and on truth in Asian religions notwithstanding, the Bible remained at the centre of his Christianity.

The Nonchurch never became a mass movement and has experienced considerable difficulties in making progress from generation to generation, due mainly to its founder's rejection of structures – these were later introduced – in favour of the teacher/disciple method. But it did attract a number of intellectuals. Moreover, Uchimura's ideas, according to Mullins (1998: 66), greatly influenced others also interested in developing Japanese forms of Christianity.

Among these were Matsumura Kaiseki (1859–1939), who in 1907 founded The Way, and Kawai Shinsui (1867–1962), founder in 1927 of the Christ Heart Church. Although Uchimura influenced their thinking, both of these founders stressed to a much greater extent than he did the importance of self-power and self-cultivation, themes central to the modern subjective spirituality movement (see, for example, Chapters 1, 4 and 5). This was in contrast to Western Christian missionary emphasis on 'Other-Power' (Mullins, 1998: 69). On the other hand, like several of the Japanese NRMs related to Shinto-Buddhist teachings and rituals, among them Sekai Kyusei Kyo, The Way, whose practice was strongly influenced by Confucianism, was concerned to integrate Eastern and Western spirituality and culture.

These, and similar attempts by Japanese Christians to indigenize Christianity and make it an attractive, viable option for the Japanese, met with little success. The Spirit of Jesus Church, started as an independent body in Tokyo in 1941, has been by far the most successful of the Christian-related NRMs, and indeed the most successful Protestant church, in Japan. By the early 1990s it was claiming with some considerable exaggeration a membership of 420,000, spread among more than 200 churches and 400 house churches. This church performs a number of rituals similar to those of many of the Buddhist-Shinto-related NRMs, among them Seicho no Ie

(House of Growth) and Agonshu, including a ritual for the ancestors of its living members, a popular ritual as the majority of Japanese believe that a person's spirit remains with the family after death.

The considerable progress made by the Spirit of Jesus Movement notwithstanding, one of the interesting lessons provided by the New Japanese-related Christian NRMs is that indigenization does not necessarily lead to the success of foreign religions in Japan. On the other hand, where Japanese NRMs have failed to adapt and/or indigenize abroad they have made virtually no impact and attracted only a few members most of whom are of Japanese origin.

Japanese NRMs abroad

With economic migration, which began in the last quarter of the nineteenth century to Hawaii, Peru, Mexico, Brazil and Canada, and with the Japanese colonization of foreign lands such as Manchuria, Korea, and Taiwan, Japanese old and new religions began to establish branches overseas essentially to care for Japanese immigrants.

From the 1960s most of the Japanese NRMs and to a lesser extent the older Japanese religions – the Zen and Jodo shu (Pure Land) schools of Buddhism, and Shinto – began actively to proselytize among non-Japanese and many of them in the process developed more refined forms of reflexive syncretism, giving rise to new forms of Japanese-Chinese, Japanese-Brazilian, and Japanese-African religion. Interesting forms of Amerindian-African-Brazilian-Shinto, Spiritist-Shinto and Catholic-Shinto groups have also emerged in Brazil. Since there has already been some discussion of Japanese NRMs abroad (see, for example, Chapter 9), comment on this topic here will be brief.

With the exception of Soka Gakkai, which reportedly has an estimated 900,000 followers in Korea alone (author's interview, Tokyo, 2005), Japanese religions, whether old or new, have had relatively little success outside Japan, with the exception of Brazil and Thailand. Adaptation, as was mentioned above, was not the main priority for Japanese religions abroad prior to the Second World War and for some time after it had ended. The intention of migrants was to return home. Up to the 1960s, thus, the Japanese NRMs were ethnic religions and this is largely true even today in Brazil of some of them, including Tenrikyo. A similar situation exists in San Francisco where this same church has been present for over one hundred years. The majority of the members, who total less than one hundred, are still Japanese or of Japanese descent.

The Tenrikyo pastor in San Francisco would welcome a more multi-ethnic congregation and strives hard to build one, but the liturgy of Tenrikyo constitutes a major obstacle to the realization of this goal. The question of control is also a problem. After a presence in Honolulu of almost one hundred years, Tenrikyo, with a shrinking membership, and in need of winning the support of the younger generation of Japanese Americans, appointed (in 1996), to the disappointment of local, committed church members, a non-English-speaking bishop from Japan. By way of contrast with the evangelist on the spot who seeks to adapt and acculturate, some of the international departments in Japan appear to be more preoccupied with the question of control and the preservation of Japanese culture and religion overseas, however much these policies limit the church's wider appeal. An anxiety at the heart of the administration over possible centrifugal tendencies on the part of overseas branches greatly influences mission thinking and strategy.

As we have seen (Chapter 9) the success of, if not the largest, then one of the largest, Japanese new movements religious in Brazil, Seicho no Ie (House of Growth), can be attributed, at least in part, to the ambiguity surrounding its identity. This movement allows itself to be defined by members and non-members alike as either a philosophy or a religion and, thus, removes any obstacle that might prevent followers of other religions from joining. At the same time Seicho no Ie does encourages members to learn more about Jesus and Christianity. This strategy has been described by Inoue (1991) as neo-syncretist and consists of the rational adaptation of a religion's beliefs and rituals to local culture and circumstances.

It is a strategy that is widely practiced by Japanese NRMs abroad with some exceptions, namely, the above named Tenrikyo, and to a lesser extent Perfect Liberty Kyodan and Soka Gakkai. While in the case of Tenrikyo the avoidance of syncretism has been a serious obstacle to the movement's growth everywhere outside Japan except Korea, and has led to stagnation in the case of Perfect Liberty Kyodan, at least in Brazil and the United States, it has hardly affected Soka Gakkai's progress, perhaps because this movement is recognizably Buddhist and, therefore, enjoys a more global appeal. But even Soka Gakkai has begun to relax its regulations regarding participation in other religions and even multiple membership (Clarke, 2000).

I now turn to the question of NRMs and violence in the Japanese context with special reference to Aum Shinrikyo. Often there is little evidence at the outset, little in a movement's ideology or practice that would suggest that it might turn to violence to achieve its objectives. The latter can, of course, especially where charismatic movements are concerned, change over time and new methods are then devised to attain them. As will be seen, Aum Shinrikyo, renamed Aleph (the first letter of the Hebrew alphabet) in 2000, underwent this kind of development. It provides a clear example of how what begins as a spiritual cause gradually comes to legitimate the use of violent means to attain its ends.

Aum Shinrikyo: the path to violence

Two of the most detailed accounts of Aum Shinrikyo's path to violence, which resulted in the murder and carnage perpetrated by members of the movement in March 1995 on the Tokyo underground, have been provided by Shimazono (1995) and Reader (2000). In attempting to trace the spiritual path to violence followed by the movement's leader, Shoko Asahara, found guilty of ultimate responsibility and sentenced to death for the violence by a court in Tokyo in 2000, both of these scholars have pointed to the importance of the ideological factor to an understanding of this phenomenon.

Aum illustrates, further, more clearly than any other NRM in the contemporary Japanese context the lethal potential of charismatic power that protects itself from every form of questioning and investigation. By charismatic power is meant here a relationship between a leader and his followers based on faith in the claims made by the former or on his behalf to supernatural powers. It is on that basis that the charismatic leader demands and obtains the unswerving loyalty and obedience of disciples to his teachings.

As was previously mentioned, Aum did not begin with destructive intentions. However, leaders of charismatic movements such as Aum, as Wallis (1993) has shown, have of necessity to be continuously inventing new stratagems if they are to retain their absolute power, such as inverting the standard, widely accepted meaning of a belief or ritual. We made reference to this in the case of Heaven's Gate (see Chapter 5). In the case of Aum, Asahara developed the notion of compassionate cruelty with devastating effects (Reader, 2000). Equally devastating was his new interpretation of the concept of *poa*, a notion that traditionally means in Tibetan Buddhism the transference of the soul of a person to a higher realm. Also in the case of Asahara, as Shimazono (1995) has pointed out, there was an important shift in emphasis from a this-worldly to an other-worldly orientation that was not obvious from the outset, but is reflected in the changing content of his writings and activities.

The change in Asahara's self-understanding that was to have most influence on the ethos of his movement occurred in 1986 in the Indian Himalayas where he began to see himself as a divine being with a divine mission. This shift occurred in someone who had been known for his lack of self-confidence. Born Chizuo Matsumoto in Kyushu in 1955, Asahara was almost totally blind from birth and was sent to a boarding school for the blind in Kumamoto prefecture, where he was reputedly a domineering personality. The future founder of Aum then went to Tokyo where he practised as an acupuncturist while waiting to enter Tokyo University and, according to Shimazono (1995: 384), it was at this point in time that he became interested in religion.

His failure to gain entrance to Tokyo University produced a deep sense of emptiness and seemed to imply that he would not be able to fulfil the most important ambition in his life. Instead of retreating into himself, however, Asahara responded in a practical way by deciding to make a living by setting up a business in Chinese medicine. At the same time he developed an interest in Taoism and began to study various forms of fortune telling, but most importantly, from the point of view of his future career, he became a member of Agonshu (see above) and undertook the practice of *senzangyo* in which, as Reader (1988: 253) explains, 'believers chanted Buddhist texts before an image of Juntei Kannon'. Drawing on the writings of the founder of Agonshu, Kiriyama Seiyu, Reader adds that this practice: 'performed over a period of a thousand days . . . was believed to remove all karmic hindrances from one's family, oneself, and lastly from one's descendants' (1988: 252. According to Shimazono (1995: 385), Asahara's opinion of his performance of *senzangyo* was that it had resulted in his being less rather than more spiritual.

This notwithstanding, Asahara began to make extraordinary claims on his own behalf, including the claim to messianic status. He reported that while carrying out religious practices on a beach in Kanagawa Prefecture the Hindu deity Shiva appeared to him, appointed him the *Abiraketsu no Mikoto* or the god of light, leader of the armies of the gods, and entrusted him with a divine mission to create a perfect society called the Kingdom of Shambala, which was to come into existence around 2010 or 2020. The location was to be Japan, which he was to turn into a federation of independent communities called Lotus villages. Entry would be limited to only those who had attained the requisite levels of psychic power by following Asahara's teachings, methods and example. This millenarian element in Asahara's thought is traced back by Shimanzono (1995: 388) to an esoteric Buddhist text, the *Kalachakra Tantra*, which contains the idea that the ideal king will be reborn as a messiah to conquer the infidels and establish the reign of Buddhism.

Some have detected a sense of elitism in the attitude and behaviour of the Aum members also and have speculated about their inability to come to terms with simply being ordinary. They were driven, it has been suggested, by their sense of superiority to go further and further beyond the normal, eventually finding in Aum the means and the outlet to experiment with ways and means of actually becoming higher beings. The psychological motives that led individual members to join Aum were doubtless highly complex, but in themselves do not offer a complete explanation for their behaviour.

However, over time, with failure in his political and personal life, Ashara led Aum into ever greater isolationism and hostility toward the outside world. Events and those in power who he encountered reinforced his conviction that Armageddon was nigh. On his visit to India in 1986, moreover, Asahara met several sages and swamis who allegedly predicted that Japan was destined to face a catastrophe that only he could prevent (Reader, 2000: 89–90). This role of saviour of Japan greatly enhanced Asahara's sense of his own importance, as did his belief that he had attained ultimate enlightenment. Any remaining self-doubt had by now vanished. After returning to Japan in February 1987, Asahara was soon back in India, in Dharamsala, meeting the Dalai Lama who, he claimed, identified him as an authentic Buddha and assigned him a special mission to spread true Buddhism throughout Japan. His spiritual and mental powers now knew no limits.

There developed a preoccupation with transcendence, with going beyond human limitations, with overcoming the physical, psychological barriers to immortality, in other words with conquering death, and, in this sense, with salvation. Training was provided in, among other things, acquiring the capacity to levitate, an ability Asahara claimed to possess from his time with Agonshu. This preoccupation attracted a number of very successful graduates and postgraduates who were to become his devoted and obedient disciples. In an attempt to explain this paradox it has been suggested that it was not so much elitism but the fact that the emotional, moral and social life of these brilliant students had been neglected at the expense of their intellectual development, a neglect that resulted in their search for an integrated sense of themselves.

Although most of the ideas discussed above were present earlier on in the history of the movement, they were not stressed until the late 1980s and early 1990s. For example, prior to 1989 Asahara had already developed his own interpretation and application of the above-mentioned Tibetan Buddhist concept of *poa* or the transference of the soul of a person to a higher plane. Although he knew this meaning, Asahara was later to teach, Watanabe (1997) explains, that a deliberate act of murder by a superior being was a case of *poa*, and, therefore, a justifiable and merciful act. We see here the elevation of destruction and violence to the status of instruments of salvation.

Destruction and violence, a preoccupation with Armageddon, legitimated by recourse to the prophecies of Nostradamus and the book of Revelation, and an emphasis on his role as saviour, as the Christ of the present age, feature in a number of Asahara's writings, particularly from 1989, and assumed greater importance as his political ambitions failed. In keeping with the apocalyptic genre, he began to teach that a harmful power or energy was spreading widely across the planet and that a major catastrophe would occur by the year 1999. Catastrophe could, however, be avoided if 30,000 individuals were to accept and practise Aum's teachings. This would have the effect of providing sufficient positive energy to counteract the evil effects of that negative energy now destroying the world.

Moreover, while Asahara's message always contained the idea of catastrophe, he also always left open the possibility that this could be avoided. Later, however, he was to rule out this possibility of avoiding Armageddon and, as he did so, his movement became increasingly introverted and elitist in outlook and attitude. The goal switched from saving humanity as a whole to saving a small group of specially chosen people who would survive to build a new civilization. Aum members who renounced the world came to believe, like members of Heaven's Gate (see Chapter 5), that they were on a higher spiritual plane than others, whom they described as mere humans stuck in the mud of suffering. This idea of a spiritual elite gave plausibility to Asahara's reinterpretation of *poa*, which, as we have just seen, regarded an act of violence on the part of a true disciple as an act of salvation.

Despite their spiritually elevated status, Aum members would need protection from the twin evils of negative energy and nuclear war, which they believed would inevitably destroy the world. Thus, Asahara and his close advisers at the movement's headquarters in the small village of Kamikuishiki at the foot of Mount Fuji began to address the question of constructing nuclear shelters. The plan for a federation of Lotus villages was also looked into and abandoned in favour of a model of government and administration under the dominion of Asahara himself, which replicated that of the secular state which was about to be destroyed. All the ministries including those of health, defence, education, and science and technology had their Aum counterpart and all were under Asahara's authority, turning Aum into a miniature model of a state within a state. Every effort was made to ensure that Aum had all the basic necessities to defend itself and survive a nuclear war.

All obstacles simply reinforced the movement's rejection of the world. In 1990 Shinrito, the political branch of Aum, campaigned for twenty-five seats in the Lower House of the Japanese Parliament and failed to obtain any. This failure, along with difficulties with the Tokyo Prefecture the previous year over recognition as a religious body, police raids following on difficulties with residents in other prefectures over the use of land, and difficulties with the press, contributed to the emergence of a more introverted, violence-prone Aum, whose distrust for the wider society deepened. Even before 1990 people had come to see Aum as a violent organization that had begun to retaliate against critics. It was believed, for example, that the movement was involved in the disappearance and murder of the lawyer Tsutsumi Sakamoto and his family, on the grounds that he had opposed its request for legal recognition as a religious body. Even within the organization any sign of dissent was severely dealt with. Close associates suspected of this were demonized and others who spoke out against violence and threatened to expose it became victims of 'poa', murdered by Asahara's 'superior' beings for the greater good of the movement (Reader, 2000: 145).

Global developments including the collapse of Communism in the Soviet Union and Eastern Europe in the late 1980s and early 1990s, the movement's access to ammunition and weapons in Russia where it had its largest following of around 30,00 members, the Gulf War of 1991, all of these events increased Asahara's sense of himself as a messianic figure. In 1991 and subsequent years the apocalyptic content of his writings increased, as did the emphasis he placed on his own universal salvific role. The following titles published in 1991 and 1992 provide an idea of his deeper mental engagement with the themes of humanity's impending destruction and his own messianic role: 'The Truth of Humanity's Destruction', 'Proclamation as Christ Part 1' – Part 2 of this treatise followed in 1992 – and 'The Great Secret Prophecy of Nostradamus'.

Public lectures reiterated the same themes, as Asahara became more precise about the date of Armageddon. He predicted it would occur in the year 2000 and that over 90 per cent of the urban population would perish unless they became 'superhuman' through his spiritual training methods, which would provide resistance to atomic, biological and chemical weapons.

Aum's preparations for this calamity were stepped up and included the construction of an underwater city. Meanwhile, hostility to the wider society became more marked in 1994, as did Aum's militant disposition. While prepared to use violence on single individuals and their families, the sarin gas attack on the Tokyo underground on March 20th 1995 marked the worst of what is now believed to have been a number of outrages committed by Aum against members of the public from 1994. Means had become ends. Meta-phorically speaking, God and the Devil had finally changed faces and places as charisma, in this final act, became utterly graceless.

The Aum tragedy did not occur independently of the rest of society and the answers, thus, to what became known as the Aum Affair do not all reside in the form and content of Asahara's mind. The culture, religious, educational and political, of mainstream society also requires analysis in the search for a rounded explanation of the Aum case, as in similar cases elsewhere. It is a case that in the interests of improving our understanding of the causal links between religion and violence can be usefully compared with the tragedies that have afflicted NRMs elsewhere (see Chapter 3), including: the People's Temple of Jonestown, Guyana (Hall, 1987); the Branch Davidian church in Waco, Texas (Hall, 2002); the Canadian- and Swiss-based magico-religious group, the Solar Temple (Introvigne and Mayer, 2002); the American UFO religion, Heaven's Gate (Balch and Taylor, 2002); and the Ugandan Movement for the Restoration of the Ten Commandments (Bromley and Melton, 2002).

The violence perpetrated by Aum Shinrikyo on March 20th 1995, in which 12 people died and 5,000 were injured from sarin gas on the Tokyo underground, not surprisingly intensified the public hostility in Japan and worldwide to new religions, but did not cause it. Hostility to NRMs in Japan had always been present in government circles and among the public even as far back as the nineteenth century.

While many former members have renounced Aum Shinrikyo and its founder and changed the name of the movement to, as we have seen, Aleph, a rump – about 1600 – of Asahara devotees remains, and makes its living from the sale of purification caps through which weak electrical currents are passed to enable wearers to experience the same brain waves as their leader and in this way be 'cleansed'. Also available is hot water training, which involves keeping the body temperature at a high level for as long as possible. Again the purpose is purification of bad energy.

Asahara himself has already been given one sentence, death (in February 2003), and now awaits trial in prison on other charges. His behaviour, meanwhile, is causing some concern as to his present state of mind. So far he has refused to admit guilt or responsibility for any of the violence carried out by Aum.

Conclusions

Although heavily dependent on them, Japanese NRMs constitute a critique of the older, more established religions, whose rituals and spiritual teachings in the form they are presented are considered irrelevant to the modern world. Furthermore, it is to the advantage of many NRMs that unlike the older religions they have little or no history of involvement with the Establishment. Some were even banned and their leaders imprisoned for their opposition to the Government.

Japan was forced by the Second World War to completely re-evaluate its global objectives, its relationship to and position in the wider world. The NRMs, partly from a determination to restore the image of their country, began to present it to the world as peacemaker and protector of the global environment. They also saw it as their mission to bring together Eastern and Western civilizations in the hope of creating a new world order, a goal symbolically expressed by the establishment both at home and abroad of models of an earthly paradise of peace, harmony, happiness (Clarke, 2000).

Since the 1980s most of Japan's NRMs have either been in decline or have ceased to grow, while 'unchurched' spirituality has been gaining in importance. As Shimazono (2004: 291) notes, 'it [spirituality] became visible and began to attract a considerable number of participants' supported by a new class of 'spiritual intellectuals'.

Guru-led movements became increasingly suspect after the Aum affair, as we have seen, and, generally, also, the model of Japan and Japanese life and culture on which many of the older Japanese NRMs had built their success – Earhart describes them as a 'miniature contemporary version' of Japan's heritage' (1989: 10) – is now considered ineffectual and obsolete. These developments have contributed to the progress made in recent times by new spirituality groups and associations.

References and select bibliography

Balch, Robert W. and Taylor, David (2002) 'Making Sense of Heaven's Gate' in David G. Bromley and J. Gordon Melton (eds) *Cults, Religion and Violence*, Cambridge: Cambridge University Press, pp. 209–29.

Blacker, Carmen (1971) 'Millenarian Aspects of the New Religions in Japan' in David H. Shively (ed.) *Tradition and Modernization in Japanese Culture*, Princeton, NJ: Princeton University Press, pp. 579ff.

Blacker, Carmen (1994) 'The Goddess Emerges from the Cave: Fujita Hmiko and Her Dragon Palace Family' in Peter B. Clarke and Jeffrey Somers (eds) *Japanese New Religions in the West*, Eastbourne: Japan Library, pp. 25–32.

Bouma, Gary, Smith, Wendy and Vasi, Shiva (2000) 'Japanese Religion in Australia: Mahikari and Zen in a Multicultural Society' in Peter B. Clarke (ed.) *Japanese New Religions: In Global Perspective*, Richmond, Surrey: Curzon Press, pp. 74–112.

Bromley, David G. and Melton, J. Gordon (2002) *Cults, Religion and Violence*, Cambridge: Cambridge University Press.

Clarke, Peter B. (2000) 'Modern Japanese Millenarian Movements' in Peter B. Clarke (ed.) *Japanese New Religions: In Global Perspective*, Richmond, Surrey: Curzon Press, pp. 129–81.

Cohn, Norman (1970) *The Pursuit of the Millennium*, London: Paladin Books.

Earhart, Byron (1982) *Japanese Religion: Unity and Diversity*, Belmont, CA: Wadsworth Publishing.

Earhart, Byron (1989) *Gedatsu-Kai and Religion in Contemporary Japan*, Bloomington: Indiana University Press.

Hall, John H. (1987) *Gone From the Promised Land: Jonestown in American Cultural History*, New Brunswick, NJ: Transaction Books.

Hall, John H. (2002) 'Mass Suicide and the Branch Davidians' in David G. Bromley and J. Gordon Melton (eds) *Cults, Religion and Violence*, Cambridge: Cambridge University Press, pp. 149–70.

Hardacre, Helen (1986) *Kurozumikyo and the New Religions of Japan*, Princeton, NJ: Princeton University Press.

Hardacre, Helen (1990) 'Gender and the Millennium in Omotokyo, a Japanese New Religion' in Tadao Umesao *et al. Japanese Civilization in the Modern World, VI, Religion*, Osaka: National Museum of Ethnography, pp. 47–63.

Inoue, Nabutaka (1991) 'Recent Trends in the Study of Japanese New Movements' in I. Nabutaka (ed.) *New Religions*, Tokyo: Kokogaguin University, pp. 4–24.

Inoue, Nabutaka (2000) *Contemporary Japanese Religion*, Tokyo: Foreign Press Center.

Introvigne, Massimo and Mayer, Jean-François (2002) 'Occult Masters and the Temple of Doom: The Fiery End of the Solar Temple' in David G. Bromley and J. Gordon Melton (eds) *Cults, Religion and Violence*, Cambridge: Cambridge University Press, pp. 170–89.

Kamstra, J. H. (1994) 'Japanese Monotheism and New Religions' in Peter B. Clarke and Jeffrey Sumers (eds) *Japanese New Religions in the West*, Eastbourne: Japan Library, pp. 103–17.

Kisala, Robert (1999) *Prophets of Peace. Pacifism and Cultural Identity in Japan's New Religions*, Honolulu: University of Hawai'i Press.

Kitagawa, Joseph M. (1990) *Religion in Japanese History*, New York: Columbia University Press.

Lortie, Bret (2004) 'Our World, Our Jewel: Engaged Buddhism and the Lotus Sutra', *Dharma World*, 31(Sept/Oct), 11–17.

McFarland, H. Neill (1967) *The Rush Hour of the Gods*, New York: Macmillan.

Mullins, M. (1998) *Christianity: Made in Japan. A Study of Indigenous Movements*, Honolulu: University of Hawi'i Press.

Nakamaki, Hirochika (2003) *Japanese New Religions at Home and Abroad*, London: Routledge/Curzon.

Ooms, Emily Groszos (1993) *Women and Millenarian Protest in Meiji Japan*, Ithaca, NY: Cornell University Press.

Reader, Ian (1988) 'The "New" New Religions of Japan: An Analysis of the Rise of Agonshu', *Japanese Journal of Religious Studies*, 15(4), 235–61.

Reader, Ian (1991) *Religion in Contemporary Japan*, Basingstoke: Macmillan.

Reader, Ian (2000) *Religious Violence in Contemporary Japan: The Case of Aum Shinrikyo*, Richmond, Surrey: Curzon Press.

Shimazono, Susumu (1986) 'The Development of Millenaristic Thought in Japan's New Religions: From Tenrikyo to Honmichi', in J. Beckford (ed.) *New Religious Movements and Rapid Social Change*, London: Sage, pp. 55–86.

Shimazono, Susumu (1995) 'In the Wake of Aum: the Formation and Transformation of a Universe of Belief', *Japanese Journal of Religious Studies*, 22(3/4), 381–415.

Shimazono, Susumu (2004) *From Salvation to Spirituality*, Melbourne: Trans Pacific Press.

Smith, Robert John (1983) *Japanese Society*, Cambridge: Cambridge University Press.

Stark, Rodney, Hamberg, Eva and Miller, Alan S. (2005) 'Exploring Spirituality and Unchurched Religions in America, Sweden and Japan', *Journal of Contemporary Religion*, 20(1), 3–25.

Wallis, Roy (1993) 'Charisma and Explanation' in Eileen Barker *et al. Secularization, Rationalism and Sectarianism*, Oxford: Clarendon Press, pp. 167–81.

Watanabe, Manubu (1997) 'Reactions to the Aum Affair: The Rise of the Anti-Cult Movement in Japan', *Bulletin of the Nanzan Institute for Religion and Culture*, 21, 32–48.

Yamashita, A. (1998) 'The "Eschatology" of Japanese New and New, New Religions: From Tenrikyo to Kofuku no Kagaku', *Japanese Religions*, 23(1/2), 125–42.

Chapter 13

East Asia (2)

NRMs in China, Taiwan and Korea

The approach to the discussion of NRMs in this chapter, as in others, is an integrated one in that it considers developments in what might be called the standard religions – Confucianism, Daoism and Buddhism – in the same context as the rise of NRMs. Some of the latter have remained local movements, concerned as they were with issues of national identity during periods of colonial rule. The Korean movement Ch'ondogyo is a case in point.

Others include Yiguandao, which began in mainland China; Foguangshan (Buddha's Light Mountain) and the Buddhist Compassion and Relief (Tzu Chi) foundation (henceforth Buddhist Compassion Relief), both of which originated in Taiwan; and Won Buddhism and the Unification Church and/ or Moonies, both of which are of Korean origin. Some of these are among the largest of the global NRMs, and leading exponents of Engaged Buddhism. Although, it should be pointed out, their understanding of engagement differs, some emphasizing the importance of a political dimension while others reject this approach and insist that their intent is entirely religious. Movements such as Falun Gong and Zhong Gong that offer more individualistic and personal routes to liberation insist they are entirely apolitical. This, however, is not always how governments have seen or continue to see new forms of spirituality and religion, or even what appears to be spirituality or religion, engaged or otherwise, as the cases of the Taiping (peaceful) rebellion (1848–65) against the Manchu dynasty in China, Falun Gong and Zhong Gong, just mentioned, graphically illustrate.

Most, if not all, of the NRMs in all three countries under review in this chapter, as in Japan (see Chapter 12) and elsewhere, are messianic movements and await with anxious anticipation the complete and total transformation of society. As will be seen below, different movements offer a different version of the form and content of that transformation.

Not only are old, long-established religions undergoing profound change, and new religions and spiritualities emerging throughout East Asia, as in South and Southeast Asia, but also underway is a shift in interpretation of the notion of religion itself and of its functions, revealing a move to a more Western understanding of the idea. But before addressing this and the other developments and innovations in the sphere of religion and spirituality I will attempt a brief overview of pre-Communist and Communist Government attitudes toward and treatment of religion in China.

Governments and religion in China

There are only five officially recognized religions in China – Buddhism, Daoism, Catholicism, Protestantism and Islam.

Recent events, including the massive destruction of temples during the Cultural Revolution (1966–69) and the even more recent suppression of Falun Gong beginning in the second half of the 1990s, have given rise to a widespread perception of Communist rule as inherently hostile to new religion, and indeed to religion of every kind. Hostility on such a scale did not, however, begin when the Communist regime came to power under the leadership of Mao Tse-tung in 1949, nor has all condemnation of religion either before or since then been totally unqualified.

Prior to Communist rule intellectuals advocated the replacement of 'negative' religion by an education in aesthetics, while supporting the retention of what they considered to be the positive aspects of religion under the label of Aesthetics (Pong and Caldarola, 1982: 553). In this debate, as in others, differences frequently emerged over the question of the definition and content of religion. Some of the intellectuals made little or no distinction between religion and culture while others, convinced that the unity of Western nations was founded on a national religion, began from the early years of the twentieth century to adopt the Western understanding of the phenomenon, which they referred to as *zongjiao*. They then applied this notion of religion to the Chinese context for the purpose of providing the country with its own national religion, the content of which would be a revised, updated, modernized version of Confucianism (Goossaert, 2003: 433).

This new approach was at odds with what was widely believed about the incapacity of religion to unite the nation. From the end of the Opium War (1840–42), and long before the Communist regime took power in 1949, Chinese religion had come to be seen increasingly not only as having failed to contribute to the development of a national spirit, but also to have collaborated with the enemies of the nation. Christianity and Buddhism were accused of furthering Western and Japanese imperialism, respectively. Reformers such as the Venerable Taixu (1890–1947) shared some of these criticisms levelled at Buddhism and Chinese religion in general. In the case of the former, he attempted to rid it both of superstition and commercialism and, although he won the backing of intellectuals and the middle classes, he met with staunch opposition from the largely conservative elements of the Sangha or Buddhist community. One of Taixu's other main objectives was to encourage greater lay participation and to gain legitimacy for Buddhist engagement in politics, controversial aims that are shared by Foguangshan in Taiwan.

Like Marx, Mao Tse-tung was convinced that religion, an ingredient of the 'twin mountains' of imperialism and feudalism from which the Chinese people needed to be liberated, would wither away. Religion was a non-antagonistic contradiction, which the people themselves would resolve, for it could not be abolished by administrative decree. Nor could people be forced to renounce such false idealism no more than they could be forced to become Marxists. Mao's stated conviction was that the only means to resolve questions of an ideological nature was by discussion and debate, in other words by democratic means. This line of reasoning was behind the decision to include guarantees of religious freedom in the Constitution of the People's Republic of China, promulgated for the first time in 1954.

However, this has never meant genuine freedom to promulgate religious teachings or to practise religious rituals openly. While the Communist regime has never pursued with consistency a policy of oppression, religions and whatever movements might closely resemble religions, have experienced close control and even persecution during the politically radical phases of Communist rule, particularly during the period 1966–69, the high point of the Cultural Revolution which aimed at the removal of the 'four olds': old culture, thinking, habits and customs. During this time religious practice virtually ceased and the monasteries and monks of Tibet whose country was brought under Chinese rule in 1951 were particularly badly hit by this revolution. Although repression by the Communist regime is not the reason for all the losses, the figures show a decline in the number of Buddhist temples from over one million in *c.*1900 to less that a few thousand in *c.*2000 (Goossaert, 2003: 429). Other religions have experienced similar losses.

Periods of greater tolerance of religion have frequently followed periods of oppression, during times of relative prosperity and greater openness to the outside world. The economic liberalization in the late 1970s was one such period, only to be succeeded once again by severe restrictions and even persecution as movements – even those that were patronized by members of the ruling elite – began to attract wide support. What Communist government in China fears most is that an independent organization with widespread appeal will emerge to challenge its ideological hegemony.

However great the repression has been and continues to be, it has done little to curb enthusiasm for popular religion or to prevent the emergence of countless new forms of religion, many of them, as we have already mentioned, strongly millenarian. But before turning to the new forms of messianic movement I want to consider first some of the developments underway in the older religions of China and Taiwan.

The religious landscape of China and Taiwan

Religions in China and Taiwan are considered here mainly from the vantage point of the three teachings – sanjiao – of Confucianism, Daoism and

Buddhism, beginning with some basic observations on the history, content and purpose of the first of the three, and its attempt to fashion for itself a new identity appropriate to the modern world (Yao, 2001a).

Confucianism, which is thought to have been started by Confucius, a sixth-century BC sage, had, historically, as its primary concern the maintenance of the balance or harmony between heaven and earth by teaching the unalterable 'Mandates of Heaven'. The utopian dimension to this philosophy was developed by later teachers who described the Way of Heaven as involving a progression from this imperfect physical world towards a future utopia (*ta-tung*) or Age of Grand Unity.

Though it has lost the prominent role it once played at the heart of government, Confucianism is not without influence in contemporary China, where a number of thinkers – the new Neo-Confucians (Cha, 2003: 481ff.) – have resorted to using Confucian philosophical thought as the vehicle for interpreting Western positivism, particularly in the field of science. Their aim is to demonstrate the value to the scientific theory and methodology of the modern world of Confucian philosophical thinking, which is concerned with ethics and meaning rather than simply the facts. What is of most importance to some scholars is to identify the inner spirit of Confucianism which consists of an 'intimate experience in one's inner heart of benevolence or humaneness [sic]' (Liu quoted in Yao, 2001a: 321).

Others, including Tu (1993), are concerned to present Confucianism as a religion and to ground it on its inherent spiritual values, claiming that faith in Tian Ming or the Mandate or Will of Heaven is the cornerstone of what is a very special, indeed unique, religion. Tu adds that there are no specific identifiers regarding being a Confucian, nor is Confucianism limited in terms of culture, geography and form of organization. In parts of the world, for example, in Indonesia (see Chapter 11), Confucianism has taken on a specific form of worship and organization, and a specific set of beliefs and practices, something that the Constitution of that country demands of all would-be religions.

Daoism is sometimes referred to as the 'indigenous' religion of China. The primary goal is to achieve union with the *Dao*, which may mean the pursuit of physical immortality or spiritual transcendence. Based on the idea of the correspondence of all forces under Heaven, the most important Daoist concept is that of qi or energy, spirit, breath. Traditionally believed to have been founded by Lao Tzu – about whom there are countless legends, one of which says he was born in 604 BC in Henan province. Daoism's most sacred book is the *Dao Teh Ching* (*Daodejing*), thought to have been written by Lao Tzu and the *Chuang Tzu* (*Zhuangzi*).

Divination using astro-geomantic techniques and the use of techniques (qigong) for acquiring longevity are two of its main practices. Most practitioners 'belong' to the Complete Reality School or *Quanzhen Dao*, which is also popular among Daoists in Hong Kong and Indonesia. Once dismissed as superstition by the Communist authorities with the introduction of the liberalization policy of the late 1970s, Daoism, while it is less widely practised than Buddhism, began at that time to attract larger numbers, which led to the building of more temples, while others, closed for peddling superstition, were reopened. Moreover, the study of its scriptures and practices became part of the curriculum of a number of universities.

Though it is heavily influenced by what, from a Durkheimian sociological perspective, might be described as magical elements, Daoism fits more readily into the category of religion as traditionally understood in the West than, for example, Confucianism. It asserts the existence of an unseen, inexpressible absolute, the *Dao* (Way) that pervades the Universe. It also tends to focus on the individual independently *of* society, whereas Confucianism's concern is with the individual *in* society. Another striking difference between Daoism and Confucianism lies in the more spontaneous approach of the former compared with the disciplined, rational, systematic approach of the latter.

Daoism orientates the individual to look inward, rather than to external decrees or Mandates of Heaven as in the case of Confucianism, for the rationale behind and for the motivation to discover the truth. Daoism, however, is not only about spontaneity, for it also holds that every concept is complimented by its opposite, a principle reflected in the two fundamental concepts of opposites at the root of Chinese religion and culture, *ying* and *yang*, each of which both contains and gives rise to the other. Hence spontaneity gives rise to the necessity for order or law, and, thus, makes possible a coming together at the intellectual level of Daoism and Confucianism.

The influence of Folk Religion remains strong. Unorganized and unstructured, this form of religion consists of a complex amalgam of ancestor veneration, Buddhist and Daoist practices, Confucian ethics, devotions to local divinities and deified heroes, and a series of practices related to divination, magic and sorcery.

Buddhism, which became part of religious life of the imperial court in China in the middle of the first century of the Christian era, after having been introduced from India, came to resemble Daoism to such an extent that it was widely perceived as a foreign branch of the latter, with the same founder, Lao Tzu. Though this belief in a common founder and its use of Daoist ideas and practices facilitated Buddhism's entry into China, it remained largely the religion of foreigners until well into the third century when, carried principally by laymen, it began to move beyond its base in northern China to the Yangtze region and further south and east.

Initially, and for some time after its arrival, Buddhism was strongly opposed by Confucianism, which contended that the former's monastic way of life was unproductive and a drain on the community and that its insistence on celibacy undermined fundamental social values including family life. There were also fears that the Sangha would become a powerful political body independent of the state, a development seen later in Japan. Buddhism, nevertheless, spread across China assisted by the crisis of values that ensued upon the break up of the Han dynasty (206 BC–220 AD), a crisis for which Confucianism appeared to have no remedy. Despite its stress on celibacy, Buddhism stepped into the vacuum, as it was to do later in different circumstances in Vietnam (see Chapter 11), and attracted followers from all classes, reaching a peak in terms of its numerical growth over a period of some 200 years from the seventh to ninth century. Particularly appealing, Harvey (1990: 149) maintains, was 'its concept of all people having the Buddha-nature, an equal potential for enlightenment, which introduced to China the notion of the equal worth of all people'.

Decline began with the re-emergence of Confucianism during the Song dynasty (960–1279) as a universal doctrine in the sense of a vast synthesis of philosophical and ethical systems, which appealed to the political and intellectual elite. Simultaneously, the old idea of the Unity of the Three Religions – Buddhism, Confucianism and Daoism – began to regain much of its appeal. While Confucianism restored its grip over the intelligentsia and ruling classes, Buddhism came to be valued increasingly not as a philosophy but more for the contribution it could make to everyday life through the provision of rituals for funerals, ancestor veneration, the production of crops, and safety and security.

As we have seen, in modern times, as in the past, Buddhism has often been attacked and its institutions destroyed by government. Many of its temples and monasteries were torn down during the Tai ping uprising (1850–64). As we have seen, in 1900 there were an estimated one million Buddhist and Daoist temples in China and this compares with only a few thousand temples open today (Goossaert, 2003: 429). The twentieth century was mostly one of temple destruction on a grand scale, though the 1920s and 1930s saw an improvement in Buddhist fortunes with, as in Japan, the emergence of numerous lay Buddhist movements promoting education and social welfare. This short period of improvement in its fortunes was followed by manipulation and suppression from the start of Communist rule in 1949. It is important to note, however, that, as was previously mentioned, such suppression and manipulation was not only a feature of Communist rule but also occurred at different times under successive imperial governments, which displayed an equal dislike and intolerance for any institution that might challenge their thinking or weaken the loyalty of the masses.

Government manipulation of monks and religious teachings has been frequent and has taken many forms, including the reinterpretation of doctrine to make it comply with and give moral and ethical legitimacy to its own actions. Killing opponents of the Government and those the Government considered to be enemies of society, for example, was interpreted as an act of compassion, while implementing the Communist social policy was held up as the authentic way of the bodhisattva or way of compassion. The Communist Government has also made use of Buddhism as a tool in its foreign policy, seeing in it a useful means of forging links with the predominantly Buddhist countries of southeast Asia.

From 1980 Buddhist seminaries began to reopen under the aegis of the Government-funded Chinese Buddhist Academy and the ordination of monks was once again permitted. As in Japan, new lay Buddhist associations formed in many parts of the country, are especially active along the east coast and play a crucial role in enabling Buddhism, regarded by many of the younger generation as outmoded, to address some of the existential and moral questions raised by the rapid pace of modernization now underway.

Christianity, growing rapidly today after many setbacks, also has a long history in China having arrived from Syria, in the form of Nestorianism, in the seventh century. Despite its efforts to change the image most Chinese have of it as an alien religion, it is still widely referred to, as is the case in parts of Southeast Asia including Thailand, as a foreign religion (*yangjiao*). Christianity is, nevertheless, relatively powerful as an institution, and its foreign identity has become for some Chinese, and in particular for the growing number of young and well-educated Chinese, part of its growing appeal. This is happening, paradoxically, at a time when Christianity has begun to demonstrate its loyalty to Chinese society and its acceptance of Chinese culture. But for those who look outwards, Christianity in China provides an opportunity for experimentation and innovation not only in religious and spiritual matters but also in intellectual thought and lifestyle, and facilitates the transition they seek to make to a more international and/or global outlook.

Islam arrived in China in much the same way as it arrived in many other parts of the world, through trade and commerce, having been introduced by Persian merchants in the eighth century. The main groups are the Hui or Chinese Muslims in the strict sense of the term, the Uighur and the Kazakhs. Minority groups include the Dongxiang, the Kyrgyz and the Salar, an ethnonym for a sinicized Turkish group, and the Shi'ite Tadjik who are Persian speaking, the Uzbek, Baoan and the Tartar, a small group but with international links stretching from Helsinki to Kazan to Tokyo (Berlie, 1998). With the exception of the sinicized Hui people who are widely scattered, most Muslims live in the northwestern provinces, including the Xinjiang Autonomous region, and in Yunnan province in the southwest.

With the exception of its relatively small and uninfluential Muslim population, religion in Taiwan shares much in common with China. However, despite this overlap there is not complete identity between the two. For example, observers of Buddhism in Taiwan point to the relatively small number of Chinese Buddhist organizations on the island in pre-modern times. In Taiwan, moreover, the scale of investment in temple building and in hospitals, educational establishments and museums by lay Buddhist movements in modern times is unprecedented. What is also particularly striking about contemporary lay Buddhism in Taiwan is its strong commitment to active engagement in the social life of the country and on the international stage. Buddhism in Taiwan has, since the 1970s, been highly visible, well funded and well organized.

New Religions in China and Taiwan: world transformation as self-transformation

Some of the New Religions, officially classified as 'Evil Cults', have emerged from within one or other of the officially recognized groups, others have entered the country from abroad, while still others were founded independently by charismatic leaders. Although they display considerable innovation, many of China's NRMs derive mainly from Confucianism, Daoism and Buddhism, and often incorporate elements of Folk Religion. Christian ideas and practices have also been drawn upon in the formation of Chinese NRMs, including the Eastern Lightning Sect or Church of Almighty God, which was started in 1995.

One of the main strands of post-1960 new religion in China and Taiwan has been engaged religion, particularly, although not exclusively, in the form of Engaged Buddhism (see also Chapters 5, 10 and 11). Another is subjective spirituality (see Chapters 1, 4, 5 and *passim*), which on occasion gives the appearance of being self-referential in the extreme. Both strands, and in particular the subjective kind, have fed the new spirituality that is presently gaining ground in the West (see Chapters 1, 4 and 5). By contrast, the socially engaged religion shares much in common with the Engaged Buddhism and applied spirituality of South and Southeast Asia and the United States, and with socially engaged Christian movements, some of which have acted as catalysts of this new development.

Almost all of the NRMs discussed here, as in other chapters, are enthusiastically millenarian proclaiming and are awaiting with intense expectation the total transformation by divine means of life on earth. Several of the more contemporary movements entertain expectations similar to those of earlier millenarian movements such as the twelfth century White Lotus movement, which predicted the imminent advent of the Maitreya or future Buddha. The White Lotus was considered a 'dangerous sect' at the time by the authorities on account of its support for militant movements of social and political protest. It was also a strict vegetarian movement.

Among written sources of religious inspiration and innovation with an impact on present day NRMs are the treatises of Luo Qing (1442–1527), whose thinking was shaped by Chan (Zen) Buddhism. One of these is his discussion of salvation as an inner experience or form of enlightenment in which the inner self becomes one with the source of all things. In describing this source, Luo used terms taken from different traditions, including the Buddhist terms 'Emptiness' (*Kong*), 'Buddha' (*Fo*), 'Non-Being' (*Wu*), and Daoist and Confucian words 'Limitless' (*Wuji*), and 'Supreme Ultimate' (*Taiji*). The purpose was to be inclusive by expressing a belief in the unity of all these traditions.

While none of this amounted in itself to an innovation, Luo Qing did introduce new ways of understanding and interpreting traditional beliefs, an example being his use of the term 'Mother' (*mu*) for the ultimate source of reality. This term allowed him to depict, in a way that resembles the Pure Land tradition, liberation as a return to the home of the mother where the wheel of rebirth (*samsara*) stops and the experience of the Land of Bliss begins. His writings are also concerned to show the importance of the belief in the imminent advent of the Maitreya or future Buddha. Though one or other may be given priority at different times, depending on social and political conditions, variations of his idea of liberation as an *inner experience*, his conviction that the advent of the Maitreya was fast approaching, and his notion of the Mother as the ultimate source of reality are all to be found in the teachings of many of China's new religions, including in those of the Yiguandao Tian Dao (Way of Heaven) movement.

While messianic movements were often peaceful, militant millenarian NRMs were never absent for long, and flourished in the nineteenth century. One of the most tragic movements of this kind in terms of the loss of human life was the God Worshipping Society (*Pai Shang-ti-Hui*), started by Hung Hsiu-Ch'uan in 1847 in Kwangsi. Hung weaved together an eclectic message of salvation from Christian, Buddhist, Confucian and Daoist beliefs and his movement attracted the support of tens of thousands of impoverished peasants embittered by the failure of successive governments to tackle the problem of land reform. They, thus, joined the march of the Taipings to establish the Heavenly Kingdom of Great Peace (*T'ai P'ing T'ien Kuo*), which Hung proclaimed to be imminent. By 1868 some 35 million people had been killed and the movement brutally suppressed.

It is worth noting before turning to the numerically large, influential and increasingly global movements such as Yiguandao Tian Dao (The Way), Foguangshan, Buddhist Compassion Relief, Falun Gong (Practice of the Dharma Wheel) and Zhong Gong (China Healthcare and Wisdom Enhancement Gong), that there were, and are, countless, mostly peasant-supported rural-based NRMs that are unknown outside of China. In recent times some of these movements, which count their members in thousands rather than millions, have succeeded, according to reports from the Ministry of Public Security, in penetrating the state bureaucracy and the ruling Communist Party to the extent that 'in certain regions the basic level of organization of society has fallen entirely under the control of sects' (Siewart, 1995: 10).

From Yiguandao (Way of Pervading Unity) to Tian Dao (The Way)

While its historical and social origins are rooted more in local conditions of socio-economic deprivation in the second half of the nineteenth century, Tian Dao's (henceforth: Tian Dao) spectacular growth in the 1930s and 1940s is best understood if seen as a response to unprecedented levels of political and social turmoil. Political, social and economic factors should not of course in this case, or in any other, be so strongly emphasized in accounting for the rise and success of a movement to the exclusion of religious concerns and interests. In the case of Tian Dao the belief that initiation ensures an individual's entry into Heaven and liberation from the endless round of rebirth (samsara) constitutes an important part of the reason for its appeal. This belief, which gives a sense of being one of the elect by being free of the cycle of rebirth, is given tangible form by issuing of a passport to Heaven to all members.

Under the leadership of Zhang Tianran (1889–1947) this small, highly ritualistic, puritanical movement was transformed from a minority group, then known as Yiguandao (the Way of Pervading Unity), into a mass movement. Changes in the rules governing diet and conduct, which resulted in a more liberal regime, and the reduction to essentials of long-drawn-out, elaborate rituals led in part to this improvement in the movement's fortunes. Thus, while vegetarianism was retained as an ideal, meat eating was allowed, celibacy was dropped as a requirement for membership and ancestral rites were simplified. Essential rituals include the invitation to the movement's numerous deities to visit the altar, repeated bowing and saluting to each of the deities, the lighting of incense, and the giving of offerings.

Tian Dao, with its strong millenarian strain, places at the centre of all worship the veneration of the Ancient Mother, Lao Mu, who is said to have ordered the future Buddha, Maitreya, to return to earth to enable lost souls to enter heaven and sit at her right side. The Ancient Mother is believed to be present in the flame of the oil lamp that stands in the centre of the altar. Other icons on the altar include an image of Maitreya and of the highly popular bodhisattva of compassion Guanyin, who exercises a strong appeal not only in China and Taiwan but also across much of the rest of East Asia and in Southeast Asia, as has already been mentioned. There are clear parallels here with the ideas spread by Luo Qing outlined above. However, as with most, if not all, Chinese NRMs, the sources of Tian Dao's teachings are many and varied, reflecting the desire to appeal widely across different belief systems in order to ensure that religion fulfils its function of ensuring harmony and stability. Thus, ideas and practices from Buddhism, Confucianism, Daoism and Chinese Folk Religion are all present. Though the obstacles to actively participating in community life in a modern, urban setting are affecting temple going, communal meals and attendance at lectures continue to be the principal activities of this movement.

Just as important in reversing the movement's fortunes as the changes in diet, lifestyle and ritual introduced by Zhang in the 1930s and 1940s was the stress placed on proselytization, which he promoted as one of the most effective ways of gaining merit for one's family. For example, by recruiting one hundred members it became possible to have a rite performed which would ensure that the soul of a departed relative would be drawn or pulled up to heaven.

Tian Dao began to establish a network of temples across China in the 1930s focusing in particular on cities and towns undergoing rapid modernization and industrialization. A similar development was taking place at the same time in Japan, where NRMs such as Soka Gakkai (Value Creation Society) were beginning to attract the new urban dwellers who had left the rural areas for work in the towns. In the case of Tian Dao, which was to enjoy the favour of the puppet Chinese Government installed by the Japanese in Nanjing (1937–45), people leading busy lives in a new and unfamiliar environment were able to fulfil their traditional ritual obligations to their ancestors, now greatly simplified, and join friendly, stable communities in a situation of political upheaval.

Its close contacts with the Japanese and later with the Nationalists in China, and the new Communist Government's campaigns against 'superstitious movements', made it impossible for Tian Dao to function in China after 1949. At that time virtually leaderless – Zhang having died in 1947 – it sought a new future in Taiwan, where it also came under suspicion as a Trojan horse for Communist spies seeking to infiltrate the country.

In the case of Taiwan, hostility from the Government and law enforcement agencies was counter-productive both in this case and in others. The Nationalist Government's virtual suppression of religion after it took control for a period of over twenty years had the effect of unleashing large numbers of NRMs with liberalization in the 1980s. Tian Dao, although it suffered repeated harassment and was several times suppressed by the Taiwanese police, developed close links with local business and commerce during the period of economic prosperity (1960s–1980s) and by the time it was eventually legalized in 1987 it had become the second largest NRM in Taiwan. Once again in Taiwan, as in the 1930s and 1940s on the mainland, Tian Dao provided a streamlined, efficient, rational way of fulfilling traditional ritual obligations to family, and through its temples and adult education courses in the Chinese classics and Buddhism, offered community and continuity to many who were having to face urban life without the traditional support of their extended family.

Foguangshan

Many Taiwanese NRMs including Foguangshan (Chandler, 2004; 2005) and Buddhist Compassion Relief (Tzu Chi) (Huang, 2005) have as their mission the dissemination of Humanistic and/or Engaged Buddhism (renjian fojiao or rengshen fojiao). They do not, however, agree on all aspects of the implementation of this kind of Buddhism. For example, Foguangshan, founded in 1967 in Kaoshsiung, Taiwan, by Master Xingyun (b.1927), maintains that

Engaged or Humanistic Buddhism should translate into political action by both the Sangha and Community of Buddhist monks and lay people. By contrast, the founder of Buddhist Compassion and Relief (Tzu Chi) believes that spirituality and politics should be kept strictly apart (Laliberté, 2003: 180). Paradoxically, the latter's radical insistence on austerity and service to others could well be construed as being more opposed to the liberal capitalist policies of successive Taiwanese governments than the endorsement of these policies by Foguangshan.

Neither Foguangshan nor any of the new Buddhist movements of Taiwan that believe in political participation could be described as radical, nor do they advocate a middle way between liberal capitalism and fully fledged socialism. Nor do they endorse such policies associated with Liberation Theology as the preferential option for the poor. Indeed, they are among the least politically radical of all the various types of Engaged Buddhism so far discussed in this volume (for examples see Chapters 4, 10 and 11).

For an understanding of the radical and innovative character of the new Buddhist movements of Taiwan one must turn to issues of religious belief and practice. As Chandler (2004) has shown, Foguangshan's 'newness' or originality consists mainly in its inversion of the traditional understanding of the location of the Pure Land. This is not seen, as is traditionally the case, as being situated elsewhere in the universe but in this world. Moreover, unlike millenarian movements in other places and at other times – for example, those of Medieval Europe described by Cohn (1970) – which rely exclusively on divine intervention to bring about transformation, Foguangshan's approach relies heavily on human effort.

Followers are encouraged to transform this world into a Pure Land, thereby guaranteeing enlightenment for all, by meditation, self-reflection, the cultivation of wisdom and compassion, by becoming better informed Buddhists, and by engaging in activities that will improve the spiritual and material well-being of others. For these purposes Foguangshan sponsors various social and educational projects and has established its own schools and a university. Its founder also calls for 'ethical democracy', stressing that sound ethics are the foundation of good government and a good society.

Foguangshan's mission is global and with the consecration of the Hsi-lai temple in Los Angeles in 1989 it formally began its campaign of 'Coming to the West'. The Buddha's Light International Association, its lay branch, is responsible for missionary work overseas and to date has enjoyed only very limited success among non-ethnic Chinese outside Taiwan. For example, in London there are fewer than twenty members of non-Chinese origin. The numbers of non-ethnic Chinese are higher in the United States but small, nonetheless, when compared with a total estimated membership of between half a million and one million members. In Africa, India and elsewhere, cultural difficulties have meant slow growth, and the drop-out rate of African, European, Indian and North American students brought to the Nanhua Temple Seminary in Taiwan for monastic training is reportedly very high (Chandler, 2005).

Buddhist Compassion Relief (Tzu Chi)

This movement is, as was pointed out above, another remarkably successful Taiwanese initiative in Humanistic and/or Engaged Buddhism, with a global outreach. Composed of nuns and lay followers, Buddhist Compassion Relief was started in Hualien province, a deprived region in eastern Taiwan, in 1966 by the charismatic Taiwanese lady, Dharma Master Zhengyan, who rarely engages in theological discourse but instead stresses the fundamental importance of planting the seeds of good fortune, or *fu* (merit, fortune, blessing) (Yao, 2001b: 116). Poor and rich alike are reminded of the necessity to realize *fu* (*zhfu*), to appreciate *fu* (*xifu*) and to create *fu* (*zhaofu*) by cultivating self-awareness and by striving to improve their own and other people's material and spiritual condition, and that of society by, for example, creating harmony. The result has been the provision of free health care and vocational education for many of the poor of Taiwan and wherever the movement has established itself around the world.

This emphasis on Buddhism as a this-worldly, socially engaged religion is a constant theme of Zhengyan's lectures and discussions. Asked by a medical student how he might be reborn as a human being, her advice was that he should study hard now in order to be able to better care, when qualified, for his patients (Yao, 2001b: 117). The core Chinese virtue of filial piety and the importance of acquiring wisdom are also interpreted in such a way as to turn them into reasons for social action on behalf of others. Regarding the virtue of filial piety Zhengyan states: 'Our bodies are given to us by our parents. The best way you can show gratitude to them is by helping others' (Yao, 2001b: 118). Wisdom is to be acquired not only through study and meditation but even more so by performing good deeds and learning from one's interaction with others.

Master Zhengyan, who initiates only women, having begun with just five disciples and thirty followers in 1966, has now over 100 nuns as disciples and some four million followers. There is a preponderance of lay women in the administration under Zhengyan's leadership and this gives Buddhist Compassion Relief the appearance of a matriarchy.

Most of the membership in Taiwan are middle-aged, come originally from rural areas, and have been helped by the movement to establish contacts in urban society. The movement illustrates the link often made by sociologists between sectarianism and upward economic and social mobility. Considerable numbers from poor backgrounds who joined the movement are now earning above average incomes. For many who took on the challenge of being self-employed Buddhist Compassion Relief introduced them to helpful business contacts from among their new 'spiritual relatives' (*faqin*). Though not university graduates themselves, a majority of Buddhist Compassion Relief families are committed to a university education for their children.

Thus, like Foguangshan, Buddhist Compassion Relief provides not only one of the clearest examples of the objectives and strategies employed by Engaged Buddhism, but also a classic illustration of the 'sect' as vehicle of upward social mobility, of the empowerment of women through an NRM (see also Brahma Kumaris Movement, Chapter 11), of the dynamics and impact of charismatic power, and of the increasingly global character of many Chinese NRMs. The movement is now established across Asia and in, among other places, North America and Europe. Although it is seeking to diversify its ethnic composition, it is still, as is Foguangshan, composed overwhelmingly of ethnic Chinese.

Falun Gong

Falun Gong, translated variably as Law Wheel Cultivation or the Practice of the Dharma Wheel, is also known as Falun Dafa, the Great law or Teachings of the Dharma Wheel. It is one of the most publicized of the new Chinese movements related to qigong on account of the persecution it has undergone. Zhong Gong (China Healthcare and Wisdom Enhancement Gong) is another similar movement and there are countless others.

The circumstances in which Falun Gong emerged differ greatly from those of the 1930s and 1940s when Tian Dao began to experience growth, and even from those of the 1960s in Taiwan when Foguangshan and Buddhist Compassion Relief were established.

Falun Gong arose at a time of relative political and economic optimism, and at a time when the Government was encouraging the practice of qigong. In this relatively liberal atmosphere followers may understandably have hoped for greater freedom of thought and self-expression. The Chinese Government had already committed itself to modernize in the economic, scientific, military and agricultural spheres, and it was logical people should think that this willingness to experiment and innovate would be extended to a broader range of philosophical and spiritual activities.

Falun Gong members whom I have met do not define their movement as a religious movement, although the term 'gong' usually refers to a spiritual practice or technique. The leader, Li Hongzhi (b.1951?/1952), moreover, has described it as the most complete form of Buddhism. Furthermore, it preaches an apocalyptic, millenarian message that holds out the offer of escape and salvation to those who study its teachings and perform its practices.

Like founders of NRMs and millenarian movements in many parts of the world, Li Hongzhi was largely self-educated. He grew up in the heavily industrialized northeast of China, widely known as Manchuria, before taking up the post as a junior officer in the army and police, and then a relatively junior position in the state-run Cereals and Oil Company of Changchun, which he left voluntarily in 1991. His teachings are based on secondary accounts of original Buddhist and Daoist materials and on his personal experience derived from qigong exercises.

Li Hongzhi's philosophy is partly a response to the Maoist mass public education and information campaigns of his childhood and adolescence, campaigns, which demonized the Capitalist world and proclaimed its total destruction through violent conflict. By contrast, Li Hongzhi places the stress on patience, forbearance and non-violence. It is also in part a response to what he sees as the moral decadence pervading contemporary China, a decadence which he attributes to the Western scientific approach to knowledge and its understanding of the human condition, its rampant materialism and unbridled permissiveness (Chang, 2004).

From 1992 oral lectures and meetings became Li Hongzhi's main media for delivering his messages. These were then turned into written form by close followers and released in print and through the Internet. These messages have acquired the status of sacred texts among members. Like many other comparatively recent NRMs, Falun Gong makes the maximum use of modern means of communications to spread its teachings.

In 1992 Li Hongzhi also founded the Falun Xiulian Dafa Research Society in Beijing, which joined the Qigong Research Society the following year. In 1994 the *Zhuanfalun* (Turning the Dharma Wheel) written in highly colloquial language was published, in the form of nine lectures. The production of texts intelligible to virtually everyone is part of the success not only of his movement but of many others including the Japanese NRMs Tenrikyo (Religion of Heavenly Wisdom) and Omoto (Great Origin) and more contemporary movements such as Kofuku no Kagaku (Institute for Research in Human Happiness) (see Chapter 12). The *Zhuanfalun* has become the core text of the Falun Gong movement, with translations in most modern foreign languages. Later lectures given by Li Hongzhi outside China were also published and partly translated into various different languages.

Falun Gong teachings are mostly derivative and can also be found in widely known Chinese philosophical and religious sources. The founder, Li Hongzhi, does not deny this. He does, however, claim to be original in the sense of having developed a higher, more advanced form of Buddhism by adding, as we have seen, the virtue of tolerance or forbearance to those of benevolence and compassion. As to his own status, although he does not explicitly refer to himself as a Buddha, Falun Gong visual and teaching materials – including its formal portrait of the founder, videos of him performing the Falun Gong exercises, and pictures on the Internet – suggest to followers that he is actually enlightened in such a way as to be on a higher plane even than those members who also attain this state.

The movement holds to a spiritual notion of causality, particularly where illness, disease and misfortune are concerned and, convinced that karma is the root of all illness, it discourages recourse to Western medicine, as do the

Aladura or praying churches of Western Africa (see Chapter 8) and a number of Japanese NRMs including Sekai Kyusei Kyo and Mahikari (see Chapter 12). Though not prohibited, 'Western' medicine is considered to be of no value, since it cannot affect one's accumulated karma. What then beomes crucially important to healing is moral rectitude and this can be acquired by cultivating the above-mentioned virtues of truthfulness, benevolence, and forbearance. By practising forbearance when harassed and persecuted, karma is greatly reduced and at the same time the victims absorb the energy or potency of their persecutors, an idea that echoes the saying from the above-mentioned Dao Teh Ching: 'Let him not strip from you, however strong he be, Compassion, the one wealth which can afford him' (Bynner, 1972: 87).

The main point of Falun Gong's teaching is a variation on a theme encountered so often in this volume: human beings are capable of achieving infinitely more than they have to date. They are ultimately capable of becoming God or the Buddha through studying Fa or the Dharma Law and by practising Li's version of qigong which consists of five sets of exercises (Chang, 2004: 86). While humans share in, they cannot on account of their karmic nature, apprehend the basic properties of the universe and/or the Great Law (*Dafa*), which are truthfulness, benevolence, and forbearance. Their karmic condition keeps them trapped in a state of ordinary consciousness. Hence the need to practise and learn about the teachings.

Falun Gong's millenarian message proclaims that the current cycle of the universe is the 'Final Period of the Last Havoc' and will inevitably end in catastrophe in the near future, to be followed by a new age of progress and calm based on material improvement. This will not be the first apocalyptic event. There have already been, Li Hongzhi maintains, many human civilizations, some of which had reached a very advanced state, but all were destroyed with the survivors moving to other planets. To avoid the coming apocalypse (jienan), repayment must be made of the debt of karma by 'cultivation practice' or the practise of the five sets of qigong exercises developed by Li Hongzhi, which with the study of Fa or the Dharma Law, will eventually lead dedicated practitioners to enlightenment. At this stage the person concerned will be transformed into a living god or Buddha and acquire countless supernormal attributes and powers.

The proliferation of millenarian movements such as Falun Gong in contemporary China cannot be explained solely in terms of their message. Indeed Falun Gong's message contains much that is controversial and unattractive even for the most deprived, whether that deprivation be in terms of status or material well-being. It is in many respects an extremely conservative vision, which not only places the blame for the moral decadence that is driving the world towards catastrophe on Western knowledge – the knowledge that is believed to be turning human beings who are essentially spiritual into material creatures – but also opposes every liberal advance made in terms of women's liberation and equal rights for same-sex partners.

Falun Gong's strident opposition to modernization in China parallels that of the Japanese movement Omoto (Great Origin) to the modernizing reforms of the Meiji dynasty (1868–1912) (see Chapter 12). At the same time its millenarianism provides a sharp contrast with the more world-affirming kind espoused by Won Buddhism (see below).

Falun Gong's widespread popularity suggests that there is considerable, deeply felt dissatisfaction with the quality of life of many, from both an existential and a material point of view. Like many new movements in Chinese history, as we have seen, Falun Gong was initially a mainly grass-roots movement of rural workers who had recently moved to the towns in search of employment only to lose their jobs during the restructuring that went hand in hand with modernization. As Cohn (1970) illustrated in his studies of medieval millenarianism in Europe, it is people like these who are both uprooted and voiceless, not necessarily starving, who are attracted to millenarianism.

Following a silent, 10,000-strong demonstration on April 25th 1999 out-side the headquarters of the Chinese Communist Party (CCP) at Zhongnanhai in Beijing, the Falun Gong movement was declared dangerous and prohibited by the Government. It was also dismissed, in line with the Marxist position on religion as an instrument of imperialism, as an agent of the CIA. An intensive campaign of suppression followed, in the course of which many members were arrested and are alleged to have been placed in camps or psychiatric institutions, with several hundred people reportedly dying in the process. Already some years previously, in 1996, Li Hongzhi had left China for the United States, from where the movement has actively protested against its persecution in China by raising public awareness through lectures, seminars, demonstrations outside Chinese embassies and the distribution of literature.

Falun Gong offers some a myth that rivals the Communist myth and it also seeks to dispel fear, fear of torture and even death, and these are adequate reasons in themselves for incurring the wrath of the Chinese Government. Moreover, as Chang (2004: 141) comments, 'It was Falun Gong's large membership, ability to organize, and facility with modern tools of com-munication that made it especially alarming to the authorities.'

Falun Gong is not the only modern NRM to have been persecuted by the Chinese Government. Zhong Gong is one of several others. Founded in 1988 by Zhang Hongbao (b.1955), it also teaches a version of qigong based on exercises as the means of stimulating *qi* or energy, which when flowing uninterruptedly through the veins leads to better health and greater mental acuity. It has likewise been singled out for suppression by the Government despite receiving for a period favourable coverage in the official media. Moreover Zhong Gong, some of whose schools attracted as many as several thousand students, was reportedly patronized by high ranking government officials. There appeared, thus, to be no ideological divide between Zhong Gong and the Communist Party.

This tolerance, even tacit support, on the part of Government came to an end in January 2000 when one of the movement's leaders was arrested in Zhejiang province and sentenced to two years in prison for practising medicine without a licence. The Government then issued new, more restrictive regulations concerning both the content and organization of all qigong groups. Clearly they were now seen as a potential challenge to the Government's desire to manage individual thought and action, and to prevent the organization of mass campaigns of protest.

Qigong and Chinese martial arts outside China

Qigong exercises and the philosophy underpinning them are presently widely practised outside of China. Qigong was little known in the West until the 1980s but experienced an upsurge in interest during the 1990s in line with the broader uptake of Asian meditative disciplines. The reasons behind this growing appeal in the West are many and varied, with some practitioners adopting the art as a preventative holistic health tool and others more for purposes of spiritual self-development (see Chapters 1, 2, 4 and 5).

Tai chi ch'uan ('supreme ultimate fist') – widely interpreted by Westerners as moving meditation – is but one of a number of martial arts connected to qigong that have been integrated into the New Age spirituality and the holistic health culture of the West. Tai chi ch'uan is linked conceptually to the yin–yang theory of cosmic emergence in the Confucian text I-Ching, a text now widely read in the West. As a practice Tai chi ch'uan is taught by practical transmission from master to student, although more often in a modern class format, rather than the traditional discipleship mode. Among relatively well-known masters teaching the art in the West is Cheng Man-ch'ing who began classes in the United States in the 1960s. As a discipline, it involves the performance of a flowing sequence of movements and postures, with qigong exercises and training in the use of various weapons and partnered sparring practice. It shares with qigong the aim of refining the quality of human 'qi' or energy, in order to develop greater harmony between earth, man and heaven.

Other Chinese martial arts practised in the West include the lesser known Wing Chun (McFarlane, 1989: 241–53). Described as a 'soft' and 'hard' fighting system, this art is believed to have been developed by a Shao Lin-trained nun, Ng Mui, in the eighteenth century. As a system, McFarlane tells us, it is characterized by 'its simplicity, directness and subtle use of motion and effort'. He continues, 'It is particularly noted for its cultivation of reflex sensitivity through the practice of Chi Sau (sticking hands)' (1989: 241). Wing Chun, which teaches a non-dualistic understanding of body and mind, lays great stress on bodily self-awareness.

In comparison with their recent popularity in the West, the influence of Chinese religious thought and spiritual techniques has long been felt elsewhere in East Asia, including Korea, and it is to an overview of religious innovation and the rise of new religions in that country that I will turn after a brief consideration of Chinese Christian groups.

Chinese Christian NRMs

While the focus has been on Daoist-Confucianian-Buddhist-related NRMs and qigong spirituality groups, the Chinese NRM phenomenon is more diverse. Other NRMs, many Christian-related, have emerged in China in recent times, one of which is Eastern Lightning and/or Church of Almighty God. A messianic movement that bases its core belief on Matthew's Gospel (Chapter 24), Eastern Lightning believes that the Second Coming of Jesus has already occurred in the East, with lightning, when Jesus incarnated in a woman. The notion of Jesus as woman is not explained. However, such a possibility would seem to be supported by the Church's belief that God is androgynous. With this incarnation of Jesus in a woman who remains unknown, the era of the third dispensation began.

This movement's mission is to establish the Kingdom of Jesus by crushing all evil forces. Officially, it is in the category of 'Evil Cults' and as such operates in secret due to surveillance on the part of the authorities. Members use a false name and meet in cells composed of ten people. Thirty members form a church and when the number reaches fifty the church divides to avoid being discovered as an unlawful gathering. Eastern Lightning, which provides an interesting example of the ritual and doctrinal adaptation of Christianity in contemporary China, has spread to other parts of East Asia, and to Europe and the United States.

Korea

Historically, diversity and inclusiveness have been two of the most notable features of Korean religion, as in much of the rest of Asia. People tend to belong to more than one religion simultaneously, and to seek different advantages from different religions and philosophies – education from Confucianism, offspring from Buddhism, and protection from dangers and evil forces through the mediation of a shaman (*mudang*), a role which is mostly hereditary and performed by women. While the advance of Christianity has changed considerably the religious outlook and reduced the level of multiple religious belonging in modern times, the older religions, including what might be called Korean Shamanism, which the authorities have often attempted to suppress and replace with what they regarded as more sophisticated belief systems and/or philosophies, remain influential.

One of the features of Korean Shamanism that distinguishes it from the Siberian variety and likens it to the African-Brazilian (Candomblé) (see Chapter 9) variety is that in the former and in Candomblé the shaman is usually possessed by spirits who come to her, whereas in the case of Siberian Shamanism the shaman makes heroic journeys into the realm of the spirits. Of course, the practice of Shamanism in Korea does not depend on the presence of a *mudang* but can be carried on by individuals independently of intermediaries. Its content and practice have also been influenced by Westernization and the advent of Christianity. For example, its ancient belief in a Supreme Being has possibly been strengthened in modern times by contact with Christianity.

During ceremonies or *kuts*, in which there is much drumming and chanting, *mudang* placate the spirits not only of the living but also of the dead. The belief in the influence of the departed spirits of the ancestors remains strong and greatly influences behaviour, as does the belief in the spiritual essence of all material and physical things, which must be controlled by *mudang* to ensure safety and well-being. Exorcism and healing rites are popular. It is also worth noting here for the purpose of drawing parallels with the Unification Church or Moonies, a Korean NRM, that the *mudang* is sometimes called upon to satisfy the desires of a dead spirit, which may include the latter's desire to marry. This desire is satisfied by conducting the appropriate ceremony, in which the spirits of the departed are married in the spirit world.

The Mahayana tradition of Buddhism is the one most widely practised in Korea and it arrived in the north of the country from China in the fourth century BC. It soon gained a strong foothold among the ruling elite and throughout government circles, as it did on its arrival in Japan, also from China via Korea (see Chapter 12). By coming from outside and bringing with it the concept of rebirth, particularly through the cult of *Kshitigarbha*, a bodhisattva (one who out of compassion postpones enlightenment in order to help others attain it), Buddhism helped to foster the idea of salvation as a universal possibility for all living beings, thus offering all the possibility of escape from suffering.

Buddhism in Korea was at its height from the middle of the tenth century until it was disestablished in the late fourteenth century by General Yi and replaced by Confucianism, which had entered Korea, again from China, in the late ninth century. Though the Japanese who invaded in 1592 attempted to impose Shinto, and a Christian presence was established at the same time by a Jesuit priest who accompanied the Japanese invading forces, Korea remained closed to Christianity, apart from one or two individual missionaries who gained access through China, until the signing of the Korean treaty with the United States in 1882.

More recent developments in the late nineteeth and the twentieth centuries include a revival in Buddhist fortunes and particularly in those of the Chogye school of Korean Buddhism whose origins date back to the arrival of the Son Buddhist monk Chinul (1158–1210) from China in the late twelfth century. By the close of the twentieth century this school, which is based on Chinul's particular approach to sudden enlightenment, had successfully survived disestablishment, two Japanese occupations, one in the 1590s and the other from 1895 to 1945, and was responsible for twenty-five monastic complexes and over two thousand branch temples and shrines in the Republic of Korea. Won Buddhism, founded in 1916 by Pak Chungbin (1891–1943), who is better known as Sot'aesan, has also experienced considerable success. It is treated below as a New Religion.

Korea's NRMs

Whenever the discussion turns to Korean NRMs, the focus is immediately on the previously mentioned Holy Spirit Association for the Unification of World Christianity, known more widely as the Unification Church (UC) and/ or the Moonies. While this is the most widely known, discussed and reviled Korean movement in the West, the country has several hundred other NRMs, some of which predate the UC and some of which emerged later. It is also home to a range of Japanese New Religions, some of which have acquired a large membership. The membership of Soka Gakkai (Value Creation Society) is estimated to be around 900,000 (interview, March 27th 2005). Millenarianism features as a core component of the message of all of these movements.

Delimiting the field of new religion (*sin chongyo*, new religion or *minjung chongyo*, religion of the people) is as problematic in Korea as it is elsewhere. Some writers, including Syn Duk Choi (1986), include in this category the Yoido Full Gospel Central Church, founded on Yoido island in Seoul in 1958 by Paul and/or David Yonghi Cho (b.1936). Now one of the largest Pentecostalist churches in the world, this church belonged initially to the Assemblies of God, an American evangelical and Pentecostalist denomination founded at Hot Springs, Arkansas, in 1914. The discussion here is limited mainly to Tonghak/Ch'ondogyo, the Unification Church and Won Buddhism.

Tonghak/Ch'ondogyo

In Korea, as in China and in other parts of Asia and of the world, millenarianism, fed by extreme forms of social, economic, psychic and status deprivation, has often been the core belief of modern NRMs in their early history. Religious factors have also been important in their development. For centuries and into modern times Korea's ruling elite sought to justify the heavy taxation which they imposed on the peasantry by resorting to Confucian teachings to legitimate their oppression. Hard pressed and under severe strain, and greatly resentful and alienated, the peasantry led by local prophets turned to such well-known sources of divination as the Book of Omens (*Chonnggamnok*) for some indication of a better future. Not unexpectedly, predictions of the fall of the ruling Yi dynasty were given great credence. One such politically dangerous prophecy foretold the coming of a new dynasty headed by Chong, who would rule from Mount Kyerong.

These were the social, economic and political circumstances in which Eastern Learning (Tonghak) was founded by Ch'oe-Cheu (1824–64) in 1860, circumstances which did not differ greatly from those in which the new and highly influential religion Omoto (Great Origin) came into existence in Japan in 1892 (see Chapter 12). Ch'oe-Cheu, son of a well-known Confucian scholar but regarded, nonetheless, as lower class on account of his mother's position as a concubine, despaired of finding an answer to society's ills in the traditional teachings of Buddhism, Confucianism, Daoism, Christianity and Folk Religions, and instead sought a remedy for these in a new form of Eastern Learning (Grayson, 1989).

With regard to Christianity the movement was particularly critical of its concept of a transcendent God who stood apart from humanity and the natural world. God, Ch'oe-Cheu believed, was the Great Totality innate in human beings, the 'Great I' to which everyone could aspire. And importantly, in terms of its millenarian belief, Tonghak taught that heaven and hell were not places that souls departed to after death but states that could be realized on earth, depending on behaviour. Chongdoryong (the one with God's truth), it was believed, from his position on Mount Kyerong, would proclaim the *chongdo* or right way for the new heaven on earth in which all nations, laws and teachings would be united. Unification was a constant theme in most nineteenth-century Korean new religion and is also at the centre of Unification Church (UC) theology (see below).

Tonghak's description of paradise on earth also displays a deep concern for the plight of the poorest, beset with the inconveniences and even intractable problems created by climate, and the forces of Nature generally, and a desire to escape from disease and attain immortality. Also evident is a deep concern with the profound disruption to social and economic life and culture, resulting from the introduction of a new form of exchange based on money, a new system of taxation and the threat to the Korean language posed by the opening up of the country to the West. In the new world, the movement proclaims:

> there will be no cold or hot weather, no poor harvest, no flood, no typhoons, and no diseases. Man will live as long as he wants . . . till 500 years of age at the medium, and till 300 years at the minimum . . .. There will be things to eat and clothes. There will be no poor and rich. There *will be no need for money. All transactions will be by barter.* The international language will be the Korean language and its alphabet . . .. At Mount Kyerong there will be built a palace of precious stones and a bank of all nations. In the new world there will be no tax [my italics].

> (Citation from: Chryssides, 1991: 89–90)

Though its teachings were contrasted with Western Learning/Christianity this new religion, like the Vietnamese movement Cao Daism (see Chapter 11) and many Japanese NRMs (see Chapter 12), was to contain ideas and practices derived from Catholicism, and from Confucianism, Buddhism, Daoism and Folk Religion. Claiming that he had been commissioned by the Lord of Heaven, the Great Totality, the ultimate energy (*chigi*), to save humanity from destruction, Ch'oe-Cheu devised the following mantra which encapsulated the movement's basic teachings:

> Infinite Energy being now within me, I yearn that it may pour into all living beings and all created things. Since this Energy abides in me, I am identified with God, and of one nature with all existence. Should I ever forget these things all existing things will know of it.
>
> (Citation from: Chryssides, 1991: 85)

Tonghak was organized into branches or units (*jops*) of between 30 to 50 believers. The foundation date of the movement, April 5, and the dates of the ordination of the leaders are kept as holy days. Services, as in Catholicism and other Christian denominations, are held on Sundays.

Amid strong opposition, at first from Confucian scholars and later from the Government, the founder of this movement began spreading his message of the Eastern or Heavenly Way as opposed to the Western (Catholic) Way, and predicting with the help of the Ch'amwisol – The Theory of Interpretation of Divinations – that the ruling Yi dynasty, after 500 years in power, would fall in 1892. The Government became increasingly hostile to what it considered to be 'subversive' teachings and in 1864 Ch'oe-Cheu was executed and his followers either exiled or imprisoned.

Tonghak's core idea that all individuals possessed a God-like nature – or the doctrine that humans and God are one but different (*In Nae Chon*) – and were, therefore, equal in dignity and worth, had obvious revolutionary implications. It developed in followers the strong belief that injustice and inequality could and would be eradicated and that those responsible for the oppression that existed in Korea – in this case the ruling Yi dynasty – would be overthrown and punished. It was predicted that the oppressive old order would be destroyed by an invading force, a destruction which Tonghak members could avoid by the use of incantations and magical means, and subsequently as immortal beings enjoy everlasting bliss in an earthly paradise (*Chisang Chonguk*).

Under the leadership of Chou Pong-jun, succcessor to Ch'oe-Cheu, the Tonghak movement, which enjoyed widepread support among the heavily taxed peasants, mounted a rebellion against the Government to eradicate injustice and inequality. This was quashed but only with the assistance of Japanese and Chinese forces.

Though greatly reduced in numbers and forced to work underground,

Tonghak continued its campaigns against corruption and injustice, and against foreign influence, and this resulted in further arrests, executions and the exiling of leaders and members. The outcome of such forceful repression was a change of name from Tonghak to Ch'ondogyo in 1904, principally for the purpose of convincing the Government that it was now a non-political, purely religious body. Its revised list of core beliefs, eight in all, included the belief that God and humanity were one, that mind and matter form a unity and the belief in the transmigration of the spirit. This new found religious orientation lasted for only a short time, as political activities recommenced with the occupation of Korea by the Japanese in 1910. Tonghak/Ch'ondogyo became a resistance movement working for Korean independence underground, which was achieved in 1947. Though its headquarters are in Seoul, capital of South Korea, where it is estimated it has over one million members, Tonghak/Ch'ondogyo also has an estimated two million members in North Korea.

There are, as we shall see, several interesting parallels between Tonghak/Ch'ondogyo beliefs and the Unification Church and Won Buddhism.

Unification Church (UC) (T'ongil-gyo)

The Unification Church (UC) was founded in Korea in May 1954 by the Reverend Sun Myung Moon, who was born into a Christian, Presbyterian, family in 1920 in what is today North Korea. Like Tonghak/Ch'ondogyo, the UC (formerly the Holy Spirit, or more accurately the Spiritual Association for the Unification of World Christianity) is also strongly millenarian in orientation, believing that in these last days the Lord of the Second Advent will appear to complete the mission left unfinished by Christ, and establish the Kingdom of Heaven on Earth. Notwithstanding its objective, the Unification of Christianity, UC teachings, as Chryssides (1991) among others has pointed out, must be seen in the context of a pluralistic Korean religious and cultural context. This is not to suggest that the UC cannot, as many observers believe, consider itself to be a legitimate Christian denomination, 'a Korean indigenization of Christianity' to use Chryssides's (1991: 8) description of its claim.

The UC's founder, Sun Myung Moon, studied engineering first in Korea and later in Japan, where he became involved in the Korean independence movement and was arrested for political activities. Moon returned to Korea in 1945 and concentrated on developing the Divine Principle, the UC's most authoritative sacred text (Barker, 1984). However, in the 1990s a new type of gathering was formed, the Hoon Dok Hae, for reading and reflection on Moon's many sermons, and these have acquired an almost equivalent status. The UC insists that the Divine Principle can only be understood if studied in conjunction with the life of the Reverend Moon, who is said to have struggled with great persistence and fortitude, having had at one stage to engage in fierce combat with the spirits, including Lucifer, to receive the revelations granted to him. From adolescence Moon was preoccupied with the problem of how a God who is infinitely good and perfect could allow evil, and was informed by Jesus that humans through their unbelief had prevented him from completing his divine mission to save the world. Jesus then commissioned Moon to complete the task, and hence the concept of the Lord of the Second Advent.

Moon's ideas were rejected as heretical by Christian groups in the South so he moved to North Korea to preach his message of the imminent arrival of the Lord of the Second Advent and the establishment of the Kingdom of God on earth, an activity that was construed by the authorities in the North as espionage on behalf of the South. He was imprisoned and tortured more than once and even spent time, as prisoner 596, in the notoriously repressive and harsh labour concentration camp of Hungnam for inciting 'social chaos'. Liberated by UN troops at the start of the Korean War in 1950, Moon fled south accompanied by a number of close associates. In 1952 he completed the draft of the Divine Principle at Pusan and founded the Unification Church, as was previously mentioned, on May 1st 1954 in Seoul. Soon afterwards he was imprisoned again for alleged illicit sexual practices, a change that was later dropped. The Church was given legal status by the South Korean Government in 1963.

Prior to that, in 1960, a major event took place when Moon married the 'true mother', Hak Ja Han. As Chryssides (1991: 158) points out this decisive event is held to have restored Eden, and marked the origin and source of new life for all humankind. Together the couple constitute the 'True Parents' and to mark the occasion a Holy Day known as Parents' Day was instituted. Other major festivals, which along with Parents' Day 'restore' the situation of life on earth to what it would have been had the Fall not taken place, are the festivals of: Children's Day (the day that commemorates the first sinless parents and their children inheriting the earth), the Day of All Things (the day on which the first sinless parents and their children would have accepted dominion over all things), and God's Day (the joyful day for God on which the first man and woman attained perfection).

According to Unification theology, Jesus completed the spiritual salvation of humanity but because he did not marry and have a family failed to restore the perfect family lineage destroyed by the sin of Adam and Eve, on which the physical salvation of humanity rested. Moon's marriage made it possible for the Lord of the Second Advent, who many are convinced from their reading of the Divine Principle is Moon, to complete the mission left unfinished by Jesus. The principal task of the Lord of the Second Advent whose birth, according to Unification calculations would occur between 1917 and 1920 after a time of preparation lasting nearly 2,000 years, was to accomplish this physical salvation by the creation of a sinless new family from which the Kingdom of God on earth would emerge. Heaven and earth meet symbolically at the movement's main shrine, situated north of Seoul at Chungpyung Lake Training Centre, a holy site with an abundance of sacred trees and healing springs, which gives the worldwide movement a sense of unity.

The Unification vision of the Creation, Fall and restoration of humanity is not unique. As Chryssides (1991) has shown, there are parallels between Unification thought and Korean Shamanism, Christianity, Confucianism, Daoism and Buddhism. As in Shamanism great importance is attached by the UC to the spirit world and it was there that the contents of the Divine Principle were ratified. In a way similar to Confucianism the main goal of Unificationism is to enable humanity to follow the plan of the Way of Heaven on which the Universe is founded, or as Chryssides states, 'The Unification Principle is fundamentally about how it is possible for human kind to follow the divine pattern which undergirds the universe and its history' (1991: 59). The Divine Principle also makes explicit references to *I-Ching* in support of such core notions in Unificationism as that of the 'central figure'. This concept resembles the ancient Chinese idea that a great man or saviour-like figure appropriate to the occasion would emerge at defining moments in history. Parallels with the messianic ideas found in Mahayana Buddhism and Christianity are also evident: the Lord of the Second Advent, for example, parallels the notion of the Maitreya, the future Buddha, and the Christian belief in the Second Coming of Jesus.

In common with Ch'ondogyo and/or Tonghak and other Korean new religions, UC is this-worldly in orientation, proclaiming, as we have seen, the advent of a Korean messiah who will unify the world and establish the Kingdom of God on earth. In this respect it has recourse to notions long known in Korea, such as those found in the apocalyptic work, the *Chung Gam Nok*, which predict the establishment of a new dynasty and the advent of the Herald of the Righteous Way from the southern ocean (Korea) who would establish a new capital in Seoul.

Many UC teachings on the spirit world resemble those not only of Folk Shamanism but also of Korean movements such as the millenarian Eden Cultural Institute which holds that spiritual beings were capable of sexual activity, an important belief for the UC, which attributes the Fall to a sexual act between a spirit, Lucifer or Satan, and a human being, Eve. The UC does not seek to deny its indebtedness to the older Korean religions or to several of the newer religions – the Eden Cultural Institute Holy Lord Monastery, the Israel Church – whose beliefs on the Creation, the Fall, the mission of Jesus, and the restoration through the arrival of the Lord of the Second Coming were of significance for its theology.

The Unification Church has developed into an international movement known as the Unification Movement (UM). The UM includes the University of Bridgeport in Connecticut in the United States, the Bolshoi Ballet Academy in Washington, DC, the ecumenical-orientated Unification Theological seminary in New York, and the Sun Moon University in Korea. The flagship of its media enterprise is the *Washington Times*. Among its other newspapers are the Korean daily *Segye Illbo*, the *Sekai Nippo* in Tokyo, and the Latin American daily *Tiempos Del Mundo* published in Buenos Aires, Argentina. The 'political' wing of the UM is CAUSA (Confederation of Associations for the Unity of the Societies of America) whose principal function has been to undermine Communism and for this purpose it has published treatises that propose the replacement of dialectical materialism and atheism with 'Godism', its own ideology. It was also alleged to have supported the Contras in Nicaragua, who were committed to preventing the more radical, socialist, Marxist-inspired movement, the Sandinistas, from coming to power in the 1980s. This and similar alliances undermined in many people's view any claim the UM might have had to being a pacifist movement.

While its activities have been concentrated mainly in the United States, the UC from the early 1970s began sending missionaries across the world and organizing conferences mainly on science and religion that brought together academics from many different countries. It also organized training centres for the purpose of defeating what it considers to be humanity's most dangerous enemy, Communism. However, there has been a softening in the way it approaches Communism in recent times. Having supported political opposition to Communism in the United States and elsewhere, the UC was quick to welcome officials and the media from Russia after the collapse of Communism in the Soviet Union, which signalled the beginning of the fulfilment of Moon's millenarian dream, or as the movement's leadership described it, the 'Completed Testament Age'.

The ending of Communism in the Soviet Union and Eastern Europe provided an ideal opportunity for engaging in activities that would bring together people from the East and West once rigidly separated by ideology, and the occasion for furthering the building of the perfect human family through large-scale international mass wedding ceremonies or 'Blessings'. These involve many thousands of couples under the auspices of the Family Federation for World Peace and Unification (FFWPU), and are presided over by Mr and Mrs Moon, the 'True Parents of all humanity' and the 'Saviour, the Lord of the Second Advent'. Though it is not known how strong the movement is numerically, the many mass weddings that have taken place over the years suggest that the adult membership is in the region of several hundred thousand.

The 1990s appeared far more favourable to the movement than the 1970s and 1980s. During those decades accusations of brainwashing, heavenly deception and tax evasion were levelled at the UC by Anti-Cult groups in various parts of the world and the Reverend Moon was jailed in the United States on charges of tax evasion. Expectations intensified as the second millennium drew to a close. The millenarian dream, the content of which differs greatly from that of Ch'ondogyo, looked to be near at hand as preparatory enterprises, including what was viewed by the UC as the reclaiming of a pure and restored Garden of Eden in the deep interior of South America, were undertaken.

Held together by the Reverend Moon's charismatic authority the Unification Church and Movement have so far avoided serious fragmentation. There are, however, signs of routinization and the loss of motivation among some long-term and second-generation members. Some of the former regret having dedicated so much time and energy to the neglect of their families and friends, no longer have a sense of commitment and remain involved as much for practical reasons as out of conviction.

Won Buddhism

Won Buddhism, like the two previously discussed NRMs, is also emphatically millenarian in outlook, although the version of paradise on earth which it offers is less ambitious in terms of the transformation it anticipates, and more pragmatic, utilitarian and small scale than that envisaged by Ch'ondogyo or the Unification Church.

Won Buddhism, founded in 1916 by Pak Chungbin (1891–1943), also known by his literary name Sot'aesan (Park, 1997), was one of several new forms of Buddhism that began to emerge with the collapse (1912) of the Yi dynasty. As with founders of many of the NRMs, Sot'aesan was ambiguous regarding his own enlightenment vision of the nature of ultimate reality and over the claims he made for his teachings. He appeared to argue that they were both original and independent of any other religious tradition but at the same time acknowledged that all the ancient sages and religious thinkers had been aware of their content. The same kind of ambiguity arises with the claim that his enlightened vision of ultimate reality is symbolized by a perfect circle, which is then equated with the notion of the Dharmakaya, the body of law or teaching of conventional Buddhism.

Like much of the new Buddhism in Asia and elsewhere, Won Buddhism is concerned with updating the image of conventional Buddhism. For example, this movement uses more contemporary language than conventional Buddhism. Whereas according to the latter the way to understand the nature of ultimate reality is through the Threefold Learning, *samadhi* (meditation), *prajna* (wisdom) and *sila* (morality), these are expressed by Won Buddhism in modern terms as 'the cultivation of spirit', 'the study of facts and principles' and 'choice of conduct'.

Won Buddhism insists on the importance of Buddhist teachings while pointing out that they are not to be understood in an exclusive sense. Moreover, it is critical of Buddhism's failure to concern itself with the practical side of life. Other differences between Won Buddhism and traditional Buddhism centre on the different interpretations of the monastic rule. Won Buddhist monks do not shave their head and can marry. Nuns, however, cannot marry, although they can become masters, even the head dharma master, and give dharma talks.

Won Buddhism represents an innovation in these ways and in rejecting the traditional understanding of liberation as nihilistic and in replacing it with the idea of a paradise on earth in which people develop their talents and abilities. It insists on the importance of understanding that there is no difference between this world and Truth or essential reality. The purpose of life as Won Buddhism understands it is to realize the Truth or one's innate Buddha nature, and to serve others with a view to saving all sentient beings. In serving others one not only helps them to find the Truth, but also the world becomes interconnected. Being a Won Buddhist is, I was informed, about 'trying to be an enlightened person serving the public' (interview with a Won Buddhist monk and nun, March 28th 2005).

Since there is no difference between this world and Truth and/or essential reality, there is an imperative to build paradise on earth. Won Buddhism's earthly paradise is unusual, as was mentioned above, not only in relation to Buddhist notions on this subject but also when seen in a wider comparative framework. It promises nothing truly spectacular or idyllic but simply that those basic facilities that will help to offset some of the more serious emotional, social and economic consequences of modern living will be readily available. The provision of such facilities may, of course, lead to some people's world being completely transformed:

> In the coming world . . . more employment agencies will serve those who are looking for jobs, and marriages offices will assist those who wish to get married; a day nursery will be established in many places so that mothers can go out to work and not worry about their children. Old people without a protector will live comfortable lives without anxiety at homes for the aged which will be established by the government, by organizations, or by social and charitable workers . . . . Life in even the remotest places will be surrounded by the most convenient cultural facilities, a fast food cafeteria will provide us with food adequate for our needs, so that we may not have to cook all the time at home; there will be many tailors, dressmakers, and laundries to help people in making their clothes and doing their laundry.
>
> (Citation from: Chryssides, 1991: 90)

As was previously pointed out, Won Buddhist beliefs are derived from the movement's principal sacred texts written by Sot'aesan, and the transcriptions of his words and of those of his successor, Son Kyu (1900–62). Practice consists essentially in reciting, as in the Pure Land Tradition, the name of the Buddha Amitabha (also Amida), when venerating the One-Circle-Figure and/or Black Circle. This One-Circle-Figure represents the Dharma-body or emptiness and replaces the widespread veneration of the countless images of the Buddha. In this the movement resembles the Santi Asoke movement in Thailand, which also prohibits the installation and veneration of images of the Buddha in its monasteries and temples (see Chapter 11).

Won Buddhism is a simplified form of Buddhism which has been greatly influenced by Western culture. Mainly an urban phenomenon it is also an example of Engaged Buddhism. The movement attaches great importance not only to inner calm and peace but also to social service and education. In recent times resources have been put into higher education and the training of leaders and monks, who attend the movement's Wonkwang University which houses a College of Won Buddhist Studies. Moreoever, since the 1950s it has built many schools and has been activily engaged in various kinds of charitable work both in Korea and abroad. With over one and a quarter million members, around 450 temples served by more than 1,500 monks, and over 10,000 religious specialists, Won Buddhism is not only a relatively large NRM but also an international movement with branches in Japan and the United States.

Conclusions

During the past 150 years numerous and significant changes, even transformations, have taken place in the way religion in East Asia has been perceived and its functions understood. And so far we have hardly begun to be aware of the impact of virtual religion there. There are allegedly an estimated 100,000 Internet graveyard sites in China alone which serve as places for the veneration of the ancestors by migrant workers and urban dwellers, in particular, who cannot return to the traditional family home for such practices. These sites are frequented by large numbers on such occasions as the Tomb Sweeping Festival.

The fortunes of religion in China can only be understood if seen in the context of a vigorous, determined attempt to advance materially, to modernize while preserving Chinese civilization and the unity and integrity of the nation. In the context also of what appears to be an ever-increasing concern over the ideological vacuum left since Maoism was allowed to become little more than empty rhetoric.

This vacuum has left openings for preachers of all kinds to attempt to fill the void. The present leadership of the Communist Party of China under President Hu Jintao clearly believes that serious problems lie ahead for Chinese society if the vacuum is not filled and they have started to advocate a Confucianist revival to provide a philosophical base for Chinese society and at the same time legitimate their own political position. It would also facilitate the perceived need to switch the emphasis away from the traditional socialist concern with hard to softer development goals such as health, education, environment, and poverty alleviation. Such a revival could also be useful as a way of strengthening common ties with China's near neighbours.

This present interest in Confucianism on the part of Government should not be seen as the beginning of a new wave of toleration for all religions, as, for example, the Uighur Muslims of the western Xinjiang region, and not only the separatists among them, are aware. The present development is but one further illustration of how the fortunes of religion, or of one in particular, can change depending on the political and economic circumstances of the time.

Religion has been dismissed in modern Chinese history as unscientific and anti-modern: successive regimes have accused Buddhism of inculcating an anti-worldly bias and, thereby, fostering passivity and undermining the creative powers of the Chinese people. Confucianism was attacked for similar reasons and specifically for suffocating individual talent and creativity, by turning the notions of filial piety and harmony and its philosophy of the fundamental importance to society of the family and kinship relations into inviolable dogmas. Its teaching of history was also severely criticized as anti-modern and in particular that aspect of it which located the Golden Age or utopia in the past. Likewise, the core of Chinese Folk Religion, ancestor worship, has frequently been ridiculed in modern times for predisposing those involved to look back to the past for guidance and inspiration rather than to the future. Daoism was also dismissed as anti-modern, escapist and fatalistic. Modern movements such as Falun Gong have been accused of disseminating similar reactionary, antediluvian notions.

While most new religion in China, Taiwan and Korea has been millennial, it has not necessarily been escapist, as the Buddhist Compassion Relief (Tzu Chi), Foguangshan, and Won Buddhism cases, among the more contemporary modern movements, illustrate. Most NRMs, moreover, seek to, as they see it, release the energies of the laity and preach the absolute importance for liberation of engagement in 'real' life, in social service.

References and select bibliography

Barker, Eileen (1984) *The Making of a Moonie. Choice or Brainwashing?*, Oxford: Blackwell.

Berlie, Jean (1998) 'Islam and Change in Contemporary China' in Peter B. Clarke (ed.) *New Trends and Developments in the World of Islam*, London: Luzac, pp. 119–39.

Bynner, Witter (1972) *The Way of Life According to Lao Tzu*, New York: Penguin Putnam Inc.

Cha, Seong Hwan (2003) 'Modern Chinese Confucianism: The Contemporary Neo-Confucian Movement and its Cultural Significance', *Social Compass*, 50(4), 481–91.

Chandler, Stuart (2000) 'Globalizing Chinese Culture, Localizing Buddhist Teachings: An Exploration of the Dynamics Underlying the internationalization of Fo-Kuang-shan', paper presented at Globalization of Buddhism Conference, Boston University.

Chandler, Stuart (2004) *Establishing a Pure Land on Earth. The Foguang Buddhist*

Perspective on Modernization and Globalization, Honolulu: University of Hawai'i Press.

Chandler, Stuart (2005) 'Spreading Buddha's Light: The Internationalization of Foguang Shan' in Linda Learman (ed.) *Buddhist Missionaries in an Era of Globalization*, Honolulu: University of Hawai'i Press, pp. 162–85.

Chang, Maria Hsia (2004) *Falun Gong*, New Haven, CT: Yale University Press.

Choi, Syn-Duk (1986) 'A Comparative Study of Two New Religious Movements in the Republic of Korea: The Unification Church and the Full Gospel Central Church' in James A. Beckford (ed.) *New Religious Movements and Rapid Social Change*, London: Sage, pp. 113–46.

Chryssides, George D. (1991) *The Advent of Sun Myung Moon: The Origins, Beliefs and Practices of the Unification Church*, Basingstoke: Macmillan.

Cohn, Norman (1970) *The Pursuit of the Millennium*, London: Paladin Books.

Goossaert, Vincent (2003) 'Le Destin de la religion chinoise au XXème siècle', *Social Compass*, 50(4), 429–41.

Grayson, James H. (1989) *Korea: A Religious History*, Oxford: Oxford University Press.

Harvey, Peter (1990) *An Introduction to Buddhism: Teachings, History and Practices*, Oxford: Oxford University Press.

Huang, C. Julia (2005) 'The Compassion Relief Diaspora' in Linda Learman (ed.) *Buddhist Missionaries in the Era of Globalization*, Honolulu: University of Hawai'i Press, pp. 185–210.

Laliberté, André (2003) 'Religious Change and Democratization in Postwar Taiwan: Mainstream Buddhist Organizations and the Kuomintang, 1947–1996' in Philip Clart and Charles B. Jones (eds) *Religion in Modern Taiwan: Tradition and Innovation in a Changing Society*, Honolulu: University of Hawai'i Press, pp. 158–86.

Lizhu, Fan (2003) 'Popular Religion in Contemporary China', *Social Compass*, 50(4), 449–57.

Lopez, Donald S. (ed.) (1996) *Religions of China: In Practice*, Princeton, NJ: Princeton University Press.

McFarlane, Stewart (1989) 'Bodily Awareness in the Wing Chun System', *Religion*, 19, 241–53.

Park, Kwangsoo (1997) *The Won Buddhism (Wonbulgyo) of Sot'aesan: A Twentieth Century Religious Movement in Korea*, San Francisco, CA: International Scholars.

Pong, Raymond and Caldarola, Carlo (1982) 'China: Religion in a Revolutionary Society' in Carlo Caldarola (ed.) *Religions and Societies: Asia and the Middle East*, Amsterdam: Mouton, pp. 549–68.

Siewart, Hubert (1995) 'Modern Popular Buddhist Sects in China', unpublished paper presented at the conference on New Religions, King's College, London, December 9th.

Tu, Wei-ming (1993) 'Confucianism' in Arvind Sharma (ed.) *Our Religions*, New York: Harper Collins, pp. 139–227.

Yao, Xinzhong (2001a) 'Who is a Confucian Today? A Critical Reflection on the Issues Concerning Confucian Identity in Modern Times', *Journal of Contemporary Religion*, 16(3), 313–29.

Yao, Yu-shuang (2001b) 'The Development and Appeal of the Buddhist Compassion Relief Movement in Taiwan', PhD Thesis, King's College, University of London.

Part VI

Conclusion

Chapter 14

Future trends

This volume has attempted to identify the distinctive features of New Religious Movements (NRMs) and new types of spirituality within a framework that included discussion of the change occurring in so-called standard or mainstream religions, a change which is in no small measure a response to the appeal of the former. What I would like to attempt at this point, in order to draw further attention to continuities and breaks in the modern history of religion, is briefly to compare and contrast NRMs and new forms of spirituality with Bellah's (1969) ideal type construct of modern religion, which bears so close a resemblance to his early modern type as to be almost indistinguishable from it.

The distinguishing features of NRMs and of new forms of spirituality

Bellah identified the defining characteristic of early modern religion as 'the collapse of the hierarchical structuring of both this and the other world' (1969: 280) and traced its origins to the Protestant Reformation in Europe of the sixteenth century. This Reformation abandoned in principle the whole idea of a mediated system of salvation. Early modern religious symbolism, Bellah suggests, concentrated on the direct relationship between the individual and transcendent reality and made the latter accessible to all, regardless of their material or spiritual condition. As to religious action, this began to be conceived as commensurate with the whole of life. A similar development occurred with the rise of True Pure Land Buddhism in medieval Japan.

In Bellah's version of modern religion, whose origins coincide roughly with the period of religious change under review in this volume, these same principles receive even greater emphasis, and once again are also evident not only in Europe, North America, Australia and New Zealand, and elsewhere traditionally classified as the West, but also in Japan (Mullins, 1998). Modern religion of the Protestant and other kinds consists essentially of thinking for oneself about religion. As a consequence, it tends to regard individuals as responsible in the last analysis for the choice of their beliefs and the selection of their own sacred symbols and spiritual practices, and even for their own salvation or liberation. To describe this process in Bellah's (1969: 288) words modern religion, 'is beginning to understand the laws of the self's own existence and so to help man [sic] take responsibility for his own fate'.

From this emphasis on self-responsibility for one's own salvation, understood in very different ways depending on the religious or spiritual tradition in question, it is only a short step to the idea of unmediated spiritual growth that eventually leads to self-perfection or self-liberation or enlightenment, an idea also central to modern religion and NRMs and new spirituality movements (see Chapters 1, 12 and 13). In these respects, therefore, many NRMs, but by no means all, as will be seen below, provide some of the most advanced forms of modern religion. Moreover, they not only accept the principles of modern religion but also actively promote them on the assumption that a fundamental element of the search for religious and spiritual development consists of a search for personal maturity.

NRMs, and the new forms of spirituality spoken of in this volume, also differ from certain forms of early modern and modern religion. For example, they allow for multiple belonging, acknowledging that the answers to questions of ultimate concern are not necessarily to be found in a single religious organization, and in this they are most unlike certain Reformation Protestant sects, including Calvinism. NRMs are even prepared to accept that answers cannot necessarily be found in organizations or institutions labelled religious and, thus, leave open the possibility of their being discovered in secular interests and pursuits, including philosophy, art and music. All of this does not make the religious organization redundant but does mean a change in its role. While traditionally this was to give legitimacy to society's norms, values and goals, and to provide believers with a set of ready-made answers to questions of ultimate concern and with fixed, unalterable rituals to go with them, it now becomes one of creating the context in which individuals can arrive at their own solutions.

Other differences between NRMs and Bellah's ideal type of early modern and modern religion centre on ideas about the natural state of the individual and the nature and causes of evil. NRMs generally provide, if not a Pelagian, then a much more positive view of the natural condition or state of the human being than Bellah's early modern and modern religion. Where the Calvinist notion of God is concerned almost all of them would join Milton in his rejection of it in *Paradise Lost*: 'Though I may be sent to Hell for it such a God will never command my respect' and endorse his belief that 'a Paradise within thee is happier far' than the one offered by such an unbending Deity.

The soteriology of many NRMs has a different starting point from that of traditional Christianity, which rests on the assumption that the human being is so sinful and flawed as to be in need of redemption by divine intervention. Rather, human beings are considered to have the capacity to perfect themselves – to become clear in Scientology's terminology or to become a Buddha in Falun Gong's language – in the here and now. The Calvinist notion, thus, of predestination would be anathema to most NRMs. As to the source of evil, again this is not attributed to sin transmitted through first parents to their human offspring, but is regarded as a matter of ignorance that can be fully cleared up through the acquisition of certain kinds of knowledge.

NRMs, furthermore, are not founded on the idea of faith in a set of beliefs derived from external sources of revelation. Indeed, as we saw in Chapter 1 in the case of Scientology, The Friends of the Western Buddhist Order, Soka Gakkai and other NRMs, faith is not even a requirement for spiritual advancement and eventual perfection. This makes for a different epistemology that runs completely contrary to the Christian idea of seeing now (in this life) 'but through a glass darkly' and clearly only without hindrance and limitation in the next life. From an NRM perspective one can not only be spiritual and/or religious without belonging but also, as we saw, without believing, as the term is understood in faith-based religions such as Christianity (see Chapter 1).

NRMs are not, of course, exclusively modern, but juxtapose both modern and traditional forms of religion. The main characteristics of the latter are: the close relationship it maintains between the mythical and actual world; its cosmological monism; the centrality of rituals which when performed tend to blur any distinction between humans and mythical beings; the fusion of religious and other roles; the absence of religious organization as a separate form of social structure; and the importance of differentiation along lines of sex, age and kin group. In terms of its functions, traditional religion is an agent of socialization and a means of reinforcing social conformity. It also contains a strong belief in destiny and looks to spiritual explanations in certain cases of sickness, disease, misfortune and death. There is also an absence of any real distinction between this life and the afterlife, this world and the rest of the cosmos.

Several of these characteristics can also be found in NRMs and new spirituality movements, and not only, as might be expected, in Neo-Pagan movements and modern forms of Wicca. The Spiritual Frontiers Fellowship (SFF), with its headquarters in Evanston, Illinois, is but one example from the West of an NRM that sees the world essentially in personal and subjective terms and fuses this world with the rest of the cosmos. Many other examples could be provided from Japan and elsewhere, and even in popular forms of standard or mainstream religions the world over, including Buddhism in Thailand (see Chapter 11). Moreover, much New Age spirituality makes a close link between the physical environment and the fortunes of the human self.

Furthermore, NRMs, and in this case especially those of the Neo-Pagan and Wiccan type, and new forms of Christianity including some but not all the new Charismatic, Pentecostal and Evangelical churches (for examples see

Chapters 7 and 9), tend to view the universe as peopled with forces, powers and spirits, some of which are considered dangerous to the self. Seen from this angle, the cosmology of such NRMs as those just mentioned and others appears to reflect a pre-Copernican vision of the universe that makes them stand out as anomalous institutions in the modern world, which responds to them accordingly (Chapter 4).

This return, in a metaphorical sense, to the past is no doubt in some instances an attempt to transcend both the present and the past and to forge a new identity, as we saw in the case of those New Agers in Australia who have become involved in Aboriginal religion (see Chapter 6). It can also be seen as a way of returning thought, which many feel has become overly objective and scientific, to its subjective foundations in an effort to learn more about the functions and potentialities of the individual as a human being and not just as a rational, technological being.

The presence of certain traditional features notwithstanding, most NRMs are best understood if seen as more advanced forms of that modern religion described above. There are, however, those who believe that the defining impact on the modern religious outlook comes not from the kind of Protestantism described above but from another source, Oriental religions, and that most of the radical innovations mentioned above, such as unmediated salvation and taking responsibility for one's own fate, have always been central features of these religions. With increasing globalization, Oriental religions have begun to act as catalysts of change everywhere in relation to the form and content of religion and spirituality, in the way they are understood, organized and practised, and in the way the boundaries between the religious and secular are drawn.

There are researchers, thus, who point not so much, or not only, to the protestantization of the religious outlook of the world but to the increasingly wide appeal of Oriental spiritual ideas and practices and speak of their revolutionary impact on the Western mind in particular (Campbell, 1999). While there is some evidence that many in the West have acquired an Oriental perspective on religion and that Oriental beliefs, including karma and the idea of God as an impersonal transcendent source of reality, are becoming more widespread, even more so than the theistic notion of a personal deity and Christian ideas of heaven and hell, one cannot help but be struck by the Hegelian-like nature of much of the subjective spirituality that now appeals to Westerners, including the understanding of the self – the individual mind – as part of the Universal Mind and the belief that humanity can be liberated by abolishing self-alienation through self-knowledge. Moreover, there is no clear evidence that one particular religious tradition or form of spirituality– say Eastern or Western – is in its classical, or even present, form displacing all the rest.

Thus, while Oriental religions have supplied and continue to supply many NRMs and new spirituality movements with their sources and techniques, I would hesitate to speak of processes either of Easternization or of Westernization, principally for the reason that there is much evidence of religious beliefs and practices that originate in one culture undergoing in another extensive domestication or 'glocalization', and even transformation (Robertson, 1992) (see also Chapter 1). All religions are exposed to the porous pluralism of late modernity, which means, among other things, greater levels and newer and more complex forms of hybridity the more they cease to be geographical 'facts' so to speak, and loose their classical character. Simultaneously, in the case of religion, like much else, the breaking down of old boundaries, doctrinal and ritual, under the impact of globalization and modernization, means that everything is coming to look a bit like everything else, creating the illusion of sameness everywhere, a process that in itself can act as the trigger for further changes and innovations that will seek to emphasize differences as opposed to similarities.

The changes and innovations experienced by Buddhism, or for that matter Hinduism, in modern times should be mentioned once again, for these have been perhaps as profound as at any time in their history. One major innovation, as we saw, was that of socially engaged Buddhism and another what I have called Neo-Hindu applied spirituality of which Raja Yoga is an example (see Chapters 5, 10, 12 and 13). Other related developments of potentially profound significance include the change in understanding of nirvana or enlightenment. Traditionally understood to be the end in itself of the spiritual quest and the foundational belief of the monastic life of Buddhism, it is now being interpreted as a means to an end, the end being the social and moral transformation of the world. Examples abound of this from Thailand to Taiwan to Japan to Korea. As we have seen, Buddhism has undergone what has been termed a process of protestantization (Gombrich and Obeyesekere, 1988) in other contexts where it also stresses the importance of work as a calling and inner-worldly asceticism. We have seen, moreover, Oriental religion in parts of Asia become more church-like in structure and theistic in belief, including a number of Neo-Hindu religions (see Chapter 10) and Buddhism and Hinduism in Indonesia (see Chapter 11), and Christianity become more Asian (Chapter 12) and African (Chapter 8). In the West, as was pointed out above, many of the beliefs and practices that derive from Oriental religions, including nirvana, karma and yoga, are seeing their meaning and purpose change radically as they come to be regarded from the standpoint of a utilitarian, individualist mentality (see Chapter 1).

The future of NRMs, the new spirituality and/or congregational religion

While what can be said about the future of NRMs and of the new spirituality must inevitably remain highly speculative, some recent research (Bainbridge, 2004; Heelas and Woodhead, 2005) provides some helpful insights into the likely progress of NRMs such as the New Age Movement (NAM) and subjective spirituality (see Chapter 1) in relation to congregational or standard or mainstream religion. This research suggests that if present trends were to continue then the probability is that in Britain during the next thirty years or so involvement in subjective forms of spirituality will match involvement in congregational religion. On the other hand, Stark *et al.* (2005) writing of, among other developments, unchurched spirituality, conclude that although the numbers of those who claim to be spiritual without belonging to a church are increasing, present data does not allow them to make any predictions about the future impact of this trend on congregational religion in the United States.

Bainbridge (2004), speculating about the future of the New Age Movement (NAM), believes that if this movement is going to move in from the margins where he believes it to be situated – others believe it is already mainstream (see Chapter 2) – and make a serious impact on the spiritual life of Americans it will have to develop more permanent, solid, recognizable structures. This, however, is to assume that the NAM lacks structures, that well-structured religions are also the religions of the future, and that there is little interaction between its spirituality and the old or standard kinds. As I attempted to show in Chapter 2, the NAM is more structured than is usually thought and the degree of interdependence between its new type of spirituality and the old types of religion and spirituality are considerable. Moreover, being well structured has not prevented some religious organizations from going into rapid decline in recent times.

Speaking generally about the future functions of religion, these will be confined mostly to the private, intimate sphere of life. It is highly unlikely, with the possible exception of parts of the Muslim world, that in the future religion in a specific institutional form will act as the main source of explicit and formal legitimization where a society's fundamental norms and values are concerned. As to the future form of religious organizations, this is likely to take the shape of loosely structured religious associations. Where doctrine is concerned, if the present trend towards the objectification of religious knowledge continues this could result in the further loss of control by the traditional institutions, elites or specialists over religious discourse, creating a much enlarged pool of autonomous, independent-minded seekers. It is highly unlikely that even Islamist (Chapter 7) and Christian fundamentalist circles (Chapter 5) – neither of which are as literal in their interpretation of their core scriptures as is often thought – and hierarchical churches such as the Catholic Church where the official institution continues to insist on providing its members with the final answers on questions of belief and morality, will be unaffected by this development whereby followers increasingly decide issues of faith and morality according to their own conscience. In the future, thus, even more so than at present, the most common way of thinking about religion is likely to be thinking about it for oneself.

This does not mean that more people will only be thinking about themselves as individuals without concern for the welfare of humanity as a whole, which Durkheim (1915) believed, would be the core element of future religion. As we have seen in various chapters, part of the agenda of old and even more so of some NRMs and spirituality movements, is the moral, ecological, environmental and social consequences of the global expansion of an all-pervasive Capitalistic economic ethic, largely devoid of spiritual or religious foundations or purpose (Weber, 1992). Even governments, including that of China, are hinting that they will need to have the support of religion if they are to address this issue effectively (Chapter 13).

The further opening up to the rest of the world through modernization and globalization of microcosms such as those of China and other parts of Asia, including Central Asia, until relatively recently sealed off, and the consequent higher levels of convergence between religions and between religions and humanistic and secular systems of thought, will doubtless result in increasing religious diversity and pluralism. These developments and the collapse of the remaining strongholds of monopolistic political ideologies opposed to religion are likely to offer an unprecedented opportunity for creative innovation in the spheres of religion and spirituality.

The impulse, thus, to profusion, multiplication and replication of NRMs, and new forms of spirituality, will doubtless be stimulated by these processes, by the World Wide Web, the media and generally by the forces of supply and demand operating in the religious market place. Some of these, it can be said with some confidence, will be like the fugitive shapes of dreams, or like images that can be multiplied at will by mirrors, and will quickly disappear. Others will have more substance and be more enduring. Stark and Bainbridge (1985) have attempted to provide reasons for such failure and success. The more successful kinds of new religion and spirituality will very likely contain in modified form the basic, by now built-in, features of what was described above as modern religion. These are: epistemological individualism associated in sociological circles with cults which are undogmatic, largely unregulated and unstructured movements; personal experience as the measure of truth claims; the notion of religion as a self-revising system; the principle of unmediated salvation or liberation; multiple membership; and the goal of liberating humanity either through abolishing self-alienation through self-knowledge, which involves understanding the self as part of the universal Self, or through self-transformation through world transformation, as in Engaged Buddhism.

References and select bibliography

Bainbridge, William Sims (2004) 'After the New Age', *Journal for the Scientific Study of Religion*, 43(3), 381–95.
Bellah, Robert (1969) 'Religious Evolution' in Roland Robertson (ed.) *The Sociology of Religion*, Baltimore, MD: Penguin Books, pp. 262–93.

Campbell, Colin (1999) 'The Easternization of the West' in Bryan R. Wilson and Jamie Cresswell (eds) *New Religious Movements. Challenge and Response*, London: Routledge, pp. 35–49.

Durkheim, Emile (1915). *The Elementary Forms of the Religious Life*, London: George Allen & Unwin.

Gibb, H. A. R. (1978) *Islam*, Oxford: Oxford University Press.

Gombrich, Richard and Obeyesekere, Gananath (1988) *Buddhism Transformed: Religious Change in Sri Lanka*, Princeton, NJ: Princeton University Press.

Heelas, Paul and Woodhead, Linda (2005)*The Spiritual Revolution: Why Religion is Giving Way to Spirituality*, Oxford: Blackwell.

Hefner, Robert W. (1998) 'Mutliple Modernities', *Annual Review of Anthropology*, 27, 83–104.

Jenkins, Philip (2000) *Mystics and Messiahs: Cults and Religions in American History*, Oxford: Oxford University Press.

Levy-Bruhl, L. (1936) [1931] *Primitives and the Supernatural*, trans. L. A. Clare, London: Allen & Unwin.

Luckmann, Thomas (1967) *The Invisible Religion*, Basingstoke: Macmillan.

McFarland, H. Neill (1967) *The Rush Hour of the Gods*, New York: Macmillan.

Mullins, M. (1998) *Christianity: Made in Japan. A Study of Indigenous Movements*, Honolulu: University of Hawai'i Press.

Robertson, Roland (1992) *Globalization: Social Theory and Global Culture*, London: Sage.

Sen, Amiya P. (ed.) (2004) *Social and Religious Reform: The Hindus of British India*, Oxford: Oxford University Press.

Shimazono, Susumu (2004) *From Salvation to Spirituality*, Melbourne: Trans Pacific Press.

Stark, Rodney and Bainbridge, William Sims (1985) *The Future of Religion*, Berkeley: University of California Press.

Stark, Rodney, Hamberg, Eva and Miller, Alan S. (2005) 'Exploring Spirituality and Unchurched Religions in America, Sweden and Japan', *Journal of Contemporary Religion*, 20(1), 3–25.

Weber, Max (1992) *The Protestant Ethic and the Spirit of Capitalism*, London: Routledge.

Wilson, Bryan R. (1982) 'The New Religions: Some Preliminary Considerations' in Eileen Barker (ed.) *New Religious Movements: A Perspective for Understanding Society*, New York: Edwin Mellen Press, pp. 16–32.

Wuthnow, Robert (1982) 'World Order and Religious Movements' in Eileen Barker (ed.) *New Religious Movements: A Perspective for Understanding Society*, New York: Edwin Mellen Press, pp. 47–69.

General bibliography

Ahlstrom, Sydney E. (1985) 'Ralph Waldo Emerson and the American Transcendentalists' in Ninian Smart *et al.* (eds) *Nineteenth Century Religious Thought in the West*, Volume II, Cambridge: Cambridge University Press, pp. 29–67.

Albanese, Catherine L. (1990) *Nature Religion in America: From American Indians to the New Age*, Chicago, IL: University of Chicago Press.

Bainbridge, William Sims (2004) 'After the New Age', *Journal for the Scientific Study of Religion*, 43(3), 381–95.

Barker, Eileen (1984) *The Making of a Moonie: Choice or Brainwashing?* Oxford: Blackwell.

Barrett, Leonard E. (1988) *The Rastafarians: Sounds of Cultural Dissonance*. 2nd rev. edn, Boston, MA: Beacon Press.

Beckford, James A. (1985) *Cult Controversies: The Social Response to the New Religious Movements*, London: Tavistock Publications.

Beit-Hallahmi, Benjamin (1992) *Despair and Deliverance: Private Salvation in Contemporary Israel*, Albany, NY: State University of New York Press.

Bellah, Robert, Marsden, Richard, Sullivan, William M., Swidler, Ann, and Tipton, Steven M. (1985) *Habits of the Heart: Middle America Observed*, London: Hutchinson Education.

Bromley, David G. and Richardson, James T. (eds) (1983) *The Brainwashing/Deprogramming Controversy: Sociological, Psychological, Legal and Historical Perspectives*, New York: Edwin Mellen Press.

Bromley, David G. and Melton, J. Gordon (eds) (2002) *Cults, Religion and Violence*, Cambridge: Cambridge University Press.

Campbell, Colin (1999) 'The Easternization of the West' in Bryan R. Wilson and Jamie Cresswell (eds) *New Religious Movements: Challenge and Response*, London: Routledge, pp. 35–49.

Chandler, Stuart (2004) *Establishing a Pure Land on Earth: The Foguang Buddhist Perspective on Modernization and Globalization*, Honolulu: University of Hawai'i Press.

Chang, Maria Hesia (2004) *Falun Gong*, New Haven, CT: Yale University Press.

Chryssides, George D. (1991) *The Advent of Sun Myung Moon: The Origins, Beliefs and Practices of the Unification Church*, Basingstoke: Macmillan.

Clarke, Peter B. (ed.) (2000) *Japanese New Religions: In Global Perspective*, Richmond, Surrey: Curzon Press.

Cosentino, D. (1995) *The Sacred Arts of Haitian Vodou*, Los Angeles: Fowler Museum.

Dawson, Lorne. L. (ed.) (2003) *Cults and New Religious Movements*, Oxford: Blackwell.

De Michaelis, Elizabeth (2004) *A History of Modern Yoga*, London: Cassell Continuum.

Earhart, Byron (1989) *Gedatsu-Kai and Religion in Contemporary Japan*, Bloomington: Indiana University Press.

Ellwood, Robert (1993) *Islands of the Dawn: The Story of Alternative Spirituality in New Zealand*, Honolulu: University of Hawai'i Press.

Flood, Gavin (1996) *Introduction to Hinduism*, Cambridge: Cambridge University Press.

Gibb, H. A. R. (1978) *Islam*, Oxford: Oxford University Press.

Gombrich, Richard and Obeyesekere, Gananath (1988) *Buddhism Transformed: Religious Change in Sri Lanka*, Princeton, NJ: Princeton University Press.

Hall, John H. (1987) *Gone From the Promised Land: Jonestown in American Cultural History*, New Brunswick, NJ: Transaction Books.

Hall, John H. (2003) 'The Apocalypse at Jonestown' in Lorne L. Dawson (ed.) *Cults and New Religious Movements*, Oxford: Blackwell, pp. 186–208.

Harvey, Peter (1990) *An Introduction to Buddhism: Teachings, History and Practices*, Oxford: Oxford University Press.

Heelas, Paul (1996) *The New Age Movement*, Oxford: Blackwell.

Heelas, Paul and Woodhead, Linda (2005) *The Spiritual Revolution: Why Religion is Giving Way to Spirituality*, Oxford: Blackwell.

Hefner, Robert W. (1998) 'Multiple Modernities', *Annual Review of Anthropology*, 27, 83–104.

Hume, Lynne (1997) *Witchcraft and Paganism in Australia*, Melbourne: Melbourne University Press.

Inoue, Nabutaka (2000) *Contemporary Japanese Religion*, Tokyo: Foreign Press Center.

Kisala, Robert J. (1999) *Prophets of Peace: Pacifism and Cultural Identity in Japan's New Religions*, Honolulu: University of Hawai'i Press.

Learman, Linda (ed.) *Buddhist Missionaries in the Era of Globalization*, Honolulu: University of Hawai'i Press.

Lofland, John (1977) *Doomsday Cult*, New York: Irvington (original version, 1966).

Lopez, Donald S. (ed.) (1996) *Religions of China: In Practice*, Princeton, NJ: Princeton University Press.

McFarland, H. Neill (1967) *The Rush Hour of the Gods*, New York: Macmillan.

McGuire, Meredith (1982) *Pentecostal Catholics: Power, Charisma and Order in a Religious Movement*, Philadelphia, PA: Temple University Press.

Martin, David (1990) *Tongues of Fire*, Oxford: Blackwell.

Melton, J. Gordon (1990) *New Age Encyclopedia*. Detroit, MI: Gale Research.

Melton, J. Gordon (1999) 'Anti-Cultists in the United States: An Historical Perspective' in Bryan R. Wilson and Jamie Cresswell (eds) *New Religious Movements: Challenges and Response*, London: Routledge, pp. 213–35.

Murphy, Joseph (1993) *Santeria: African Spirits in America*, Boston: Beacon Press.

Nakamaki, Hirochika (2003) *Japanese New Religions at Home and Abroad*, London: Routledge/Curzon.

Ooms, Emily Groszos (1993) *Women and Millenarian Protest in Meiji Japan*, Ithaca, NY: Cornell University, East Asia Program.

Palmer, Susan J. (1994) *Moon Sisters, Krishna Mothers, Rajneesh Lovers: Women's Roles in New Religions*, Syracuse, NY: Syracuse University Press.

Palmer, Susan and Hardman, Charlotte (1999) *Children in New Religions*, New Brunswick, NJ: Rutgers University Press.

Pearson, Joanne, Roberts, Richard H., and Samuel, Geoffrey (1998) *Nature Religion Today: Paganism in the Modern World*, Edinburgh: Edinburgh University Press.

Peel, John D. Y. (1968) *Aladura: A Religious Movement among the Yoruba*, Oxford: Oxford University Press.

Puttick, Elizabeth (1997) *Women in New Religions: In Search of Community, Spirituality and Spiritual Power*, Basingstoke: Macmillan.

Queen, Christopher S. (ed.) (2000) *Engaged Buddhism in the West*, Boston: Wisdom.

Queen, Christopher S. and King, Sallie B. (eds) (1996) *Engaged Buddhism: Buddhist Liberation Movements in America*, Albany, NY: State University of New York Press.

Reader, Ian (2000) *Religious Violence in Contemporary Japan: The Case of Aum Shinrikyo*, Richmond, Surrey: Curzon Press.

Robbins, Thomas (1988) *Cults, Converts and Charisma*, London: Sage.

Robbins, Thomas (2003) 'Constructing Cultist Mind Control' in Lorne L. Dawson (ed.) *Cults and New Religious Movements: A Reader*, Oxford: Blackwell, pp. 167–81.

Robertson, Roland (1992) *Globalization: Social Theory and Global Culture*, London: Sage.

Robilliard, St. John A. (1984) *Religion and the Law: Religious Liberty in Modern English Law*, Manchester: Manchester University Press.

Sen, Amiya P. (ed.) (2004) *Social and Religious Reform: The Hindus of British India*, Oxford: Oxford University Press.

Shimazono, Susumu (1999) '"New Age Movement" or New Spirituality Movements and Culture?', *Social Compass*, 46(2), 126–34.

Shimazono, Susumu (2004) *From Salvation to Spirituality*, Melbourne: Trans Pacific Press.

Smith, David (2003) *Hinduism and Modernity*, Oxford: Blackwell.

Spuler, Michelle (2003) *Developments in Australian Buddhism: Facets of the Diamond*, London: Routledge/Curzon.

Stark, Rodney and Bainbridge, William Sims (1985) *The Future of Religion*, Berkeley: University of California Press.

Stark, Rodney and Finke, Roger (2000) *Acts of Faith*, Berkeley: University of California Press.

Stark, Rodney, Hamberg, Eva and Miller, Alan S. (2005) 'Exploring Spirituality and Unchurched Religions in America, Sweden and Japan', *Journal of Contemporary Religion*, 20(1), 3–25.

Sundkler, Bengt G. M. (1970) *Bantu Prophets in South Africa*, London: Oxford University Press.

Sutcliffe, Steven and Bowman, Marion (eds) (2000) *Beyond New Age*, Edinburgh: Edinburgh University Press.

Tipton, Steven M. (1982) *Getting Saved from the Sixties*, Berkeley: University of California Press.

Wallis, Roy (1976) *The Road to Total Freedom: A Sociological Analysis of Scientology*, London: Heinemann.

Wallis, Roy (1984) *The Elementary Forms of the New Religious Life*, London: Routledge.

Wilson, Bryan R. (1973) *Magic and the Millennium*, London: Heinemann.

Wilson, Bryan R. (1979) 'The Return of the Sacred', *Journal for the Scientific Study of Religion*, 18(3), 268–80.

Wilson, Bryan R. (1990) *The Social Dimensions of Sectarianism*, Oxford, Clarendon Press.

Wilson, Bryan R. (1993) 'Historical Lessons in the Study of Sects and Cults' in David G. Bromley and Jeffrey K. Hadden (eds) *Religion and Social Order*, Vol. 3, Greenwich, CT: JAI Press, pp. 53–85.

Wilson, Bryan R. and Cresswell, Jamie (eds) (1999) *New Religious Movements: Challenge and Response*, London: Routledge.

Wilson, Bryan R. and Dobbelaere, Karel (1994) *A Time to Chant: The Soka Gakkai Buddhists in Britain*, Oxford: Oxford University Press.

Wuthnow, Robert (1982) 'World Order and Religious Movements' in Eileen Barker (ed.) *New Religious Movements: A Perspective for Understanding Society*, New York: Edwin Mellen Press, pp. 47–69.

Wuthnow, Robert (1986) 'Religious Movements and Counter-movements in America' in James Beckford (ed.) *New Religious Movements and Rapid Social Change*, London: Sage, pp. 1–29.

Wuthnow, Robert and Cadge, Wendy (2004) 'Buddhists and Buddhism in the United States: The Scope of Influence', *Journal for the Scientific Study of Religion*, 43(3), 363–81.

York, M. (1995) *The Emerging Network: A Sociology of the New Age and Neo-pagan Movements*, Lanham, MD: Rowman & Littlefield.

Zahab, Miriam Abou and Roy, Olivier (2002) *Islamist Networks: The Afghan-Pakistan Connections*, London: Hurst.

Index

Related titles from Routledge

Researching New Religious Movements
Responses and Redefinitions

Elisabeth Arweck

'Powerful and original . . . it succeeds triumphantly in being at the same time an important, high-quality academic study and a book for our times.'

Professor David Marsland, Brunel University

New religious movements such as Scientology, the Jehovah's Witnesses and the Unification Church (Moonies) are now well established in mainstream cultural consciousness. But responses to these 'cult' groups still tend to be overwhelmingly negative, characterized by the furious reactions that they evoke from majority interests. Modern societies need to learn how to respond to such movements, and how to interpret their benefits and dangers.

Researching New Religious Movements provides a fresh look at the history and development of 'anti-cult' groups, and the response of mainstream churches to these new movements. In this unique reception study, Elisabeth Arweck traces the path of scholarship of new religious movements, exploring the development of research in this growing field. She considers academic and media interventions on both sides, with special emphasis on the problems of objectivity inherent in terminologies of 'sects', 'abduction' and 'brainwashing'. Ideal for students and researchers, this much-needed book takes the debate over new religious movements to a newly sophisticated level.

Elisabeth Arweck is a Research Associate at King's College London, and a Research Fellow at the University of Warwick's Religions and Education Research Unit. She co-edits the *Journal of Contemporary Religion*, and has co-edited books including *New Religious Movements in Western Europe* (1997) and *Theorizing Faith* (2002).

Hb: 0–415–27754–X
Pb: 0–415–27755–8

Available at all good bookshops

For ordering and further information please visit:

www.routledge.com

Related titles from Routledge

New Religious Movements in the 21st Century: Legal, Political and Social Challenges in Global Perspective

Edited by
Phillip Charles Lucas and Thomas Robbins

New religious movements are proliferating in nearly every region of the world. From new sects within larger global movements such as Islam, Christianity, or Buddhism, to the growth and spread of minority religions (e.g. ISKON, Unification Church, and Scientology) and the development of completely new religions, the future of these new religious movements will increasingly come to be played out on a political battlefield. Governments in many countries in both the industrialized and the developing worlds have enacted new policies and legislation that dramatically affect not only marginal and minority religious groups but also the broader power relationships between states and the religious freedom of their citizens.

New Religious Movements in the 21st Century is the first volume to examine the urgent and important issues facing new religions in their political, legal, and religious contexts in global perspective. With essays from prominent new religious movement scholars and usefully organized into four regional areas covering Western Europe, Asia, Africa, and Australia, Russia and Eastern Europe, and North and South America, as well as a concluding section on the major themes of globalization and terrorist violence, this book provides invaluable insight into the challenges facing religion in the twenty-first century. An introduction by Tom Robbins provides an overview of the major issues and themes discussed in the book.

Hb: 0–415–96576–4
Pb: 0–415–96577–2

Available at all good bookshops

For ordering and further information please visit:

www.routledge.com

Related titles from Routledge

New Religions and the Nazis

Karla Poewe

This book highlights an important but neglected part of Nazi history – the contribution of new religions to the emergence of Nazi ideology in 1920s and 1930s Germany. Karla Poewe argues that Nazism was the unique consequence of post-World War I conditions in Germany, a reaction against the decadence of nineteenth-century liberalism, the shameful defeat of World War I, the imposition of an unwanted Weimar democracy, and the post-war punishment of the Treaty of Versailles. Aiming towards national regeneration, leading cultural figures such as Jakob Wilhelm Hauer, Mathilde Ludendorff, Ernst Bergman, Hans Grimm, and Hans F. K. Günther wanted to shape the cultural milieu of politics, religion, theology, Indo-Aryan meta-physics, literature and Darwinian science into a new genuinely German faith-based political community. Instead what emerged was a totalitarian political regime known as National Socialism, with an anti-Semitic worldview. Looking at modern German paganism as well as the established Church, Poewe reveals that the new religions founded in the pre-Nazi and Nazi years, especially Jakob Hauer's German Faith Movement, would be a model for how German fascism distilled aspects of religious doctrine into political extremism.

New Religions and the Nazis addresses one of the most important questions of the 20th century – how and why did Germans come to embrace National Socialism? Researched from original documents, letters and unpublished papers, including the SS personnel files held in Berlin's Bundesarchiv, it is an absorbing and fresh approach to the difficulties raised by this deeply significant period of history.

Hb: 0–415–29024–4
Pb: 0–415–29025–2

Available at all good bookshops

For ordering and further information please visit:

www.routledge.com